RESEARCH ON SERVICE LEARNING

Volume 2A

IUPUI Series on Service Learning Research

Series Editors
Robert G. Bringle and Julie A. Hatcher

Vol. 1: *International Service Learning*
Vol. 2A: *Research on Service Learning: Students and Faculty*
Vol. 2B: *Research on Service Learning: Communities, Institutions, and Partnerships*
Vol. 3: *Research on Student Civic Outcomes*
Vol. 4: *Research on Service Learning, Diversity, and Persistence*

RESEARCH ON SERVICE LEARNING

Conceptual Frameworks and Assessment

VOLUME 2A: Students and Faculty

EDITED BY

Patti H. Clayton, Robert G. Bringle,

and *Julie A. Hatcher*

IUPUI Series on Service Learning Research

STERLING, VIRGINIA

Sty/us

COPYRIGHT © 2013
BY STYLUS PUBLISHING, LLC.

Published by Stylus Publishing, LLC
22883 Quicksilver Drive
Sterling, Virginia 20166-2102

Library of Congress Cataloging-in-Publication Data
Research on service learning : conceptual frameworks and
assessment : students and faculty / edited by Patti H.
Clayton, Robert G. Bringle, and Julie A. Hatcher.
    p.   cm. — (LUPUI series on service learning and
research ; v. 2A)
Includes bibliographical references and index.
ISBN 978-1-57922-340-3 (cloth : alk. paper)
ISBN 978-1-57922-341-0 (pbk. : alk. paper)
ISBN 978-1-57922-838-5 (library network e-edition)
ISBN 978-1-57922-839-2 (consumer e-edition)
    1. Service learning.   2. Service learning—Research.
I. Clayton, Patti H.   II. Bringle, Robert G.   III. Hatcher,
Julie A., 1953–
LC220.5.R477   2013
361.37—dc23   2012020695

13-digit ISBN: 978-1-57922-340-3 (cloth)
13-digit ISBN: 978-1-57922-341-0 (paper)
13-digit ISBN: 978-1-57922-838-5 (library networkable
e-edition)
13-digit ISBN: 978-1-57922-839-2 (consumer e-edition)

Printed in the United States of America

All first editions printed on acid-free paper
that meets the American National Standards Institute
Z39-48 Standard.

Bulk Purchases

Quantity discounts are available for use in workshops
and for staff development.
Call 1-800-232-0223

First Edition, 2013

10   9   8   7   6   5   4   3   2   1

CONTENTS

CONTENTS

PREFACE

C hange does not come easily to higher education, but service learning has demonstrated its capacity to have an influence on dimensions of the academy that are among the most difficult to change: the curriculum, faculty work, organizational infrastructure, budget allocations, promotion and tenure, assessment of student learning, and community-campus partnerships. These changes have manifested themselves across institutional types, with a tenacity that suggests that they are not mere fads but enduring trends. More than 1,000 institutions are now members of Campus Compact, which reports increasing numbers of students, faculty, and community partners involved in service learning (Campus Compact, 2010). Stimulated by the model of service learning, institutions of higher education have examined how civic engagement more broadly can change the nature of faculty work, enhance student learning, advance institutional missions, provide a basis for public accountability, and improve quality of life in communities (e.g., Boyer, 1994, 1996; Bringle, Games, & Malloy, 1999; Calleson, Jordan, & Seifer, 2005; Colby, Ehrlich, Beaumont, & Stephens, 2003; Edgerton, 1994; Harkavy & Puckett, 1994; O'Meara & Rice, 2005; Percy, Zimpher, & Brukardt, 2006; Rice, 1996; Saltmarsh & Hartley, 2011).

However, when the degree and nature of the changes associated with service learning and, more broadly, civic engagement are assessed for their quality, breadth, and depth, interpretations vary. Saltmarsh, Giles, et al. (2009) analyzed applications for the Carnegie Foundation's Community Engagement classification, finding uneven evidence of institutional change: Change has occurred in all classified institutions, but there is also evidence of resistance to change (e.g., in the arena of promotion and tenure) and of consistent shortcomings (e.g., with respect to community-campus reciprocity). Butin's (2005) edited volume presents multiple perspectives that raise issues about the degree to which the assumptions, values, and operations of service learning are incompatible with the ingrained culture of higher

---

Portions of this preface are from Bringle, Hatcher, and Jones (2011).

education—constraining the capacity of the pedagogy to generate transformational institutional change. Saltmarsh, Hartley, and Clayton (2009) question the degree to which the changes associated with civic engagement more generally have been fundamental and systemic.

Regardless of how full or how empty the glass is thought to be, service learning has produced change not only in the curriculum but also more broadly, and this is not a trivial outcome. In the absence of a consensual goal, among either civic engagement practitioners or leaders in higher education in general, to produce systemic transformation, the amount of change service learning has produced in higher education can be viewed as an extraordinary accomplishment. Many criticisms (change has been slow, small, and incomplete or has otherwise fallen short of ideal) underacknowledge and perhaps undervalue the significant changes that have occurred. Furthermore, the very existence of these interpretations, analyses, and critiques indicates that (a) scholars have some progress to review; (b) they care enough about the impact of service learning to invest their resources in studying it; and (c) there are aspirations and standards against which incomplete, though significant, accomplishments can be evaluated. Ongoing reflection on the extent and nature of change within institutions and throughout the academy as a whole can inform future development of service learning and civic engagement. These volumes, and the series of which they are a part, contribute research-grounded perspectives on the processes and outcomes of service learning to this national and international conversation.

The growth of service learning and civic engagement on the Indiana University–Purdue University Indianapolis (IUPUI) campus mirrors national developments. Starting with opening an IUPUI Office of Service Learning in 1993 (now incorporated into the IUPUI Center for Service and Learning [CSL]), service learning has been purposefully nurtured on a campus of more than 30,000 students with strong traditions of community involvement among its many professional schools. Through strategic decisions by executive leadership (Bringle & Hatcher, 2004; Bringle, Hatcher, & Holland, 2007; Plater, 2004), significant commitments to infrastructure were made to support the growth of service learning. That growth has been guided by a Comprehensive Action Plan for Service Learning (CAPSL) that identified 10 key tasks (planning, increasing awareness, developing a prototype of good practice, gathering resources, expanding programs, providing recognition, monitoring, evaluating, conducting research, and institutionalizing) and four key stakeholders (the institution, faculty, students, and community) (Bringle & Hatcher, 1996). There is evidence of institutional progress across all areas of CAPSL at IUPUI (Bringle & Hatcher, 2004: Bringle, Hatcher, & Clayton, 2006; Bringle, Hatcher, Hamilton, & Young, 2001; Bringle et al., 2007; Bringle, Hatcher, Jones, & Plater, 2006).

In addition, independent external reviews support the assessment of significant institutional progress at IUPUI around service learning and civic engagement. For example, IUPUI's service learning program has been recognized every year since 2003 as one of the top programs in the country by *U.S. News & World Report*. In 2006, IUPUI was recognized in the Saviors of our Cities national report by the New England Board of Higher Education as one of 25 urban colleges and universities that have dramatically strengthened the economy and quality of life of neighboring communities; IUPUI was the highest ranked public university receiving this distinction and was again recognized in 2009. Most noteworthy, in 2006, the inaugural year for the award, IUPUI was selected by the Corporation for National and Community Service as one of three universities in the country (out of 510 campuses that applied) to receive the Presidential Award for exceptional accomplishments in General Student Community Service activities. In 2006, IUPUI was a member of the first group of colleges and universities to receive the Carnegie Foundation's Community Engagement classification, in the two categories of Curricular Engagement and Outreach and Partnerships.

With the intention to build on these accomplishments and to continue its field-building leadership, the IUPUI CSL applied for and received an internal designation in 2007 as an IUPUI Signature Center and established the CSL Research Collaborative. The mission of the CSL Research Collaborative is to

- Increase the capacity of faculty to engage in research on service learning practice.
- Convene service learning scholars to develop new conceptual frameworks and methodological tools to improve the quality of service learning research.
- Disseminate high-quality scholarship through books, research briefs, monographs, a website that provides information on resources (e.g., grant opportunities, tools for research), presentations at scholarly conferences, and publications in peer-reviewed journals.

The CSL Research Collaborative has provided the basis for launching several new initiatives for advancing scholarship on campus, nationally, and internationally, including the *IUPUI Series on Service Learning Research*.

This series was designed by identifying themes around which scholarship that would advance the field and meet strategic goals of IUPUI could be organized. The theme for the first volume in the series, *International Service Learning: Conceptual Frameworks and Research*, grew out of a collaboration between CSL and the IUPUI Office of International Affairs that emphasized service learning as a distinctive aspect of the development of both study abroad and strategic international partnerships. That collaboration included partnering with the International Partnership for Service-Learning and Leadership and Indiana Campus Compact to host two conferences at IUPUI focused on international service learning and two symposia at IUPUI at which authors and discussants shaped the chapters for the first volume.

The present two volumes—Volume 2A, *Students and Faculty* and Volume 2B, *Communities, Institutions, and Partnerships*—that together comprise the second work in the series, grew out of CSL's long-standing commitment to advancing service learning research through improved assessment (Bringle, Phillips, & Hudson, 2004). As used here, assessment encompasses measurement and is not limited to gauging student performance in a course for the sake of giving a grade; measurement is relevant to qualities of process and to outcomes and, in the case of service learning, includes but transcends a focus on students. Furthermore, assessment and measurement are not isolated endeavors. Implicit or explicit in any measurement procedure, whether quantitative or qualitative, is a conceptual understanding of the constructs that are being studied. Each construct that is part of systematic research is, or should be, embedded in a theoretical context that explains the manifestations of the construct and the relationships between it and other constructs. In addition, how the measurement is taken (i.e., research design) and its implications for practice are both critical to its meaningfulness. Although elsewhere we have focused on quantitative measurement (Bringle et al., 2004; Bringle & Hatcher, 2000), here measurement is construed broadly as any procedure that is used to collect evidence, data, or indicators of a construct.

The authors contributing chapters to these books were convened in a symposium at IUPUI in 2009 to discuss the overall vision for the book and the specific content of individual chapters. Authors were asked to take on a task that was expansive and forward looking: Develop a research agenda and recommendations for practice within a particular topic area (e.g., student civic learning, faculty motivations, community outcomes, institutional leadership, organizational partnerships) that draw upon theory from cognate areas and are informed by critique of extant research through the lens of that theory as well as by review of relevant assessment methods and tools. As a result, we expect this work to advance understanding of, investigation of, and implementation of service learning in innovative and meaningful ways. This was an intellectual challenge, and the authors are to be commended for their work in producing chapters that will shape future research on service learning.

Dean Uday Sukhatme, executive vice-chancellor and dean of the faculties at IUPUI, provided support for the CSL Research Collaborative through the Signature Center initiative. Several graduate student colleagues provided key support in the development of these books: Megan Gehrke and Matthew Williams helped to organize the convening of contributing authors at IUPUI and facilitated many aspects of the book project in its early phases; Kristi S. Combs provided substantial project coordination and editorial assistance as chapters were revised and combined into a single, coherent manuscript; and Kathleen E. Edwards brought strong editorial and project management skills when she joined our editorial team in the final stages of production. Finally, a special note of appreciation is extended to William M. Plater, who served as executive vice-chancellor and dean of the faculties at IUPUI from 1987 to 2006 and then as the director of the Office of International Community Development. Dean Plater has been the architect for advancing much of IUPUI's work on civic engagement and service learning, providing persistent and pervasive support to CSL and the work associated with the CSL Research Collaborative.

For the convenience of readers who may choose to buy only one of the two books that comprise this two-volume set, the preface and first two chapters appear in both volumes. Volume 2A comprises the preface and chapters 1.1 through 3.3. Volume 2B comprises the preface, chapters 1.1 and 1.2, and chapters 4.1 through 6.3. Each volume includes an integrated index to both books and an About the Contributors section.

Robert G. Bringle
April 2012

References

Boyer, E. L. (1994, March 9). Creating the new American college. *The Chronicle of Higher Education*, A48.

Boyer, E. L. (1996). The scholarship of engagement. *Journal of Public Service and Outreach, 1*(1), 11–20.

Bringle, R. G., Games, R., & Malloy, E. A. (1999). Colleges and universities as citizens: Issues and perspectives. In R. G. Bringle, R. Games, & E. A. Malloy (Eds.), *Colleges and universities as citizens* (pp. 1–16). Needham Heights, MA: Allyn & Bacon.

Bringle, R. G., & Hatcher, J. A. (1996). Implementing service learning in higher education. *Journal of Higher Education, 67*, 221–239.

Bringle, R. G., & Hatcher, J. A. (2000). Meaningful measurement of theory-based service-learning outcomes: Making the case with quantitative research [Special issue]. *Michigan Journal of Community Service Learning, Fall*, 68–75.

Bringle, R. G., & Hatcher, J. A. (2004). Advancing civic engagement through service-learning. In M. Langseth & W. M. Plater (Eds.), *Public work and the academy: An academic administrator's guide to civic engagement and service-learning*. Bolton, MA: Anker.

Bringle, R. G., Hatcher, J. A., & Clayton, P. H. (2006). The scholarship of civic engagement: Defining, documenting, and evaluating faculty work. *To Improve the Academy, 25*, 257–279.

Bringle, R. G., Hatcher, J. A., Hamilton, S., & Young, P. (2001). Planning and assessing campus/community engagement. *Metropolitan Universities, 12*(3), 89–99.

Bringle, R. G., Hatcher, J. A., & Holland, B. A. (2007). Conceptualizing civic engagement: Orchestrating change at a metropolitan university. *Metropolitan Universities, 18*(3), 57–74.

Bringle, R. G., Hatcher, J. A., & Jones, S. G. (Eds.). (2011). *International service learning: Conceptual frameworks and research*. Sterling, VA: Stylus.

Bringle, R. G., Hatcher, J. A., Jones, S. G., & Plater, W. M. (2006). Sustaining civic engagement: Faculty development, roles, and rewards. *Metropolitan Universities, 17*(1), 62–74.

Bringle, R. G., Phillips, M. A., & Hudson, M. (2004). *The measure of service learning: Research scales to assess student experiences*. Washington, DC: American Psychological Association.

Butin, D. W. (Ed.). (2005). *Service-learning in higher education: Critical issues and directions*. New York, NY: Palgrave.

Calleson, D. C., Jordan, C., & Seifer, S. D. (2005). Community-engaged scholarship: Is faculty work in communities a true academic enterprise? *Academic Medicine, 80*, 317–321.

Campus Compact. (2010). *Annual member survey results: Executive summary 2010*. Retrieved from http://www.compact.org/about/statistics/?zoom_highlight = statistics

Colby, A., Ehrlich, T., Beaumont, E., & Stephens, J. (2003). *Educating citizens: Preparing America's undergraduates for lives of moral and civic responsibility*. San Francisco, CA: Jossey-Bass.

Edgerton, R. (1994). The engaged campus: Organizing to serve society's needs. *AAHE Bulletin, 47*(1), 2–3.

Harkavy, I., & Puckett, J. L. (1994). Lessons from Hull House for the contemporary urban university. *Social Science Review, 68*, 299–321.

O'Meara, K., & Rice, R. E. (Eds.). (2005). *Faculty priorities reconsidered: Rewarding multiple forms of scholarship*. San Francisco, CA: Jossey-Bass.

Percy, S. L., Zimpher, N., & Brukardt, M. (Eds.). (2006). *Creating a new kind of university*. Bolton, MA: Anker.

Plater, W. M. (2004). Civic engagement, service-learning and intentional leadership. In M. Langseth & W. M. Plater (Eds.), *Public work and the academy: An academic administrator's guide to civic engagement and service-learning* (pp. 1–22). Bolton, MA: Anker.

Rice, R. E. (1996, January). *Making a place for the new American scholar*. Paper presented at the AAHE Conference on Faculty Roles and Rewards, Atlanta, GA.

Saltmarsh, J., Giles, D. E., Jr., O'Meara, A., Sandmann, L., Ward, E., & Buglione, S. M. (2009). The institutional home for faculty engagement: An investigation of reward policies at engaged campuses. In B. E. Moely, S. H. Billig, & B. A. Holland (Eds.), *Creating our identities in service-learning and community engagement* (pp. 3–29). Charlotte, NC: Information Age.

Saltmarsh, J., & Hartley, M. (Eds.). (2011). *'To serve a larger purpose': Engagement for democracy and the transformation of higher education*. Philadelphia, PA: Temple University Press.

Saltmarsh, J., Hartley, M., & Clayton, P. H. (2009). *Democratic engagement white paper*. Boston, MA: New England Resource Center for Higher Education.

PART ONE

ORIENTATION TO RESEARCH ON SERVICE LEARNING

I.I

RESEARCH ON SERVICE LEARNING

An Introduction

Robert G. Bringle, Patti H. Clayton, and Julie A. Hatcher

Over the past 25 years, the prevalence of service learning courses has steadily increased in higher education. This expansion has occurred across all types of institutions of higher education in the United States and across the spectrum of disciplines, with a reported rate of 7% of faculty teaching with service learning (Campus Compact, 2010). Internationally, there is a growing interest in the pedagogy, as represented by organizational networks across the globe (e.g., Australian Universities Community Engagement Alliance, Canadian Alliance for Community Service-Learning, Latin American Center for Service-Learning), scholarship documenting regional case studies (Annette, 2005; Badat, 2003; McIlrath, Farrel, Hughes, Lillis, & Lyons, 2007), and cross-cultural comparisons (Hatcher & Erasmus, 2008; Thomson, Smith-Tolken, Naidoo, & Bringle, 2011). Service learning has gained prominence in higher education as a high-impact educational practice (Kuh, 2008) and as an active learning strategy that provides both a rich set of potential learning outcomes and opportunities for educators to explore teaching and learning in ways that have implications for all pedagogies (Conway, Amel, & Gerwein, 2009; Eyler, Giles, Stenson, & Gray, 2001; Finley, 2011).

Research by instructors and other practitioner-scholars who support teaching and learning involves systematic inquiry and reflective practice. Such investigation into the processes and outcomes of service learning and other pedagogies can improve instructional design, enhance abilities, and increase confidence among teachers and learners alike; model scholarly practices for others; and contribute to a campus culture of inquiry related to teaching and learning. High-quality research can also inform campus policy, public policy, and funding activities of private foundations. In addition, such research holds the promise of deepening the understanding and practice of service learning, which has significant implications for a wide range of community and campus stakeholders. Service learning is rooted in the public purposes of higher education (Boyer, 1995); careful attention must be paid to its design, implementation, assessment, and outcomes to ensure that it fulfills these purposes.

The broadest goal of this two-volume set and other books in the *IUPUI Series on Service Learning Research* is to enhance the breadth, depth, and quality of research conducted in the context of service learning. Establishing a solid research agenda based on theory and building on prior work in order to improve the quality of subsequent research is the ultimate aim. Guiding, advancing, and improving research in any field of study requires a number of steps, including agreement on clear definitions, theory building, and mapping the terrain of what is already known (Hodgkinson, 2004). The chapters in this two-volume set address these steps, examining research related to service learning in five broad areas—students, faculty, communities, institutions of higher education, partnerships—from a variety of disciplinary and interdisciplinary perspectives (e.g., higher education, leadership, learning sciences, organizational theory, political science, psychology). Each chapter considers questions of theory, measurement, research design, and practice in surveying a particular topical arena of research (e.g., students' intercultural competence, faculty development, institutionalization). Together, these chapters have important implications for research as well as for program and course design and assessment. All of these activities are dependent on systematic inquiry, analysis, and dissemination of results for peer review, which are characteristics of scholarship work. Thus, research on service learning has the additional benefit that it can contribute to the professional development of instructors in ways that should be acknowledged through the reward structure of institutions of higher education.

Many chapters have relevance to other forms of civic engagement (e.g., volunteering, political participation, advocacy, professional service in the community) and to related research activities (e.g., community-based participatory research), even though these are not the primary foci of these two volumes. Furthermore, although all of the chapters are intentionally focused on service learning within the context of higher education, researchers with an interest in other contexts (e.g., precollegiate educational settings, service learning based in community organizations) may also find them relevant.

This chapter conceptualizes and defines service learning by articulating many of the components and variables that comprise the complexity of and inform the research on this teaching and learning strategy. Characteristics of high-quality service learning courses are introduced here and further examined in subsequent chapters. In addition, this chapter defines research and differentiates among research, program evaluation, and assessment. The chapter also serves as an introduction to both volumes in this set and provides a context for and description of the template used by the contributing authors.

Conceptualizing Service Learning

The beginning of wisdom is to call things by their right names.

—Chinese Proverb

Researchers in any field of inquiry must pay close attention to details, nuances, and conceptual clarity. Clearly delineating what is to be studied is one of the first steps in research, regardless of disciplinary perspective or methodology. Similar to other terms related to community-based activity (e.g., civic engagement, public scholarship, engaged scholarship, community service, volunteerism), service learning is "a complex phenomenon . . . comprised of multiple dimensions and, hence, many possible variables in research, which complicates inquiry" (McBride & Sherraden, 2007, p. 4). This complexity poses challenges to—and opportunities for—conducting research on service learning.

There are many definitions of *service learning* (e.g., Jacoby, 1996; Pragman & Flannery, 2008; Rama, Ravenscroft, Wolcroft, & Zlotkowski, 2000), and each may emphasize a slightly different orientation to or aspect of the pedagogy. Service learning is a socially embedded practice (Conway et al., 2009), and, therefore, different words are used—and avoided—in reference to it, reflecting the different assumptions, ideologies, norms, and identities of different personal, organizational, and cultural contexts. Although variation in language, conceptualization, and practice may be unavoidable, both within the United States and in international contexts, it can complicate the research process, particularly if the differences, along with their underlying rationales and implications, are not made explicit. When there are multiple definitions and multiple practices associated with a single concept, "confidence in being able to accurately assess the meaning of this concept is compromised" (Finley, 2011, p. 18).

Defining service learning precisely and explicitly identifying variations in forms and structures provide a level of certainty about the construct in any particular context for inquiry and, in turn, enhance the ability of researchers and practitioner-scholars to test and advance theory and to understand and improve practice (McBride & Sherraden, 2007). Using a consistent definition within this series is, therefore, intentional. Despite variations, there is broad consensus that service learning involves the integration of academic material, relevant service activities, and critical reflection and is built on reciprocal partnerships that engage students, faculty/staff, and community members to achieve academic, civic, and personal learning objectives as well as to advance public purposes (Bringle & Clayton, 2012). For this series, service learning is defined as follows:

> a course or competency-based, credit-bearing educational experience in which students (a) participate in mutually identified service activities that benefit the community, and (b) reflect on the service activity in such a way as to gain further understanding of course content, a broader appreciation of the discipline, and an enhanced sense of personal values and civic responsibility. (Bringle & Clayton, 2012, pp. 114–115, adapted from Bringle & Hatcher, 1996)

This definition identifies service learning as a pedagogical component of the formal curriculum that benefits the community in tangible ways and that incorporates reflection to support the academic, civic, and personal development of students. It also establishes that service learning necessarily involves civic education; civic learning comprises civic knowledge, skills, and habits (Battistoni, 2002; Billig & Eyler, 2003; Eyler & Giles, 1999; Eyler et al., 2001; Westheimer & Kahne, 2003; Zlotkowski, Longo, & Williams, 2006).

Each of the dimensions of the pedagogy encompasses variables that can be identified, measured, and explored through research. Variables that can be incorporated into research designed to explore and understand the design and impact of service learning as a curricular strategy include types of courses (e.g., first-year success seminars, general education, capstone), frequency and sequencing of courses within the curriculum (prerequisites, learning communities), and instructional roles (e.g., faculty, peer mentors, community mentors, graduate assistants). Partnerships encompass a range of variables that can be explored to understand their influence on the process and outcomes of service learning; they also constitute a variable in course design that can be measured as a mediating variable, and they represent a tangible outcome insofar as they provide a foundation for additional activities. Student outcomes have received the most attention in research on service learning, yet little is known about what variables under what conditions lead to desired outcomes or about why documented outcomes are, in fact, achieved. This volume focuses on high-quality research related to many, but by no means all, dimensions of service learning.

Designing Service Learning

Requisite for high-quality research on service learning is well-designed and well-implemented service learning. Service learning has an explicit student learning focus, which is integrated with an equally explicit community focus; fundamental to strong design, therefore, is the conviction that it is not a form of volunteerism and is not the addition of service activities to otherwise unchanged learning activities. Intentional curricular design—grounded in well-articulated goals for both learning and service—is required to achieve the integration of service processes and learning processes that characterizes high-quality service learning. Service activities function analogously to the texts to be studied and analyzed in a course; thus, they must be selected or designed carefully based on how they supplement, illustrate, and augment other academic material. When designed and implemented appropriately, service learning encompasses multiple factors that are known to help students achieve in-depth understanding, including, for example, active learning, feedback, collaboration, cognitive apprenticeship, and real consequences with a safety net as a buffer against high-stakes mistakes (Marchese, 1997). These elements, which lead service learning to be identified as a high-impact pedagogy (Kuh, 2008), contribute as well to establishing a context that lends itself to high-quality research on a rich array of processes and outcomes across a wide range of stakeholders.

Within this set of features, pedagogical design is customized based on local context and the objectives and constraints of those involved. Service learning courses can range from the first-year to graduate level, and service learning can transcend a focus on individual courses and operate across courses in minors or entire degree programs (e.g., chapter 5.2; Jameson, Clayton, & Bringle, 2008). Service learning may involve short- or long-term community-based activities, which, in turn, may consist of direct or indirect service (or both). Community may be on campus, in the local area, in another state or country, or online; it may include grassroots initiatives, nonprofit organizations, for-profit businesses, and government agencies. Explicitness and transparency regarding the specific form that each of these design variables takes in any given situation is necessary in order for research in that setting to inform theory, contribute to a knowledge base, and guide practice. Investigating the outcomes of service learning as a phenomenon without reference to the specific form it takes in any given instance is rarely helpful in advancing understanding. The same holds for designing and investigating particular components of the pedagogy.

Regardless of these design choices, community members are to be partners in the process of developing and implementing service learning, not merely recipients of service. Sigmon (1979) suggested that all participants in service learning learn, serve, and are served; such reciprocity in service learning partnerships is now seen as requiring "shared voice and power and insist-[ing] upon collaborative knowledge construction and joint ownership of work processes and products" (Jameson, Clayton, & Jaeger, 2011, p. 264). Not all relationships in service learning are reciprocal partnerships (Bringle, Clayton, & Price, 2009; chapter 6.1), and not all relationships or partnerships involve the same stakeholder populations. The SOFAR Model (Clayton, Bringle, Senor, Huq, & Morrison, 2010; chapter 6.1) differentiates campus constituents into students, faculty, and administrators and community constituents into organization staff and residents (or clients); service learning activities and projects generally involve most, if not all, of these populations. Enos and Morton (2003) distinguish between onetime events, short-term placements, ongoing placements that involve mutual dependence, interdependent core partnerships, and transformational partnerships that involve joint creation of work and knowledge; they also distinguish between transactional and transformational orientations to partnerships. High-quality service learning is designed with attention to the full range of stakeholder perspectives and avoids the conceptual and practical confusion that can emerge from characterizations of campus and community as monolithic entities or of partnerships as homogeneous phenomena (chapter 6.1). Principles such as those developed by Community-Campus Partnerships for Health (2005)—establishing agreed-upon goals and outcomes, being trustworthy and respectful, building on assets while addressing areas for improvement, sharing resources, engaging in open communication, encouraging input from all participants, continually improving the partnership and its outcomes, sharing credit—can provide helpful guidance in developing the partnerships on which high-quality service learning–enhanced courses depend and, consequently, in establishing a setting for high-quality research. These principles can also inform research on service learning in that the commitments of service learning to reciprocal partnerships transcend courses to include the full range of service learning–related activities.

The critical examination of service experiences and academic material through carefully designed reflection is the component of the process that generates meaning, new questions, and enhanced understanding and practice—for students in particular but also for any of the participants in service learning who see themselves as co-learners in the process. Reflection provides a vehicle through which service and associated activities (e.g., project planning, teamwork) can be analyzed and interpreted—much like a text is read and studied for deeper understanding—as well as improved. Reflection activities may be written, oral, kinesthetic, or audiovisual; they may be individual, collaborative, or both. They may take on a wide variety of forms, including journal entries, online chat sessions, poster presentations, essays, worksheets, drawings, audiovisual products, and discussion sessions. They may occur on a regular schedule and at serendipitous moments. Critical reflection may involve feedback—from student peers, instructors, community members, or service learning staff—and opportunities for revision. Principles of good practice call for service learning course design to integrate guided reflection activities that contribute to the intended learning and service outcomes by linking the service activities to the course content, and vice versa (Ash & Clayton, 2009; Hatcher & Bringle, 1997). Relatedly, critical reflection is especially powerful in improving the quality of learning and of service when integrated with assessment—using the same set of objectives, standards, and tools to generate learning (through reflection prompts), deepen learning (through formative assessment or feedback), and document learning (through summative assessment or grading and reporting outcomes) (Ash & Clayton, 2009; Bringle & Clayton, 2012; Whitney & Clayton, 2011). As with service learning overall and with partnerships, being intentional and specifying the details of and rationale for the design of reflection in any given situation is necessary in order for related research to inform theory and guide practice.

Conceptualizing Research on Service Learning

Research is a complex term because it can have so many interpretations. Elsewhere, the case has been presented that the term *research* should have a particular meaning, specifically, that it should refer to inquiry that is theory based (Bringle, 2003; Bringle & Hatcher, 2000; Bringle, Hatcher, & Williams, 2011; Steinberg, Bringle, & Williams, 2010). We suggest here that *research* should be used to describe activities that reflect convergence of theory, measurement, design, and practice (see Figure 1.1.1).

By contrast, program evaluation is largely descriptive in nature, does not typically test theory, and lacks generalizability because it is primarily concerned with the relevance of the data and inferences to a particular program. Program evaluation asks question about *what* is happening in a particular context; research, on the other hand, inquires into *why* it is happening and the conditions under which it does and does not happen. As Patton (2002) notes,

FIGURE 1.1.1
Research Situated Within the Context of Theory,
Measurement, Design, and Practice

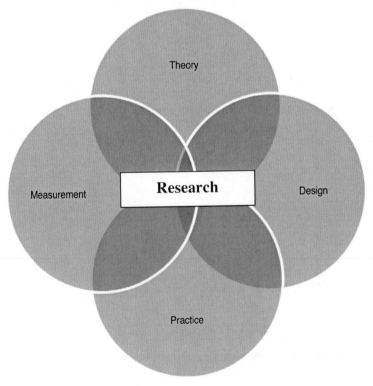

Research, especially fundamental or basic research, differs from evaluation in that its primary purpose is to generate or test theory and contribute to knowledge for the sake of knowledge. Such knowledge, and the theories that undergird knowledge, may subsequently inform action and evaluation, but action is not the primary purpose of fundamental research. (pp. 10–11)

We would add to Patton's thoughts that research should have a connection not only to theory but also to practice.

In a review of past research on service learning, Eyler (2011) offers the following appraisal:

Even well-designed research studies of [service learning] programs will be of limited value if they primarily replicate the growing body of literature linking service learning and particular service learning course characteristics to specific outcomes at only a descriptive level. There are many surveys that show small but marginally significant impacts of service learning on students; but there is little in these program evaluation studies that increases understanding of precisely how students experience and process the challenges they face in their work with community partners. (pp. 232–233)

The chapters in this two-volume set were guided by the recommendation that more and better research, not program evaluation, is needed to advance understanding of service learning and, in turn, of teaching and learning and civic engagement more generally. Research and program evaluation can be integrated into program evaluation research, which Furco (in Gelmon, Furco, Holland, & Bringle, 2005) identifies as a hybrid that encompasses meaningful feedback on a particular program but also is guided by research design and theory in such a way as to contribute to generalizable knowledge that informs others.

Another issue of terminology that is important to clarify is the distinction between research and assessment. Assessment can be undertaken in a variety of ways and for multiple purposes that include improving the implementation of a practice (formative assessment) and providing summaries of outcomes for reporting or grading (summative assessment); in higher education, formative and summative assessment most often concern student learning outcomes. As noted previously in the distinction between research and program evaluation, assessment may be concerned primarily with questions of *what* students are (and are not) learning, often in one particular context and as a means to improving teaching and learning strategies in that context. Systematically asking *why* and *under what conditions* students are (and are not) learning so as to enhance the overall knowledge base related to teaching and learning builds on assessment in a way that becomes research.

Drawing on and generalizing the discussion of assessment in chapter 2.1, the work here is relevant to both of the distinct but interrelated tasks of assessment for research purposes and assessment for course (program) enhancement purposes. According to Steinke and Fitch (2011; chapter 2.1) strong assessment shares with research—as conceptualized here—an emphasis on the use of theory. Assessment at its best, they argue, is grounded in theory that can shape the articulation of outcomes, informs the development of appropriate instructional activities to cultivate those outcomes, provides direction for identifying indicators of those outcomes, uses multiple measures to assess complex constructs, and clarifies the interpretation of assessment results. Given this strong link to theory, assessment that targets improved practice (e.g., more effective teaching and learning) "can be viewed as action research to solve an immediate problem such as how to deepen student learning by improving service learning design" (chapter 2.1, p. 59).

The chapters in these volumes were guided by the intention to support more and better research—not program evaluation and not atheoretical assessment of outcomes—on service learning. The following sections in this chapter examine each of the four dimensions that we view as integral to conducting high-quality research, as expressed in Figure 1.1.1.

Theory

"All research, both quantitative and qualitative, is most beneficial when the design of research is guided by a theory and when the information that is gained through data collection is relevant to supporting, developing, refining, and revising a theory" (Bringle & Hatcher, 2000, p. 69). Qualitative researchers may or may not agree with that statement, depending on the degree to which they conceive qualitative research as generating theory but neither guided by nor testing theory. Accordingly, theory and theory testing might be associated only with a positivist view of research. However, action research, including on pedagogical topics such as service learning, can be theory oriented and can use theory to understand causal relationships among aspects of individuals, programs, contexts, and environments that enhance learning (Friedman & Rogers, 2009).

Giles and Eyler (1994) note that "service-learning, as a relatively new social and educational phenomenon, suffers from the lack of a well articulated conceptual framework" (p. 77). Dewey's (1933) educational theory and Kolb's (1984) experiential learning theory (based on Dewey's work) are most frequently used as a basis for practice, research, and analysis. Bringle (2003) has advocated for theory from cognate areas to be clearly used as a basis of research. These could include, for example, theories from psychology about motivation, interpersonal relationships, and cognitive and moral development; from business about interorganizational relationships, leadership, and change management; from philosophy about value systems and decision making; from political theory about individual and collective action; from history about social movements; and from communication about conflict resolution. These theories can also enrich the logic models that are used to design service learning–enhanced courses.

There is an integral connection between theory and measurement because measurement must be clearly linked to constructs, which, in turn, are embedded in theories that should be formal and explicit (Bringle, 2003; Eyler, 2011). The theory or conceptual framework might precede the data collection, or it might emerge from or be modified based on data analysis and interpretation. Procedures for measuring quantitative or qualitative aspects of attributes do not stand alone, and their meaningfulness is often a function of how solidly they are situated in theory. This point begins to develop the interdependency among theory, measurement, design, and practice.

Measurement

Measurement is an underdeveloped component of research on service learning (Bringle & Hatcher, 2000; Bringle, Phillips, & Hudson, 2004). Measurement as used here refers to any systematic procedure that gathers information or evidence about the process and outcomes of service learning. As Wolcott (1994) notes, "Everything has the potential to be data, but nothing *becomes* data without the intervention of a researcher who takes note— often makes note—of some things to the exclusion of others" (pp. 3–4). Measurement is the process through which data are created.

All measurement needs to be meaningful as well as practical. One form is quantitative measurement, in which numbers are assigned to attributes of an entity, a situation, or an event according to some specified rule (Stevens, 1946). The term *attribute* is intended to be interpreted very broadly and to encompass any feature that is of interest and that varies in some manner (e.g., intensity, frequency, duration, length). All approaches to quantitative measurement share the expectation of consistency when applied by different researchers to the same entity (i.e., reliable), and they will be meaningful (i.e., valid) insofar as they embody and document differences in the attribute of interest (Bringle et al., 2004; Steinberg et al., 2010). The numbers might reflect rank order (ordinal measurement) or equal intervals (e.g., intensity, time, frequency, amount). Whereas quantitative measurement focuses on the amount or intensity of an attribute, qualitative measurement focuses on kinds or categories. Numbers may be used to denote different kinds or categories (e.g., 1 = Republican; 2 = Democrat; 3 = Independent), in the case of nominal variables. Alternatively, qualitative data may be represented by words or phrases that are documented and represented in a non-numeric manner (e.g., themes, patterns).

Connections can be made between quantitative and qualitative measurement. Sandelowski, Volls, and Knaft (2009) contend that all quantitative data have qualitative attributes underlying them and that all qualitative data have quantitative properties. Furthermore, as clear as the distinction between quantitative (e.g., intensity, duration) and qualitative (e.g., kind, themes) data may seem, there are similarities between the two approaches. In either case, the best measurement will make clear the construct that is being examined and the integrity with which the procedures or rules align with the construct; the more transparent this process is, the greater the integrity or trustworthiness it will have. Both types of information can be gleaned from the same sources, including both individuals (e.g., verbal reports, interviews, observations) and documents (e.g., reflection products, written reports, webpages). Both approaches to measurement can be used to investigate processes, outcomes, and the relationship between them. Finally, in neither case should raw data be confused with attributes. Raw data (e.g., written narratives) are representations (samples) that may or may not be indicative of the attribute that is being investigated. The attribute is a hypothetical construct that is embedded in a theory, and the meaningfulness or trustworthiness of the research process must demonstrate the degree of connection between the raw data (e.g., IQ test score) and the attribute (e.g., intelligence). The rationale that establishes that relationship will depend on the theories, implicit or explicit, that guide the selection and interpretation of sampled evidence.

Design

Research design refers to the procedures that are associated with collecting and analyzing data. Just as measurement may be quantitative or qualitative, so too can research designs be quantitative (e.g., quasi-experimental, experimental) or qualitative (e.g., ethnography, case study, phenomenological inquiry). Designs can also be mixed-methods. Creswell and Plano Clark (2006) provide a typology of methods that mix quantitative and qualitative methods, including (a) triangulation designs in which quantitative and qualitative data are collected concurrently, (b) exploratory and (c) explanatory designs in which data are gathered in two sequential phases, and (d) embedded designs in which one form of data is embedded in the other.

The appropriate design is best determined within the context of a theory and a particular set of research questions. It is the research design, whether quantitative or qualitative or mixed, that determines the integrity with which inferences can be made or conclusions generated based on the information or evidence collected. Theories typically implicate causal statements, and, for quantitative research, research designs differ in their capacity to support causal inferences from the research (Campbell & Stanley, 1963; Steinberg et al., 2010; chapter 1.2). Qualitative research designs focus on interpretation of information and typically emphasize not testing theory but uncovering theoretical connections. Research designs are discussed in more detail in chapter 1.2.

Practice

Perhaps the most obvious connection between practice and research is the conviction that the choices made in the process of instructional design—for example, whether students will receive feedback on reflection products and, if so, from whom; which decisions are made by faculty and community organization staff and which are made by students; how civic learning is to be defined; and what criteria are to be used to assess student learning outcomes—need to be informed by what has been learned through research and scholarly practice. The conceptualization of research as comprising theory, measurement, design, and practice, however, assumes a multifaceted understanding of the relevance of practice, well beyond it being merely an arena of application for results of research.

First, strong research requires a strong foundation of pedagogical design. As discussed earlier, although service learning invites—indeed, requires—customization to context, there are defining parameters, necessary conditions, and well-established principles of good practice that need to be adhered to, both in order to produce strong outcomes for all involved and in order to provide a context for conducting high-quality research in the context of service learning courses. *Principles of Good Practice for Combining Service and Learning: A Wingspread Special Report* (Honnet & Poulson, 1989) identifies, for example, (a) opportunities for critical reflection; (b) clear service and learning goals for everyone involved; (c) clarification of responsibilities of everyone involved; (d) training, support, recognition, and evaluation related to both service and learning goals; and (e) participation by and with diverse populations. Howard (2001) synthesizes such principles of good practice as (a) give credit for learning not for service, (b) establish learning objectives, (c) establish criteria for selection of service placements, (d) prepare students for learning from the community, and (e) minimize the distinction between the students' community learning role and classroom learning role.

Second, given the philosophical commitment to and practical necessity of customized design of the pedagogy—customized with consideration of the characteristics and goals of the full range of constituents and the particular opportunities and constraints of the situation—research on service learning needs to explicitly acknowledge and be designed in light of variables in implementation. Otherwise, investigations that purport to be of the same phenomenon in fact are not, and comparisons become meaningless. When the implementation of service learning is intended to provide a context for investigating the pedagogy's processes or outcomes, that implementation needs to be designed intentionally with an eye to both the immediate desired outcomes and the requirements of good research design. Approaching service learning as the scholarship of teaching and learning enables strong linkages between design for learning and design for research. Perhaps more often in service learning than in other pedagogies that involve fewer stakeholders and that present everyone involved with less dissonance (Clayton & Ash, 2004; Howard, 1998), these two foci—research and learning—may be in tension with one another (e.g., an instructor may need to modify planned reflection strategy in response to challenges that students are facing learning through reflection even though doing so will distort the desired data set).

Ultimately, the same commitment to using theory to guide research and to design research so as to generate and refine theory applies to practice. Paraphrasing Lewin (1952, p. 169), there is nothing more practical than a good theory. Lewin's message was twofold. Theorists should try to provide new ideas for understanding or conceptualizing a (problematic) situation, ideas that may suggest potentially fruitful new avenues of dealing with that situation. Conversely, applied researchers should provide theorists with key information and facts relevant to solving a practical problem, facts that need to be conceptualized in a detailed and coherent manner. More generally, theorists should strive to create theories that can be used to solve social or practical problems, and practitioners and researchers should make use of available theory. Service learning research builds on this acknowledgment of the interconnections between theory and practice and invites a more nuanced understanding of the relationship among researchers, theory and theorists, and practice and practitioners. It positions everyone involved as a co-generator of knowledge and, more generally, challenges dichotomies, such as those often perceived between theoretical and applied research or between researchers and practitioners. Service learning researchers are frequently themselves practitioners, and vice versa—thus, the significance of the integrated identity of practitioner-scholar or scholar-practitioner.

Chapter Template

The goal of *Research on Service Learning: Conceptual Frameworks and Assessment* is to stimulate more and better research on service learning. The conceptualization of research as involving theory, measurement, design, and practice guided the development of the chapters. We invited the authors to discuss research in their particular topic areas in terms of all four of these dimensions. We asked them to introduce theories and measurement approaches from cognate areas, to use those theories to critique extant research studies (including designs and analyses), and to integrate those theoretical lenses with what has and has not been undertaken and learned in work to date in order to generate recommendations for practice and an agenda for future research. Table 1.1.1 summarizes the template provided to the authors.

Each chapter provides useful information to practitioners and researchers alike. The structure of each chapter is intended to make transparent the rationale for practice recommendations in terms of both theory and past research. In addition to highlighting aspects of practice that may be particularly salient from the perspectives of theory and research, the chapters support deepening program evaluation into program evaluation research that is grounded in and advances theory. The concise summaries of relevant theories—many of them not well established in the service learning literature to date—as well as the reviews of past studies, the compilation of tools and methods, and the recommendations for future research are intended to facilitate high-quality research by new and veteran researchers and by

TABLE 1.1.1
Chapter Template

Introduction and Scope of Chapter: Why is this topic important to issues of research and assessment in service learning? What are the key definitions related to this topic of inquiry?
Theoretical and Conceptual Frameworks: What are key relevant theories from both within and beyond the field of service learning that can be used to advance research on this topic?
Critical Evaluation of Past Research: What has been done? What do we know from that work? What are the limitations of past research? What remains unanswered? What are the strengths and shortcomings of research to date in light of the theoretical frameworks discussed earlier? In terms of research design?
Measurement Approaches and Instruments: What are the existing tools, approaches, and instruments that could be used or modified? What are their strengths and weaknesses?
Implications for Practice: What are the recommendations for interventions and programs? What should practice and programs look like given what we know? How should service learning be designed so as to support both best practice and future research?
Future Research Agenda: Based upon the theoretical frameworks and the research that has been conducted to date, what implications and recommendations are there for future research? What are the most significant and pressing questions?
Summary and Conclusion
Recommended Reading

practitioner-scholars. The range of topics addressed includes but goes well beyond student outcomes, calling attention to the significance of current and future research related to faculty, communities, institutions, and partnerships as well.

Future Directions

We admire the skill with which the authors contributing to this volume have developed and refined perspectives that can enhance future research on service learning. We expect that the theoretical perspectives they bring, their critiques of past research, the measurement approaches and tools they review, and the recommendations they offer for practice that is informed by research and can enhance settings for research will all contribute not only to the visions for research that they have presented but also to additional research possibilities.

The thinking generated by and documented in these chapters was framed by a particular understanding of service learning and catalyzed by a particular set of guidelines that we, as editors, specified to the authors, whom we invited to focus on particular topic areas. The definition of service learning that framed this project limits the pedagogy to a course-based context and, therefore, carries with it certain assumptions about the activities (e.g., for credit) and does not invite exploration of alternative conceptualizations (e.g., co-curricular service learning). Many of the same theoretical perspectives and questions that are considered here are relevant to other understandings of service learning and other approaches to civic engagement more generally. Much could be learned, for example, by comparing and contrasting the development of intercultural competence (chapter 2.5) and the sources of faculty motivation (chapter 3.2) in curricular and co-curricular service learning; by designing and investigating partnerships that intentionally integrate curricular and co-curricular service learning to target multiple systems and levels of analysis (chapter 4.1); by examining the dynamics of student affairs units as engaged departments (chapter 5.2); and by viewing multiunit collaboration within an institution through the lens of interorganizational relationships and partnership entities (chapter 6.2). We invite such application of the wide-ranging theoretical frameworks gathered in this volume to a much broader set of contexts for service learning.

Many additional focal topics that are not included here certainly fall within the realm addressed by each section of this work. Part Two, on students, for example, lacks explicit consideration of graduate students as a potentially somewhat distinct student population with its own particular set of key outcomes (e.g., research capacities, professional development). Additional theory related to adult learning, professional socialization, mentoring, and identity formation in the context of academic disciplines could be brought to bear to advance understanding and practice of service learning and civic engagement with this population. A focus on P–12 schools could inform research on community outcomes of service learning (Part Four)—for example, outcomes experienced by P–12 students, their parents and other caretakers, and community organizations that provide programming for youth—and research on partnerships in service learning (Part Six)—for example, partnerships among P–12 schools, between P–12 schools (of various types) and higher education institutions (of various types), between faculty in Colleges of Education and cooperating P–12 teachers, and between university students and youth. The examination of learning outcomes for students (Part Two) and faculty (Part Three) needs to be broadened with parallel consideration of community organization staff, residents, and administrators as learners in service learning. Relatedly, the exploration of faculty as co-learners with students in chapter 3.3 only begins to uncover the complexity of positioning all partners in service learning as co-educators, co-learners, and co-generators of knowledge; theory from a variety of disciplines related to the dynamics of reciprocity, paradigm shift, and epistemology could advance research and practice well beyond this rhetorically powerful, but perhaps not yet fully operationalized, framing of partnerships. More comprehensive use of the SOFAR Model that helps to frame Part Six (see chapter 6.1) than is attempted there invites investigation of the full range of partnerships in service learning, including, for example, those that faculty do or can engage in with faculty developers or other campus-based professional staff, with staff at community organizations, and with community residents; those between community organization staff and community residents; those between campus-based staff and community organization staff; and those within any particular stakeholder population (e.g., faculty with faculty).

That this set of volumes has as its guiding framework the use of theory from a variety of cognate areas is both a strength and a limitation. The approach is multidisciplinary, with each chapter emphasizing one or more theories that can contribute to research on service learning. However, very little attempt has been made to integrate these perspectives so that the discussion is interdisciplinary in nature. Furthermore, and perhaps most significantly, this approach directs attention to the value of borrowing from other fields and disciplines rather than emphasizing the development of novel theoretical frameworks, measurement tools, research designs, or practices that are inherent to—if not unique to—and, thereby, perhaps best suited for service learning as its own emerging field. In effect, the approach used here maintains and replicates as the status quo the work of existing disciplines from which the authors borrowed. One significant consequence is that the analyses of extant research and the recommendations for future research offered in the chapters are heavily anchored in a normative, social science orientation to research. In some ways, then, the approach taken can be viewed as antithetical to and incompatible with the ethos of service learning and with emerging models of civic engagement that emphasize democratic, participatory processes that are focused on justice and social change (Saltmarsh & Hartley, 2011). Researchers, practitioners, and practitioner-scholars should continue to explore and debate the integrity and usefulness of alternative epistemologies and their associated methods of inquiry (e.g., ethnographic, feminist, phenomenological) in the process of systematically investigating service learning, with an eye to the possibilities for ever-tighter alignment between the ultimate purposes of the work and the processes that we use to understand and advance it.

References

Annette, J. (2005). Community, service learning and higher education in the UK. In J. Arthur & K. E. Bohlin (Eds.), *Citizenship and higher education: The role of universities in communities and society* (pp. 39–48). New York, NY: RoutledgeFalmer.

Ash, S. L., & Clayton, P. H. (2009). Generating, deepening, and documenting learning: The power of critical reflection in applied learning. *Journal of Applied Learning in Higher Education, 1*(1), 25–48.

Badat, S. (2003). *Transforming South African higher education, 1990–2003: Goals, policy initiatives, and critical challenges and issues* (Unpublished paper). Retrieved from http://www.che.org.za/che_secretariat/ceo_papers/2003/SA-Transform_Dec 2003.pdf

Battistoni, R. M. (2002). *Civic engagement across the curriculum: A resource book for service-learning faculty in all disciplines.* Providence, RI: Campus Compact.

Billig, S. H., & Eyler J. S. (Eds.). (2003). *Deconstructing service-learning: Research exploring context, participation, and impacts.* Greenwich, CT: Information Age.

Boyer, E. L. (1995, October). *The scholarship of engagement.* Talk given to the American Academy of Arts and Science, Cambridge, MA.

Bringle, R. G. (2003). Enhancing theory-based research on service-learning. In S. H. Billig & J. S. Eyler (Eds.), *Deconstructing service-learning: Research exploring context, participation, and impacts* (pp. 3–21). Greenwich, CT: Information Age.

Bringle, R. G., & Clayton, P. H. (2012). Civic education through service learning: What, how, and why? In L. McIlraith, A. Lyons, & R. Munck (Eds.), *Higher education and civic engagement: Comparative perspectives* (pp. 101–124). New York, NY: Palgrave Macmillan.

Bringle, R. G., Clayton, P. H., & Price, M. F. (2009). Partnerships in service learning and civic engagement. *Partnerships: A Journal of Service Learning & Civic Engagement, 1*(1), 1–20.

Bringle, R. G., & Hatcher, J. A. (1996). Implementing service learning in higher education. *Journal of Higher Education, 67*, 221–239.

Bringle, R. G., & Hatcher, J. A. (2000). Meaningful measurement of theory-based service-learning outcomes: Making the case with quantitative research [Special Issue]. *Michigan Journal of Community Service Learning, Fall,* 68–75.

Bringle, R. G., Hatcher, J. A., & Williams, M. J. (2011). Quantitative approaches to research on international service learning: Design, measurement, and theory. In R. G. Bringle, J. A. Hatcher, & S. G. Jones (Eds.), *International service learning: Conceptual frameworks and research* (pp. 275–290). Sterling, VA: Stylus.

Bringle, R. G., Phillips, M., & Hudson, M. (2004). *The measure of service learning: Research scales to assess student experiences.* Washington, DC: American Psychological Association.

Campbell, D. T., & Stanley, J. C. (1963). *Experimental and quasi-experimental designs for research on teaching.* Boston, MA: Houghton Mifflin.

Campus Compact. (2010). *Annual report.* Retrieved from http://www.compact.org/wp-content/uploads/2008/11/2010-Annual-Survey-Exec-Summary-4-8.pdf

Clayton, P. H., & Ash, S. L. (2004). Shifts in perspective: Capitalizing on the counter-normative nature of service learning. *Michigan Journal of Community Service Learning, 11*(1), 59–70.

Clayton, P. H., Bringle, R. G., Senor, B., Huq, J., & Morrison, M. (2010). Differentiating and assessing relationships in service-learning and civic engagement: Exploitive, transactional, and transformational. *Michigan Journal of Community Service Learning, 16*(2), 5–21.

Community-Campus Partnerships for Health. (2005). *Principles of good community-campus partnerships.* Retrieved from http://depts.washington.edu/ccph/principles.html#principles

Conway, J., Amel, E., & Gerwein, D. (2009). Teaching and learning in the social context: A meta-analysis of service-learning's effects on academic, personal, social, and citizenship outcomes. *Teaching of Psychology, 36,* 233–245.

Creswell, J. W., & Plano Clark, V. L. (2006). *Designing and conducting mixed methods research.* Thousand Oaks, CA: SAGE.

Dewey, J. (1933). *How we think: A restatement of the relation of reflective thinking to the educative process.* Boston, MA: Heath.

Enos, S., & Morton, K. (2003). Developing a theory and practice of campus community partnerships. In B. Jacoby (Ed.), *Building partnerships for service-learning* (pp. 20–41). San Francisco, CA: Jossey-Bass.

Eyler, J. S. (2011). What international service learning research can learn from research on service learning. In R. G. Bringle, J. A. Hatcher, & S. G. Jones (Eds.), *International service learning: Conceptual frameworks and research* (pp. 225–242). Sterling, VA: Stylus.

Eyler, J. S., & Giles, D. E., Jr. (1999). *Where's the learning in service-learning?* San Francisco, CA: Jossey-Bass.

Eyler, J. S., Giles, D. E., Jr., Stenson, C. M., & Gray, C. J. (2001). *At a glance: What we know about the effects of service learning on college students, faculty, institutions and communities, 1993–2000* (3rd ed.). Washington, DC: Learn and Serve America's National Service Learning Clearinghouse.

Finley, A. (2011). *Civic learning and democratic engagements: A review of the literature on civic engagement in post-secondary education.* Paper prepared for the U.S. Department of Education as part of Contract ED-OPE-10_C-0078. Retrieved from http://www.civiclearning.org/SupportDocs/LiteratureReview_CivicEngagement_Finley_July2011.pdf

Friedman, V. J., & Rogers, T. (2009). There is nothing so theoretical as good action research. *Action Research, 7*(1), 31–47.

Gelmon, S. B., Furco, A., Holland, B. A., & Bringle, R. G. (2005, November). *Beyond anecdote: Challenges in bringing rigor to service-learning research.* Panel presented at the Fifth International Service-Learning Research Conference, East Lansing, MI.

Giles, D. E., Jr., & Eyler, J. S. (1994). The theoretical roots of service-learning in John Dewey: Towards a theory of service-learning. *Michigan Journal of Community Service Learning, 1*(1), 77–85.

Hatcher, J. A., & Bringle, R. G. (1997). Reflections: Bridging the gap between service and learning. *Journal of College Teaching, 45*(4), 153–158.

Hatcher, J. A., & Erasmus, M. (2008). Service learning in the United States and South Africa: A comparative analysis informed by John Dewey and Julius Nyerere. *Michigan Journal of Community Service Learning, 15*(1), 49–61.

Hodgkinson, V. A. (2004). Developing a research agenda on civic service. *Nonprofit and Voluntary Sector Quarterly, 33*(4), 184S–197S.

Honnet, P. P., & Poulsen, S. J. (1989). *Principles of good practice for combining service and learning: A Wingspread special report.* Racine, WI: The Johnson Foundation.

Howard, J. (1998). Academic service learning: A counternormative pedagogy. *New Directions for Teaching and Learning, 1998*(73), 21–29. doi:10.1002/tl.7303

Howard, J. (2001). *Service learning course design workbook.* Ann Arbor, MI: OCSL Press.

Jacoby, B. (Ed.). (1996). *Service-learning in higher education: Concepts and practices.* San Francisco, CA: Jossey-Bass.

Jameson, J. K., Clayton, P. H., & Bringle, R. G. (2008). Investigating student learning within and across linked service learning courses. In S. H. Billig, B. A. Holland, & M. A. Bowden (Eds.), *Scholarship for sustaining service-learning and community engagement* (pp. 3–27). Charlotte, NC: Information Age.

Jameson, J. K., Clayton, P. H., & Jaeger, A. J. (2011). Community-engaged scholarship through mutually transformative partnerships. In L. M. Harter, J. Hamel-Lambert, & J. Millesen (Eds.), *Participatory partnerships for social action and research* (pp. 259–278). Dubuque, IA: Kendall-Hunt.

Kolb, D. (1984). *Experiential learning: Experience as the source of learning and development.* Upper Saddle River, NJ: Prentice-Hall.

Kuh, G. D. (2008). *High-impact educational practices: What they are, who has access to them, and why they matter.* Washington, DC: Association of American Colleges and Universities.

Lewin, K. (1952). *Field theory in social science: Selected theoretical papers by Kurt Lewin.* London, UK: Tavistock.

Marchese, T. J. (1997). The new conversations about learning: Insights from neuroscience and anthropology, cognitive science and work-place studies. In American Association for Higher Education (Ed.), *Assessing impact: Evidence and action* (pp. 79–95). Washington, DC: American Association for Higher Education.

McBride, A. M., & Sherraden, M. (Eds.). (2007). *Civic service worldwide: Impacts and inquiry.* Armonk, NY: M. E. Sharpe.

McIlrath, L., Farrel, A., Hughes, J., Lillis, S., & Lyons, A. (Eds.). (2007). *Mapping civic engagement within higher education in Ireland.* Retrieved from http://www.compact.org/wp-content/uploads/2011/03/Mapping_Civic_Engagement_final.pdf

Patton, M. Q. (2002). *Qualitative research and evaluation methods* (3rd ed.). Newbury Park, CA: SAGE.

Pragman, C., & Flannery, B. (2008). Assessment of service-learning outcomes: Examining the effects of class size, major, service-learning experience, and sex. *The International Journal of Learning, 15*(4), 217–225.

Rama, D. V., Ravenscroft, S. P., Wolcroft, S. K., & Zlotkowski, E. (2000). Service-learning outcomes: Guidelines for educators and researchers. *Issues in Accounting Education, 15,* 657–692.

Saltmarsh, J., & Hartley, M. (Eds.). (2011). *"To serve a larger purpose": Engagement for democracy and the transformation of higher education.* Philadelphia, PA: Temple University Press.

Sandelowski, M., Volls, C. I., & Knaft, B. (2009). On quantitizing. *Journal of Mixed Methods Research, 3*(3), 208–222.

Sigmon, R. L. (1979). Service-learning: Three principles. *Synergist, 8*(1), 9–11.

Steinberg, K. S., Bringle, R. G., & Williams, M. J. (2010). *Service learning research primer.* Scotts Valley, CA: National Service-Learning Clearinghouse.

Steinke, P., & Fitch, P. (2011). Outcome assessment from the perspective of psychological science: The TAIM approach. *New Directions for Institutional Research, 2011*(149), 15–26. doi:10.1002/ir.377

Stevens, S. S. (1946). On the theory of scales of measurement. *Science, 103*(2684), 677–680.

Thomson, A. M., Smith-Tolken, A., Naidoo, A. V., & Bringle, R. G. (2011). Service learning and civic engagement: A comparison of three contexts. *Voluntas, 22*(2), 214–237.

Westheimer, J., & Kahne, J. (2003). What kind of citizen? Political choices and educational goals. *Campus Compact Reader, 3*(3), 1–13.

Whitney, B. C., & Clayton, P. H. (2011). Research on the role of reflection in international service learning. In R. G. Bringle, J. A. Hatcher, & S. G. Jones (Eds.), *International service learning: Conceptual frameworks and research* (pp. 145–187). Sterling, VA: Stylus.

Wolcott, H. F. (1994). *Transforming qualitative data: Description, analysis, and interpretation.* Thousand Oaks, CA: SAGE.

Zlotkowski, E., Longo, N. V., & Williams, J. R. (Eds.). (2006). *Students as colleagues: Expanding the circle of service-learning leadership.* Providence, RI: Campus Compact.

ATTRIBUTES OF HIGH-QUALITY RESEARCH ON SERVICE LEARNING

Kathryn S. Steinberg, Robert G. Bringle, and Lisa E. McGuire

One of the strengths of service learning is its varied nature (Billig & Eyler, 2003). It (a) draws on multiple theories of learning; (b) focuses on individuals and individual outcomes (e.g., students, faculty, residents); (c) encompasses relationships between individuals (e.g., between students and others, between community-based organizations, between campus and communities); (d) targets a broad range of outcomes (e.g., civic education, character education, student development, academic learning, quality of life in communities); and (e) draws on multiple disciplinary perspectives in design, implementation, and application. Along with the strengths of this versatility and broad scope, however, comes the challenge of conducting high-quality research; variations in design, objectives, methods, and potential sources of evidence complicate the endeavor.

Low-quality research is unethical research because it is a waste of resources and runs the risk of misinforming the understanding and practice of service learning. This chapter focuses on the nature of research at a general level and discusses the issues of quality and rigor of both qualitative and quantitative research. Based on this discussion, an evaluation of the current status of the quality of research on service learning is offered and recommendations for improving research in the future are proposed.

Portions of this chapter are based on and adapted from Steinberg, Bringle, and Williams (2010) and Bringle and Steinberg (2010).

Conceptual Frameworks That Guide Research

Shavelson and Towne (2002, p. 51) describe the scientific process in terms of six interrelated principles of inquiry:

1. Pose significant questions that can be investigated empirically.
2. Link research to relevant theory.
3. Use methods that permit direct investigation of the question.
4. Provide a coherent and explicit chain of reasoning.
5. Replicate and generalize across studies.
6. Disclose research to encourage professional scrutiny and critique.

All research on service learning should aspire to meet these principles or explain why some need to be modified or are not relevant to a particular mode of inquiry. Although most researchers may contend that the work they have disseminated aligns with these principles, there is variability in the degree to which past research on service learning exhibits these characteristics (Bringle & Hatcher, 2000; Bringle & Steinberg, 2010).

The second of Shavelson and Towne's (2002) principles identifies the importance of connecting research to a theoretical or conceptual base. Theory is a set of speculations about a phenomenon and its nature. Theories identify concepts and coherently interrelate those concepts in a way that aids in organizing, understanding, and predicting events. Theories can provide a rich set of heuristics through which to explore generalizations and boundary conditions, auxiliary phenomena, and connections between and among constructs. In doing so, theories suggest additional means for analyzing phenomena, provide a context for subsequent predictions, and offer a basis for relating research findings to other research and theories. Bringle (2003) contends that research on service learning has suffered from a lack of attention to theory. He suggests that service learning research can be improved by developing theories or drawing on theories from cognate areas, which is one of the key purposes of this two-volume set.

Theory and research are both important to the process of accumulating knowledge (Bringle, 2003; Bringle & Hatcher, 2000). The process can begin at different points on the diagram shown in Figure 1.2.1. It may start with a preliminary theory that, through a deductive process, generates research questions and testable hypotheses that are evaluated through research, the results of which produce decisions about the applicability and relevance of the theory (e.g., supported, needs modification, refuted). Alternatively, specific observations may be used to generalize principles that are inductively

FIGURE 1.2.1
The Relationship Between Research and Theory

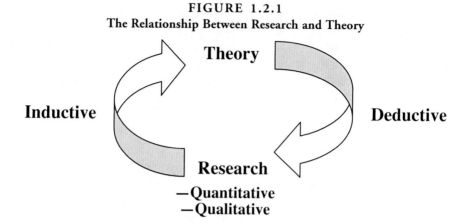

developed into a theory that then guides subsequent research and practice. The presumption is that, in every case, there is a symbiotic relationship between theory and research, such that theory guides the research process and research results arbitrate an evaluation of the appropriateness of the theory.

Research on service learning, and on education more generally, typically sorts into two conceptual frameworks that can be differentiated on paradigmatic issues, theoretical perspectives, research design, and measurement strategies: (a) *qualitative* research design, which focuses on systematic interpretation of information (e.g., documents, artifacts, words, pictures) and may position the researcher as a participant in the process; and (b) *quantitative* research design, which uses scientific methods of data collection and analyzes numerical data and which typically values a detached researcher. The type of data (information collected) does not define the type of design; the design (qualitative or quantitative) and the type of data (qualitative or quantitative) are independent.

Although there are many adherents to each approach, some (e.g., Trochim, 2006) have posited that the dichotomy is false, at least in terms of the data that are collected. For example, researchers who are inclined toward the quantitative approach may utilize interviews or focus groups, which yield qualitative data, to explore ideas, elaborate theories, or develop questionnaires. Investigators who prefer a more qualitative approach may quantify qualitative data (e.g., interview responses) into categories that are coded numerically and statistically summarized. Sandelowski, Volls, and Knaft

(2009) contend that all quantitative data have underlying qualitative attributes and that all qualitative data have quantitative properties.

In practice, many of the assumptions, philosophical approaches, and procedures of quantitative researchers are different from those of qualitative researchers. Some scholars contend that one approach is not inherently better than the other and that a mixed-methods approach may be best in that it can capitalize on the strengths and compensate for the limitations of each (Tashakkori & Teddlie, 2003). However, because of the sometimes dramatic differences in approaches to research (e.g., static design in quantitative research versus dynamic design in qualitative research, sampling preferences), mixing quantitative and qualitative methods without a clear rationale and purpose does not necessarily lead to better evidence to support inferences. A full discussion of mixed-methods research is beyond the scope of this chapter; for a typology of methods that mix quantitative and qualitative methods, see Creswell and Plano Clark (2006).

This chapter's analysis of the conceptual frameworks that guide both research and the evaluation of its quality is organized around the conceptual, paradigmatic, and methodological distinctions that are traditionally identified for qualitative and quantitative research. Issues that support an evaluation of quality, rigor, and relevance for each approach are delineated in this chapter.

Qualitative Research Methods

Qualitative inquiry is consistent with the premise that "not everything that counts may be counted" (Remshardt & Flowers, 2007, p. 20). Qualitative research has received considerable attention in the academy over the past 25 years as the definition of scholarship has expanded to include not only the scholarship of discovery but also the scholarships of integration, application, and teaching (Boyer, 1990). Qualitative inquiry provides a strategy to develop new theory or to expand applications and interpretations of existing theories. Moving beyond a positivist or a postpositivist tradition that stresses a single knowable reality, qualitative research grows out of constructivist paradigms, which assume multiple realities, as well as critical or transformative paradigms, which emphasize the pervasiveness and impact of power differentials and the value of participant voice (Lincoln & Guba, 2000).

In general, qualitative research designs focus on discovery and description rather than quantification and generalizability (Patton, 2002). In relation to service learning, this could mean that qualitative research designs might lead to the development of new theories or insights that were previously not identified using traditional designs or existing theory.

Common Attributes of Qualitative Research

The focus on discovery, description, and synthesis is facilitated by three attributes of qualitative research: naturalistic inquiry, emergent design flexibility, and purposive sampling (Patton, 2002).

Naturalistic Inquiry

Drawing on its constructivist roots, qualitative design begins with the proposition that each research situation is unique and that data should be gathered from their situated context (Lincoln & Guba, 1985). Qualitative researchers reject the ideas that the laboratory is an appropriate approximation for the natural setting and that controlling for variables during data analysis is sufficient, desirable, or even possible. The strategy of naturalistic inquiry in service learning research guides researchers to collect data in the field (i.e., community or classroom) as close to the implementation of the service and learning activities as possible. Qualitative researchers also consider the unique context of any given study, understanding that the nature of the learning environment is an important factor shaping the knowledge to be gained from the particular study.

Emergent Design Flexibility

Unlike in quantitative research design, in which specific hypotheses and measurement procedures are developed prior to data collection, qualitative studies do not generally begin with a specific frame for data collection (i.e., survey items, interview questions) that is unmalleable; rather, the focus of the research and the nature of the data collection may emerge while the data are being collected. The best example of this may be the constant comparative method from grounded research (Glaser & Strauss, 1967) in which the findings of, for example, interviews are systematically compared with those from previous interviews throughout the data-gathering process to identify themes. These preliminary themes are then utilized to ask questions during subsequent interviews, and, again, themes are supported or amended as the data-gathering process continues. This process continues until saturation is reached (i.e., until no new themes are identified).

Purposive Sampling

"Perhaps nothing better captures the difference between quantitative and qualitative methods than the different logic that undergirds sampling approaches" (Patton, 2002, p. 230). In qualitative research, sampling is not formulated to strengthen statistical power or generalizability but rather to provide depth of experience with the topic in question. Participants in a qualitative study are chosen for their particular experiences, and sample size is not important except as it may fulfill the expectations of the particular research design and research question.

Qualitative Designs

Naturalistic inquiry, emergent design flexibility, and purposive sampling are apparent in the diverse designs available in qualitative inquiry. One of the greatest strengths, as well as criticisms, of qualitative research is the proliferation of designs (Denzin & Lincoln, 2000, 2005). The most relevant to future research on service learning are ethnography, case study, grounded theory, phenomenology and narrative inquiry, and participatory research, each of which is briefly discussed next.

Ethnography

Anchored in anthropology (Patton, 2002), ethnographic designs are used to study a given culture, with an emphasis on fieldwork and participant observation that seeks "to make the strange familiar and the familiar strange" (Glesne, 2006, p. 51). Data are collected through interviews, observation of events, and review of documents and artifacts (Glesne, 2006). The well-developed ethnographic data collection strategy may be of interest to students and faculty involved in unique cultures at service learning sites as a means for them to enhance their understanding of the nature of the settings and contexts (Gaughan, 2002).

Case Study

Although case studies take different forms in different disciplines, the major feature of this design is to focus on the research situation itself. Stake (2000) defines the context of a case as a bounded, integrated system with functioning subsystems. In service learning, those subsystems might include faculty, students, community partners, university administrators, campuses, or partnerships (Zlotkowski, 1998). The case study may be intrinsic (specifically case focused), instrumental (providing insight into a specific issue), or collective (case studies of multiple individual cases) (Stake, 2000). Case studies are appropriate for gaining knowledge in new situations, particularly those that are highly successful or problematic. Much of the existing literature on service learning could be viewed as case studies that have been the basis for subsequent research.

Grounded Theory

Grounded theory most exemplifies the inductive approach of qualitative research in that the focus is on building theory rather than testing it (Strauss & Corbin, 1998). In this design, the process of generating theory occurs through the constant comparative method (Glaser & Strauss, 1967). In this process the findings of, for example, interviews are iteratively compared with the findings of previous interviews throughout the data-gathering process to identify and revise common themes. Coding procedures are the analytical tool for handling large amounts of data that will provide support for the theory developed. Although grounded theory emphasizes systematic analysis, it also encourages creativity by allowing researchers to consider alternative meanings of observed phenomena (Strauss & Corbin, 1998).

Phenomenology and Narrative Inquiry

Phenomenology seeks to understand the lived experience of respondents, while narrative inquiry focuses on the structure and nature of the personal stories of respondents. Both seek to gain knowledge from an intense study and analysis of individual experiences and to identify common themes that provide a deeper understanding of the focus of study (Peters, 2004). Narrative accounts of the early service learning practitioners and scholars (e.g., Stanton, Giles, & Cruz, 1999) and of students (e.g., Coles, 1993) are examples of how narrative and phenomenological approaches may elucidate new ideas in the early stages of knowledge building. Peters (2004) utilized narrative inquiry methods to conduct interviews with a landscape architecture faculty member to study how scholars understand and pursue the civic mission of higher education. Baldwin, Buchanan, and Rudisill (2007) studied the narratives of teacher candidates as they explored diversity and social justice issues in relation to a service learning experience.

Participatory Research

Emerging from the critical or transformative paradigm in which "increased sensitivity to issues of power and authority has encouraged a rethinking of research design and implementation" (Glesne, 2006, p. 13), participatory methods emphasize including the voices of those being studied throughout the entire research process, from design through analysis to interpretation and use of the information. Abowitz (2001) highlights the common ground between critical discourses and service learning discourses in that they both build on Dewey (1933) as a foundational theorist and emphasize a less hierarchical relationship between student and teacher. Participatory research may be an appropriate design for service learning researchers because the goals of community voice and change are central to critical research and civic engagement (Crabtree, 1998; Strand, Marullo, Cutforth, Stoecker, & Donohue, 2003).

Quality and Rigor in Qualitative Research

The basic steps of all qualitative research designs can be compared and contrasted with Shavelson and Towne's (2002) description of the six principles of inquiry. Consistent with the first principle, qualitative researchers pose research questions that require the systematic collection of evidence. The selection of the qualitative research design must be appropriately matched to the question(s) posed, and qualitative research may be evaluated by the existence of a well-articulated rationale for the choice of the research design. Qualitative inquiry may be especially appropriate for questions that involve the identification or development of new theory or for the application of theory to new situations or populations.

In terms of the second principle of inquiry, linking research to theory, the purpose and timing of the literature review may be unique in qualitative designs (Patton, 2002). Some literature may be reviewed prior to data collection to (a) confirm that the research topic is justifiable, (b) identify the focus for the research, (c) inform the selected research design and interview questions, and (d) provide an ongoing process to identify new literature that may inform the study or assist in interpreting results (Glesne, 2006). However, in qualitative research an additional literature review is often conducted after data analysis to provide a deepening of themes identified or to support the identification of unique theory developed in and resulting from the research.

The third principle in Shavelson and Towne's (2002) research process involves the collection of data that permit direct investigation of the research question. Qualitative data collection is marked by unique features including purposive sampling (Patton, 2002), collection techniques that yield thick description (Geertz, 1973), acknowledgment of the subjective nature of the participatory process with efforts to maintain empathic neutrality (Glesne,

2006), and a dynamic systems perspective that highlights the role of research in the change process (Patton, 2002).

For the fourth principle of Shavelson and Towne's (2002) research process, one means to evaluate the quality of a qualitative research study is to review the description of the data analysis process to determine its consistency with the traditions of the research designs that we have discussed. For example, it is not appropriate for a narrative analysis to utilize the constant comparative process for data analysis, because this technique is specific to grounded theory. Rigorous qualitative research requires knowledge of specific methods with information provided about the plan for gathering and analyzing data that build on the established scholarly traditions.

The fifth principle in Shavelson and Towne's (2002) model is most contradictory to qualitative research because the goals of discovery and description are not the same as those of replication and generalization. However, qualitative research may stimulate further research and may lead to quantification of the themes and patterns identified. Qualitative results are often presented using the specific words and images (i.e., of respondents) to provide the opportunity for empirical verifiability that supports the identification of themes from the analysis. The findings of qualitative studies may also have implications for application in similar situations, thus meeting the identified need for research to be transferable (generalizable). And finally, according to the sixth principle, qualitative research should be disseminated in ways that invite the scrutiny of peer review and critique.

Lincoln and Guba (1985) initially proposed trustworthiness as the standard of quality in constructivist inquiry, with the indicators of credibility, transferability, auditability, and confirmability. Creswell (1998) identified the following eight verification processes that further specify the means for qualitative researchers to increase trustworthiness of findings:

1. Prolonged engagement with the research situation, including multiple observations
2. Triangulation, or multiple data collection methods, sources, theories, or researchers
3. Peer review and debriefing, including personal and external reflection
4. Negative case analysis, which encourages presentation of information that does not fit the patterns or categories identified in the results
5. Clarification of researcher bias and subjectivity as well as mention of how they were monitored
6. Member checking by sharing drafts and final reports with the respondents

7. Rich, thick description in the data collection process, capturing actual words and images
8. External audit involving an outside person in reviewing research notes, coding, and other materials related to the research process

Although not every strategy is possible, or even appropriate, for each of the qualitative designs, researchers should identify and fully articulate how multiple strategies were used to ensure the trustworthiness of their study in order to meet standards for rigor in their research.

Lather (1986) identified an additional criterion for rigor: catalytic validity. This criterion refers to whether the research brings about change or transformation in the research participants and their circumstances. This criterion has been less popular than Lincoln and Guba's criterion of trustworthiness; however, it is appropriately consistent with research conducted under the transformative or critical paradigm. Given the aspirational purposes of service learning, this criterion may be interesting to explore for qualitative research that seeks to bring about change in the academy, the community, and the individual (e.g., student, faculty, community member) participants themselves.

Quantitative Research Methods

In contrast to qualitative research, quantitative research focuses on particular scientific methods and analyzes numerical data. The quality of quantitative research is evaluated based on the completeness of the literature review, the rigor and appropriateness of the research design, the use of theory to generate hypotheses, the sampling framework and strategy, the measurement approaches, the statistical analysis and interpretation, and the appropriateness of the conclusions reached (i.e., alignment of conclusions with the design, theory, and measures). Quantitative research is based on empirical evidence and must be replicable and generalizable. Quantitative research can be classified into three types: non-experimental, experimental, and quasi-experimental (Trochim, 2006; see Table 1.2.1).

Non-Experimental Designs

The simplest and most common forms of quantitative research involve non-experimental designs or pre-experimental designs (Campbell & Stanley, 1963; Cook & Campbell, 1979) that do not include random assignment of subjects to groups and that have no control or comparison group. This type

TABLE 1.2.1
Quantitative Research Designs

Research Design	Random Assignment of Subjects to Groups	Control Group or Multiple Waves of Measurement
Non-experimental	No	No
Experimental	No	Yes
Quasi-experimental	Yes	Yes

of design is very useful for answering descriptive questions such as the following:

- What percentage of students on campus is involved in community service?
- Do male students have different attitudes than female students about the need for social service agencies in American society?
- How many faculty members on a campus have taught a service learning course in the past three years?

One very common form of non-experimental design is a one-shot (or onetime) survey. For example, an investigator might survey student perspectives on community activism at the end of a semester in a service learning course. This design lacks a comparison and, therefore, the ability to conclude that the outcome was the result of the service learning experience.

An improvement on the one-shot survey is the single group, pretest-posttest design. For example, Williams, King, and Koob (2002) gave an attitude measure of self-efficacy to students in a service learning course at the beginning and end of the semester. This non-experimental design provides comparisons of the student group to itself, which can be important to inferences of change or learning. This design is appropriate for determining whether change (i.e., learning, attitude shift) occurred during the time period of the course. However, without a comparison group, there is no way to know whether a non–service learning section of the same course would have produced the same degree of change.

A third approach is the correlational research design, which evaluates the nature and degree of association between two naturally occurring variables. For example, Steinberg, Hatcher, and Bringle (2011) found that the number of service learning courses that a student had taken was positively correlated ($r = +.34$) with their civic-mindedness. The correlation coefficient summarizes the nature of the linear pattern between two constructs and provides two pieces of information: (a) a number, which summarizes the degree to which the two variables are associated; and (b) a positive or negative sign, which summarizes the nature or direction of the relationship. Correlational studies have limited ability to generate valid causal inferences about either the relationships between two variables or the likelihood that a correlation is the result of the influence of a third variable.

Experimental Designs

In contrast to correlational methods that assess the patterns between naturally occurring variables, experiments manipulate a variable, the independent variable, to determine what consequence that manipulation has on an outcome variable, the dependent variable. Not all experimental designs are equally good at allowing the researcher to make causal inferences.

The gold standard of quantitative research is the randomized control group design, in which subjects are randomly assigned to different groups or treatments. Traditionally these groups are referred to as the experimental or treatment group(s) (e.g., students in a service learning course) and the comparison or control group(s) (e.g., students in a traditional or non–service learning course). Random assignment controls for preexisting differences between groups. Well-designed randomized experiments allow the researcher to have greater confidence about appropriate cause-and-effect conclusions. Random selection, or sampling, is a research method distinct from random assignment. Random sampling is relevant to the generalizability (external validity) of the research; random assignment is relevant to controlling for preexisting differences in groups (internal validity).

True experimental studies, which can be conducted in natural settings or laboratories, are relatively rare in service learning research, as in most educational research. There may be opportunities to assign students randomly to different conditions in service learning courses; for example, students may be randomly assigned to (a) written reflection or (b) reflection through group discussion. Blind selection, which occurs when students are not aware which sections of a course will include service learning when they register, can be used to approximate random assignment of students to groups (e.g., service learning and non–service learning groups). Markus, Howard, and King's work (1993) involved both pretest and posttest comparisons of two nonequivalent (nonrandom) groups (service learning and traditional course sections) and controlled for self-selection through blind selection.

Quasi-Experimental Designs

Like experimental designs, quasi-experimental designs involve the manipulation of an independent variable to examine the consequence of that variable on another (dependent) variable. The key difference between experimental and quasi-experimental designs is that the latter do not involve random assignment of subjects to groups but, instead, incorporate preexisting groups. A large portion of quantitative research on service learning involves quasi-experimental design (Bringle & Steinberg, 2010).

A prevalent problem in service learning research is self-selection bias. This form of bias occurs when students knowingly choose to enroll in a service learning course or when they elect to engage in an optional service learning component of a course. In this case, students are not randomly assigned to the treatment group (service learning course) but are self-selecting the treatment. These conditions make it difficult to assume that these students were equivalent to students participating in non–service learning courses or components, which makes it difficult for the researcher to determine why the two groups of students are different at the end of the course. Self-selection also complicates knowing whether the outcomes are generalizable to students who do not possess the same characteristics as the self-selecting students (e.g., interest in community service).

There are a number of ways that researchers have dealt with self-selection bias. In addition to random assignment and blind selection, another option is delayed treatment, in which students are randomly assigned to groups that participate in service learning at different points in the calendar. For instance, one group of students (experimental group) is identified by the researcher (possibly through a random sampling procedure) to participate in a service learning opportunity in one semester, while another group (control group) is delayed until the next semester in its involvement in service learning. The second group is a control group during the first semester and then becomes the experimental group during the next semester. A researcher can also address self-selection bias by administering to the treatment and control groups pre- and posttests and then utilizing statistical controls to isolate the effect of the treatment while controlling for preexisting differences between groups based on pretest scores. Astin, Sax, and Avalos (1999) and Eyler and Giles (1999) used this design strategy. A limitation of this approach is that it can statistically control only for variables measured in the pretest; there may be other variables that the groups differ on that were not measured in the pretest.

There are two approaches to designing research to answer questions about service learning across time. In a cross-sectional design, data are gathered from several different groups of subjects (e.g., first-year students, sophomores, juniors, seniors) at approximately the same point in time. Longitudinal studies involve gathering information from the same group of persons at several different points in time. For example, Astin et al. (1999) analyzed survey data from entering first-year students in 1985; a second survey was given to the same group of students four years later, in 1989; and a third survey was administered to the then-alumni in 1994–95. Longitudinal studies are extremely valuable sources of information for studying long-term consequences of service learning, although they present some sampling (e.g., loss of persons in the sample), practical, technical, and financial difficulties associated with the researcher following a group of people over time.

Characteristics of Good Measurement Approaches and Instrumentation

Measurement procedures can be judged on a variety of merits, including practical as well as technical or psychometric issues. No one procedure is perfect for every task because all measurement procedures, whether qualitative or quantitative, have strengths and limitations and are context specific in their meaningfulness.

In general, a measurement procedure that incorporates multiple indicators is stronger, whether one is examining behavioral indices (e.g., attendance, communication skills); written communications (e.g., journal entries, formal papers); testimony by others (e.g., from community partners, from other students); outcomes or products; or self-reported beliefs, attitudes, and values (e.g., scales, inventories; see Bringle, Phillips, & Hudson, 2004). Aggregation can occur across occasions in the same situation (e.g., multiple observations at the service site), across situations (e.g., at the service site, in the classroom), across modalities (e.g., written, verbal), and across domains of a construct (e.g., social responsibility behaviors, social responsibility attitudes). In all cases, aggregation can improve the quality of the measure, presuming that the individual components that are being aggregated are coherent and meaningful. For this reason, researchers should consider collecting multiple samples and forms of evidence (e.g., a log of activities completed at the service site, multiple items for each construct on a self-report satisfaction survey, reflection narratives, focus group reports, peer evaluations, evaluations from site supervisors) that can then be aggregated or triangulated as appropriate to create a composite picture of an outcome (Bringle et al., 2004).

Practical Issues

Some of the practical issues that need to be considered for each measurement procedure are as follows:

- Cost
- Availability of the evidence
- Training required (e.g., for conducting interviews or focus groups)
- Ease of administration, scoring, and analysis
- Time and effort required on the part of respondents
- Completeness of the data gathered (e.g., return rates)
- Potential sources of bias (e.g., social desirability response bias)
- Relevance to the research question

Practical considerations for various measurement procedures must be evaluated against the richness of the information, the meaningfulness of the information, and the relevance of the information to the research question or hypothesis.

Psychometric Properties

Along with the practical issues, quantitative measurement procedures (especially surveys, tests, and scales) may be judged on the psychometric properties of the instruments, outlined in Table 1.2.2. There are two major categories of psychometric properties—reliability and validity—both of which are important for good quantitative measurement. Although qualitative researchers may not be concerned about all of the aspects identified in Table 1.2.2, many are relevant for qualitative techniques; for example, qualitative researchers might need to consider the consistency between different raters using a particular coding scheme that is being applied to written products.

Improving Future Research on Service Learning

Based on the limitations and deficiencies of past research (Bringle & Steinberg, 2010) and the importance of theory, measurement, design, and practice

TABLE 1.2.2
Psychometric Properties of Research Instruments

Type	Description	Other Names, Subtypes	Measured By
RELIABILITY	The instrument produces consistent scores when measuring the same entity.	Consistency	Coefficient (numerical summary)
Test-retest reliability	The instrument has the ability to give similar scores of the same entity from one time to another.	Temporal consistency	Correlation coefficient
Internal consistency reliability	There is consistency of results across items within a measure.	Split-half reliability	Interitem correlation; Cronbach's coefficient alpha
Interrater reliability	There is consistency for different observers using the same instrument, rating scale, or rubric.	Scoring agreement; interobserver reliability	Correlation coefficient; intraclass correlation; kappa
VALIDITY	The instrument does a good job of measuring the concept it purports to measure. Refers to a specific purpose for the instrument with a specific group of people.	Meaningfulness	Varies
Construct validity	The instrument is measuring the desired construct because obtained results or scores conform to theoretical predictions.	Convergent validity; discriminant validity; factor structure	Correlation coefficient; factor scores; other evidence of confirmation
Content validity	The instrument includes items or indicators that are representative of a clearly delineated conceptual domain.	Face validity	Ratings by independent reviewers
Criterion-related validity	The instrument is associated with a criterion (e.g., future behavior, scores on a behavioral index) that is implicated by the theory of the construct.	Concurrent validity; predictive validity	Correlation coefficient; regression results

in informing future research, there is a developing consensus (e.g., Billig & Eyler, 2003; Bringle et al., 2004) that good service learning research, whether quantitative or qualitative, should embody the characteristics explored in the following sections.

Connecting Research With Theory

More service learning research needs to have interventions and outcomes linked in systematic ways to theory so that results across studies can be compared and contrasted (see Figure 1.2.1). Theories posit answers to "Why?" questions: Why did the students change? Why did a particular type of reflection improve learning? Why did faculty stop teaching a service learning course? Why did service learning student involvement produce community results? Simply describing outcomes from a service learning course (e.g., on students, faculty, the community) severely limits enhancing our understanding why the outcomes occurred. Unfortunately, research on service learning too often consists of isolated evaluations of specific courses that do not incorporate or develop theory in a way that extends our understanding of what is being studied (e.g., student learning, attitude change, community outcomes). Furthermore, rarely does service learning research return to theory when discussing the implications and generalizations of the research (Bringle, 2003). Theories provide a basis for understanding outcomes, and good (quantitative) research will evaluate theory. Theories can come from multiple sources, including new theories developed specifically for service learning or from cognate disciplines (Bringle, 2003; chapters 2.1 through 6.3). Theories from the social sciences (e.g., education, cognitive sciences, psychology, sociology, anthropology, communications studies) can contribute to the development and interpretation of service learning research.

Clearly Identifying and Defining Constructs

One difficulty in comparing results across research studies is the lack of common agreement on definitions (e.g., service learning, community service, volunteering, reflection, civic outcomes, civic engagement, learning outcomes). For example, some researchers include co-curricular service in their studies, whereas others limit their studies to service learning experiences that occur in credit-bearing academic courses. In addition to defining the independent and dependent variables, researchers need to identify and explore the role of important moderator variables (e.g., type of community organization, size and type of institution) and mediating variables (e.g., self-efficacy, civic-mindedness) (Bringle, 2003).

Controlling for, or Accounting for, Differences Among Groups

Many quantitative and qualitative studies in service learning research have not included adequate control or comparison groups to contrast one intervention (e.g., service learning) with other interventions (e.g., research paper, volunteering) in ways that would permit appropriate conclusions related to differences and similarities. Both quantitative and qualitative researchers need to base their conclusions on appropriate contextualization of results. Qualitative investigators should clearly describe the characteristics of the participants in each study, so that other researchers can evaluate the transferability of results to another context (Guba, 1981). Quantitative researchers should use scientific research designs or procedures (e.g., experimental method, analysis of covariance to control for preexisting differences) that control for extraneous explanations, including self-selection, and that allow causal inferences about well-measured outcomes (see Bringle & Hatcher, 2000). For multicourse, multicampus studies, statistical procedures that account for the nesting of students within courses and of courses within institutions should be used.

Controlling for, or Accounting for, Self-Selection Bias

As discussed earlier, when students (or faculty members) choose to be in a service learning course, there are likely to be differences between them and any comparison group (Astin & Sax, 1998; Eyler & Giles, 1999), which confounds the quantitative researcher's ability to determine why the students (or faculty or community members) are different at the end of the experiences. Some options for dealing with self-selection include blind selection, delayed treatment using a pretest to compare equivalence of groups at the beginning of the study, and statistical procedures (e.g., hierarchical or stepwise regression, analysis of covariance) to control for differences between treatment and nontreatment groups (but only for measures that are obtained prior to the educational intervention).

Avoiding Over-Reliance on, or Exclusive Use of, Self-Report Measures

Many measures in service learning research are based on self-reports by students, faculty, staff, or community partners (e.g., students self-report that they improved their communication skills in a service learning class). Self-report instruments can be useful, convenient, and meaningful; however, their reliability and validity are limited (Bowman & Brandenberger, 2010;

Bringle et al., 2004; Steinke & Buresh, 2002). For example, they may be influenced by social desirability response sets, they may be affected by inaccurate or biased memories, they may be influenced by response-shift bias (Bray, Maxwell, & Howard, 1984), or they may not correspond to past or future behavior. A few service learning studies (e.g., Ash, Clayton, & Atkinson, 2005) have utilized more authentic measures of student learning outcomes, including independent evaluation of student products. Collecting this type of authentic information or direct evidence, and in some cases behavioral ratings by external observers, is useful in triangulating results to lead to justifiable conclusions.

Using Psychometrically Defensible Measures That Have Multiple Indicators

Service learning researchers should focus on using measurement procedures that possess demonstrable reliability and validity (Bringle et al., 2004) and that are not susceptible to social desirability response bias. Some measures of behaviors and attitudes (e.g., civic-mindedness, social responsibility) are socially desirable, and respondents are inclined to make themselves look good when they record responses (e.g., to survey questions). One way to counteract this bias is for researchers to include neutral or negatively worded items in a survey or interview protocol (i.e., to write items in ways that control for the bias). In addition, researchers can state that there are no right or wrong answers because the questions are designed to assess respondents' judgments rather than facts (Oskamp & Schultz, 2005). To measure the strength of the social desirability bias, researchers can also include an instrument to assess an individual's tendency to respond in a socially desirable manner; a low correlation would indicate that the primary instrument is not heavily related to social desirability bias. Finally, researchers can statistically remove the variance arising from individual differences in social desirability (Moley, Mercer, Ilustre, Miron, & McFarland, 2002; Oskamp & Schultz, 2005).

Using Multiple Methods if Possible and Establishing Converging Results Across Different Methods

Research is strengthened when it incorporates multiple measures and multiple designs that allow triangulation of converging results to increase understanding, confidence, and generalizability (Creswell, 1998; Patton, 2002). This is relevant to both qualitative and quantitative research design.

Using Designs That Result in Confidence in the Conclusions Reached

Service learning research is plagued by pre-experimental designs and small sample size or limited data, such as basing the research on a single course experience measured only at the end of a semester (Bringle & Steinberg, 2010). Small sample size does not necessarily indicate a purposive sample, which is an aspiration for some qualitative researchers. Small sample size makes it difficult for researchers to have confidence in the results and in the implications of those results because it can limit the reliability, generalizability, or trustworthiness of the data. This is an important limitation for researchers who use quantitative methods and is an issue for both the statistical power of the design and the generalizability of the results. Researchers should avoid conducting a single case study with limited descriptive data; cross-case analysis can help to increase understanding and transferability to other contexts (Patton, 2002). Finally, researchers should provide clear articulation of the rationale for how the research questions are matched with the research designs and data collection methods.

Using Designs That Lead to Results That Can Be Generalized or Transferred

Poor research design or sampling procedures can lead to results that cannot be generalized or applied to other situations or populations; that is, they lack relevance or external validity (Campbell & Stanley, 1963; Cook & Campbell, 1979). In either qualitative or quantitative research, the nature of some studies limits the usefulness of the conclusions for other contexts. Regardless of which design a research study incorporates, generalizability can be compromised in a variety of ways (e.g., sampling, nature of the intervention, context-specific elements, and measurement procedures). Generalizability is enhanced when the sample of respondents is heterogeneous and representative (e.g., age of students, discipline of the faculty member, type of institution, sector in which the community organization operates). Multicourse and multicampus studies have the advantage of gathering and examining data across a heterogeneous set of contexts. Investigators, however, must provide a complete description of the context, methodology, samples, and assumptions of a study (Guba, 1981). Discussion of the generalizability of conclusions and of how they are limited should reflect the restrictions of the research procedures (Bringle et al., 2004). Again, cross-case or comparative analysis can increase understanding and transferability since the researcher looks for themes and patterns across several cases (Patton, 2002). Research findings that are not relevant to other settings or contexts do not contribute to a body of knowledge that advances the field.

Avoiding Over-Interpreting Results Based on the Design of the Study

Investigators need to pay attention to how they interpret results when conducting research that is limited to students, faculty, and community members who are heavily involved in or committed to service learning, community service, or volunteering (i.e., "creaming"). The difficulty occurs when the investigator over-interprets or over-generalizes the results to draw conclusions about a larger group of students (e.g., all students in a writing course, all college students). This issue applies to the capacity of the researcher to generalize the results about the intervention, because an intervention that is effective with a group of motivated and committed students, faculty, or organization staff might not have the same impact on a group of less motivated individuals. Nor might it have the same impact when its elements are implemented within a different context. There are many issues in addition to the nature of the students, faculty, and community partners (e.g., context, measurement procedures, content of the course) that can limit the generalizability of results. Not addressing these issues limits the credibility and transferability of the conclusions reached (Guba, 1981).

Drawing Appropriate Conclusions Based on the Design of the Study

Researchers sometimes conduct a correlational study but draw inappropriate causal (cause-and-effect) conclusions. Causal inferences are very difficult to make from a single correlation because the correlation does not assist in determining the direction of causality. For instance, a positive correlation between volunteering and self-esteem indicates that more volunteering is associated with higher self-esteem. However, the correlation does not differentiate among at least three possibilities: (a) that volunteering promotes self-esteem, (b) that self-esteem promotes volunteering, or (c) that a third variable (e.g., self-efficacy) is responsible for the correlation between self-esteem and volunteering. This same issue also applies to qualitative research in which inferences are made (e.g., by the researcher, by the participants) about why an outcome occurred; accounts that purport to analyze causality are not always reliable (Nisbett & Wilson, 1977).

Considering Implications of the Research for Teaching and Learning in General

Service learning as an engaging and active pedagogy may have implications for all teaching and learning (e.g., cognitive processes, student-centered instruction, collaborative learning). As assessment of instruction becomes more outcome oriented and assessment of learning becomes more focused on authentic evidence, there will be opportunities to assess how different pedagogical approaches, including service learning, contribute to achieving many desired student learning outcomes. Studies focused only on service learning courses not only can inform practice for service learning but also may have relevance to teaching and learning more generally when the research is testing theory that is relevant to all learning or to particular types of teaching. These studies on service learning may also be relevant to other forms of instruction when moderator variables (i.e., under what conditions and for which students the results occur) and mediating variables (i.e., how pedagogies differ in why certain outcomes occur and do not occur) have applicability to instruction more generally.

Taking Into Account Ethical Considerations

Researchers must be aware of ethical considerations that are particularly relevant to the service learning context. Although research on service learning in higher education settings usually involves minimal risk to participants, there may be situations that involve decisions with ethical implications, which must be reviewed by institutional review boards (IRBs) or an equivalent. Some of these situations are discussed next.

Research on the Researcher's Own Students

Because of the power differences between faculty and the students whose work they evaluate, researchers should be careful and cautious when undertaking research on their own students' experiences and outcomes, particularly during the semester in which students are enrolled in a course taught by the researcher (American Psychological Association, 2002). If a course has a requirement for research participation, students must be given the opportunity to choose another option, such as a research paper, without penalty. The students' capacity to refuse to participate in the research and to choose an alternative assignment might be severely constrained when the researcher is also the students' instructor.

Multicampus Studies

Researchers involved in projects on multiple campuses must consult with the IRB office of each campus. Depending on the nature of the study and the status of colleagues as co–principal investigators, the researcher may be required to apply for IRB approval on each campus.

International Studies

Investigators should be aware of applicable laws, regulations, and norms in the country (or countries) in which they are conducting research. Researchers working in the context of international service learning courses or programs need to consult with the IRB (or equivalent) office of any non-U.S. institution. The criteria against which research might be judged in another country could be based on principles that deviate from Western or American standards (Wells, Warchal, Ruiz, & Chapdelain, 2010).

Research in K–12 Settings

Studies involving minor children require particular care with regard to informed consent. Some procedures, if they are not part of the standard teaching and learning environment, require separate parental consent. An IRB must review research protocols to determine whether and how informed consent will be handled for minors.

Research That Involves Community Partners

Many of the agencies that provide sites for service learning activities involve both public and nonprofit services. These agencies may be dependent on public opinion for funding, through either governmental or private fundraising efforts. Findings that highlight challenges and problems in an agency can have a potential negative impact on its funding base. One strategy is to share results with agency administrators prior to dissemination; however, doing so raises additional ethical concerns when making decisions as to what to publish or present if an agency administrator expresses reservations. In addition, depending on the nature of the involvement of community agency personnel in the research process, they may have to qualify as co–principal investigators according to current regulations.

Conclusion

This chapter has presented the fundamentals of designing high-quality research on service learning in the context of both quantitative and qualitative approaches to research. The selection among these different approaches should be intentionally aligned with and guided by the research question and the theoretical framework that guides any given study. Practical matters related to the institutional context might also shape design issues (e.g., availability of comparable courses that do not include service learning), measurement issues (e.g., practicality of accessing information), and ethical issues (e.g., conducting research on one's students). There is tremendous opportunity in all institutional contexts for serious inquiry into the pedagogy of service learning, which can continue to contribute significant, if not transformational, change to higher education.

Recommended Reading

Bringle, R. G., Phillips, M. A., & Hudson, M. (2004). *The measure of service learning: Research scales to assess student experiences.* Washington, DC: American Psychological Association.

Campbell, D. T., & Stanley, J. C. (1963). *Experimental and quasi-experimental designs for research on teaching.* Boston, MA: Houghton Mifflin.

Cook, T. D., & Campbell, D. T. (1979). *Quasi-experimentation: Design and analysis issues for field settings.* Boston, MA: Houghton Mifflin.

Creswell, J. W., & Plano Clark, V. L. (2006). *Designing and conducting mixed methods research.* Thousand Oaks, CA: SAGE.

Denzin, N., & Lincoln, Y. S. (Eds.). (2005). *Handbook of qualitative research* (3rd ed.). Thousand Oaks, CA: SAGE.

Patton, M. Q. (2002). *Qualitative research & evaluation methods* (3rd ed.). Thousand Oaks, CA: SAGE.

Steinberg, K. S., Bringle, R. G., & Williams, M. J. (2010). *Service learning research primer.* Scotts Valley, CA: Learn and Serve America's National Service Learning Clearinghouse.

Trochim, W. M. (2006). *Research methods knowledge base* (2nd ed.). Retrieved from http://www.socialresearchmethods.net/kb/

References

Abowitz, K. K. (2001). Getting beyond familiar myths: Discourses of service learning and critical pedagogy. *The Review of Education/Pedagogy/Cultural Studies, 21*(1), 63–77.

American Psychological Association. (2002). *Ethical principles of psychologists and code of conduct, 8.04: Client/patient, student, and subordinate research participants.* Retrieved from http://www.apa.org/ethics/code/index.aspx

Ash, S. L., Clayton, P. H., & Atkinson, M. P. (2005). Integrating reflection and assessment to capture and improve student-learning. *Michigan Journal of Community Service Learning, 11*(2), 49–60.

Astin, A. W., & Sax, L. J. (1998). How undergraduates are affected by service participation. *Journal of College Student Development, 39,* 251–263.

Astin, A. W., Sax, L. J., & Avalos, J. (1999). The long-term effects of volunteerism during the undergraduate years. *The Review of Higher Education, 21*(2), 187–202.

Baldwin, S., Buchanan, A., & Rudisill, M. (2007). What teacher candidates learned about diversity, social justice and themselves from service-learning experiences. *Journal of Teacher Education, 58,* 315–327.

Billig, S. H., & Eyler J. S. (2003). The state of service-learning and service-learning research. In S. H. Billig & J. S. Eyler (Eds.), *Deconstructing service-learning: Research exploring context, participation, and impacts* (pp. 253–264). Greenwich, CT: Information Age.

Bowman, N. A., & Brandenberger, J. W. (2010). Quantitative assessment of service-learning outcomes: Is self-reported change an adequate proxy for longitudinal change? In J. Keshen, B. A. Holland, & B. E. Moely (Eds.), *Research for what? Making engaged scholarship matter* (pp. 25–43). Charlotte, NC: Information Age.

Boyer, E. (1990). *Scholarship reconsidered: Priorities of the professorate.* San Francisco, CA: Jossey-Bass.

Bray, J. H., Maxwell, S. E., & Howard, G. S. (1984). Methods of analysis with response-shift bias. *Educational and Psychological Measurement, 44,* 781–804.

Bringle, R. G. (2003). Enhancing theory-based research on service learning. In S. H. Billig & J. S. Eyler (Eds.), *Deconstructing service learning: Research exploring context, participation, and impacts* (pp. 3–21). Greenwich, CT: Information Age.

Bringle, R. G., & Hatcher, J. A. (2000). Meaningful measurement of theory-based service-learning outcomes: Making the case with quantitative research [Special issue]. *Michigan Journal of Community Service Learning, Fall,* 68–75.

Bringle, R. G., Phillips, M. A., & Hudson, M. (2004). *The measure of service learning: Research scales to assess student experiences.* Washington, DC: American Psychological Association.

Bringle, R. G., & Steinberg, K. S. (2010). Educating for informed community involvement. *American Journal of Community Psychology, 46,* 428–441.

Campbell, D. T., & Stanley, J. C. (1963). *Experimental and quasi-experimental designs for research on teaching.* Boston, MA: Houghton Mifflin.

Coles, R. (1993). *The call of service: A witness to idealism.* Boston, MA: Houghton Mifflin.

Cook, T. D., & Campbell, D. T. (1979). *Quasi-experimentation: Design and analysis issues for field settings.* Boston, MA: Houghton Mifflin.

Crabtree, R. (1998). Mutual empowerment in cross-cultural participatory development and service learning: Lessons in communication and social justice from projects in El Salvador and Nicaragua. *Journal of Applied Communication Research, 26*(2), 182–209.

Creswell, J. W. (1998). *Qualitative and research inquiry design: Choosing among five traditions.* Boston, MA: Houghton Mifflin.

Creswell, J. W., & Plano Clark, V. L. (2006). *Designing and conducting mixed methods research.* Thousand Oaks, CA: SAGE.

Denzin, N., & Lincoln, Y. S. (Eds.). (2000). *Handbook of qualitative research* (second ed.). Thousand Oaks, CA: SAGE.

Denzin, N., & Lincoln, Y. S. (Eds.). (2005). *Handbook of qualitative research* (3rd ed.). Thousand Oaks, CA: SAGE.

Dewey, J. (1933). *How we think: A restatement of the relation of reflective thinking to the educative process.* Boston, MA: Heath.

Eyler, J. S., & Giles, D. E., Jr. (1999). *Where's the learning in service learning?* San Francisco, CA: Jossey-Bass.

Gaughan, M. (2002). Ethnography, demography and service-learning: Situating Lynwood Park. *Critical Sociology, 28*(1/2), 217–234.

Geertz, C. (1973). *The interpretation of cultures.* New York, NY: Basic Books.

Glaser, B., & Strauss, A. (1967). *The discovery of grounded theory: Strategies for qualitative research.* Chicago, IL: Aldine.

Glesne, C. (2006). *Becoming qualitative researchers: An introduction* (3rd ed.). Boston, MA: Pearson Educational.

Guba, E. G. (1981). Criteria for assessing the trustworthiness of naturalistic inquiries. *Educational Technology Research and Development, 29*(2), 75–91.

Lather, P. (1986). Research as praxis. *Harvard Educational Review, 56,* 257–277.

Lincoln, Y., & Guba, I. (1985). *Naturalistic inquiry.* Beverly Hills, CA: SAGE.

Lincoln, Y., & Guba, I. (2000). Paradigmatic controversies, contradictions, and emerging confluences. In N. Denzin & Y. Lincoln (Eds.), *Handbook of qualitative research* (2nd ed., pp. 163–188). Thousand Oaks, CA: SAGE.

Markus, G. B., Howard, J. P. F., & King, D. C. (1993). Integrating community service and classroom instruction enhances learning: Results from an experiment. *Educational Evaluation and Policy Analysis, 15,* 410–419.

Moley, B. E., Mercer, S. H., Ilustre, V., Miron, D., & McFarland, M. (2002). Psychometric properties and correlates of the Civic Attitudes and Skills Questionnaire (CASQ): A measure of students' attitudes related to service-learning. *Michigan Journal of Community Service Learning, 8*(2), 15–26.

Nisbett, R., & Wilson, T. (1977). Telling more than we can know: Verbal reports on mental processes. *Psychological Review, 84,* 231–259.

Oskamp, S., & Schultz, P. W. (2005). *Attitudes and opinions* (3rd ed.). Mahwah, NJ: Erlbaum.

Patton, M. Q. (2002). *Qualitative research & evaluation methods* (3rd ed.). Thousand Oaks, CA: SAGE.

Peters, S. (2004). Educating the civic professional: Reconfigurations and resistances. *Michigan Journal of Community Service Learning, 11*(1), 47–58.

Remshardt, R. M. A., & Flowers, D. L. (2007). Understanding qualitative research. *American Nurse Today, 2*(9), 20–32.

Sandelowski, M., Volls, A. A., & Knaft, G. (2009). On quantitizing. *Journal of Mixed Methods Research, 3*(3), 208–222.

Shavelson, R. J., & Towne, L. (Eds.). (2002). *Scientific research in education.* Washington, DC: National Research Council, National Academy.

Stake, R. (2000). Case studies. In N. Denzin & Y. Lincoln (Eds.), *Handbook of qualitative research* (2nd ed., pp. 435–454). Thousand Oaks, CA: SAGE.

Stanton, T. K., Giles, D. E., Jr., & Cruz, N. L. (1999). *Service learning: A movement's pioneers reflect on its origins, practice, and future.* San Francisco, CA: Jossey-Bass.

Steinberg, K. S., Bringle, R. G., & Williams, M. J. (2010). *Service learning research primer.* Scotts Valley, CA: Learn and Serve America's National Service Learning Clearinghouse.

Steinberg, K. S., Hatcher, J. A., & Bringle, R. G. (2011). A north star: Civic-minded graduate. *Michigan Journal of Community Service Learning, 18*(1), 19–33.

Steinke, P., & Buresh, S. (2002). Cognitive outcomes of service-learning: Reviewing the past and glimpsing the future. *Michigan Journal of Community Service Learning, 8*(2), 5–14.

Strand, K., Marullo, S., Cutforth, N., Stoecker, R., & Donohue, P. (2003). *Community-based research and higher education: Principles and practices.* San Francisco, CA: Jossey-Bass.

Strauss, A., & Corbin, J. (1998). *Basics of qualitative research: Techniques and procedures for developing grounded theory* (2nd ed.). Thousand Oaks, CA: SAGE.

Tashakkori, A., & Teddlie, C. (2003). *Handbook of mixed methods in social & behavioral research.* Thousand Oaks, CA: SAGE.

Trochim, W. M. (2006). *Research methods knowledge base* (2nd ed.). Retrieved from http://www.socialresearchmethods.net/kb/

Wells, C., Warchal, J., Ruiz, A., & Chapdelain, A. (2010). Ethical issues in research on international service learning. In R. G. Bringle, J. A. Hatcher, & S. G. Jones (Eds.), *International service learning: Conceptual frameworks and research* (pp. 319–343). Sterling, VA: Stylus.

Williams, N. R., King, M., & Koob, J. J. (2002). Social work students go to camp: The effects of service learning on perceived self-efficacy. *Journal of Teaching in Social Work, 22*(3/4), 55–70.

Zlotkowski, E. (Ed.). (1998). *Successful service learning programs: New models of excellence in higher education.* Bolton, MA: Anker.

PART TWO

RESEARCH ON STUDENTS
AND SERVICE LEARNING

RESEARCH AND THEORETICAL PERSPECTIVES ON COGNITIVE OUTCOMES OF SERVICE LEARNING

Peggy Fitch, Pamela Steinke, and Tara D. Hudson

P rimary among the goals of higher education is learning that lasts, which Mentkowski and associates (2000) posit includes the "integration of learning, development, and performance" (p. 1). Although Mentkowski and associates do not explicitly mention service learning as a way to achieve learning that lasts, as explored in this chapter, the pedagogy of service learning has the potential to enhance intellectual development and related cognitive processes. The service learning experience can, in turn, be enhanced by the intentional inclusion of activities that are scaffolded and developmentally designed.

Well-designed service learning experiences serve as bridges between the curriculum and the world outside the classroom, where problems are ill structured and the stakes are often high for communities and students alike. These opportunities build students' capacities to develop, use, and refine their knowledge, skills, and critical thinking abilities. The capacity for critical thinking requires a set of cognitive skills as well as personal dispositions that enhance confidence and good judgment in using these skills (Fascione, 1990). The disposition to engage in reflective critical thinking, which goes

The authors thank Ben Allen for his assistance with the graphic design of the figures included in this chapter.

beyond pure cognitive skills, requires the development of a set of epistemic assumptions that are part of overall intellectual development (King & Kitchener, 1994). Extensive longitudinal research at Alverno College evaluated the relationship between intellectual development and cognitive process related to critical thinking and found that these were independent factors (Mentkowski & Associates, 2000). Whereas intellectual development reflects qualitative changes over time in epistemological understanding about the nature of knowledge and knowing and is necessarily connected to identity of oneself as a learner, cognitive processes are demonstrated in a quantitative way through more use or less use and are not necessarily connected to self.

Successful critical thinking requires both attainment of higher levels of intellectual development and the use of cognitive processes such as metacognition, transfer, and problem solving. These cognitive processes also advance students' intellectual development—a primary goal of higher education that contributes to success in college and beyond. Indeed, these processes underlie student outcomes in the arenas of academic learning (chapter 2.2), civic learning (chapter 2.3), personal development (chapter 2.4), and intercultural competence (chapter 2.5).

Service learning, when designed appropriately, has the potential to promote intellectual development and these associated cognitive processes by encouraging students to examine how they and others interpret and attempt to resolve ill-structured problems, by requiring them to integrate different perspectives (some of which contradict one another and are not easily reconciled), and by providing guidance in their reflection process as they co-construct meaning with academic and community experts and redefine themselves as learners and as agents of social change. Given this potential, the purpose of this chapter is to review theory and research on intellectual development and on specific cognitive processes that interact with it to produce good critical thinking and to discuss implications of this work for service learning practice and research.

Theoretical and Conceptual Frameworks

This chapter is intended to be useful both to those interested in assessment for research on cognition in service learning and to those interested in assessment of student learning outcomes for program enhancement. Although the purposes of these two uses of assessment are different, they share best practices informed by psychology (Steinke & Fitch, 2011). Our approach begins with the assumption that high-quality assessment is grounded in theory and research that can shape the articulation of outcomes, inform the development of appropriate instructional activities to cultivate those outcomes, provide direction for identifying indicators of those outcomes, emphasize the importance of using multiple measures to assess complex constructs, and clarify the interpretation of assessment results. Within this framework, the key difference between assessment for research and assessment for program enhancement is the purpose of the assessment. Assessment for enhancement can be viewed as action research to solve an immediate problem such as how to deepen student learning by improving service learning design. Faculty and other practitioner-scholars who begin assessing for enhancement may intentionally proceed in such a way that the work also advances their research agendas (Steinke & Fitch, 2007a).

Selected theories and concepts that are relevant to the study of cognition in service learning are presented in the following sections. As shown in Figure 2.1.1, cognition encompasses intellectual development and critical thinking as constructs that are broader and more complex than specific cognitive processes such as metacognition, transfer, and problem solving, which, in turn, are more complex than specific cognitive skills such as inference, categorization, and deductive reasoning. As intellectual development progresses from dualism to commitment within relativism (Perry 1968/1970/1999, 1981), the cognitive processes of transfer, metacognition, and problem solving grow increasingly complex, all ultimately leading to self-regulated learning.

Intellectual Development

Theories of intellectual development are grounded in epistemology, the study of the nature of knowledge and knowing. Hofer (2001) defines *personal epistemology* as "beliefs about the definition of knowledge, how knowledge is constructed, how knowledge is evaluated, where knowledge resides, and how knowing occurs" (p. 355). Hofer and Pintrich (1997) review various conceptualizations of personal epistemology—including such developmental models as King and Kitchener's reflective judgment, Baxter Magolda's epistemological reflection, Belenky and colleagues' women's ways of knowing, and Kuhn's argumentative reasoning, as well as Schommer's system of epistemological beliefs (which is not developmental)—and conclude that all make reference to, and are derived from, original work by Perry, Steinke and Fitch (2003) summarize Perry's model (see Figure 2.1.1):

> Perry's scheme of intellectual and ethical development describes how college students' conceptions of knowledge, truth, learning, and commitment

FIGURE 2.1.1
Relationships Between Intellectual Development and
Cognitive Processes Related to Critical Thinking

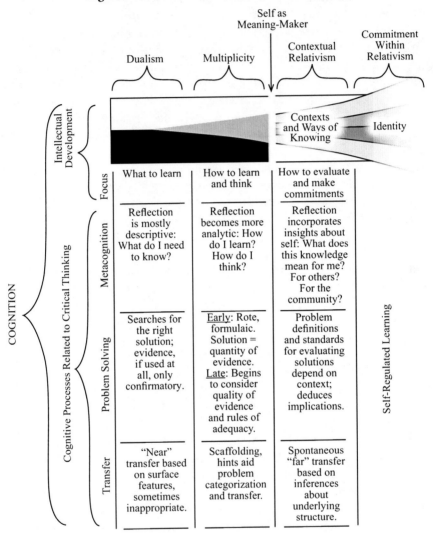

evolve through nine positions within four broad stages, from *Dualism* (i.e., all knowledge is known by the "right" Authorities and it is black and white; thus, Truth is absolute) through *Multiplicity* (i.e., knowledge includes some "gray" areas and things we do not know yet; authorities disagree, thus any opinion is as good as another) and *Contextual Relativism* (i.e., knowledge is constructed by learners in specific and limited contexts; the best opinions are supported by quality evidence, thus standards exist to judge the adequacy of opinions) to *Commitment Within Relativism* (i.e., commitments that reflect one's identity—to an area of study, a career, a relationship, a value system—must be made within an essentially relativistic world). (emphasis added, p. 183)

In this chapter, the term *intellectual development* refers to the family of theories or models about students' personal epistemologies that are grounded in Perry's work. Hofer and Pintrich (1997) report that regardless of which specific theory is used, the majority of studies investigating intellectual development have found that students typically enter college in the epistemological stage of dualism and leave in the stage of late multiplicity.

Critical Thinking and Its Related Cognitive Processes

Fascione's (1990) report of consensus on the meaning of critical thinking concludes that critical thinking represents a set of cognitive skills and affective dispositions, such as inquisitiveness and open-mindedness, that provide useful insights and powerful resources for personal and civic life. Paul and Elder (2008) use the following definition in their work with the Foundation for Critical Thinking: "Critical thinking is the art of analyzing and evaluating thinking with a view to improving it" (p. 2). Some of the recommendations in Fascione's (1990) report that are particularly relevant here are that education be guided by a holistic understanding of critical thinking that does not reduce it to a particular skill feature, that educational strategies be designed holistically, and that critical thinking be taught in a variety of contexts.

Whereas the experts on critical thinking in Fascione's work identified a set of specific cognitive skills including interpretation, analysis, evaluation, inference, explanation, and self-regulation as components of critical thinking, this chapter focuses on more complex cognitive processes related to critical thinking that have been the subject of cognitive and educational research: metacognition, transfer, and problem solving. Each of these higher level processes has a body of theory and research grounded in basic psychological science and a history of applied educational relevance and research.

In addition, each is clearly implicated in service learning, and how these processes are enacted is related to a student's level of intellectual development: The higher the level of intellectual development, the more sophisticated the use of these cognitive processes, and vice versa.

As shown in Figure 2.1.1, the relationship between cognitive processes and intellectual development is not simply correlative but, rather, dynamic and synergistic; intellectual development is an ongoing process in which students' epistemological (i.e., Perry) levels function as lenses through which they interpret their experiences, which subsequently leads them to employ these three cognitive processes either more or less successfully (Steinke & Fitch, 2003). For example, students in dualism may find it difficult to apply what they learn in the classroom to their service learning experience, or this transfer may occur randomly or inappropriately based on the surface features of the two contexts. Students in multiplicity may be able to apply academic learning to service activities when given explicit guidance, as through structured reflection prompts. Those in contextual relativism, however, are most likely to transfer learning appropriately between classroom and community because they can identify the deep structural similarities and differences between these contexts. In turn, while using these cognitive processes in limited ways, students encounter situations in which their approach is not accurate or adequate, prompting them to question why. This doubt about their current understanding leads to the adaptation of assumptions about knowledge and knowing that is the core of intellectual development and that, in turn, fosters the use of somewhat more sophisticated cognitive processes.

Metacognition

Both Fascione (1990) and Paul and Elder (2008) contend that teaching critical thinking includes helping students develop the ability and disposition to reflect on the process and quality of their own thinking, a phenomenon psychologists refer to as metacognition—broadly, thinking about thinking. Veenman, Van Hout-Wolters, and Afflerbach (2006) note that Brown and Flavell are typically credited with introducing the term *metacognition*, defined as "the knowledge about and regulation of one's cognitive activities in learning processes" (p. 3). They indicate that many terms—such as *feeling of knowing, theory of mind, higher-order skills, learning strategies, meta-memory,* and *self-regulation*—have been associated with metacognition and note that it can be difficult to separate metacognition from these other processes when assessing reasoning, particularly if these processes are not explicitly defined during task performance. Metacognition encompasses beliefs about the self as a learner in the context of a particular domain of knowledge. With respect to intellectual development, metacognition is an indicator of movement toward the stage of contextual relativism as it provides evidence of recognizing oneself as a meaning-maker versus as a receiver of knowledge from the "right" authorities. The development of metacognitive skills also promotes transfer (Bransford, Brown, Cocking, Donovan, & Pellegrino, 2000).

Transfer

One characteristic of a good critical thinker is the ability to apply cognitive skills to a range of contexts for a variety of purposes, including personal and civic (Fascione, 1990). This ability to apply knowledge and skills from one context to another is known as transfer. Transfer is an important outcome in higher education because it determines whether the skills and content that students learn in one academic setting can be used appropriately and effectively in future academic, civic, professional, or personal contexts. For this reason, Bransford et al. (2000) identify transfer as the "ultimate goal of schooling" (p. 73). Of particular importance is "far transfer," in which relevant knowledge and skills are appropriately applied in contexts that are clearly dissimilar to the ones in which they were learned (Barnett & Ceci, 2002). Typical dissimilar contexts experienced by students include the classroom, a service learning community setting, an internship, a job, a lab, a residence hall, and a favorite bar. Thus, the challenge of far transfer could be between any of these learning contexts. After decades of research on transfer, many questions remain, including: To what degree does transfer regularly occur (Bransford et al., 2000; Ritchhart & Perkins, 2005)? However, transfer is more likely to happen when understanding is at a deep, structural level rather than a surface, replicating level and when knowledge and skills are organized around a conceptual framework (Bransford et al., 2000; Halpern, 1998). For example, students who have learned how to apply concepts of scaffolding and Vygotsky's (1978) zone of proximal development in a child development course (e.g., to case studies) are more likely to transfer these concepts to their service learning tutoring experiences. Seeing the relevance of a principle to multiple contexts allows a student to state the principle more abstractly (Wagner, 2006). Thus, appropriate transfer indicates recognition of context, and this insight reflects the epistemological transition from multiplicity to contextual relativism in Perry's scheme.

Problem Solving

Learning critical thinking across contexts equips students to be able to apply critical thinking skills to a wide range of problems (Fascione, 1990). Problem solving involves not only finding solutions to problems that have already been defined but also recognizing new problems. As defined here, problems include those that are ill structured and cannot be described completely or solved with certainty (King & Kitchener, 1994). Recognizing when problems exist is a key component of successful navigation of everyday events (Sternberg, 1997). Expert problem solving relies not only on well-organized knowledge but also on the ability to monitor one's own problem-solving approach (metacognition) and flexible adaptation of knowledge to new situations (transfer) (Bransford et al., 2000). Because ill-structured problems necessarily involve ambiguity, students at the lowest levels of intellectual development likely will not demonstrate good problem-solving skills across multiple problem types.

Relevance of Intellectual Development and Cognitive Processes to Service Learning

Collaborating with others in the community, utilizing guided reflection on service learning experiences, and working on authentic ill-structured issues and problems in the community that are relevant to academic content are specific aspects of service learning that, taken together, have the potential to promote outcomes related to enhanced intellectual development and critical thinking. Ideally, service learning creates opportunities for shared cognition, or active social construction of knowledge, as students collaborate with others in the classroom and the community. In both settings students encounter people who think differently than they do about what they know and how they know it, make different assumptions about knowledge and truth, and define and approach problems in different ways. In other words, collaboration during service learning exposes students and those with whom they interact to other ways of knowing, which has the potential to enhance intellectual development.

Engaging in critical reflection in relation to a community-based service experience also helps students identify themselves as agents in their own learning, not simply as receivers of knowledge from authorities. According to Mentkowski and associates (2000), the use of metacognitive strategies, which can occur in the structured critical reflection that is part of service learning, can stimulate evaluation of one's own performance and potentially transform the learning process into one that may eventually lead to a consistent pattern of self-regulated learning. In turn, this process can enhance intellectual development as students learn to claim their own perspective while situating it within the context of multiple divergent perspectives.

At its best, service learning can create what Ritchhart and Perkins (2005) refer to as "cultures of thinking" (p. 792), a term they use to describe outcomes of pedagogies that make thinking visible by engaging students in opportunities for socially constructing knowledge with others and for using critical thinking skills to address meaningful problems. They cite examples such as cognitive apprenticeships, learning communities, and inquiry-based teaching and note that

> at the heart of these efforts lies reflection on one's thinking and cognitive monitoring, the core processes of metacognition. Ultimately, teaching students to be more metacognitive and reflective, providing rich opportunities for thinking across various contexts, setting up an environment that values thinking, and making the thinking of group members visible contribute a great deal to the formation of a culture of thinking. (p. 794)

As previously established, service learning also has this potential.

Critical Evaluation of Past Research

Large-scale studies have reported positive effects of service learning on cognitive outcomes. Astin, Vogelgesang, Ikeda, and Yee (2000) conducted national longitudinal studies and found increases in self-reported critical thinking among students who participated in service (both service learning and community service) compared with those who did not, though this effect was stronger for the students who had taken service learning courses (Astin & Sax, 1998; Astin et al., 2000). Eyler and Giles (1999) found that students involved in service learning reported greater openness to new perspectives (related to intellectual development and critical thinking), deeper understanding of the complexity of social problems (related to intellectual development, critical thinking, and problem solving), and stronger ability to apply class material to such problems (related to transfer) than those not involved in service learning. The presence of service learning by itself did not increase critical thinking as measured by an intellectual development index; however, it did when its design included a high level of integration into course activities through regular application of relevant material and high-quality reflection. Eyler and Giles (1999) address the critique that perhaps a highly integrated service learning experience simply supports students' current level of intellectual development with the following interpretation:

> Critical thinking . . . is dependent on both knowledge and the students' level of cognitive [intellectual] development [p. 101]. . . . Whether a semester of well-integrated, highly reflective service learning helps students consolidate or exhibit previous gains or helps them develop to a higher level, the findings support the value of service learning in intellectual development. (p. 125)

Novak, Markey, and Allen (2007) conducted a meta-analysis of cognitive outcomes of service learning in higher education. Nine studies met the criteria for inclusion in the meta-analysis because they compared service learning and non–service learning groups and included quantitative measures of cognitive outcomes (some self-reported by students), specifically: understanding of course material, application of knowledge and skills across settings, and/or reframing of complex social issues. Of these, application is the most relevant to this discussion because it reflects the cognitive process of transfer, though understanding and reframing may implicate intellectual development, critical thinking, and problem solving. They found that for all three outcomes combined, the average advantage of service learning was a statistically significant, though moderate, effect. This meta-analysis included some studies that relied on self-reported outcomes and some that lacked information about whether students chose service learning courses or were randomly assigned, both important limitations.

Four studies that were not included in this meta-analysis investigated intellectual development as an outcome and found small pretest-posttest increases in measures of students' cognitive change in courses with well-integrated service learning. The consistency of these results is notable given that the investigators used three different Perry-based measures of intellectual development: Learning Environment Preferences (Fitch, 2004), Measure of Epistemological Reflection (Wang & Rodgers, 2006), and two Reflective Judgment indexes labeled critical thinking (Eyler & Giles, 2002; Li & Lal, 2005). One challenge with assessing intellectual development is that it may change slowly; therefore, gains are rarely seen over one semester (Eyler & Giles, 1999).

In the authors' review of studies that investigated critical thinking, the four that were theoretically grounded in Paul and Elder's (2008) model all showed increases over time as measured by pretest-posttest comparisons of written reflection products for students involved in well-integrated service learning experiences (Ash, Clayton, & Atkinson, 2005; Jameson, Clayton, & Bringle, 2008; Pinzón & Arceo, 2005; Sedlak, Doheny, Panthofer, & Anaya, 2003). None used comparable control groups. Two studies that used Fascione's (1990) theoretical approach found opposite effects of community-based learning (not service learning per se, because the projects did not include reciprocity with community partners) on critical thinking. Quitadamo, Faiola, Johnson, and Kurtz (2008) reported pretest-posttest increases in California Critical Thinking Skills Test (CCTST) scores for student groups who conducted biology research on pressing community issues such as water quality and amphibian decline using community-based inquiry (CBI) compared with partial-CBI and no-CBI groups. By contrast, Nokes, Nickitas, Keida, and Neville (2005) found pretest-posttest decreases in California Critical Thinking Disposition Inventory (CCTDI) scores, especially in self-confidence, for a small voluntary sample of nursing students after completing their required clinical practicum. Furco's reminder that "service learning is not the same as clinical experience" (as cited in Sedlak et al., 2003, p. 103) is one possible explanation for this negative outcome. Additionally, these opposite effects could be attributed to differences between the direct, objective CCTST measure of critical thinking skills (interpretation, analysis, evaluation, inference, explanation, and self-regulation) as applied to specific problems, arguments, or materials and the indirect, self-report CCTDI measure of dispositions (inquisitiveness, open-mindedness, truth seeking, flexibility, self-confidence, maturity) in which test takers rate their level of agreement with a series of statements about critical thinking–related attitudes and values. The latter are subject to response-shift bias if students' standard for evaluating themselves shifts between the pretest and posttest as a function of the service learning intervention itself. As Howard (1980) explains, unless a retrospective pretest is used, it is impossible to determine whether self-reported changes are actually due to the intervention (here, service learning) or to this shifting self-evaluation standard.

Three studies found evidence of transfer by service learning students via application of course material, which would be considered far transfer, as defined previously by Barnett and Ceci (2002). Each used analyses of students' narrative responses about social problems in journal reflections, essay exams, or focus groups, and in each course in the study service learning was well integrated. Only Batchelder and Root (1994) used a non–service learning control group, and they reported more positive outcomes for service learning students than for non–service learning students, especially for those who received high-quality supervision compared with those who received low-quality supervision at their service learning site. Two of these studies (Batchelder & Root, 1994; Hirschinger-Blank & Markowitz, 2006) also reported that service learning students demonstrated greater understanding of the complexity of social problems, an outcome related to critical think-ing—intellectual development, and problem solving—than those who did not engage in service learning. Govekar and Rishi's (2007) four-year longitu-dinal study of two undergraduate business courses noted that some students found the inherent ambiguity in service learning projects particularly chal-lenging, a finding that would be consistent with the hypothesis that ill-structured problems are more difficult for students at lower levels of intellec-tual development.

Metacognition was explicitly assessed in only one study, which found improvement on the Learning and Study Strategies Inventory over two years for students in problem-based learning groups compared with students matched on demographic characteristics who were not involved in problem-based learning (Downing, Kwong, Chan, Lam, & Downing, 2009). Problem-based learning and service learning are similar in their use of authentic ill-structured problems; thus, service learning students might be expected to show similar gains. Finally, Parker-Gwin and Mabry (1998) com-pared three types of service learning placements (whole class; individual, required service; individual, optional service) on students' self-assessments of critical thinking and analytic and problem-solving skills; they found that only the whole-class group reported improvement over the semester. This finding was unexpected because structured reflection was used less often in this group than in the two individual-placement service learning conditions; however, it is conceivable that in the whole-class placement condition more unstructured reflection occurred through class discussion and student inter-action within or outside of class than in the individual-placement groups. On the other hand, both of these studies reported gains in metacognition for students involved in group-based learning, which supports intellectual development theories about the benefits of co-construction of knowledge for seeing oneself as a meaning-maker rather than simply as a receiver of knowl-edge (Hofer & Pintrich, 1997; Perry, 1968/1970/1999, 1981).

Overall, these empirical investigations of cognition in service learning and related pedagogies support the importance of well-integrated service learning, the role of critical reflection, and the value of assessment methods that are grounded in theory.

Measurement Approaches: Existing Tools and Suggested Strategies

There is no single approach to measurement that will provide a complete understanding of complex cognitive processes such as metacognition, transfer, and problem solving. Steinke and Fitch (2007a) provide a table of selected tools used to assess the cognitive outcomes of intellectual development, critical thinking and problem solving, and knowledge application and transfer. They suggest that measurement approaches to assess cognitive outcomes of service learning would be strengthened with a shift from indirect, self-report of students' perceptions to direct and/or mixed measures of students' performance. Self-report is generally considered an indirect approach to assessment because it does not directly measure what students know or can do but rather what students believe they know or can do. Mixed measures still rely on some form of self-report, but students' responses are scored using external criteria developed by someone with expertise in the field to assess directly the quality of students' thinking in a way that aligns with a specific theory. Examples described in Hofer and Pintrich (1997) are the Measure of Intellectual Development, the Measure of Epistemological Reflection, and the Reflective Judgment Model coding procedure.

To facilitate assessment of students' optimal learning as represented by products that reflect students' best efforts, assessment tools that are course-embedded are preferable. This approach requires researchers to attend to the assignments used to develop and assess cognitive outcomes. Quitadamo et al. (2008) provide an example of incorporating multiple course-embedded tools in their study of CBI classes, including small-group proposals for a community-based scientific research project, peer evaluations, and reflective journals; these assignments both fostered and assessed student learning. Course-embedded direct measurement tools to assess cognitive outcomes are most valid as indicators of higher order thinking when they use systematic processes for eliciting and scoring student products of critical reflection. Being intentional about how best to systematize approaches to generating and assessing these products is crucial to good outcomes assessment research. Ash and Clayton (2009) demonstrate the value of connecting assessment approaches and learning outcomes to theory and of incorporating assessment into and throughout service learning courses to improve and document student learning outcomes (see chapter 2.2). Teaching and student products can also be intentionally aimed at having students reflect on the quality of their own thinking (metacognition), the application and abstraction of their knowledge (transfer), and how they approach everyday challenges (problem solving).

Course-embedded systematic assessments such as context-specific problems or cases (Pinzón & Arceo, 2005; Steinke & Fitch, 2007b) provide a consistent protocol that may be integrated into service learning courses and that can be used to promote discussion and development of critical thinking (Quitadamo et al., 2008). Two examples of such standardized protocols for assessing cognitive outcomes of service learning are the Problem Solving Analysis Protocol (P-SAP) (Steinke & Fitch, 2007b) and the DEAL (Description, Examination, Articulation of Learning) Model for Critical Reflection (Ash & Clayton, 2009). The P-SAP starts with a course-related issue or problem and asks students to write their thoughts about the causes of and solutions to the problem through a series of directed questions. One example of an issue used in Environmental Economics and Public Policy is "Even when recycling is encouraged people often do not comply." Another example used in Adaptive Physical Education is "Teaching units for physical education are rarely designed with the needs of special populations in mind." The prompts presented after the statement of the issue are as follows:

- Do you consider this to be a problem? If *yes*, explain how it is a problem. If *no*, explain how other people might consider it to be a problem.
- What do you or other people think causes this problem?
- What do you or other people think could be done to try to solve this problem?
- What are the strengths and limitations of these possible solutions to this problem?

The DEAL Model guides participants through critical reflection in three sequential steps. Step one involves "Description of experiences in an objective and detailed manner"; step two involves "Examination of those experiences in light of specific learning goals or objectives"; and step three involves "Articulation of Learning, including goals for future action that can then be taken forward into the next experience for improved practice and further refinement of learning" (Ash & Clayton, 2009, p. 41). Each step is structured with prompts, and in the Examination step those prompts are aligned with the particular academic, civic, and personal growth learning goals of the service learning component of the course, generally expressed as assessable (i.e., Bloom-based; Bloom, 1956) learning objectives.

Both protocols can be used repeatedly throughout a course, and both include rubrics that can be applied to student products to assess cognitive outcomes. For example, both rubrics have multiple scoring levels and multiple criteria (locus and complexity for the P-SAP and two sets of critical thinking criteria for the DEAL Model). The P-SAP has seven scoring levels for locus and four levels for complexity and includes descriptions and examples for each level. The DEAL Model has four scoring levels on one rubric and six on another and includes descriptions of each criterion at each level. Rubrics such as these two incorporate properties of good measures, such as clear, precise descriptions of performance that vary in degrees of quality and reflect specific outcomes.

Given the importance of measurements aligning with pedagogy and the importance of teaching for transfer, assessing cognitive outcomes of service learning will be most relevant if rubrics are applied to authentic products that allow students to demonstrate their knowledge and skills and their ability to apply material to new problems and contexts in out-of-classroom settings. Portfolios provide a way of assembling a range of products from courses in various disciplines as well as from community-based projects. These products can be assessed with tools that are broad enough to be employed on a variety of assignments. The Association of American Colleges and Universities' (AAC&U, 2010) VALUE Rubrics, designed to assess common general education outcomes, are examples of such tools. Particularly relevant to this discussion are the rubric to assess integrative learning skills, which includes transfer, reflection, and self-assessment among its components, and the rubrics to assess problem solving and critical thinking.

Implications for the Practice of Service Learning

This review of service learning research, as well as the literature on intellectual development and cognitive processes, provides direction for how service learning practitioners might use the pedagogy to enhance intellectual development, critical thinking, metacognition, transfer, and problem solving. One of the best ways to enhance student performance is to use assessments that provide a basis for feedback to students on those dimensions. Whether assessments are used for research or for evaluation of student performance in the course, student performance is more likely to be optimal when results not only are useful to the researcher or instructor but also provide helpful feedback to the student (Steinke & Fitch, 2003). This feedback could take the form of a comparative profile or a summary of strengths and weaknesses and could be distributed to each participant or used as a topic of class discussion. Feedback can also be integrated into the course when using critical reflection tools such as the DEAL Model or the P-SAP by sharing and discussing the rubric that is used to assess reasoning demonstrated in the reflection products and/or by providing opportunities for students to continue to deepen their thinking through feedback-informed revision of draft products. Indeed, to develop the metacognitive skills needed for critical thinking, students must be able to evaluate their own progress toward the goals or outcomes of the learning experience (Loacker, 2000). Shifting the focus from teaching to student learning is an important component of the constructivist approach (Huba & Freed, 2000) and begins by clarifying learning outcomes and sharing these with students (Ash et al., 2005; Loacker, 2000).

Making incremental adjustments to teaching and learning strategies based on students' cognitive understanding is consistent with the developmental principle of scaffolding (Rogoff, 1990). In building construction, the purpose of a scaffold is to enable one to reach higher than one could without it, and the same dynamic occurs in student learning and development. Service learning instructors can intentionally cultivate cognitive outcomes by employing developmental course design. Moore (1994) describes Knefelkamp and Widick's model of developmental instruction, which integrates Perry's (1968/1970/1999) scheme with Sanford's (1962) concept of balancing challenge and support and applies them to the design of activities, courses, and, ultimately, curricula. The model identifies four variables—diversity, structure, involvement, personalism—that can challenge or support students differently depending on their level of intellectual development. For example, students at lower levels are challenged by high diversity in a course (e.g., multiple readings, many perspectives) and feel supported by high structure (e.g., clear expectations, rehearsal of evaluation tasks), whereas those at higher levels seek out high diversity and require less structure to master the material successfully.

This model of developmental instruction suggests that students at any level benefit from involvement in active learning (e.g., problem-based learning, service learning, collaborative learning) and from personalism (e.g., instructor availability, small-group discussion), although those at higher levels of intellectual development need these strategies less than those at lower levels. One implication of developmental instruction for service learning practice is that although students at lower levels of intellectual development may be supported by service learning as active learning, they are often challenged by the diversity of perspectives and ambiguity of expectations that they encounter in their service learning experiences. For these students, instructors can balance this challenge with higher structure (e.g., specific reflection prompts, models of completed assignments) and personalism (e.g., comprehensive and timely feedback on reflection products, sharing of reflection products with other students for the purpose of feedback). This analysis is consistent with Eyler and Giles's (1999) conclusion that whether service learning students see the complexity of social problems as "a revelation that enhances their service or as a barrier that discourages them may depend to some extent on their intellectual development" (p. 101).

Guided reflection also enhances critical thinking about the complex issues that service learning students encounter (e.g., Ash et al., 2005; Grossman, 2008; Jameson et al., 2008). Given the importance of metacognition, transfer, and problem solving, practitioners may need to reexamine the role of reflection in their service learning courses to ensure that their reflection strategies enhance critical thinking. Reflection activities can encourage students not only to make meaning of the service learning experience in the context of course content but also to use course content to solve problems that they encounter in the community and to examine their own ways of knowing, learning, and self-regulating. When students are able to identify, evaluate, and take responsibility for their own cognitive processes, they will be more likely to develop the core skills and dispositions that characterize good critical thinkers (Fascione, 1990).

When students take responsibility for learning it broadens the focus of learning from only the immediate context to encompass the students' ability to learn in a multitude of contexts (Mentkowski & Associates, 2000). Using service learning to teach students to transfer knowledge and skills across multiple contexts requires instructors to be comfortable with students' disequilibrium and failure, even when students are not. Instructors can help teach problem-solving skills and enhance intellectual development by modeling a willingness to try new ways of approaching ill-structured problems and articulating the process by which they evaluate potential solutions and learn from mistakes (King & Kitchener, 1994). Another way to enhance problem solving and intellectual development is to encourage students to view problems from a variety of perspectives while suspending their initial judgments (King & Kitchener, 1994). Instructors can help model this process by not forming conclusions until they have considered all aspects of an issue and not sharing with students their own conclusions until they have explored all aspects of the issue with the class.

Implications and Recommendations for a Future Research Agenda

A viable research agenda on cognition in service learning will use theory and research on intellectual development and cognitive processes to develop research questions, measures, and designs that address why and under what conditions service learning enhances intellectual development and cognitive processes. It is insufficient for future research to demonstrate merely that enhanced cognitive outcomes in a particular context are related to the presence of service learning. What is needed is research that provides evidence of the role that service learning can play in the sustained growth of students' intellectual development, critical thinking skills, and related cognitive processes, as well as the role that these cognitive processes play in the effectiveness of service learning and performance beyond college. The research agenda proposed here is predicated on the evidence that cognitive processes and high-quality service learning experiences mutually reinforce each other.

Methodological Implications and Recommendations

In chapters 1.1 and 1.2 of this volume, the authors explain how the quality of service learning research can be enhanced by paying closer attention to issues of research design, measurement, and theory. Although large-N, randomized control group designs are often held up as the gold standard of explanatory quantitative investigations, most researchers have difficulties conducting such studies because of limited resources, access to populations, and authority over administrative processes such as registration and staffing. Higher education practices frequently do not lend themselves to this level of control. Bringle and Hatcher (2000), however, suggest that researchers must explore using designs and procedures that reduce confounds and maximize control within limited parameters. Furthermore, complex cognitive processes do not lend themselves to single measures (Steinke & Fitch, 2011). How, then, might scholars improve research on cognition in service learning under such conditions?

Beyond just paying better attention to research design and measures, researchers and practitioners should become more intentional about the outcomes they are cultivating and investigating. Much of the research in service learning does not clearly define the critical components of the course, the outcomes being investigated, or how and why the course components are related to the outcomes. Future research can make stronger connections between service learning course design and anticipated cognitive outcomes, to demonstrate the effectiveness of intentionally designing the course to meet those outcomes rather than expecting service learning to deliver learning gains automatically (Ash et al., 2005). Furthermore, when working with complex cognitive outcomes, researchers need to be clear about the indicators of the outcomes that they want to measure (Steinke & Fitch, 2011) and which of these are likely to change during the time frame of an investigation. For example, the AAC&U (2010) critical thinking VALUE Rubric identifies the following criteria or indicators for critical thinking: explanation of issues, evidence, influence of context and assumptions, student's position and conclusion, and related outcomes. Using common criteria for outcomes across institutions, as can occur with the use of the VALUE Rubrics, allows research to be conducted collaboratively with multiple researchers all providing data from their own institutions.

Another recommendation is to design studies that use regression and predictive/structural equation modeling analyses. Such procedures measure and attempt to account for the natural multicollinearity (i.e., redundancy) within the often complex relationships between latent and observed variables. These analyses could provide a basic framework for creating latent variable models to use for research on the relationships among service learning, intellectual development, and cognitive processes and on how they change across time. This recommendation suggests the importance of using mixed-methods in which qualitative data can enrich findings from quantitative analyses and provide some degree of reliability across methods.

Moreover, research on cognitive outcomes of service learning should move beyond one-shot designs. As Jameson et al. (2008) suggest, learning outcomes can also be assessed across the curriculum, examining both the intended and unintended cumulative effects across several courses. How can a well-structured curriculum that incorporates service learning across multiple courses cumulatively build gains in intellectual development, critical thinking, and other cognitive outcomes? This type of question often requires longitudinal analyses that assess the degree to which a focus on enhancing intellectual development and cognitive processes through service learning develops the type of self-regulated learning that leads to optimal performance beyond college (Mentkowski & Associates, 2000) and helps students to construct a world in which they see themselves as active agents in communities.

Recommendations for Future Research

The theories about intellectual development and cognitive processes reviewed in this chapter suggest directions for future research that will enhance pedagogical practice as well as understanding of the theories themselves. We offer three different designs to investigate research questions on cognition in service learning.

Experimental Design

A pretest-posttest, randomized control group design could be used to examine a research question such as: How much guided reflection is needed to enhance cognitive (or other) outcomes of service learning? The basic design would involve randomly assigning service learning courses that are comparable (e.g., content, integration of service learning) to varying amounts of guided reflection through the use of tools such as the DEAL Model or P-SAP and measuring outcomes before and after service learning. The independent variable would be the frequency with which a guided reflection tool is integrated into the course and would vary from never (control) to occasionally or often (two or more experimental groups). The dependent variables would include critical thinking and problem solving as measured by the rubrics associated with the reflection tools themselves (critical thinking for the DEAL Model and problem solving for P-SAP) as well as by the parallel VALUE Rubrics for critical thinking and problem solving, which would provide measures for convergent validity. The control group would be measured only before and after service learning, whereas the course-embedded reflection tools would provide additional midcourse assessments for the experimental groups. Intellectual development is a slow, incremental process, and it may take longer than a single course to detect changes in this outcome, so we recommend measuring it over at least one year. Researchers who have access to large populations of students and multiple sections of comparable service learning courses could use a true experimental design, whereas those who have limited access to these conditions would need to use a quasi-experimental design and attempt to control statistically for potential confounding variables.

Predictive Modeling Design

Figure 2.1.2 illustrates a broad conceptual model that could be used as a starting point to investigate the question: Under what conditions does service learning promote intellectual development and the types of cognitive processes that are the foundation of self-regulated learning? In this model,

FIGURE 2.1.2

Proposed Design for Predictive Modeling Study on Interaction Among Cognitive Processes, Intellectual Development, and High-Quality Service Learning as Predictors of Self-Regulated Learning

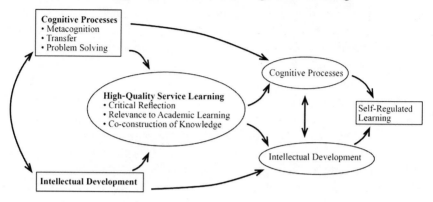

initial levels of cognitive processes and intellectual development are posited as exogenous variables or characteristics and abilities that students bring with them and that affect how they approach service learning experiences and, potentially, what they learn through them. As such, we propose that they function as moderating variables, along with the quality of the service learning experience. High-quality service learning—characterized by critical reflection, service that is meaningful and academically relevant, and opportunities for students to co-construct knowledge with others in academic and community contexts (Eyler & Giles, 1999)—is expected to further enhance initial use of cognitive processes and intellectual development level. We hypothesize that the interaction of all three variables will predict self-regulated learning. Tracking how these variables are related to each other and how these relationships change over time and across contexts using structural equation modeling would enhance the understanding of both theory and practice regarding the development of cognitive processes. In keeping with standard practices employed in predictive modeling designs, each variable would be associated with one or more measures, many of which have been discussed previously in this chapter.

Developmental Design

The developmental instruction model (Moore, 1994) supports the hypothesis that development of critical thinking and related cognitive processes of transfer, problem solving, and metacognition is dependent on a student's level of intellectual development (as illustrated in Figure 2.1.1). In addition, it suggests that intellectual development functions in part as a moderator of cognitive processes, which then facilitates further intellectual development and more effective cognitive processes in an iterative fashion. Moreover, service learning has the potential to enhance intellectual development and cognitive processes, and the extent to which it does so likely depends on how it is designed. Questions that could advance this aspect of a research agenda on service learning include the following: How does a student's level of intellectual development function as a lens (i.e., mediating or moderating variable) for interpreting and responding to the challenges and supports implicated by developmental instruction that are encountered in the service learning experience? How does intellectual development, in turn, affect cognitive processes? Specific examples of each of the four developmental instruction variables—structure, diversity, personalism, and experiential learning—that could be tested are (a) level of structure in reflection activities and at the service learning community setting; (b) diversity of people encountered in the service learning experience; (c) degree of personalism in relationships with the course instructor and with people in the service learning setting; and (d) level of concrete, face-to-face versus vicarious, imagined involvement with the course instructor and the community.

These interrelated research questions would best be addressed by a series of smaller investigations leading up to a long-term study similar to that conducted by Mentkowski and associates (2000) but employing a full cross-sequential design that includes multiple cohorts measured over time at regular intervals during and after college. It would require measuring the developmental instruction model (Moore, 1994) characteristics (structure, diversity, involvement, and personalism) of particular service learning and comparable non–service learning courses as well as students' intellectual development levels and cognitive processes relevant to expected course outcomes. Ideally, this study would use both quantitative and qualitative measures, including some course-embedded assessments, and would compare outcomes of service learning in discrete courses with outcomes from courses in which service learning is linked across the curriculum (Jameson et al., 2008). This sequential design would also employ structural equation modeling. If our hypothesis is supported, intellectual development level should moderate the effects of service learning on cognitive outcomes, depending on the developmental instruction characteristics of the experience. For example, students at lower levels of intellectual development should demonstrate more positive cognitive outcomes when service learning experiences are more structured, when diversity of course material is more limited, and when they receive more frequent and personal feedback on their reflection products; whereas students at higher levels of intellectual development should perform equally well under conditions of lower structure in service learning experiences, higher diversity of course material, and less feedback from the professor on reflection products and perhaps more from peers and community partners. At this level students' learning is more self-regulated and reflects recognition of themselves as a meaning-makers, an insight tied ultimately to identity.

Conclusion

This chapter provides direction for exploring connections among the design of service learning courses, intellectual development, and cognitive processes. Recommendations are offered for measures, designs, and questions to enhance research on cognition in service learning and to encourage researchers to learn from best practices in outcomes assessment. High-quality assessment can develop into high-quality research when faculty and other practitioner-scholars take ownership of the process and integrate it into their professional development (Hutchings, 2010; Steinke & Fitch, 2007a); in turn, high-quality research can provide useful recommendations for program and course enhancement.

This chapter also discusses the relationships among these variables in the context of high-quality service learning. Moreover, all of the discussed processes—intellectual development, critical thinking, metacognition, problem solving, and transfer—are essential components of self-regulated learning that lasts beyond college and that undergirds responsible and effective engagement with communities. Furthering research on cognition in service learning as outlined in this chapter will lead to a better understanding of the relationship between these outcomes and learning that endures.

Recommended Reading

Bransford, J. D., Brown, A. L., Cocking, R. R., Donovan, M. S., & Pellegrino, J. W. (Eds.). (2000). *How people learn: Brain, mind, experience, and school* (Expanded ed.). Washington, DC: National Academy Press.
Eyler, J. S., & Giles, D. E., Jr. (1999). *Where's the learning in service learning?* San Francisco, CA: Jossey-Bass.

Mentkowski, M., & Associates (Eds.). (2000). *Learning that lasts: Integrating learning, development, and performance in college and beyond.* San Francisco, CA: Jossey-Bass.

Moore, W. S. (1994). Student and faculty epistemology in the college classroom: The Perry schema of intellectual and ethical development. In K. Prichard & R. M. Sawyer (Eds.), *Handbook of college teaching: Theory and applications* (pp. 45–67). Westport, CT: Greenwood Press.

Perry, W. G. (1968/1970/1999). *Forms of intellectual and ethical development in the college years: A scheme.* San Francisco, CA: Jossey-Bass.

Steinke, P., & Fitch, P. (2007). Assessing service-learning. *Research & Practice in Assessment, 1*(2), 1–8. Retrieved from http://www.virginiaassessment.org/rpa/2/Steinke%20Fitch.pdf

References

Ash, S. L., & Clayton, P. H. (2009). Generating, deepening, and documenting learning: The power of critical reflection in applied learning. *Journal of Applied Learning in Higher Education, 1*(1), 25–48.

Ash, S. L., Clayton, P. H., & Atkinson, M. P. (2005). Integrating reflection and assessment to capture and improve student learning. *Michigan Journal of Community Service Learning, 11*(2), 49–60.

Association of American Colleges and Universities (AAC&U). (2010). *VALUE: Valid Assessment of Learning in Undergraduate Education.* Retrieved from http://www.aacu.org/value/

Astin, A. W., & Sax, L. J. (1998). How undergraduates are affected by service participation. *Journal of College Student Development, 39,* 251–263.

Astin, A. W., Vogelgesang, L. J., Ikeda, E. K., & Yee, J. A. (2000). *How service learning affects students.* Los Angeles, CA: Higher Education Research Institute, University of California.

Barnett, S., & Ceci, S. J. (2002). When and where do we apply what we learn? A taxonomy for far transfer. *Psychological Bulletin, 128,* 612–637.

Batchelder, T. H., & Root, S. (1994). Effects of an undergraduate program to integrate academic learning and service: Cognitive, prosocial cognitive, and identity outcomes. *Journal of Adolescence, 17,* 341–355.

Bloom, B. S. (Ed.) (1956). *Taxonomy of educational objectives* (Vol. 1). New York, NY: McKay.

Bransford, J. D., Brown, A. L., Cocking, R. R., Donovan, M. S., & Pellegrino, J. W. (Eds.). (2000). *How people learn: Brain, mind, experience, and school* (Expanded ed.). Washington, DC: National Academy Press.

Bringle, R. G., & Hatcher, J. A. (2000). Meaningful measurement of theory-based service-learning outcomes: Making the case with quantitative research [Special issue]. *Michigan Journal of Community Service Learning, Fall,* 68–75.

Downing, K., Kwong, T., Chan, S. W., Lam, T. F., & Downing, W. K. (2009). Problem-based learning and the development of metacognition. *Higher Education, 57,* 609–621.

Eyler, J. S., & Giles, D. E., Jr. (1999). *Where's the learning in service learning?* San Francisco, CA: Jossey-Bass.

Eyler, J. S., & Giles, D. E., Jr. (2002). Beyond surveys: Using the problem-solving interview to assess the impact of service-learning on understanding and critical thinking. In A. Furco & S. H. Billig (Eds.), *Service learning: The essence of the pedagogy* (pp. 147–160). Greenwich, CT: Information Age.

Fascione, P. A. (1990). Critical thinking: A statement of expert consensus for purposes of educational assessment and instruction, Executive Summary. *The Delphi Report.* Millbrae, CA: California Academic Press. Retrieved from http://www.insightassessment.com/CT-Resources/Expert-Consensus-on-Critical-Thinking/Delphi-Consensus-Report-Executive-Summary-PDF/(language)/eng-US

Fitch, P. (2004). Effects of intercultural service-learning experiences on intellectual development and intercultural sensitivity. In M. Welch & S. H. Billig (Eds.), *Research to advance the field* (pp. 107–126). Greenwich, CT: Information Age.

Govekar, M. A., & Rishi, M. (2007). Service learning: Bringing real-world education into the B-school classroom. *Journal of Education for Business, 83*(1), 3–10.

Grossman, R. (2008). Structures for facilitating student reflection. *College Teaching, 57*(1), 15–22.

Halpern, D. F. (1998). Teaching critical thinking for transfer across domains. *American Psychologist, 53,* 449–455.

Hirschinger-Blank, N., & Markowitz, M. W. (2006). An evaluation of a pilot service-learning course for criminal justice undergraduate students. *Journal of Criminal Justice Education, 17*(1), 69–86.

Hofer, B. K. (2001). Personal epistemology research: Implications for teaching and learning. *Journal of Educational Psychology Review, 13,* 353–383.

Hofer, B. K., & Pintrich, P. R. (1997). The development of epistemological theories: Beliefs about knowledge and knowing and their relation to learning. *Review of Educational Research, 67*(1), 88–140.

Howard, G. S. (1980). Response-shift bias: A problem in evaluating interventions with pre-post self-reports. *Evaluation Review, 4*(1), 93–106.

Huba, M. E., & Freed, J. E. (2000). *Learner-centered assessment on college campuses: Shifting the focus from teaching to learning.* Needham Heights, MA: Allyn & Bacon.

Hutchings, P. (2010). *Opening doors to faculty involvement in assessment.* National Institute for Learning Outcomes Assessment, Occasional paper #4. Retrieved from http://www.learningoutcomeassessment.org/documents/PatHutchings.pdf

Jameson, J. K., Clayton, P. H., & Bringle, R. G. (2008). Investigating student learning within and across linked service learning courses. In M. A. Bowdon, S. H. Billig, & B. A. Holland (Eds.), *Scholarship for sustaining service learning and civic engagement* (pp. 3–27). Charlotte, NC: Information Age.

King, P. M., & Kitchener, K. S. (1994). *Developing reflective judgment: Understanding and promoting intellectual growth and critical thinking in adolescents and adults.* San Francisco, CA: Jossey-Bass.

Li, X., & Lal, S. (2005). Critical reflective thinking through service learning in multicultural teacher education. *Intercultural Education, 16,* 217–234.

Loacker, G. (Ed.). (2000). *Self assessment at Alverno College.* Milwaukee, WI: Alverno College Institute.

Mentkowski, M., & Associates. (Eds.). (2000). *Learning that lasts: Integrating learning, development, and performance in college and beyond.* San Francisco, CA: Jossey-Bass.

Moore, W. S. (1994). Student and faculty epistemology in the college classroom: The Perry schema of intellectual and ethical development. In K. Prichard & R. M. Sawyer (Eds.), *Handbook of college teaching: Theory and applications* (pp. 45–67). Westport, CT: Greenwood Press.

Nokes, K. M., Nickitas, D. M., Keida, R., & Neville, S. (2005). Does service learning increase cultural competency, critical thinking, and civic engagement? *Journal of Nursing Education, 44*(2), 65–70.

Novak, J. M., Markey, V., & Allen, M. (2007). Evaluating cognitive outcomes of service learning in higher education: A meta-analysis. *Communication Research Reports, 24*(2), 149–157.

Parker-Gwin, R., & Mabry, J. B. (1998). Service learning as pedagogy and civic education: Comparing outcomes for three models. *Teaching Sociology, 26,* 276–291.

Paul, R. W., & Elder, L. (2008). *The miniature guide to critical thinking: Concepts and tools.* Dillon Beach, CA: Foundation for Critical Thinking.

Perry, W. G. (1968/1970/1999). *Forms of intellectual and ethical development in the college years: A scheme.* San Francisco, CA: Jossey-Bass.

Perry, W. G. (1981). Cognitive and ethical growth: The making of meaning. In A. Chickering (Ed.), *The modern American college* (pp. 76–116). San Francisco, CA: Jossey-Bass.

Pinzón, D. P., & Arceo, F. D. B. (2005). Critical thinking in a higher education service learning program. In K. M. Casey, G. Davison, S. H. Billig, & N. C. Springer (Eds.), *Research to transform the field* (pp. 89–110). Greenwich, CT: Information Age.

Quitadamo, I. J., Faiola, C. L., Johnson, J. E., & Kurtz, M. J. (2008). Community-based inquiry improves critical thinking in general education biology. *CBE Life Sciences Education, 7,* 327–337.

Ritchhart, R., & Perkins, D. N. (2005). Learning to think: The challenges of teaching thinking. In K. J. Holyoak & R. G. Morrison (Eds.), *The Cambridge handbook of thinking and reasoning* (pp. 775–802). New York, NY: Cambridge University Press.

Rogoff, B. (1990). *Apprenticeship in thinking: Cognitive development in social context.* New York, NY: Oxford University Press.

Sanford, N. (Ed.). (1962). *The American college.* New York, NY: Wiley.

Sedlak, C. A., Doheny, M. O., Panthofer, N., & Anaya, E. (2003). Critical thinking in students' service learning experiences. *College Teaching, 51*(3), 99–103.

Steinke, P., & Fitch, P. (2003). Using written protocols to measure service learning outcomes. In S. H. Billig & J. Eyler (Eds.), *Deconstructing service learning: Research exploring context, participation, and impacts* (pp. 171–194). Greenwich, CT: Information Age.

Steinke, P., & Fitch, P. (2007a). Assessing service-learning. *Research & Practice in Assessment, 1*(2), 1–8. Retrieved from http://www.virginiaassessment.org/rpa/2/Steinke%20Fitch.pdf

Steinke, P., & Fitch, P. (2007b). How to measure problem-solving ability: The problem-solving analysis protocol (P-SAP). *Toolkit: The nuts and bolts newsletter from Office of Assessment Services, 5*(3). Retrieved from http://www.niu.edu/assessment/Toolkit/vol5_ish3.pdf

Steinke, P., & Fitch, P. (2011). Outcome assessment from the perspective of psychological science: The TAIM approach. *New Directions for Institutional Research, 2011*(149), 5–26. doi:10.1002/ir.377

Sternberg, R. J. (1997). *Successful intelligence: How practical and creative intelligence determine success in life.* New York, NY: Plume.

Veenman, M. V. J., Van Hout-Wolters, B. H. A. M., & Afflerbach, P. (2006). Metacognition and learning: Conceptual and methodological considerations. *Metacognition and Learning, 1*(1), 3–14.

Vygotsky, L. S. (1978). *Mind and society: The development of higher psychological processes.* Cambridge, MA: Harvard University Press.

Wagner, J. F. (2006). Transfer in pieces. *Cognition and Instruction, 24*(1), 1–71.

Wang, Y., & Rodgers, R. (2006). Impact of service learning and social justice education on college students' cognitive development. *NASPA Journal About Women in Higher Education, 43*, 316–337.

CONCEPTUALIZING, ASSESSING, AND INVESTIGATING ACADEMIC LEARNING IN SERVICE LEARNING

Jessica Katz Jameson, Patti H. Clayton, and Sarah L. Ash

Faculty, staff, and students at North Carolina State University collaborated to develop an interdisciplinary minor in nonprofit studies that is designed around *threaded service learning*, defined as

> the intentional use of service-learning as a vehicle to connect the teaching and learning processes across one or more courses in a developmentally sequenced and progressive fashion, which is designed to increase student learning and critical thinking [as well as quality and intensity of service]. It is a process of learning through reflection on multiple experiences that build cumulatively over time. (Jameson, Clayton, & Bringle, 2008, pp. 8–9)

The design of the minor's service learning component includes use of Bloom's Taxonomy[1] to articulate hierarchically structured learning objectives within five themes, which were identified by the collaborating faculty as the primary challenges facing leaders in the nonprofit sector: (a) aligning mission, methods, and resources; (b) balancing individual interests and the common good; (c) earning and maintaining the public trust; (d) capitalizing on opportunities associated with diversity; and (e) moving beyond charity toward systemic change. Critical reflection prompts within each of these five themes—categories of learning that the courses in the minor are designed to cultivate in a cumulative fashion—support and challenge students to ever-higher levels of reasoning as they progress through the minor. In the capstone course, critical reflection is intended to support students in integrating multiple service learning experiences they have undertaken in the variety of nonprofit settings and disciplines from earlier courses and in adopting the interdisciplinary perspectives of leaders in the nonprofit sector. Throughout, the critical reflection process is closely integrated with the assessment strategy—both feedback on and grading of student products—which, in turn, provides data for course and program refinement and for investigation of student learning, within and across courses.

The preceding vignette illustrates the thesis of our discussion of assessing and investigating academic learning in service learning: Academic learning takes a variety of forms, different courses may target different types and levels of learning, and if the pedagogy is to produce the desired learning then both instructional and assessment practices must be designed in a way that is consistent with and aligned with the desired learning outcomes. Precise conceptualization of different types and levels of academic learning is central to research investigating these outcomes and the processes that generate them.

Academic learning is widely understood (chapter 1.1) to be one of at least three interrelated categories of learning that define service learning—the others being civic learning (the topic of chapter 2.3) and personal growth (the topic of chapter 2.4). This breadth and the potential integration of these categories of learning are among the defining elements of the pedagogy. Further, service learning raises the possibility—if not the expectation—of unanticipated and unique student learning outcomes within each category. The pedagogy thus challenges practitioner-scholars to consider the extent and nature of their responsibility to (a) support students in achieving and articulating individualized as well as common learning outcomes in multiple categories and (b) develop approaches to assessing and investigating the full range of these student learning outcomes and the associated learning processes.

When we focus on academic learning in particular, service learning presents students with opportunities to see examples of academic material emerge in community experiences. Service learning students should recognize and perhaps use academic concepts and theories in their service; in other words, the pedagogy invites them to think at the level of application. For many instructors and curriculum designers, such as those involved in the minor described in the opening vignette, a key reason to use service learning is that its integration of disciplinary content and community-based experience makes it particularly well suited to support and challenge students to achieve higher levels of academic learning and to develop critical thinking capacities. Some instructors may be interested in using the pedagogy to nurture students' abilities to co-create academic (and other) learning goals and to develop identities and skills as producers of knowledge.

Academic learning in service learning, then, encompasses various types and levels of learning outcomes. In some cases it may be appropriate to document and measure basic levels of learning (e.g., gateway courses), whereas in others it may be important to assess higher levels of learning (e.g., intensive first-year seminars, capstones, graduate courses); levels of critical thinking might be assessed as well in either or both of these types of cases. Although some approaches to assessment—such as applying rubrics to reflection products—are well suited for assessing any level of learning, others (including some approaches to multiple-choice tests) may lend themselves more readily to assessing basic rather than higher level learning outcomes. Using an assessment mechanism that is not sensitive to or appropriate for the level(s) of desired learning or attempting to assess learning that the pedagogy has not been designed to generate limits the ability of students to improve their reasoning processes, instructors to enhance courses, and scholars to build a knowledge base on service learning.

The next section presents a conceptual framework for articulating academic learning outcomes, distilled from a set of related theoretical perspectives that speak to the nature of experiential learning and of cognitive processes more generally. This is followed by a critical examination of past research questions, methods, and instruments through the lens of this framework and by practical recommendations for implementation of service learning and assessment of resultant academic learning. Academic learning is treated as a discrete, albeit multifaceted, category of learning outcomes throughout most of the chapter. In the section on recommendations for future research the question of integration with other categories of learning is revisited.

Theoretical Perspectives and a Conceptual Model

Because service learning is a form of experiential education, any discussion of the theoretical bases for its learning potential typically begins with Dewey

(1997/1933). Dewey's educational philosophy was a reaction to the dominant educational strategy of his time: the rote memorization of facts that were identified as significant entirely by the instructor. In *How We Think*, Dewey (1997/1933) explores the role of disciplined, evidence-based inquiry that draws heavily on experience in moving beyond conventional wisdom, and he frames reflection as a process of coming to understand the meaning, sources, and consequences of knowledge. Calling attention to the importance of engaging with dissonance, or perplexity, in the learning process, Dewey suggests that when confronted with an unexpected experience, individuals are required to stop and examine—reflect on—their current beliefs in deciding what to do next. Service learning provides such an opportunity for students to face new, possibly dissonant, experiences that can cause them to see persons, places, policies, and problems in new and more complex ways. It invites thinking that, as Dewey advocated, involves more than basic knowledge and indeed requires, as well as fosters, higher levels of cognitive activity.

Schön (1983) similarly posits that all practitioners, regardless of field or level of experience, should see themselves as active learners, continually taking in new information and integrating it with previous understanding. Rather than assuming that we must always learn theory and concepts before attempting to use them in practice, he suggests that much of our most important learning is achieved through reflection-in-action, in which existing knowledge is used to solve problems in practice and to continually and deliberately test and adapt theories and concepts in new situations. This conceptualization of learning is consistent with goals of higher education in that students are expected to integrate what they learn in general education courses with their academic majors, minors, and elective course work and are encouraged to become aware of their own learning processes as they move across learning environments—sometimes as beginning learners and sometimes as expert learners, sometimes learning inductively and sometimes deductively. Especially because these outcomes rarely unfold in a predictably linear fashion, students can perhaps best achieve them if they learn to reflect continually on new concepts and to find and actively create interconnections among various theories, conceptual frameworks, learning processes, and experiences. A compartmentalized curriculum runs the risk of providing very few intentional opportunities for students to develop these capacities, whereas a design like that of the minor described in the opening vignette, which includes intentional sequencing of courses that are linked through cumulative design of a core pedagogy, may support them in learning how to learn in these ways.

Bloom's Taxonomy of the Cognitive Domain (Bloom, 1956; hereafter referred to as Bloom's Taxonomy), which undergirds the threaded service learning design in that minor, includes lower levels of reasoning that involve basic knowledge comprehension; midlevel application of knowledge; and the higher levels of analysis, synthesis, and evaluation. Bloom's Taxonomy suggests that an academic concept must be identified and explained before it can be recognized or used in practice (application) and that comparing and contrasting (analysis) one representation of it with another is an important precursor to achieving more nuanced understandings of it (synthesis) or evaluating its theoretical or practical adequacy. Reasoning, then, includes increasingly more complex, higher level cognitive tasks involving the creation of new understandings and the use of evidence to make and support judgments. Bradley (1997), Ash and Clayton (2009a, 2009b), Ash, Clayton, and Atkinson (2005), and Jameson et al. (2008) are among those who call for design of service learning based on hierarchically expressed, Bloom-based academic (and other) learning objectives.

Yet another way to conceptualize academic learning is to frame it as thinking from the perspective of a discipline. There is an important distinction between basic subject matter learning—for example, focusing on names, dates, and places in a history course—and thinking like a scholar in or practitioner of the discipline—for example, viewing recorded history as the product of multiple and often contradictory interpretations of the past. Boix Mansilla and Gardner (2008) propose four competencies of disciplinary thinking: (a) having an essential knowledge base, (b) understanding how the discipline helps make sense of the world and solve problems, (c) understanding relevant methods of inquiry, and (d) using disciplinary forms of communication (e.g., lab reports, museum exhibits, films). Thinking from the perspective of one or more disciplines invites and enables students to examine sources of information critically, integrate new information, see the world through the lens of multiple—sometimes interconnected, other times discrete—frameworks, and consider what the various disciplines that they encounter do and do not have in common.

Running through each of these perspectives on learning and thinking is the importance of critical thinking. According to the Foundation for Critical Thinking (Paul, 1993), "Critical thinking is a systematic way to form and shape one's thinking. . . . It is thought that is disciplined, comprehensive, based on intellectual standards, and as a result, well-reasoned" (p. 20). Like

Dewey, Paul (1993) points to the shortcomings of instruction focused only on basic knowledge and skills and calls for an approach to education that helps students learn the characteristics of high-quality thinking and develop the ability to assess their own and others' reasoning accordingly. Paul and Elder's (2006) universal standards of critical thinking—clarity, accuracy, precision, relevance, depth, breadth, logic, significance, and fairness—create a shared language around the characteristics of high-quality reasoning and serve as specific criteria with which thinking can be assessed, both formatively (i.e., in giving students feedback) and summatively (i.e., in grading). Regardless of the type or level of reasoning in question, these standards are key to its quality.

Taken together, these perspectives on experiential learning and on the nature of thinking provide significant guidance in designing for as well as assessing and investigating academic learning, including in the context of service learning. To support the precise conceptualization of academic learning required for undertaking high-quality teaching, assessment, and research, the following typology is proposed:

1. Basic, foundational learning (e.g., of facts, theories, formulas) and skills
2. Higher level learning associated with, for example, evaluation of knowledge and skills
3. Thinking from disciplinary and/or interdisciplinary perspectives
4. Critical thinking

Domains 1 and 2 include discipline-specific knowledge and skills as well as discipline- and profession-transcendent competencies (e.g., writing and speaking, information literacy, research). Domain 3 refers to the ability to adopt the underlying perspectives, paradigms, processes, and methods of inquiry of one or more disciplines, which can in turn enable an interdisciplinary perspective (Donald, 2002). Domain 4 includes the intellectual skills associated with high-quality, self-aware thinking (e.g., conceptual clarity, logical reasoning, the ability to interpret information from multiple perspectives, representing others' ideas with integrity).

These four domains of academic learning and the relationship between them can be conceptualized as an interconnected and dynamic set of nested circles (see Figure 2.2.1). The inner circles represent basic, foundational learning and are nested inside the midlevel circles, which indicate higher

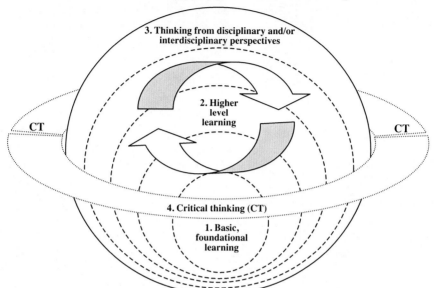

FIGURE 2.2.1
Conceptual Framework for Typology of Academic Learning Outcomes

level learning. The midlevel circles are, in turn, nested inside the outer circles, which represent thinking from disciplinary and/or interdisciplinary perspectives. The broken lines suggest the fluidity of the demarcations between and the interconnected relationships among these domains, and the arrows represent the iterative, cyclical nature of the learning process as it encompasses and moves between the domains.

The fourth domain of academic learning illustrated here is critical thinking. Whereas some scholars (e.g., Donald, 2002) include critical thinking under the umbrella of higher order reasoning, this conceptual framework posits that the three domains of academic learning are encircled and, indeed, held together by critical thinking and that critical thinking can and, in fact, should occur within all three of the other domains. Paul and Elder's (2006) standards of critical thinking (i.e., clarity, accuracy, precision, relevance, depth, breadth, logic, significance, and fairness)—and work on critical reflection in service learning that builds on those standards (e.g., Ash & Clayton, 2009a, 2009b)—suggest that critical thinking is relevant at all levels of academic learning. For example, explaining basic concepts, evaluating theoretical frameworks, and thinking like a historian all require clarity, accuracy, and logical reasoning; and moving from basic knowledge to higher level evaluation of theory involves conceptual clarity and logic. The simultaneous distinctiveness and pervasiveness of the domain of critical thinking—both its own category and key to the others—is expressed here by the encompassing outer ring.

This typology does not privilege academic outcomes in any particular domain, although it does suggest the hierarchical—in the sense of cumulatively interconnected—nature of learning. Any or all of these four domains of academic learning may be relevant in any given service learning course or course sequence as students encounter various learning goals based on their individual interests and needs as well as the design of the course or curriculum. In the example from the vignette, students in the introductory level nonprofits course are expected to identify, explain, and apply foundational concepts, terms, and theories related to each of the five leadership challenges. In the midlevel courses, learning outcomes include critical evaluation of strategic choices made by nonprofit leaders in terms of how they influence such issues as earning and maintaining the public trust or capitalizing on opportunities associated with diversity. A midlevel course on the history of nonprofits not only invites students to compare and contrast conceptualizations of the common good that have informed the work of nonprofits since the 1800s; it also challenges students to think like historians as they design and implement procedures for archival research and sift through multiple and sometimes contradictory interpretations of events in a nonprofit organization's history. In the minor's capstone, students could be expected to integrate material and experiences from the full range of earlier service learning activities across a variety of courses and disciplines, and critical reflection could be structured correspondingly for integrative reasoning across disciplinary perspectives.

Although encompassing distinct types of learning outcomes, the four domains illustrated in Figure 2.2.1 are interconnected, sometimes in an iterative fashion. Higher level learning, for instance, requires foundational knowledge as a prerequisite, and it sometimes instigates a return to that level for additional basics (e.g., clarification of terminology, nuances between related terms, reexamination of definitions in light of subsequent learning, paradoxes encountered in the application of a concept). As an example of this dynamic from the vignette, when students take the introductory nonprofits course they learn the basic concept of a mission statement and see an example of it in the work of their partner organizations. When they take the intermediate nonprofit leadership course and encounter an organization that modified its mission as its funders changed, they are expected to develop a higher level ability to analyze the evolution of mission statements over time, which may in turn change their basic understanding of the role and function of a mission statement and signal their need to learn associated foundational concepts such as *mission creep*.

The various theoretical frameworks that underlie the four domains of academic learning expressed in Figure 2.2.1 facilitate a more precise articulation of academic learning outcomes in service learning, which enables intentional design of the pedagogy and meaningful assessment of and research on these outcomes. Using this conceptual model as an analytical lens, in the following section we address the range of ways that academic learning has been defined and assessed; the importance of and challenges associated with aligning desired learning outcomes, instructional design, and assessment strategies; and the challenges of doing this kind of research more generally.

Review of Previous Research

Eyler and Giles posed the question, "Where's the learning in service learning?" in their 1999 book. Their central thesis is that service learning has the potential to produce significant learning but that the field needs better methods to facilitate as well as document that learning. This review highlights research on academic outcomes associated with service learning since the publication of that landmark book. Further, this review is limited to studies that use measures of student learning, such as graded written products and exam scores, rather than surveys of student satisfaction or self-reported outcomes.

One recurring question in the field concerns whether service learning improves student learning of course content better than other pedagogies. A common approach to shedding light on this question—illustrated here with three examples—is to compare service learning students' performance on assignments or exams with that of students in non–service learning courses. Strage (2000) compared 311 students in non–service learning sections of an introductory child development course with 166 students in service learning sections. The service learning students achieved higher scores on the essay portions of all exams (common across the two sets of students) but showed no significant difference on the multiple-choice components, suggesting to the investigator relative enhancement of academic learning primarily in terms of higher order thinking (domain 2) but not in terms of basic knowledge acquisition (domain 1). In addition to this comparison across pedagogies, Strage considered the extent to which service learning students' academic learning increased through the semester. Examination of journal entries, in which students responded to prompts specifically tied to course content, suggested that the service learning students' ability to integrate experience and course concepts increased as the course progressed; Strage reported that the journal entries became more focused, more detailed, and more accurate in their research- and theory-based analyses of everyday events. From the perspective of the conceptual framework expressed in Figure 2.2.1, this part of the study conceptualized learning in terms of critical thinking (domain 4).

Wurr (2002) compared the writing performance of 35 students in sections of a first-year composition course that included service with a community organization with that of 38 students enrolled in sections of the same course that used traditional methods (e.g., library research). He reported that the essays of the service learning students were judged by independent graders as at least half a letter grade higher than those of non–service learning students. Wurr also reported that analytic measures of the use of rhetorical appeals, logic, coherence, and mechanics were significantly higher, suggesting to him a greater understanding of the complexity of the issues at the heart of the course and the ability to engage in higher order reasoning and critical thinking (domains 3 and 4 of our conceptual framework).

Mpofu (2007) compared the learning outcomes of 65 students who opted for a service learning component of a rehabilitation services course with those of 65 students who took the same course without that experience. He found no significant differences on multiple-choice exams, which tested learning of medical facts, procedures, and outcomes (domain 1); but he did find that students in the service learning group achieved increasingly higher scores than non–service learning students on case study assignments that required them to evaluate the appropriateness of the services being given in the case study based on the patient's disability and to predict the patient's medical prognosis and future quality of life (domains 2, 3, and 4). Unlike their counterparts, the service learning students wrote reflective journals that required the same integrative thinking as the case studies. Thus, although the self-selection rather than randomization of students into the service learning component of the course raises questions about the comparability of the two groups of students in this as in other similarly designed studies, in this study enhanced academic outcomes, especially relative to higher level learning, were associated with the stronger alignment of pedagogical approaches and desired outcomes in the service learning group.

Several studies—three of which are summarized here—have focused not on comparing service learning and other pedagogies but rather on determining how service learning might best be designed so as to fulfill the claims made for its academic (and other) learning potential. Investigators have, for example, examined changes in the quality of reasoning demonstrated by service learning students throughout a course or curriculum. Ash et al. (2005) defined and assessed academic learning in terms of both critical thinking skills and movement up Bloom's Taxonomy (1956) in students' reasoning about specific, student-identified course concepts. Using two rubrics, they examined written products generated through a critical reflection process that (a) was guided to ensure tight integration of service learning experiences with Bloom-based learning objectives and (b) included the use of Paul and Elder's (2006) critical thinking standards in the feedback and revision process. In reference to the model of academic learning in Figure 2.2.1, this study examined domains 1, 2, and 4 (basic learning, higher level learning, and critical thinking) but did not attend explicitly to learning to think from disciplinary and/or interdisciplinary perspectives. The quality of students' critical thinking as well as their level of reasoning about academic concepts increased across first drafts of reflection products from the beginning to the end of the semester and across multiple drafts of the same reflection product (informed by feedback). Students had a harder time achieving the highest levels of reasoning in the category of academic learning, in contrast with the civic learning and personal growth categories. The authors suggested that asking students to critique and reconstruct academic knowledge for themselves is especially counternormative to more traditional regurgitation of facts and theories. Learning of this type thus requires even more capacity building (e.g., guided practice in critical reflection and support for taking ownership of their own learning and generating new knowledge), which, as the minor in the opening vignette demonstrates, can occur both within courses and across course sequences.

Within the context of that minor, Jameson et al. (2008) investigated the quality of student learning across linked service learning courses by applying Bloom-based rubrics to written reflection products that had been produced through the use of Bloom-based reflection prompts. Unlike the previously described study, they did not integrate critical thinking capacity-building tools or use a critical thinking rubric. Qualified by their small sample size, the investigators concluded that threaded service learning—in which critical reflection is intentionally designed in each course and across the courses to build cumulatively on itself and to support students in reasoning to ever higher levels—did support progressively more sophisticated understanding of course material, mainly focusing on domains 1 and 2.

McGuire et al. (2009) focused on academic learning in terms of critical thinking alone (domain 4) and engaged in a variety of interventions designed to build their students' critical thinking skills across the semester through critical reflection activities. The investigators gathered two written reflection products from each of six students in their service learning courses, one produced near the beginning of the semester and one produced near the end, and scored them using a critical thinking rubric (Ash & Clayton, 2009a, 2009b). Comparing changes in critical thinking across students who had scored at the bottom (weakest), middle, and top (strongest) of the grade range on a prior assignment, the investigators found greater improvement over time by the weakest and strongest students. Interestingly, they found examples of reflection products that demonstrated high levels of critical thinking but were lacking in substantive connections to the academic content of the course. They thus acknowledged the value that would have been added by integrating the critical thinking standards with Bloom-based learning objectives in formative and summative assessment of academic learning in student reflection (see Ash & Clayton, 2009a, 2009b; Ash et al., 2005).

The preceding review is not comprehensive, it provides examples of attempts to assess and investigate academic learning in service learning in recent years. Although many instructors have identified critical thinking (domain 4 in our conceptual model) as a desired learning outcome, few studies distinguish between basic and higher level academic learning outcomes (domains 1 and 2) or explicitly measure thinking from disciplinary and/or interdisciplinary perspectives (domain 3). The next section provides an overview of several types of measurement approaches and tools that are available to deepen this work.

Measurement Approaches and Tools

A variety of approaches can be used to measure academic learning outcomes, some better suited than others to one or more of the domains of learning conceptualized in Figure 2.2.1 and some more closely aligned than others with the design of the associated instructional strategies. Indicators of students' academic learning can come from a variety of sources (e.g., the students themselves, individuals collaborating with them in the service learning process), take a variety of forms (e.g., perceptions, demonstrations), and be gathered in a variety of ways (e.g., asking questions, making observations, evaluating products). The conceptual framework expressed in Figure 2.2.1 provides one typology of the range of ways that the outcomes at stake in the category of academic learning might be conceptualized.

Using grades (e.g., from exams) to investigate academic learning in service learning has the appeal of readily available data (from both service learning and non–service learning students). However, this approach has the significant limitation that standard exam questions may not be well aligned with the full range of levels of learning toward which service learning has been designed in any given instance. As an example, if items on a multiple-choice exam require that students be able to identify or define or recognize examples of course concepts, then that exam is not well suited to measure higher level reasoning, thinking from the perspective of a discipline, or critical thinking. The same exam could provide better insight into such abilities if the items were written differently—perhaps if it provided students with a complex problem to reason through from various theoretical perspectives before selecting which response option best expresses the primary tension points among the theories as they emerge in the case. Thus, researchers need to know, in adapting and evaluating instruments, specifically what kinds of items and questions are included in terms of the types and levels of academic learning they are best suited to measure.

Surveys or questionnaires, often including scales and/or narratives in which students are asked to assess their knowledge or skills or to report on what they have learned (Mahin & Kruggel, 2006; Marshall, Beck, Coghlan, & Kimbro, 2005), can be used to obtain quantitative and qualitative measures of student perceptions of their own learning (or perceptions of the instructor, staff, or community partners). Eyler (2000), however, warns against relying solely on student self-report, which may conflate learning with satisfaction, and calls instead for direct evidence of academic (and other) learning. Combining surveys with other approaches designed to elicit direct evidence of student learning allows for triangulation of data and may provide more rigorous evidence of academic learning in service learning than surveys alone. Direct evidence may come from the assessment of written, oral, or audiovisual products generated, for example, through student reflection or problem-solving activities. The nature of the thinking required of students as they write essays, analyze case studies, resolve problems, or critically reflect on their service learning experiences through the lens of course concepts will depend on the content and structure of the prompts. When these prompts are aligned with the intended learning outcomes, the resultant products can provide a basis for the assessment of any or all of the domains of academic learning expressed in Figure 2.2.1.

Problem-solving interviews (Eyler & Giles, 1999) or narratives (Batchelder & Root, 1994; Steinke & Fitch, 2003)—which pose a problem and invite students to reason through such issues as potential causes, consequences, solutions, and response strategies—can provide direct, authentic evidence of academic learning in all four domains (as well as other dimensions of intellectual development; see chapter 2.1). Steinke and Fitch (2003) built on Eyler and Giles's (1999) interview protocol and designed a written version that can be more easily and less expensively administered, such as by integrating it into reflection activities. They suggest that the problem scenarios provided need to relate to the content of the course or discipline if they are to provide evidence of students' understanding of academic material. Scenarios should also be novel so as to provide evidence of students' abilities to transfer this knowledge to new situations. Bringle and Steinberg (2010) and Bullock and Clayton (2010) integrate self-report scales with problem-solving narratives. The work of these investigators suggests that a common multidisciplinary problem scenario might be posed to students or that students might be asked individually to identify a relevant problem, but in either case they would then engage with the problem using predetermined prompts designed to evoke and document the types and levels of thinking desired.

Reflection can also be an important source of evidence for documenting and investigating student learning across all four of the domains conceptualized in Figure 2.2.1 through the application of rubrics to student reflection products. Ash and Clayton (2004, 2009a, 2009b) and Ash et al. (2005) offer an approach to assessment that is integrated with learning objectives as well as with the design of critical reflection to generate the desired type or level of learning: the DEAL Model for Critical Reflection. The DEAL Model and its associated rubrics—one grounded in Bloom's Taxonomy (1956) and another in Paul and Elder's (2006) standards of critical thinking—facilitate the use of critical reflection to generate, deepen, and document learning. DEAL is a three-step, prompt-guided model for critical reflection that begins with Description of experiences; moves on to Examination of those experiences in light of specific learning goals and objectives; and concludes with the Articulation of Learning, which involves considering the sources and significance of learning as well as setting related goals for improved future action. The associated rubric for academic, content-based learning (as well as the rubrics for other categories of learning) supports both the design of prompts in the Examination step and the formative and summative assessment of student reasoning in terms of the levels of Bloom's Taxonomy (1956). The corollary critical thinking table describes 11 standards of critical thinking, adapted from Paul and Elder (2006), and provides questions designed to support students and reviewers of their work in applying the standards. The Bloom-based and critical thinking rubrics provide a basis for assessment and research, either separately or combined. Critical reflection structured with the DEAL Model can be focused on instructor- or student- (or community partner–) identified academic (and other) learning goals and objectives, giving it the flexibility to generate, deepen, and document either highly individualized or widely shared academic learning. Even when parameters for reflection are limited to particular concepts, however, students all reach and articulate their own learning rather than regurgitate their instructor's understanding. As previously described, several studies (Ash et al., 2005; Jameson et al., 2008; McGuire et al., 2009; Molee, Henry, Sessa, & McKinney-Prupis, 2010) have examined the utility of this model at the course or curricular level by having multiple raters examine written products generated by critical reflection processes structured with the DEAL Model, coding them for evidence of Bloom-based levels of academic learning and/or evidence of critical thinking.

In summary, exams, surveys, problem-solving interviews or narratives, critical reflection products, and rubrics are all potentially useful tools for assessing academic learning in service learning. Key to investigating attainment of the desired types and levels of academic learning is intentional design of well aligned pedagogical and assessment strategies. The next section explores implications of the conceptual framework proposed in Figure 2.2.1 for the practice of teaching with service learning and assessing the resultant academic learning.

Implications for Practice

Whether service learning generates and provides evidence of academic learning outcomes in any or all of the four domains illustrated in Figure 2.2.1 depends in large part on the degree of alignment among desired learning outcomes, pedagogical design, and assessment strategies. Such design and implementation issues are determined by choices made by the full range of participants—students, community members, and instructors—all of whom can be co-constructors of the service learning process (Jameson, Clayton, &

Jaeger, 2011). Although Dewey (1938) was speaking primarily of faculty at the time, his emphasis on the role of educators in experiential learning applies to any and all of the participants in service learning who assume responsibility for its design, implementation, and assessment. As Dewey (1938) writes in *Experience and Education*, it is the "teacher's business to see that the occasion is taken advantage of" (p. 84).

Eyler and Giles's (1999) conclusion, "We have discovered that the learning in service learning is in the questions" (p. 207), further refines Dewey's call for intentional design: The questions posed to guide reflective meaning making (i.e., critical reflection) should support students in achieving and demonstrating the level(s) or domain(s) of academic (and other) learning desired. Thus, a second key implication for practice that follows from the discussion in this chapter is the need to integrate critical reflection into course design and assessment practices to generate, deepen, and document learning (Ash & Clayton, 2009a, 2009b). As discussed, providing students with a context for problem-solving and structured reflection on the connection between academic content and community-engaged activities may be especially conducive to higher level learning outcomes and critical thinking. A design that aligns the focus of and guidance for critical reflection with the assessment instruments and criteria, all in light of the intended learning objectives, can help to capitalize on this potential while also establishing a context for solid research.

Learning through critical reflection in service learning—particularly higher level learning, thinking from disciplinary and/or interdisciplinary perspectives, and critical thinking—requires significant capacity building (e.g., guided practice, feedback, instruction on standards of critical thinking), especially given the counternormative nature of the pedagogy and the associated challenges of learning how to learn in unfamiliar ways (Clayton & Ash, 2004; Howard, 1998). Eyler and Giles (1999), Ash et al. (2005), Grossman (2008), and Steinke and Fitch (2003) have all found that students benefit from guidance, scaffolding, and practice—including peer and/or instructor feedback and opportunities to revise their thinking and writing—in order to improve the quality of their thinking. They also suggest that such enhancement of reasoning is facilitated by helping students become aware of their own metacognitive processes. The intentionally designed integration of critical reflection and assessment can be an important element of such capacity building. In their discussion of the paradigmatic shifts in perspective and practice associated with service learning, Clayton and Ash (2004) and Ash and Clayton (2009a, 2009b) suggest that learning through critical reflection not only requires but also fosters the development of new ways of learning.

An associated characteristic of well-designed service learning is that it can support students in moving beyond superficial engagement in learning practices. Creating an environment that encourages and facilitates deep approaches to learning (Donald, 2002; Laird, Shoup, Kuh, & Schwarz, 2008) supports students in maximizing any of the desired types and levels of academic learning expressed in Figure 2.2.1. Pedagogical strategies such as problem-based learning, active learning, peer instruction, and critical reflection are examples of methods of instruction especially well suited to fostering deep approaches to learning (Donald, 2002). Deep approaches, which are associated with self-directed and higher order learning, are contrasted with surface approaches, which are linked to memorizing and reproducing knowledge. Service learning, with its emphasis on application, integration, and co-creation, lends itself readily to instructional design that fosters deep approaches to learning.

Designing critical reflection to generate, deepen, and document learning gives rise to another important implication for service learning practitioners, especially instructors: the appropriateness of and tools for grading reflection products. Faculty may struggle to assess reflection products, sometimes inhibited by lack of confidence but as often by a sense—often shared with students—of the inappropriateness of doing so. The products of reflection understood and implemented as critical reflection, rather than as personal and private introspection, can and arguably should be graded. If higher level learning is expected and critical reflection activities are designed accordingly, then resultant products provide the evidence of outcomes on which grades can be based. Grading reflection products as pass-fail or grading students on regurgitation while espousing the use of critical reflection to support higher level learning sends contradictory messages about the value placed on deep approaches to all types and levels of academic learning. The previously discussed rubrics associated with the DEAL Model are examples of tools that are useful not only for cultivating deeper approaches to learning and assessing and investigating student learning but also for grading student work.

Growth in all four domains of academic learning expressed in Figure 2.2.1 may be maximized when service learning is intentionally designed to facilitate learning across course sequences and curricula. As demonstrated by the minor described in the opening vignette, service learning can be designed cumulatively across a curriculum such that no single course bears all the weight of student outcomes in all domains of academic learning. When we apply our conceptual framework for academic learning, introductory courses in the major might implement service learning targeting domains 1 and 2 and, thus, provide scaffolding for student achievement in domains 2 and 3 in later courses, including capstones. To accomplish these cumulative learning outcomes effectively while also promoting metacognitive development, a focus on critical thinking (domain 4) might well be incorporated within each course. Along these same lines, application might be understood in introductory courses as the ability to recognize or provide examples of course material as it emerges in the community; by contrast, application in capstones or practica could be evidenced through the use of discipline-linked knowledge, skills, and dispositions as professional practitioners in community settings. Thus, a coherent cross-course design of service learning might cumulatively develop disciplinary and professional competencies and provide evidence of student achievement of those competencies (including for program accreditation purposes).

Recommendations for Future Research

The previous section makes clear that effectively designing and implementing service learning so as to achieve and document academic (and other) learning is challenging and warrants careful attention. A key opportunity for practitioners to improve their understanding and implementation of service learning is through the scholarship of teaching and learning (SoTL). SoTL provides a bridge from what is often instructors' initial interest—enhancing student engagement in the course and improving academic learning outcomes—to a role in contributing to the broader pedagogical knowledge base as practitioner-scholars. Explicit use of the theoretical and conceptual frameworks reviewed in this chapter—as well as theory drawn from a range of other fields, such as work on learning styles and peer-assisted learning— moves SoTL into the arena of theory-testing and/or theory-generating research, which explores fundamental questions of why and under what conditions a certain service learning design produces particular academic (and other) learning outcomes. The following sections suggest four potential directions for such research related to the academic outcomes of service learning.

Operationalizing the Domains of Academic Learning and the Relationships Among Them

Given the categorization of domains of academic learning expressed in Figure 2.2.1, an important area for future work is to operationalize these domains through further conceptual and empirical work. This is especially the case for thinking from disciplinary and/or interdisciplinary perspectives, which is the least investigated of the four proposed domains of academic learning, certainly within the service learning community and arguably within higher education more generally. Using Bloom's Taxonomy (1956) as a guide, a SoTL project might bring together faculty from multiple disciplines to determine what learning objectives associated with thinking from disciplinary and/or interdisciplinary perspectives would look like (see the example in Table 2.2.1). Once such learning objectives are developed, service learning practitioner-scholars could design critical reflection activities and assess resultant products using these objectives as a rubric (perhaps in combination with a rubric for critical thinking) and, thereby, iteratively refine the objectives, prompts, and rubrics. Associated resources (e.g., activities, tutorials, peer mentoring activities) to support students in learning how to learn in domain 4 could also be generated through such a process.

Drawing on Bloom's Taxonomy (1956) and the hierarchical nature of the levels of learning, Figure 2.2.1 suggests that, with the exception of critical thinking, each domain is contingent on learning at the previous level. This premise needs further empirical evaluation in the context of service learning, and this investigation should be undertaken at the level of courses, programs,

TABLE 2.2.1
**Sample Bloom-Based Learning Objectives for Academic Learning Domain 3
(Thinking From Disciplinary and/or Interdisciplinary Perspectives)**

Identify two or more constructs or theories from the discipline.
Explain those constructs or theories in your own words so that someone not in the discipline could understand them.
Apply these constructs or theories to a given situation—how would each interpret or explain the situation?
Analyze these constructs or theories through comparing and contrasting the explanations each provides in making meaning of the situation—what does one reveal that another obscures, for example?
Synthesize these constructs or theories into a larger, integrated framework, noting the associated tension points.
Evaluate the explanatory power of the larger, integrated framework—what is enhanced and what is still incomplete, for example?

and curricula. With a conceptual foundation and tools to operationalize thinking from the perspective of one or more disciplines established (as discussed in the previous paragraph), researchers might investigate the relationships among thinking in all four domains (e.g., the role of basic foundational learning and critical thinking in higher level learning; the role of basic foundational learning, higher level learning, and critical thinking in enabling thinking from disciplinary and/or interdisciplinary perspectives).

Examining Relationships Between Academic and Other Categories of Learning

Another area for future research pushes the conceptualization of academic learning offered here by considering its relationship with other types of learning: its affective dimensions as well as its role in and connection with civic learning and personal growth. The examination and potential revision of assumptions about knowledge, which often accompany the exposure to novel situations that is characteristic of service learning, are at the heart of transformative learning (Cranton, 2006; Mezirow & Associates, 2000), and the resultant perspective transformation often involves emotional responses associated with dissonance. Felten, Gilchrist, and Darby (2006) note that while emotion has traditionally been discussed by service learning scholars as a trigger for sense making and critical thought, more work should be done that acknowledges and examines the ways in which affect and cognition are integrated and inform each other in the learning process.

Similarly, service learning problematizes the academy's traditional distinctions between content learning and learning about one's self and about communities and citizenship. Understanding the public purposes of a discipline or the social drivers for and consequences of its development and use is a function of learning squarely at the intersection of academic and civic arenas, as is professional ethics. Professional development within the disciplines also implicates learning about one's own evolving skills, attitudes, and values. Various conceptions of civic-mindedness (e.g., Bringle & Steinberg, 2010; Steinberg, Hatcher, & Bringle, 2011) explicitly include knowledge of one or more particular disciplines and an inclination to use that knowledge as a public steward.

One way to investigate the interrelationships among academic learning, civic learning, and personal growth would be to develop Bloom-based learning objectives, critical reflection prompts, and rubrics for the intersections of two of the three categories (i.e., academic and civic learning, academic learning and personal growth, civic learning and personal growth) and for the intersection of all three categories. Applied to student products, such rubrics could quantify evidence of the extent and quality of connections made among the three learning categories. These scores could then be examined with respect to such potentially moderating variables as student learning styles and such potentially mediating variables as degree of structure in critical reflection prompts or approach to feedback on and revision of student products. These analyses—which, here again, could be undertaken at the course, program, and curricular levels—would provide insights into how the three categories of learning interact and how instructors can improve pedagogical techniques to help students make these connections in the context of academic course work.

Examining Relationships Between Approaches to Teaching and Approaches to Learning

A third area for future research involves the relationship between students' identities and habits as learners and instructional design choices underlying the generation of academic learning outcomes in service learning. As an example, Donald (2002) suggests that while students may come to a course with either surface or deep approaches to learning, instructors can encourage and cultivate either orientation through their course design, including their choice of pedagogies and how they implement them. Research on academic learning in service learning can advance understanding of these relationships between teaching and learning strategies, on the one hand, and students' evolving identities and habits as learners, on the other.

In this context, the tight alignment among outcomes, strategies, and assessment that is needed to both build students' capacities for learning within and across all four domains and provide a foundation for assessing learning outcomes and processes can also establish a somewhat controlled set of circumstances for research, including on such issues as (a) the differential outcomes of deep approaches to teaching on students with surface approaches to learning and students with deep approaches to learning and (b) the ways in which deep approaches to teaching can facilitate growth in students' identities and habits as learners. Determination of students' positioning along a continuum from surface to deep could be triangulated with assessment of academic learning outcomes per the four domains in Figure 2.2.1 to provide a basis for examining patterns of association between characteristics of students as learners and pedagogical design choices. Service learning and other nontraditional pedagogies (e.g., inquiry-guided learning, problem-based learning) increasingly provide evidence-based alternatives to the dominant teacher-centered strategies of higher education (Buskist & Groccia, 2011). Research can contribute to understanding of the specific ways that these nontraditional pedagogies must be designed in order to cultivate students' identities and habits as learners who are responsible for their own learning and able to integrate their learning with their roles as professionals and citizens.

Investigating the Relationships Between Student and Faculty Learning

A final important and emerging area of research on service learning involves the relationship between students' academic (and other) learning and that of their instructors (McGuire et al., 2009; chapter 3.2) and community partners (Clayton, Bacon, Hess, Moore, & Snow, 2010). Service learning at its best positions students; faculty/staff; and community members as co-learners, co-educators, and co-generators of knowledge (Jameson et al., 2011). Research is needed to enable better understanding of the dynamics and identities associated with these coroles and, in turn, to enable deeper enactment of them. Much, if not all, of the theory underlying the conceptual framework for academic learning expressed in Figure 2.2.1 should hold for all learners, regardless of their particular role in the service learning process; many of the same methodologies used with students for generating, assessing, and investigating their learning may prove relevant when applied to faculty and community member learning as well. Research can inform understanding of such issues as the ways that faculty and community partners' learning (e.g., about critical thinking) plays a role in their students' learning (e.g., their development of critical thinking capacities); the similarities and differences in the processes whereby each partner can best engage in learning (e.g., about critical thinking); and the ways that students, faculty, and community partners can best support one another's learning (e.g., about critical thinking). Further, such research can inform the development of partnerships that enable faculty and community members' identities as co-learners. Such research will be most authentically undertaken in the spirit of reciprocity, with students, faculty, and community members working closely together to conceptualize the questions, design and implement the methods, analyze the resultant data, and disseminate their learning.

Conclusion

What Eyler and Giles said in 1999 remains relevant today: "Before we can understand the academic value of service learning programs we need a clear idea of what learning might be expected from this approach and the extent to which these outcomes are consistent with the goals of higher education" (p. 3). Academic learning is a category of learning for which the pedagogy is well suited, and that category need not be—arguably, should not be— narrowly defined. Although service learning can and should promote student learning of basic content-linked knowledge and skills, perhaps its fullest potential is tapped when it is understood, designed, and implemented so as to also nurture as well higher level learning, thinking from disciplinary and/ or interdisciplinary perspectives, and critical thinking. The framework illustrated in Figure 2.2.1 attempts to articulate these various ways of conceptualizing academic learning as well as the connections among them. One goal of this chapter has been to call attention to the particular utility of service learning in facilitating learning beyond basic foundational knowledge and skills and to the potential of curricular level, cumulative design, implementation, and assessment in achieving that learning.

Research in the context of well-designed course- and curricular-level service learning can serve not only to enhance implementation and contribute to the growing knowledge base on nontraditional pedagogies but also to strengthen support for the choice to use the pedagogy and, in turn, its institutionalization within the academy. Further, there are many difficult questions yet to be resolved regarding best practices of service learning as well as of teaching and learning more generally. Rigorous investigation of academic (and other) learning (appropriately conceptualized) and of the processes that generate it will be most meaningful when the pedagogy in question has been well designed to produce and document such learning.

Note

1. Bloom's Taxonomy of the Cognitive Domain (Bloom, 1956) explicitly distinguishes "lower" and "higher" levels of reasoning and frames the relationship between the levels in hierarchical terms. It should be noted that multiple revisions of the original taxonomy have been proposed, reordering and adding to the higher levels, and it may be that a newer version is most appropriate in some disciplines or service learning contexts.

Recommended Reading

Ash, S. L., & Clayton, P. H. (2009). Generating, deepening, and documenting learning: The power of critical reflection in applied learning. *Journal of Applied Learning in Higher Education, 1*(1), 25–48.

Eyler, J. S., & Giles, D. E., Jr. (1999). *Where's the learning in service learning?* San Francisco, CA: Jossey-Bass.

Paul, R., & Elder, L. (2006). *Critical thinking: Tools for taking charge of your learning and your life* (2nd ed.). Saddle River, NJ: Prentice Hall.

Schön, D. (1983). *The reflective practitioner: How professionals think in action.* New York, NY: Basic Books.

References

Ash, S. L., & Clayton, P. H. (2004). The articulated learning: An approach to guided reflection and assessment. *Innovative Higher Education, 29*(2), 137–154.

Ash, S. L., & Clayton, P. H. (2009a). Generating, deepening, and documenting learning: The power of critical reflection in applied learning. *Journal of Applied Learning in Higher Education, 1*(1), 25–48.

Ash, S. L., & Clayton, P. H. (2009b). *Learning through critical reflection: A tutorial for service-learning students (instructor version).* Raleigh, NC: Authors.

Ash, S. L., Clayton, P. H., & Atkinson, M. P. (2005). Integrating reflection and assessment to improve and capture student learning. *Michigan Journal of Community Service Learning, 11*(2), 49–60.

Batchelder, T. H., & Root, S. (1994). Effects of an undergraduate program to integrate academic learning and service: Cognitive, prosocial cognitive, and identity outcomes. *Journal of Adolescence, 17*, 341–355.

Bloom, B. S. (Ed.). (1956). *Taxonomy of educational objectives book 1: Cognitive domain.* New York, NY: McKay.

Boix Mansilla, V., & Gardner, H. (2008). Disciplining the mind. *Educational Leadership, 65*(5), 14–19.

Bradley, L. R. (1997). Evaluating service-learning: Toward a new paradigm. In A. S. Waterman (Ed.), *Service-learning: Applications from the research* (pp. 151–171). Mahwah, NJ: Erlbaum.

Bringle, R. G., & Steinberg, K. S. (2010). Educating for informed community involvement. *American Journal of Community Psychology, 46*, 428–441.

Bullock, B., & Clayton, P. H. (2010, March). *International MS education and dual degrees in forestry: The Atlantis Program.* Paper presented at the University Education in Natural Resources Conference, Blacksburg, VA.

Buskist, W., & Groccia, J. (Eds.). (2011). Evidence-based teaching [Special issue]. *New Directions for Teaching and Learning, 2011*(128).

Clayton, P. H., & Ash, S. L. (2004). Shifts in perspective: Capitalizing on the counter-normative nature of service learning. *Michigan Journal of Community Service Learning, 11*(1), 59–70.

Clayton, P. H., Bacon, B., Hess, G., Moore, A., & Snow, A. (2010, February). *Who's doing the learning: Faculty and community partners as learners in service-learning.* Paper presented at Pathways to Achieving Civic Engagement (PACE) Conference, Elon, NC.

Cranton, P. (2006). Fostering authentic relationships in the transformative classroom. *New Directions for Adult and Continuing Education, 2006*(109), 5–13. doi:10.1002/ace.203

Dewey, J. (1938). *Experience and education.* New York, NY: MacMillan.

Dewey, J. (1997/1933). *How we think.* Mineola, NY: Dover Publications.

Donald, J. G. (2002). *Learning to think: Disciplinary perspectives.* San Francisco, CA: Jossey-Bass.

Eyler, J. S. (2000). What do we most need to know about the impact of service learning on student learning? [Special issue]. *Michigan Journal of Community Service Learning, Fall,* 11–17.

Eyler, J. S., & Giles, D. E., Jr. (1999). *Where's the learning in service learning?* San Francisco, CA: Jossey-Bass.

Felten, P., Gilchrist, L. Z., & Darby, A. (2006). Emotion and learning: Feeling our way toward a new theory of reflection in service learning. *Michigan Journal of Community Service Learning, 12*(2), 38–46.

Grossman, R. (2008). Structures for facilitating student reflection. *College Teaching, 57*(1), 15–22.

Howard, J. (1998). Academic service learning: A counter normative pedagogy. *New Directions in Teaching and Learning, 73,* 21–29. doi:10.1002/tl.7303

Jameson, J. K., Clayton, P. H., & Bringle, R. G. (2008). Investigating student learning within and across linked service learning courses. In S. H. Billig, B. A. Holland, & M. A. Bowden (Eds.), *Scholarship for sustaining service-learning and community engagement* (pp. 3–27). Charlotte, NC: Information Age.

Jameson, J. K., Clayton, P. H., & Jaeger, A. J. (2011). Community-engaged scholarship through mutually transformative partnerships. In L. M. Harter, J. Hamel-Lambert, & J. Millesen (Eds.), *Participatory partnerships for social action and research* (pp. 259–278). Dubuque, IA: Kendall-Hunt.

Laird, T. F. N., Shoup, R., Kuh, G., & Schwarz, M. J. (2008). The effects of discipline on deep approaches to student learning and college outcomes. *Research in Higher Education, 49,* 469–494. doi:10.007/s11162-008-9088-5

Mahin, L., & Kruggel, T. G. (2006). Facilitation and assessment of student learning in business communication. *Business Communication Quarterly, 69,* 323–327.

Marshall, D. B., Beck, S. L., Coghlan, L. K., & Kimbro, E. (2005). Understanding student learning outcomes through narrative transcript analysis: Assessing general education in an institution without grades or required courses. *Assessment Update, 17*(5), 4–11.

McGuire, L., Strong, D., Lay, K., Ardemagni, E., Wittberg, P., & Clayton, P. H. (2009). A case study of faculty learning around reflection: A collaborative faculty development project. In B. E. Moely, S. H. Billig, & B. A. Holland (Eds.), *Creating our identities in service-learning and community engagement* (pp. 75–101). Greenwich, CT: Information Age.

Mezirow, J., & Associates (Eds.). (2000). *Learning as transformation: Critical perspectives on a theory in progress.* San Francisco, CA: Jossey-Bass.

Molee, L. M., Henry, M. E., Sessa, V. I., & McKinney-Prupis, E. R. (2010). Assessing learning in service-learning courses through critical reflection. *Journal of Experiential Education, 33,* 239–257.

Mpofu, E. (2007). Service learning effects on the academic learning of rehabilitation services students. *Michigan Journal of Community Service Learning, 14*(1), 46–52.

Paul, R. (1993). *Critical thinking: What every student needs to survive in a rapidly changing world.* Dillon Beach, CA: Foundation for Critical Thinking.

Paul, R., & Elder, L. (2006). *Critical thinking: Tools for taking charge of your learning and your life* (2nd ed.). Saddle River, NJ: Prentice Hall.

Schön, D. (1983). *The reflective practitioner: How professionals think in action.* New York, NY: Basic Books.

Steinberg, K. S., Hatcher, J. A., & Bringle, R. G. (2011) A north star: Civic-minded graduate. *Michigan Journal of Community Service Learning, 18*(1), 19–33.

Steinke, P., & Fitch, P. (2003). Using written protocols to measure service-learning outcomes. In S. H. Billig & J. Eyler (Eds.), *Deconstructing service-learning: Research exploring context, participation, and impacts* (pp. 171–194). Greenwich, CT: Information Age.

Strage, A. A. (2000). Service learning: Enhancing student learning outcomes in a college-level lecture course. *Michigan Journal of Community Service Learning, 7*(1), 5–13.

Wurr, A. J. (2002). Service-learning and student writing. In S. H. Billig & A. Furco (Eds.), *Service-learning through a multidisciplinary lens* (pp. 103–121). Greenwich, CT: Information Age.

CIVIC LEARNING THROUGH SERVICE LEARNING

Conceptual Frameworks and Research

Richard M. Battistoni

More than a decade ago, Campus Compact issued a manifesto announcing a renewed civic engagement agenda in higher education. In the *Presidents' Declaration on the Civic Responsibility of Higher Education*, endorsed by more than 400 college and university presidents, campus leaders committed themselves "to renew [their] role as agents of our democracy, [and to] catalyze and lead a national movement to reinvigorate the public purposes and civic mission of higher education" (Campus Compact, 1999, pp. 3–4). Subsequently, the Carnegie Corporation of New York and Center for Information and Research on Civic Learning and Engagement (CIRCLE) (2003) convened some of the nation's most distinguished researchers and practitioners and produced another document, *The Civic Mission of Schools*, calling on the nation's schools to "help young people acquire and learn to use the skills, knowledge, and attitudes that will prepare them to be competent and responsible citizens throughout their lives" (p. 10). Many other organizations (e.g., the Association of American Colleges and Universities [AAC&U], the American Association of State Colleges and Universities [AASCU]) have also called for a renewal of civic education on college campuses (e.g., Musil, 2009).

The civic engagement agenda reflects a great concern about citizen disengagement from public life and anxiety over a decline in the social capital necessary for the survival of a vibrant democracy (Galston, 2001; Keeter,

Zukin, Andolina, & Jenkins, 2002; Putnam, 2000). With mounting evidence of disengagement, especially among young persons, from American politics and public life, there is an ever-deepening feeling that educational institutions are leaving students unprepared for a life of engaged, democratic citizenship (e.g., Colby, Ehrlich, Beaumont, & Stephens, 2003).

A common institutional strategy for stemming the tide of civic disengagement has been to connect work in service- and community-based learning to civic outcomes. One of the intentions behind these activities has been to capitalize on the well-documented involvement of students in community service to advance the mission of civic engagement. This strategy assumes that a clear relationship can be developed between experiences of service and the cultivation of citizenship, which depends on how concretely educators can define civic outcomes and how effectively they can design service and service learning to generate them. It also raises serious questions about how to assess whether these important outcomes are being achieved and how to conduct research to understand why these outcomes occur, which is the subject of this chapter.

Theoretical and Conceptual Frameworks

The development of theories about education for civic engagement has been made difficult by the contested nature of concepts associated with citizenship and the varied understandings of the knowledge, skills, and dispositions that are requisite for citizenship (Battistoni, 2002). Still, there are several theories that inform how service learning might work to improve students' civic learning and engagement. For some, especially mainstream political scientists, service learning might be framed as helping students to gain the kind of civic and political knowledge necessary for informed citizenship in a representative democracy (Delli Carpini & Keeter, 1996; Zukin, Keeter, Andolina, Jenkins, & Delli Carpini, 2006). This understanding of the causal pathway from service learning to civic learning outcomes most aligns with concepts of constitutional citizenship (e.g., Rawls, 1971), presented in Table 2.3.1. For those holding a more communitarian conception of citizenship (Etzioni, 1993; Table 2.3.1), service learning might be seen as important because it connects students to the larger community and its concerns, thus engendering in students an appreciation for and understanding of community norms and civic responsibilities. A third theoretical framework for studying the connection between service learning and civic engagement, and

TABLE 2.3.1
Conceptual Frameworks From the Social Sciences

Conceptual Framework	View of Citizenship	Understanding of Civic Knowledge	Associated Civic Skills	Disciplinary Affinities
Constitutional citizenship (Rawls, 1971)	Rights-bearing individual; voter	Knowledge of governmental institutions, laws, elections	Political knowledge; critical thinking	Political science; law; policy studies (health, education)
Communitarianism (Etzioni, 1993)	"Good neighbor"; duty to fulfill common good	Knowledge of community values and civic responsibilities	Civic judgment; community building	Philosophy; religious studies; social work; public health
Participatory democracy (Barber, 1984, 1992)	Active participant in public life	Knowledge of processes of democratic participation	Communication skills; collective action; civic imagination; cross-cultural competencies	Political science; education; public health
Public work (Boyte & Kari, 1996)	Cocreator of things of public value	Knowledge (through projects) of skills, habits, and values of working with others on public tasks	Public problem-solving; coalition building and cross-cultural competencies	Political science; public administration; health administration; professional disciplines
Social capital (Putnam, 2000)	Membership in associations of civil society	Knowledge of social connections and institutions	Communication skills; organizational analysis	Sociology; nonprofit management

one that has gained increasing acceptance, holds that service learning works to trigger civic identity, a person's identity as a civic agent seeking to solve a public problem or create overall change in the community. Most closely aligned with more participatory or public work conceptions of the citizen (Table 2.3.1), civic identity, formed by the collaboration and interaction with others that service learning represents, leads an individual to take action and requires the accompanying knowledge and skills necessary for effective public action (Boyte, 2008; Colby, Beaumont, Ehrlich, & Corngold, 2007; Knefelkamp, 2008; Youniss, McClellan, & Yates, 1997).

The difficulty lies in the dilemma of defining which kind of citizens educational interventions should be designed to produce (Westheimer & Kahne, 2004). Which theory forms the basis for research on the civic learning outcomes of service learning depends on how citizenship is defined and what those citizens need to know, do, and believe in order to be effective civic actors.

The dilemma of how to conceptualize civic learning originates from controversies around what it means to be a good citizen in a democracy and, in turn, what goals are held for students' civic learning. The controversy surrounding definitions stems in part from the ways that terms such as *citizenship* are used (Battistoni, 2002, 2006b). For example, some scholars prefer overtly political definitions of student learning and engagement (Battistoni, 2006a; Boyte, 2004; Colby et al., 2007). Because of the legal, historical, and ideological associations with the terms *citizenship* and *civic*, civic engagement language tends to be somewhat amorphous, implying different meanings and interpretations to different persons. This is a strength because it can be related to many different issues, including community development, student leadership, service learning as a pedagogical strategy, mission reclamation, and public perceptions of education (Saltmarsh, 2004). Civic engagement language, however, tends to lack concreteness or clarity, especially when it comes to learning goals for students, which complicates assessment and research.

Perhaps a better way to conceive of civic engagement, in the context of research on educational interventions, is to ask: What *student learning outcomes* are associated with a civic engagement perspective, divorced from ideologically based conceptual frameworks of what constitutes good citizenship? Newman (1985) argued for this approach more than 25 years ago, in a book written for the Carnegie Foundation for the Advancement of Teaching: "The most critical demand is to restore to higher education its original purpose of preparing graduates for a life of involved and committed citizenship. . . . The advancement of *civic learning* [emphasis added], there-fore, must become higher education's most central goal" (p. xiv). A number of scholars have begun to emphasize civic learning outcomes for students (Colby et al., 2003; Saltmarsh, 2005; Torney-Purta & Vermeer, 2004).

One definition of civic learning that captures a common framework that can inform any educational program comes from the *Service Learning Course Design Workbook*:

> We conceive of "civic learning" as any learning that contributes to student preparation for community or public involvement in a diverse democratic society. A loose interpretation of civic learning would lead one to believe that education in general prepares one for citizenship in our democracy. And it certainly does. However, we have in mind here a strict interpreta-tion of civic learning—knowledge, skills and values that make an explicitly direct and purposeful contribution to the preparation of students for active civic participation. (Howard, 2001, p. 45)

This definition focuses on determining the types of knowledge, skills, and values (or dispositions) to be fostered in students in order to equip them to participate actively in public life within a diverse democratic society. As with civic engagement more generally, there have been disagreement and ambigu-ity in the research frameworks about what should count as civic learning and what should constitute appropriate civic knowledge, skills, and values (or dispositions). Individual service learning instructors and programs have, in turn, made distinct determinations about how they can contribute to their students' civic learning and what knowledge, skills, and values they choose to pursue to make this contribution.

Civic Knowledge

When defining *civic knowledge*, some educators (e.g., Delli Carpini & Keeter, 1996) focus on the purely academic forms that such knowledge takes: dates and places of important civic or political events; definitions of citi-zenship and democracy; and the institutions and operations of democratic government, particularly in the United States. But students engaged in community-based experiences have demonstrated that civic knowledge is much broader than this and comes from multiple sources, including com-munity members (e.g., Battistoni, 1997). This broader understanding of civic knowledge includes a deeper knowledge of public issues, including their underlying causes as well as of how different community stakeholders understand issues. An understanding of place and the community history that provides a context for service and public problem solving—including learning about how individuals and community groups have effected change in their communities—has also been asserted as another key element of civic knowledge (Morton, 1997). An added benefit to defining civic knowledge in this broader way is that students and community members become co-creators of knowledge, rather than simply rely on expert texts or professors (Fretz & Longo, 2010).

Finally, civic knowledge can be defined in terms of the distinct perspectives that different disciplines bring to questions of democracy and public life. As discussed, a number of different conceptual frameworks of civic engagement have been developed, in particular by political and social theorists (Battistoni, 2002). These frameworks share common themes but are also distinct in their specific views of citizenship and in their understanding of civic education and associated civic skills (see the next section for further discussion of civic skills). These views, as well as the disciplinary affinities for each of the five frameworks, are illustrated in Table 2.3.1.

Rich conceptual frameworks also exist outside the social sciences, and they can be used by educators at different levels to ground their understanding of engagement and provide frameworks for research. In conversations with 13 national educational disciplinary associations as part of the Engaged Disciplines Project conducted by national Campus Compact with support from The Pew Charitable Trusts, a list of terms coming from each discipline was identified and then summarized into seven conceptual frameworks connected to civic engagement (Battistoni, 2002; Gelmon & Battistoni, 2005). These frameworks are summarized in Table 2.3.2, along with their views of citizenship, their understanding of civic education, and the associated civic skills needed for effective public life. Also included are each framework's disciplinary affinities. Which framework one adopts has implications for research and assessment because different conceptions of citizenship and civic learning will produce different questions about educational inputs and outcomes.

Civic Skills

Civic Engagement Across the Curriculum (Battistoni, 2002) delineates in some detail a set of civic skills that educators from different disciplines can instill as part of preparing students for active participation in democratic public life. This set of civic skills includes critical thinking; communication and

TABLE 2.3.2
Conceptual Frameworks From a Range of Disciplines

Conceptual Framework	View of Citizenship	Understanding of Civic Knowledge	Associated Civic Skills	Disciplinary Affinities
Civic professionalism (Sullivan, 2004)	Professional work with a civic purpose	Knowledge of the civic traditions and values of the professions	Public problem solving; civic judgment	Professional disciplines; management; law; public administration
Social responsibility (e.g., Musil, 2009)	Responsibility to the larger society	Knowledge of public problems most closely associated with chosen field of work	Political knowledge of issues; organizational analysis	Health professions; business disciplines; computer science; public health
Social justice (Hollenbach, 1988)	Bringing one's spiritual values to bear on social problems	Knowledge of the principles of social justice and their application to public life	Civic judgment; collective action; cross-cultural competencies	Philosophy; religious studies; social work
Connected knowing; ethic of care (Gilligan, 1982)	Caring for the future of our public world	Knowledge of others and their perspectives on the world	Critical thinking; coalition building; cross-cultural competencies	Women's studies; nursing; psychology; global studies
Public leadership (Greenleaf, 1996)	Citizen as "servant-leader"	Knowledge of the arts of collaborative leadership	Community building; communication	Management; leadership studies
Public intellectual (Jacoby, 1987)	Thinkers who contribute to the public discourse	Knowledge of the traditions of writers and artists who have served as public intellectuals	Civic imagination; creativity	Literature; visual and performing arts
Engaged/public scholarship (Boyer, 1996)	Participatory action researcher	Knowledge of how scholarly research might contribute to the needs and values of the community	Organizational analysis; public problem solving	Journalism; communications; professional disciplines

deliberation (speaking and listening); public problem solving; civic judgment; civic imagination and creativity; teamwork, coalition building, and
collective action; community organizing; and organizational analysis. In
addition, there are important cross-cultural skills (and values) that are critical
in educating citizens to participate in a diverse democratic society and world.
Kirlin (2003) has identified a longer set of civic skills and categorized them
into four major areas: organization, communication, collective decision making, and critical thinking. In many ways, these civic skills are ones that
traditionally have been defined as part of a liberal education or, more
recently, have been associated with employability or workforce development
(Battistoni & Longo, 2005). However, in laying out a set of questions for
future research, Kirlin (2003) suggests that many service learning programs
do not achieve their desired civic impact because they have not sufficiently
addressed the development and assessment of fundamental civic skills. This
is a key area for future development and research.

Civic Values

The category of civic values is the most contentious area of civic learning
outcomes because many educators, particularly those in public institutions,
are reluctant to broach the subject of civic values. This may be why some
proponents of civic engagement use the seemingly more neutral terms *attitudes, dispositions,* or *motivation* to describe this area of civic learning outcomes (Billig, Root, & Jesse, 2005; Colby et al., 2003, 2007; Torney-Purta &
Vermeer, 2004). Values are an important dimension of civic learning, however, and a conversation about what values are appropriate to democratic
public life, even though there may be strong disagreement over them, is
critical to improving program design, assessment, and research.

Saltmarsh (2005) presents the key democratic values as participation,
justice, and inclusion—values he believes "can be widely agreed upon and
shared" (p. 55). Boyte (2008) argues for the importance of civic agency as an
additional value or disposition crucial to the development of democratic
citizens. The authors of *Becoming Citizens* make a strong case for considering
the development of a young person's civic vocation, which they define as
being "called to 'make the world better,' to 'make a difference' in the public
sphere" (Roholt, Hildreth, & Baizerman, 2009, p. 131). And the authors of
Educating for Democracy, although they use the term political engagement
rather than *civic learning,* concentrate on the development of students' civic
motivation and efficacy (Colby et al., 2007).

Faculty from different disciplinary perspectives may frame the question of civic values differently. For example, the framework of civic professionalism positions civic values as the way that a professional's technical expertise "discovers its human meaning" (Sullivan, 2004, p. xix). This perspective assumes that students bring their own public values to the work they are doing, both in the classroom and in the community.

Additionally, civic values might be framed by the values expressed in the mission of the educational institution in question. For example, University of Minnesota President Robert Bruininks (2006) defined civic/public engagement as an "institutional commitment to public purposes and responsibilities intended to strengthen a democratic way of life in the rapidly changing information age of the 21st century." Portland State University (2011) defines civic engagement as "active involvement in the discourse dealing with the need to develop and utilize knowledge for the improvement of society, to use talents and offer wisdom for the greater good, and to provide opportunities for education in the spirit of a democratic society." Faith-based institutions may define civic values through a different lens. For example, at many Catholic colleges and universities, the way into dialogue about civic values comes through concepts such as *dignity of the human person*, the *preferential option for the poor, solidarity*, and *subsidiarity* (Hollenbach, 1988).

Review of Past Research and Existing Instruments

The current state of research on the impact of service learning on students' civic learning outcomes—particularly rich conceptions of civic learning that include knowledge, skills, values, and the creation of an action-oriented civic identity—is inadequate because of limitations of and weaknesses in the research. The most severe problem in past research assessing the impact of service learning on students' civic learning was in conceptualizing both the independent variable (i.e., the nature of the service learning experience) and the dependent variable (i.e., measuring the civic learning). On the independent variable side, most research tends to lump together a number of different educational practices as constituting service learning without particular attention to factors such as the duration and intensity of service, the connection to explicit educational goals around civic learning, teacher intentionality, student voice, and reflection (Battistoni, 2002; Eyler & Giles, 1999). Clarification of the nature of the educational experience is important not only for distinguishing among nonservice, community service, and service learning participants but also for learning more about the impact of variations in the service learning experience and for determining whether service learning has a greater impact than other possible educational interventions with the same civic learning aims (Billig et al., 2005; Cammarano, Battistoni, & Hudson, 2000; Hepburn, Niemi, & Chapman, 2000). On the dependent variable side, research studies to date tend to employ weak and indirect measures of political or civic learning outcomes.

The very best research on civic learning outcomes captures only a small portion of the knowledge, skills, values, attitudes, or dispositions that are core to civic learning. Some of the most promising approaches and studies occur in the literature on K–12 research on service learning, and future research in higher education can benefit from examining this work. Billig and colleagues, for example, have done good work identifying the most important elements of service learning practice in selecting those K–12 programmatic interventions to study for their impact—see the next section for a listing of these key elements as applied to higher education (Billig, 2000, 2004; Billig et al., 2005; Billig, Jesse, Brodersen, & Grimley, 2008). In their qualitative research on the civic outcomes of service learning, Westheimer and Kahne (2000) conducted a mixed-methods study—including classroom observations, teacher interviews, and a pre- and post-survey of students—to determine the extent to which service learning led to civic outcomes at 10 K–12 sites. They identified elements such as teacher intentionality, course construction, and operating conceptions of citizenship attached to curricular programs as crucial, ultimately finding "compelling evidence that when service experiences are combined with rigorous analysis of related social issues, students do develop attitudes, skills, and knowledge necessary to respond in productive ways" (Westheimer & Kahne, 2000, p. 3; see also Kahne & Westheimer, 2006; Westheimer & Kahne, 2004).

In higher education, a major problem in the assessment research, beyond the conceptual problems of identifying the relevant indicators of quality service learning and comprehensive civic learning, is that most studies (e.g., Cammarano et al., 2000; Hunter & Brisbin, 2000) have been conducted on a small scale, on individual campuses, or even with individual classes on a given campus. Still, promising research studies and approaches are under way. One of the better early attempts to develop measures of civic engagement and learning comes from the work of the Measuring Citizenship Project of Rutgers University's Walt Whitman Center for the Culture and Politics of Democracy. For this project a 23-item Civic Leadership scale that combined items involving civic knowledge, skills, and attitudes was developed and used to study the effect of service learning courses on several participating campuses (Walt Whitman Center, 1996). The scale incorporated a number of smaller scales, including views of democracy; civic skills; political, religious, and racial tolerance; voting and civic participation; and self-agency.

The Carnegie Foundation for the Advancement of Teaching's Political Engagement Project, though using the overarching concept of political engagement, developed constructs and indicators of political understanding, political skills, and political motivation and, using both quantitative and qualitative research methods, studied the impact of different programs and pedagogies on achieving these student outcomes (see appendix B in Colby et al., 2007 for a copy of the survey scales and results).

More recently, researchers at Indiana University–Purdue University Indianapolis developed a Civic-Minded Graduate (CMG) Scale, pulling together elements of civic knowledge, skills, dispositions, and behavioral intentions. The psychometric properties of the scale have been evaluated using three measurement procedures: self-report CMG Scale, CMG narrative and rubric, and CMG interview and rubric. The scale is used to measure the civic outcomes of students, both those involved in service learning and those participating in other courses and service programs (Bringle & Steinberg, 2010; Bringle, Studer, Wilson, Clayton, & Steinberg, 2011; Steinberg, Hatcher, & Bringle, 2011).

Implications for Practice: Programmatic Interventions With Civic Learning in Mind

With what is known and not known about the impact of service learning on students' civic learning outcomes, what are the implications for service learning practitioners, with an eye to both developing better practices and future research? Conceptual clarity around desired civic learning outcomes is essential. The theoretical frameworks informing civic engagement and learning are increasingly rich and complex but can warrant subsequent clarification of the elements that define student civic learning. There may not be one single definition and set of measurements for civic knowledge, skills, and values (especially because researchers and practitioners are not even agreed on the legitimacy of this third category). But at the very least, for research and assessment purposes, practitioners need to be intentional about what civic learning outcomes they seek and develop "local articulated understandings" of their program's goals (Vogelgesang, 2009, p. 242). As one prominent service learning assessment researcher has stated, "If you want me to evaluate the impact of your program, there needs to be conceptual clarity around the desired outcomes" (Vogelgesang, 2009, p. 242).

The assessment research done to date has limited utility in recommending particular curricular programming, but research clearly shows that effective service learning strategies aimed at civic learning outcomes share certain common characteristics (Battistoni & Longo, 2005; Billig, 2009; Eyler & Giles, 1999; Mitchell, 2008). These characteristics include the following:

- Meaningfulness, duration, and intensity of the service and work students do in the community
- Tight connections with a curriculum intentionally designed with civic learning outcomes in mind
- Student voice in designing the community projects and making decisions related to the service learning curriculum and programming
- Community voice in designing the partnership with educational institutions, implementing the programs, and setting the civic learning outcomes for students
- Diversity in the experiences and populations involved
- Critical reflection that generates civic meaning of the community-based experience

Any service learning course or program must pay attention to these factors to be successful in achieving desired civic learning outcomes.

Beyond these factors, the theoretical frameworks that have been developed to define civic learning outcomes for students, laid out in the beginning of this chapter, do suggest what practice and programs should incorporate. For example, the Political Engagement Project not only developed scales for measuring political engagement but also collected supplemental materials that include a variety of programmatic and curricular ideas and assignments for faculty to enhance student civic learning (Colby et al., 2007). One criticism emerging in the research literature of the single-course models of service learning commonly seen at all levels of education is "that one assignment, one semester, is not enough" to create a sustainable change in either the individual or the community (Bickford & Reynolds, 2002, p. 234). Research using the CMG Scale so far shows that students who have taken more service learning courses have higher overall average scores on the scale (Steinberg et al., 2011). A framework for civic learning that focuses on developing the knowledge, skills, values, and civic identity that results in a commitment to leadership and active citizenship involves a process that takes time and requires persistent engagement (Knefelkamp, 2008; Roholt et al., 2009; Youniss et al., 1997).

There is accumulating evidence that a sustained, developmental, curricular approach to civic engagement—one that goes beyond the single-course/single-experience service learning opportunities that shape most students' college years—is better able to engender the kinds of civic learning outcomes examined in this chapter (Mitchell, Visconti, Keene, & Battistoni, 2011; see Jameson, Clayton, & Bringle, 2008 for an example of such an approach to curricular design). Furthermore, because the development of civic identity and a range of civic values is inherently social, shaped and reshaped by students' interactions with others and the perspectives and experiences that they share, a cohort experience as part of the service learning program may be recommended for stronger civic learning outcomes in students (Mitchell et al., 2011). Programmatic activities that are sustained and developmental will require more sophisticated research designs to assess how and why students' civic learning outcomes are changed over time.

Implications and Recommendations for a Future Research Agenda

Weaknesses in past research on student civic learning outcomes suggest what directions a future research agenda should take. In the area of theoretical framework development, where greater precision can be developed in defining what specific civic ends and outcomes are sought for students, researchers need to ask the following questions: What causes civic learning to occur? Why does it occur for some students and not for others? What, exactly, is the role of civic identity in civic learning and action, and how does service learning assist in its development? Although the movement from civic engagement to civic learning, with the specific dimensions and indicators of civic knowledge, skills, and values, is a positive development, researchers can do more to make these concepts and their connection to broader concerns about educating students for democratic participation in public life more explicit and, through better coordination and networking, agreed upon across the K–16 field and beyond (Battistoni, 2006a).

On this point, researchers in the United States have much to learn from their international colleagues, particularly those in the United Kingdom, where, over the past decade, concerns about citizen disengagement have led to a fairly precise definition of what British researchers call *active citizenship* and the knowledge, skills, and dispositions that need to be taught to achieve it (Qualifications and Curriculum Authority, 1998, 2004). The definition of *active citizenship* contains the following six dimensions:

1. Having an awareness of issues
2. Having the desire to address and act on issues
3. Being able to make judgments and decisions
4. Taking direct, peaceful action
5. Collaborating with others to address commonly defined problems
6. Reflecting on decisions and actions

This definition, in turn, has led to the creation of a national curriculum and a common research agenda about civic learning outcomes featuring an eight-year longitudinal study of citizenship education in England (Kerr, Ireland, Lopes, & Craig, 2004).

The recent work of AAC&U to develop a model called the civic learning spiral may deepen understanding of civic learning and how it is assessed. This spiral, made up of six "braids" (self, communities and cultures, knowledge, skills, values, and public action), can be seen as a fluid continuum of characteristics, which coexist and connect with one another. AAC&U's Civic Engagement Working Group has defined outcomes related to each civic learning braid and has begun to lay out an agenda and set of rubrics for assessing the outcomes in this civic learning spiral (Musil, 2009).

So far, most understandings of civic learning assume a national (or local) focus, with a view toward educating students for citizenship in the United States. The global dimensions of civic learning need to be developed and refined further, based on preliminary research that has already been done (Battistoni, Longo, & Jayanandhan, 2009; Bringle, Hatcher, & Jones, 2010; Lewin, 2009; Longo & Saltmarsh, 2010). In an increasingly globalized world, definitions and measures of student civic learning need to align with the aspirations of global citizenship and action. These definitions and measures would include more global conceptual frameworks for citizenship and civic learning as well as the competencies and dispositions necessary for being an effective, reciprocal global citizen (see Bringle & Hatcher, 2010 and Lewin, 2009 for discussions of the kinds of conceptual frameworks that might align with more global perspectives on learning).

Beyond greater precision in our conceptual framework, there are three areas in particular that should drive the research agenda in assessing student civic learning outcomes: (a) more (and better) longitudinal and qualitative research, (b) understanding of the role and importance of educators in student civic learning, and (c) comparison of the impact of different service learning models on students' civic learning as well as comparison of the impact of service learning with that other active pedagogies aimed at student civic engagement.

Properly Funded Longitudinal and Qualitative Research

There is a great need in all service learning research to understand "how this learning impacts students years down the road" (Vogelgesang, 2009, p. 246). This is particularly important in the area of civic learning outcomes because citizenship in a democracy is a lifelong occupation, and therefore, merely examining the immediate outcomes of educational interventions is insufficient. Mitchell et al. (2011) are investigating the long-range effects on civic identity and action of three different sustained, developmental, cohort-based curricular models for service learning. Using a mixed-methods approach, the research team begins with qualitative interviews of alumni of each program and will construct a quantitative survey and later a focus-group protocol based on their analysis of the interview results (see Mitchell et al., 2011 for the conceptual framework that will guide this longitudinal research on alumni from each program). Very little longitudinal research on students has been done to date, although work at the Higher Education Research Institute (HERI) at University of California, Los Angeles (Vogelgesang, 2005) and the longitudinal study of the Bonner Scholars Program are good examples of the type of longitudinal research that is needed. The Bonner study (Keen & Hall, 2005) in particular, which surveyed nearly 400 alumni from 10 campuses using questions from several sources including HERI's Life After College survey, is a good example of a quantitative approach to longitudinal research on the impact of (co-curricular) service learning on college graduates (Keen & Hall, n.d.).

Better qualitative research on student civic learning outcomes is also needed. At the K–12 level, more research is being conducted involving experimental and quasi-experimental quantitative designs, in response to pressure to isolate interventions and ascertain causality with specific learning outcomes, particularly those that can be tested quantitatively (e.g., Billig et al., 2005). However, in the area of service learning research, especially in higher education, it is difficult to assign students randomly to anything at all, certainly not to educational institutions, majors, or courses. And many of the indicators of civic learning, particularly in the skills and values areas, are difficult to measure or assess using survey research methodology. Good examples of qualitative work exist, including studies that evaluate student and teacher understandings of what they are learning and how they conceive of civic or political engagement (see Kahne & Westheimer, 2006; Longo, Drury, & Battistoni, 2006; Roholt et al., 2009). Additional research might offer insight into how—as distinct from whether and why—service learning has an impact on student civic learning outcomes.

The Importance of Educators in Student Civic Learning

What is the role of educators in developing students' civic capacities, identity, and motivations? This was one of the key questions in the research surrounding two national student civic engagement initiatives, Project 540 and Raise Your Voice (Battistoni, 2008; Longo et al., 2006). This was also a key question for the Political Engagement Project, which surfaced important elements regarding the instructor's role in developing political understanding, skills, and motivation (Colby et al., 2007). There is a need to study further teachers' intentions and understandings, how they frame their work, their understanding of and experience with it, and how they see their role in citizen education and engagement. The study done by Billig et al. (2005) for CIRCLE on the civic impact of participation in K–12 service learning also examined some of these factors. So, too, have studies by Kahne and Westheimer (2006) in which the authors interviewed K–12 teachers. Research needs to explore how instructors are framing their work in service learning and civic engagement and the connections between instructor intentionality and educational outcomes for students.

Research on the Comparative Impact of Service Learning and Other Active Pedagogies

The future research agenda needs to include studies that compare different educational interventions and their impact on various student civic learning outcomes. What kinds of service learning programs yield the best results, and why? Is a sustained, developmental, cohort-based curricular approach to service learning better able to produce, over time, persons with stronger measures on all of the indicators of civic knowledge, skills, identity, and motivation, among other categories? Also needed are studies that compare service learning courses with other active learning pedagogies (e.g., collaborative learning, problem-based learning, simulations) aimed at enhanced civic outcomes for students. As several studies have shown, it is often not simple for an educator or a practitioner to choose between service learning and a traditional, lecture-style or banking model of educational delivery (Billig et al., 2005; Colby et al., 2007). Service learning is only one of a number of potential vehicles to greater civic learning, and research is needed to show when and whether other pedagogies can lead to better outcomes as well as under what conditions a service learning approach "confers additional benefits over other active pedagogies" (Billig et al., 2005, p. 1; see also Pritzker & McBride, 2006).

Conclusion

In this chapter I have summarized existing research on the impact of service learning on student civic learning outcomes, with a view to informing the future research agenda in this field. We must do much more in this area if we are to achieve the kind of revitalization of civic education and democratic participation envisioned by a wide range of organizations and experts. I hope this chapter provides a start in that direction.

Recommended Reading

Battistoni, R. (2002). *Civic engagement across the curriculum: A resource book for faculty in all disciplines.* Providence, RI: Campus Compact.

Billig, S. H. (2009). Does quality really matter? In B. E. Moely, S. H. Billig, & B. A. Holland (Eds.), *Creating our identities in service-learning and community engagement* (pp. 131–157). Charlotte, NC: Information Age.

Colby, A., Beaumont, E., Ehrlich, T., & Corngold, J. (2007). *Educating for democracy: Preparing undergraduates for responsible political engagement.* Stanford, CA: The Carnegie Foundation for the Advancement of Teaching.

Kahne, J., & Westheimer, J. (2006). The limits of efficacy: Educating citizens for a democratic society. *PS: Political Science and Politics, 39,* 289–296.

Lewin, R. (Ed.). (2009). *The handbook of practice and research in study abroad: Higher education and the quest for global citizenship.* Florence, KY: Taylor & Francis.

Musil, C. (2009). Educating students for personal and social responsibility: The civic learning spiral. In B. Jacoby (Eds.), *Civic engagement in higher education: Concepts and practices* (pp. 49–68). San Francisco, CA: Jossey-Bass.

Saltmarsh, J. (2005). The civic promise of service learning. *Liberal Education and the New Academy, 91*(2), 50–55.

References

Barber, B. (1984). *Strong democracy.* Berkeley, CA: University of California.

Barber, B. (1992). *An aristocracy of everyone: The politics of education and the future of America.* New York, NY: Ballantine.

Battistoni, R. (1997). Service learning as civic learning: Lessons we can learn from our students. In J. Cammarano & G. Reeher (Eds.), *Education for citizenship: Ideas and innovations in political learning* (pp. 31–49). Lanham, MD: Rowman & Littlefield.

Battistoni, R. (2002). *Civic engagement across the curriculum: A resource book for faculty in all disciplines.* Providence, RI: Campus Compact.

Battistoni, R. (2006a). Approaching democratic engagement: Research findings on civic learning and civic practice. In K. M. Casey, G. Davidson, S. H. Billig, & N. C. Springer (Eds.), *Advancing knowledge in service-learning: Research to transform the field* (pp. 3–16). Greenwich, CT: Information Age.

Battistoni, R. (2006b). Civic engagement: A broad perspective. In K. Kecskes (Ed.), *Engaging departments: Moving faculty culture from private to public, individual to collective focus for the common good* (pp. 11–26). San Francisco, CA: Jossey-Bass.

Battistoni, R. (2008). Democracy's practice grounds: The role of school governance in citizenship education. In J. S. Bixby & J. L. Pace (Eds.), *Educating democratic citizens in troubled times: Qualitative studies of current efforts* (pp. 131–156). Albany, NY: State University of New York.

Battistoni, R., & Longo, N. V. (2005). *Connecting workforce development and civic engagement: Higher education as public good and private gain.* Lynn, MA: North Shore Community College Policy Institute.

Battistoni, R., Longo, N. V., & Jayanandhan, S. R. (2009). Acting locally in a flat world: Global citizenship and the practice of service-learning. *Journal of Higher Education Outreach and Engagement, 13*(2), 89–108.

Bickford, D. M., & Reynolds, N. (2002). Activism and service-learning: Reframing volunteerism as acts of dissent. *Pedagogy: Critical Approaches to Teaching, Literature, Language, Composition and Culture, 2*(2), 229–254.

Billig, S. H. (2000, May). Research on K–12 school-based service-learning: The evidence builds. *Phi Delta Kappan, 81*, 658–664.

Billig, S. H. (2004). Heads, hearts, hands: The research on K–12 service-learning. In J. Kielsmeier, M. Neal, & M. McKinnon (Eds.), *Growing to greatness 2004: The state of service-learning project* (pp. 12–25). St. Paul, MN: National Youth Leadership Council.

Billig, S. H. (2009). Does quality really matter? In B. E. Moely, S. H. Billig, & B. A. Holland (Eds.), *Creating our identities in service-learning and community engagement* (pp. 131–157). Charlotte, NC: Information Age.

Billig, S. H., Jesse, D., Brodersen, R. M., & Grimley, M. (2008). Promoting secondary students' character development in schools through service-learning. In M. Bowden, S. H. Billig, & B. A. Holland (Eds.), *Scholarship for sustaining service-learning and civic engagement* (pp. 57–83). Charlotte, NC: Information Age.

Billig, S. H., Root, S., & Jesse, D. (2005). *The impact of participation in service-learning on high school students' civic engagement* (CIRCLE Working Paper 33). College Park, MD: University of Maryland, Center for Information and Research on Civic Learning and Engagement.

Boyer, E. (1996). The scholarship of engagement. *The Journal of Public Service and Outreach, 1*(1), 11–20.

Boyte, H. (2004). *Everyday politics: Reconnecting citizens and public life*. Philadelphia, PA: University of Pennsylvania.

Boyte, H. (2008). Against the current: Developing the civic agency of students. *Change: The Magazine of Higher Learning, 40*(3), 8–15.

Boyte, H., & Kari, N. (1996). *Building America: The democratic promise of public work*. Philadelphia, PA: Temple University.

Bringle, R. G., & Hatcher, J. A. (2010). International service learning. In R. G. Bringle, J. A. Hatcher, & S. G. Jones (Eds.), *International service learning: Conceptual frameworks and research* (pp. 3–28). Sterling, VA: Stylus.

Bringle, R. G., Hatcher, J. A., & Jones, S. G. (Eds.). (2010). *International service learning: Conceptual frameworks and research*. Sterling, VA: Stylus.

Bringle, R., & Steinberg, K. G. (2010). Educating for informed community involvement. *American Journal of Community Psychology, 46*, 428–441.

Bringle, R. G., Studer, M. H., Wilson, J., Clayton, P. H., & Steinberg, K. S. (2011). Designing programs with a purpose: To promote civic engagement for life. *Journal of Academic Ethics, 9*(2), 149–164.

Bruininks, R. S. (2006). *About the Council on Civic Engagement (COPE)*. Retrieved from http://www.umn.edu/civic/about/index.html

Cammarano, J., Battistoni, R., & Hudson, W. (2000, August–September). *Community service and citizenship: Is service-learning essential?* Paper presented at the 2000 Annual Meeting of the American Political Science Association, Washington, DC.

Campus Compact. (1999). *Presidents' declaration on the civic responsibility of higher education*. Providence, RI: Campus Compact.

Carnegie Corporation of New York & Center for Information and Research on Civic Learning and Engagement (CIRCLE). (2003). *The civic mission of schools*. New York, NY: Author.

Colby, A., Beaumont, E., Ehrlich, T., & Corngold, J. (2007). *Educating for democracy: Preparing undergraduates for responsible political engagement*. Stanford, CA: The Carnegie Foundation for the Advancement of Teaching.

Colby, A., Ehrlich, T., Beaumont, E., & Stephens, J. (2003). *Educating citizens: Preparing America's undergraduates for lives of moral and civic responsibility*. San Francisco, CA: Jossey-Bass.

Delli Carpini, M., & Keeter, S. (1996). *What Americans know about politics and why it matters*. New Haven, CT: Yale University.

Etzioni, A. (1993). *The spirit of community: Rights, responsibilities, and the communitarian agenda*. New York, NY: Crown.

Eyler, J. S., & Giles, D. E., Jr. (1999). *Where's the learning in service-learning?* San Francisco, CA: Jossey-Bass.

Fretz, E., & Longo, N. V. (2010). Students co-creating an engaged academy. In H. Fitzgerald, C. Burack, & S. Seifer (Eds.), *Handbook of engaged scholarship: Contemporary landscapes, future directions* (pp. 313–329). East Lansing, MI: Michigan State University Press.

Galston, W. (2001). Political knowledge, political engagement, and civic education. *Annual Review of Political Science, 4*, 217–234.

Gelmon, S. B., & Battistoni, R. (2005). Civic engagement: Conceptual frameworks. In E. Stefl, S. Gelmon, & A. Hewitt (Eds.), *Civic engagement in health administration education*. Arlington, VA: Association of University Programs in Health Administration.

Gilligan, C. (1982). *In a different voice: Psychological theory and women's development.* Cambridge, MA: Harvard University.

Greenleaf, R. K. (1996). *On becoming a servant leader.* San Francisco, CA: Jossey-Bass.

Hepburn, M., Niemi, R., & Chapman, C. (2000). Service learning in college political science: Queries and commentary. *PS: Political Science and Politics, 33*, 617–622.

Hollenbach, D. (1988). *Justice, peace, and human rights: American Catholic social ethics in a pluralistic context.* New York, NY: Crossroad.

Howard, J. (2001). *Service learning course design workbook.* Ann Arbor, MI: OCSL Press.

Hunter, S., & Brisbin, R. (2000). The impact of service learning on democratic and civic values. *PS: Political Science and Politics, 33*, 623–626.

Jacoby, R. (1987). *The last intellectuals: American culture in the age of academe.* New York, NY: Basic Books.

Jameson, J. K., Clayton, P. H., & Bringle, R. G. (2008). Investigating student learning within and across linked service-learning courses. In M. A. Bowdon, S. H. Billig, & B. A. Holland (Eds.), *Scholarship for sustaining service-learning and civic engagement* (pp. 3–27). Greenwich, CT: Information Age.

Kahne, J., & Westheimer, J. (2006). The limits of efficacy: Educating citizens for a democratic society. *PS: Political Science and Politics, 39*, 289–296.

Keen, C., & Hall, K. (n.d.). *Access to education through the Bonner Scholars Program: Post-graduation service and civic outcomes for high financial need students of a co-curricular service-learning college program in the United States.* Retrieved from https://files.pbworks.com/download/ubQfIhrHVn/bonnernetwork/38083485/KeenBSParticle.pdf

Keen, C., & Hall, K. (2005, November). *The Bonner Program: Student impact survey report.* Paper presented at the International Service-Learning Research Conference, East Lansing, MI.

Keeter, S., Zukin, C., Andolina, M., & Jenkins, K. (2002). *The civic and political health of the nation: A generational portrait.* College Park, MD: Center for Information & Research on Civic Learning & Engagement.

Kerr, D., Ireland, E., Lopes, E., & Craig, R. (2004). *Citizenship education longitudinal study: Second annual report: First longitudinal survey: Making citizenship education real* (Research Report No. 531). London, UK: National Foundation for Educational Research, Department for Education and Skills.

Kirlin, M. (2003). *The role of civic skills in fostering civic engagement.* (CIRCLE Working Paper 6.) Retrieved from http://www.civicyouth.org/PopUps/Working-Papers/WP06Kirlin.pdf

Knefelkamp, L. L. (2008). Civic identity: Locating self in community. *Diversity & Democracy, 11*(2), 1–3.

Lewin, R. (Ed.). (2009). *The handbook of practice and research in study abroad: Higher education and the quest for global citizenship.* Florence, KY: Taylor & Francis.

Longo, N. V., Drury, C., & Battistoni, R. (2006). Catalyzing political engagement: Lessons for civic educators from the voices of students. *Journal of Political Science Education, 2,* 313–329.

Longo, N. V., & Saltmarsh, J. (2010). New lines of inquiry in reframing international service learning into global service learning. In R. G. Bringle, J. A. Hatcher, & S. G. Jones (Eds.), *International service learning: Conceptual frameworks and research* (pp. 69–85). Sterling, VA: Stylus.

Mitchell, T. D. (2008). Traditional vs. critical service-learning: Engaging the literature to differentiate two models. *Michigan Journal of Community Service Learning, 14*(2), 50–65.

Mitchell, T. D., Visconti, V., Keene, A., & Battistoni, R. (2011). Educating for democratic leadership at Stanford, UMass, and Providence College. In N. Longo & C. Gibson (Eds.), *From command to community: A new approach to leadership education in colleges and universities* (pp. 115–148). Medford, MA: Tufts University Press.

Morton, K. (1997). Campus and community at Providence College. In *Expanding boundaries: Building civic responsibility within higher education* (Vol. II, pp. 8–11). Washington, DC: Corporation for National Service.

Musil, C. (2009). Educating students for personal and social responsibility: The civic learning spiral. In B. Jacoby (Eds.), *Civic engagement in higher education: Concepts and practices* (pp. 49–68). San Francisco, CA: Jossey-Bass.

Newman, F. (1985). *Higher education and the American resurgence.* Stanford, CA: Carnegie Foundation for the Advancement of Teaching.

Portland State University. (2011). *Civic engagement.* Retrieved from http://www.pdx.edu/cae/civic-engagement

Pritzker, S., & McBride, A. M. (2006). Service-learning and civic outcomes: From suggestive research to program models. In K. M. Casey, G. Davidson, S. H. Billig, & N. C. Springer (Eds.), *Advancing knowledge in service-learning: Research to transform the field* (pp. 17–43). Greenwich, CT: Information Age.

Putnam, R. (2000). *Bowling alone.* New York, NY: Simon & Schuster.

Qualifications and Curriculum Authority. (1998). *Education for citizenship and the teaching of democracy in schools: Final report of the advisory group on citizenship.* London, UK: Author.

Qualifications and Curriculum Authority. (2004). *Play your part: Post-16 citizenship.* London, UK: Author.

Rawls, J. (1971). *A theory of justice.* Cambridge, MA: Harvard University.

Roholt, R. V., Hildreth, R. W., & Baizerman, M. (2009). *Becoming citizens: Deepening the craft of youth civic engagement.* New York, NY: Routledge.

Saltmarsh, J. (2004). *The civic purpose of higher education: A focus on civic learning.* Unpublished manuscript, University of Massachusetts, Boston, MA.

Saltmarsh, J. (2005). The civic promise of service learning. *Liberal Education, 91*(2), 50–55.

Steinberg, K. S., Hatcher, J. A., & Bringle, R. G. (2011). A north star: Civic-minded graduate. *Michigan Journal of Community Service Learning, 18*(1), 19–33.

Sullivan, W. (2004). *Work and integrity: The crisis and promise of professionalism in America.* San Francisco, CA: Jossey-Bass.

Torney-Purta, J., & Vermeer, S. (2004). *Developing citizenship competencies from kindergarten through grade 12: A background paper for policymakers and educators.* Denver, CO: Education Commission of the States.

Vogelgesang, L. J. (2005, November). *Understanding the post-college impacts of service-learning.* Paper presented at the Fifth International Service-Learning Research Conference, East Lansing, MI.

Vogelgesang, L. J. (2009). Civic engagement and service learning: The challenge and promise of research. In B. E. Moely, S. H. Billig, & B. A. Holland (Eds.), *Creating our identities in service-learning and community engagement* (pp. 237–250). Charlotte, NC: Information Age.

Walt Whitman Center, Rutgers University. (1996). *Measuring citizenship: Assessing the impact of service learning on America's youth.* New Brunswick, Canada: Author.

Westheimer, J., & Kahne, J. (2000, January). Service learning required. *Education Week, 19*(20), 1–3.

Westheimer, J., & Kahne, J. (2004). What kind of citizen? The politics of educating for democracy. *American Educational Research Journal, 4,* 237–269.

Youniss, J., McLellan, J. A., & Yates, M. (1997). What we know about engendering civic identity. *American Behavioral Scientist, 40,* 620–631.

Zukin, C., Keeter, S., Andolina, M., Jenkins, K., & Delli Carpini, M. (2006). *A new engagement? Political participation, civic life, and the changing American citizen.* New York, NY: Oxford University Press.

INVESTIGATING PERSONAL DEVELOPMENT OUTCOMES IN SERVICE LEARNING

Theory and Research

Jay W. Brandenberger

The dominant vocation of all human beings at all
times is living—intellectual and moral growth.

—(Dewey, 1916, p. 362)

Among the many potential learning goals for engaged pedagogies such as service learning, personal development outcomes are particularly salient. Although advocates for service learning suggest a range of positive outcomes from mastery of course content to community impact, a consistent assumption—sometimes implicit—is that students will develop personally through their participation. Such an assumption comes naturally; service learning engages students (and faculty and community members) in a range of interpersonal relationships and complex social issues that have the power to challenge assumptions, stimulate critical reflection, and prompt ongoing exploration and growth. Research over the last decade has confirmed that service learning can foster personal growth in a variety of domains—as this chapter will review—yet the story is far from complete. The implicit expectations of personal development at the end of the service learning rainbow come almost too easily, without critical qualification. What processes during course-based engagement with communities lead to personal growth? Is the expected growth through service learning consistent with what is known about human development, and how can theories of human development inform research and practice in service learning? In investigations of personal development outcomes, how are the effects of student self-selection into the pedagogy dealt with (when participation is optional)? What are the critical questions in research on service learning and personal development, and how might they best be studied in a way that moves from assumptions about such outcomes to a firmly grounded knowledge base? Such questions are the focus of this chapter.

Personal development is an important outcome of higher education in the United States (Bowen, 1997), though it is more often assumed to occur than intentionally or explicitly targeted within curriculum development. The term *personal development* is also difficult to circumscribe; many constructs and capacities—from single attitudes to complex skill sets—are put forth as valuable outcomes in this domain. Indeed, any of the following could reasonably fit within the category of personal development: self-understanding and autonomy, locus of control, emotional intelligence, character, courage, political efficacy and attitudes, spiritual or religious orientation, attitudes toward social issues, conceptions of fairness and justice, openness to diversity, moral judgment, identity development, sense of integrity and purpose, motivation, interdependence, wisdom, well-being, flourishing, civic orientation, leadership skills, and personal ways of knowing. Discussion of each of these can be found in the service learning literature, but a detailed review is beyond the scope of this chapter. Rather, this chapter outlines developmental theory as a grounding for understanding the link between service learning pedagogy and the many attributes of personal development. In addition, it maps key research questions to inform ongoing practice.

Many, if not all, of the aforementioned constructs associated with personal development have a moral or prosocial component. Service learning, to the degree that it leads to such development, then, is not a neutral pedagogy; it engages students in relational and, thus, moral contexts and readily lends itself to evoking students' ethical awareness and sense of responsibility (Brandenberger, 2005). Although service learning practitioners do not always delineate what types of personal (including moral) growth are desired or expected, and may not always implement the pedagogy intentionally to achieve specific moral ends, they likely have implicit hopes about the personal growth that is possible and sense the power of the pedagogy to cultivate it. Thus, to understand the range of personal growth potentials inherent to service learning pedagogy, both implicit and explicit, we need well-grounded theory attentive to what personal outcomes might be expected and how such qualities may develop over time.

Theoretical and Conceptual Frameworks

Personal growth and development are complex processes, studied for decades through a variety of theoretical perspectives. It is important to note from the onset that development is a more complex goal than change. Change may refer to a modification or shift (in various directions), whereas development refers to growth represented by enhanced complexity: "Developmental growth is typically valued and pursued as a desirable psychological or educational end, perhaps even a moral end" (Pascarella & Terenzini, 2005, p. 17). Thus, research on service learning does well to build on developmental theory to inform both conceptual models and practice (Brandenberger, 1998; McEwen, 1996). Too often, service learning research is atheoretical, examining cohort differences or pre- and post-changes without reference to theory—in this case, theories and supporting research related to what is already known about personal development. Such shortcomings hinder the development of the field because results have limited generalizability or testability (Bringle, 2003; Bringle & Hatcher, 2000). This two-volume set in general, and this chapter in particular, offer correction to such shortcomings, outlining means to test and generate theory while informing best practice.

Theories of Dewey and Piaget

John Dewey (1916, 1938) viewed personal development as social in nature and based in experience. He thoroughly addressed the process and quality of experience, noting that personal struggle and conflict can be valuable if integrated within experience; they "carry it forward" and give it meaning and even an esthetic value (Dewey, 1934, p. 43). Note the parallels here to service learning pedagogy, with its use of reflection to help students make meaning of problems and failures in their efforts as well as their successes. Dewey (1938) argued that experiences have both an internal element that "influences the formation of attitudes of desire and purpose" (p. 39) and an external or environmental element. These aspects of experience interact continually: "The conceptions of situation and of interaction are inseparable from each other. An experience is always what it is because of a transaction taking place between an individual and what, at the time, constitutes his [sic] environment" (1938, p. 39). Furthermore, "Every genuine experience has an active side which changes in some degree the objective conditions under which experiences are had" (p. 39). Giles and Eyler (1994) provide a further analysis of Dewey's work as a theoretical basis for service learning.

Cognitive developmental theory, informed by Dewey (1938) and built on the work of Piaget (1970) and constructivist epistemology, offers further theoretical grounding. For Piaget, learning is active, and development results from exploration—from engaging with the world. Piaget (1970) asks "How is knowledge possible?" (p. 1), noting that traditional epistemologies assume that knowledge is stable and fact based. Piaget counters that knowledge (both in science and in the individual) is in a constant state of change or progression, or is *fieri*. Drawing on neo-Kantian views, he states that "this 'fieri' alone is the fact. Any being (or object) that science attempts to hold fast dissolves once again in the current of development" (Piaget, 1970, p. 3). Thus, Piaget paves the way for developmental understanding of knowledge (Muller, Carpendale, & Smith, 2009) and human education. Knowledge is not a "passive copy" of reality; rather, "to know is to transform reality" and to construct "models among which experience can enable us to choose" (Piaget, 1970, p. 15). Such processes of interaction and construction are central to service learning.

Moral Development Theory and Prosocial Research

Service learning and other community-based pedagogies are contexts for moral learning (Brandenberger, 2005). Students are engaged in relational (and thus moral) contexts for purposes that include improving lives or addressing social challenges. To understand the developmental processes that may be involved in such encounters, we can again draw from cognitive developmental theory. Piaget (1932) examined the implications of human interaction and construction for moral development, raising questions that framed the work of Kohlberg: How do individuals develop morally? What specific qualities or abilities develop? And how, in a diverse world, is one form of moral persuasion or action developed or advanced over another (Kohlberg, 1971)? Rest, Narvaez, Bebeau, and Thoma (1999), building on the work of Kohlberg, offer a four-component model of moral development that can inform service learning research. They posit that moral development involves an interaction among four active processes: (a) awareness, (b) judgment, (c) motivation, and (d) behavior. Persons may not be aware of a moral concern, but, if presented with such, they will make judgments about potential courses of action. Yet moral judgments are not always followed by corresponding action. Alternatively, one may be motivated to be moral without having the well-developed judgment or skills necessary for complex moral action. Thus, moral development requires an ongoing interplay of the four key domains, each emanating from different aspects of self. An integrated examination of these four components of moral development would be a beneficial next step in service learning research.

Because the outcomes implicit in service learning include a sense of social responsibility, awareness of social issues, and benefits to others, another relevant line of theory and research focuses on prosocial development. The term *prosocial* refers to voluntary commitment, either cognitive or behavioral, to the welfare of other persons or groups (Eisenberg, Cumberland, Guthrie, Murphy, & Shepard, 2005). Overlapping terms include *altruism, caring, helping, compassion*, and *philanthropy*. Research on prosocial development has focused on both personality factors and contextual influences. Penner, Dovidio, Piliavin, and Schroeder (2005) outline the need for multilevel analyses of prosocial development, ranging from brain functioning to group behaviors such as cooperation. Research by Eisenberg, Carlo, Murphy, and van Court (1995) delineates age-related changes in prosocial reasoning: As individuals mature, they are able to move beyond hedonistic motivations to considerations of reciprocity, and they develop the perspective-taking abilities that undergird prosocial responding (Eisenberg et al., 2005).

Research focused explicitly on prosocial development through the collegiate curriculum is limited, though there are indications that higher education has the potential to foster meaningful growth in this area. For example, research at the Higher Education Research Institute by Astin (1993) documents a significant rise in students' scores on a measure of social activism over four years. Research by Hill, Burrow, Brandenberger, Lapsley, and Quaranto (2010) outlines a means to conceptualize prosocial purpose orientations during the college years and demonstrates longitudinal outcomes; in this study, involvement in service learning during college was positively associated with prosocial purpose at graduation, which in turn predicted higher scores on measures of prosocial purpose, generativity, and integrity 13 years later.

Psychosocial and Identity Development

Erikson's (1950) theory of psychosocial development has important implications for service learning because it outlines the roles of social exploration and cultural context in development. Erikson (1975) describes the challenges that youth experience as they encounter increasingly complex social situations, with implications for the key task of late adolescence: identity development. Chickering and Reisser (1993) present a model of identity and personal development in college defined by seven "vectors": (a) developing competence, (b) managing emotions, (c) achieving autonomy and interdependence, (d) developing mature relationships, (e) establishing identity, (f) developing purpose, and (g) developing integrity.

Many service learning practitioners sense that much is stirred up within the self when students encounter difference and test their developing sense of agency in new environments (e.g., Yates & Youniss, 1996). Because identity develops in relation to the historical moment (Erikson, 1975), further explorations of identity formation may be especially important in light of the rapid social and technological changes that young people experience. For example, might the direct and complex encounters of service learning provide an important balance to the increasing time today's youth spend in electronic forms of communication and learning?

Positive Psychology

Positive psychology and research also provide important theoretical context for service learning and personal development in asking what it means to live well, to flourish. Many theorists agree that connection to something beyond the self is key (Keyes & Haidt, 2003). Research on psychological well-being has increased (e.g., Deci & Ryan, 2008; Ryff, 1989). Psychologists distinguish between hedonic or subjective well-being, characterized by pleasure or happiness, and eudaimonic well-being, defined as living optimally with meaning and purpose (Waterman, 1993). Service learning may foster eudaimonia; longitudinal studies have shown that various forms of helping and volunteering have positive effects on participants' sense of well-being (Musick, Herzog, & House, 1999; Piliavin, 2003). Such work provides a theoretical and empirical framing for research on service learning, which is addressed in more detail later in this chapter.

Review of Research Studies and Methods

Research has expanded significantly since Markus (1995) called for further study of service learning processes and impacts. Eyler, Giles, Stenson, and Gray (2001) offered an overview of what had been learned about the effects of service learning as of 2001. Citing 32 studies, they concluded that "service learning has a positive effect on student personal development" (p. 1), including efficacy, identity, spiritual growth, and moral development. In addition, they presented 22 studies that indicated impacts on interpersonal, leadership, and communication skills and 23 studies that linked service learning with the development of social responsibility and citizenship skills. Similar research has continued since 2001, with increased citation and inclusion in mainstream higher education publications (see Pascarella & Terenzini, 2005).

Five key areas for which research has demonstrated the impacts of service learning in the arena of personal development are as follows: (a) agency and identity; (b) perspective transformation and ways of knowing; (c) moral development and spirituality; (d) sociopolitical attitudes, citizenship, and leadership; and (e) career development and well-being. These areas are not empirically, conceptually, or developmentally distinct but are presented as means to mark progress and identify future research priorities. Research conducted since the late 1980s is highlighted.

Agency and Identity

Service learning can prompt examination of personal agency and identity as students consider whether they have the ability to address social issues and whether it is appropriate to do so. Various studies (Astin, Vogelgesang, Ikeda, & Yee, 2000; Stewart, 2009) suggest positive impacts of service learning on self-efficacy. Some examine a specific type of self-efficacy, from political efficacy (Kahne & Westheimer, 2006) to creativity efficacy (Tan, Ho, Ho, & Ow, 2008). Other research (Pascarella & Terenzini, 2005, p. 305) indicates that service learning may not always prompt growth in self-efficacy, perhaps because some students begin to understand that social change is complex, with initial confidence waning in the face of newly realized challenges. Beliefs about one's efficacy are central to social change (Bandura, 1995) and service learning and warrant further investigation. Reeb (2006) has refined a 10-item scale developed to measure community service self-efficacy, offering researchers a useful tool to assess participants' beliefs about their abilities to contribute within service contexts and to examine the potential impacts of service learning on self-efficacy.

Beliefs about personal agency, including self-efficacy, are also an important component of identity. According to Blasi (1993), individuals come to understand themselves as responsible or moral persons through being agents in the world and experiencing consequences for themselves and others. Youniss and Yates (1997) provide a theoretical framework for how identity formation may be influenced by service engagements and present research suggesting positive impacts of service learning on students' sense of agency. Similarly, longitudinal research by Jones and Abes (2004) suggests that service learning may enhance students' self-authorship. Recent research (Hill et al., 2010) suggests that service learning during college may also foster a sense of social or moral purpose that lasts into the young adult years. Purpose is an integrative construct that merits further exploration (Damon, Menon, & Bronk, 2003; Nash & Murray, 2010).

Perspective Transformation and Ways of Knowing

Various studies have demonstrated that service learning can prompt epistemological shifts and foster the development of "socially responsive knowledge" (Altman, as cited in Stukas, Clary, & Snyder, 1999, p. 11). Indeed,
Vandenberg (1991) argues that learning to respond "to others as 'cobeings'
and not as objects" (p. 1281) is a key developmental outcome built on direct
social experience. Research by Eyler and Giles (1999) suggests that high-
quality service learning placements with integrated reflection have the power
to foster perspective transformation on a fundamental level, yielding for
many students a "new set of lenses for seeing the world" (p. 129). Such
challenging of basic assumptions, and the learning that can result, may lead
participants to become advocates for new ways of knowing based on engagement (Brandenberger, 1998). Similarly, service learning can enhance meaning making (Bringle & Hatcher, 1999) and openness to different types of
people and experiences (Jones & Abes, 2004). Given such findings, further
research exploring the potential for service learning to enhance perspectives
on diversity and commitment to racial understanding is warranted (see Astin
et al., 2000; Bowman & Brandenberger, 2012).

Moral Development and Spirituality

Service learning is a pedagogy embedded in the moral domain, as outlined
earlier. Indeed, service learning is replete with and animated by questions of
existence (Why are we here?), responsibility (Who is my brother or sister?),
and justice and human rights (How can social groups have equal access to
beneficial goods?). Vandenberg (1991) claims that all "actions involving other
people necessarily entail ethical implications" (p. 1278) and presents a cogent
argument for service learning without explicit reference to the pedagogy.
The tensions inherent in the ethical and political issues raised by service
learning (Eyler & Giles, 1999) present challenges for educators who want to
avoid controversy, but even the most basic of service experiences raises moral
questions: Why do some have more to give than others? What does it mean
to serve? Brandenberger (2005) addresses such challenges in an overview of
experiential learning in higher education (see also Colby, Ehrlich, Beaumont, & Stephens, 2003).

Boss (1994) made an early and still relevant attempt to examine the
implications of service learning for moral development. Using the Defining
Issues Test (DIT), a comprehensive measure of principled moral reasoning
built on the work of Kohlberg, Boss compared students in two ethics courses

in which the instruction differed only with respect to service learning participation. She found the combination of cognitive disequilibrium (provided by engagement with challenging texts, done in both classes) with social disequilibrium (provided by the service learning experience in one class) to be a powerful predictor of student moral growth. Service learning participants showed significantly higher DIT scores at the end of the course. Research by Pratt (2001) using the DIT showed no significant differences among service learning participants and nonparticipants on principled moral reasoning, although there was an interaction effect between gender and service learning. Because solutions to most social challenges require moral reasoning, additional research should more fully examine the means by which engaged learning can facilitate growth in moral judgment.

Many other components of the moral realm have been explored in research on service learning. Batchelder and Root (1994) demonstrated a positive effect of service learning on prosocial reasoning, and Lundy (2007) presents evidence that service learning can have a constructive impact on the development of empathy. Furthermore, Pascarella and Terenzini (2005) cite evidence that service learning may foster commitment to social justice. From the lens of the related field of character education, Lapsley and Narvaez (2006) present a detailed analysis of the positive effects of service learning. They note that service learning and similar opportunities for direct moral interaction constitute one of Eleven Principles of Effective Character Education advocated by the national Character Education Partnership.

Moral matters can prompt questions of spirituality and religion, and a focus on service or compassion is central to all major religions (Armstrong, 2009) and conceptions of spirituality (Lama XIV, 1999). Research by Saroglou, Pinchon, Trompette, Verschueren, and Dernelle (2005) confirms links among spirituality, helping behavior, and altruism, though the relationship is complex. How might service learning relate to spirituality and matters of faith? Less research than might be expected has addressed this question (Radecke, 2007). Two relevant lines of investigation arise: Does religious faith or spirituality predict prosocial interest and engagement in service learning, and does service learning prompt spiritual or religious development? Various studies among college students suggest that personal spirituality or religious commitment may foster engagement (Andolina, Meents-DeCaigny, & Nass, 2006; Serow, 1989). In research by Eyler and Giles (1999), students in a national sample indicated that spiritual growth was a personal outcome of their service learning. Given the potential salience of spiritual and religious matters to service learning, various authors (e.g.,

Chickering, Dalton, & Stamm, 2006; Sikula & Sikula, 2005) call for increased attention to the intersection of civic engagement, service, spirituality, and higher education. The Spirituality in Higher Education Project (Higher Education Research Institute, 2004) developed at UCLA is an important step in this direction. Using national data from this project, Brandenberger and Bowman (in press) found that spiritual identification at college entry is associated with subsequent gains on measures of ethic of caring, charitable involvement, and compassionate self-concept. Similar research specifically addressing service learning, spirituality, and related constructs seems warranted given the salience of findings to date and the prominent role of religion in many aspects of American life.

Sociopolitical Attitudes, Citizenship, and Leadership

A related focus in service learning research examines the pedagogy's potential influence on sociopolitical attitudes and civic behavior. In a review of research, Pascarella and Terenzini (2005) suggest that evidence is "conclusive" (p. 304) that service learning influences sociopolitical attitudes and beliefs. Research also demonstrates a positive effect on civic responsibility (Moely, McFarland, Miron, Mercer, & Ilustre, 2002) and orientation toward future volunteerism (Tomkovick, Lester, Flunker, & Wells, 2008).

After years of decline in youth political interest, some wonder whether service learning may focus students on the local and the individual versus the systemic or political (Barber, 1992). Others emphasize the potential for service learning to promote civic and political engagement (Campbell, 2000). In a longitudinal study, Astin et al. (2006) found that service learning in particular (compared to volunteerism) during the undergraduate years predicted political engagement in the post-college years. The reflective component of service learning may play a key role in fostering links between what students observe and relevant political and policy challenges. After hitting an all-time low in the late 1990s, student political interest increased significantly in the past decade, reaching a 40-year high in 2008 (Pryor et al., 2008). Given such contexts, researchers need to examine more fully how students become engaged, and stay engaged, in political processes, and they need to make explicit how service learning can foster political learning (Colby, Beaumont, Ehrlich, & Corngold, 2007; Walker, 2002).

The service learning literature is filled with discussions of developing future leaders, and some argue that "service learning without intentional leadership development is trivial" (Des Marais, Yang, & Farzanehkia, 2000,

p. 678). However, it would be premature to claim significant understanding of leadership development in relation to service-based pedagogies. Many campus centers or service learning programs reference leadership in their name or mission statements, yet leadership is a broad term and difficult to operationalize empirically.

Astin and Sax (1998) demonstrated positive effects for service learning on leadership development in a large college sample. More recent research by Dugan (2006) suggests that service engagement may prompt leadership development. Flanagan (2004) provides a thoughtful review of research on the linkages among service, political socialization, and leadership. She argues that an ethic of civic participation develops from two psychological orientations: "identification with the public good" and "tolerance for the views of those with whom we fundamentally disagree" (p. 736)—qualities that are certainly germane to service learning. She also suggests the importance of building a theory of youth civic development. Another fruitful line of inquiry may be the link between servant leadership, as outlined by Robert Greenleaf, and service learning (see Spears, 1996).

Career Development and Well-Being

A less explored arena of potential service learning outcomes related to personal development concerns the years beyond college into adulthood. Controlling for orientations in the freshman year, Astin et al. (2000) found that service engagement during college "appears to have its strongest effect on the student's decision to pursue a career in a service field" (p. iii). Stukas et al. (1999) describe the relevance of service learning for career exploration but note the lack of research in this area (see also Pascarella & Terenzini, 2005).

A relevant and promising line of research examines the impact of volunteering at various ages on subsequent well-being. Engaging in service can serve as a protective factor or an asset in positive youth development (Penner et al., 2005) and can foster well-being among adults (Hao, 2008; Musick et al., 1999). Bowman, Brandenberger, Lapsley, Hill, and Quaranto (2010) found that college students who engaged in service learning reported enhanced forms of well-being—including life satisfaction and continued volunteering—13 years following graduation. A related area of research examines indicators of health (e.g., prevention of alcohol abuse) among college students as a function of engagement (Buettner, Andrews, & Glassman, 2009). Indeed, Aronson (2006) argues that service learning research should adopt paradigms employed in prevention science.

Implications for Practice

What implications for practice may be drawn from the research since the late 1980s? Service learning is a powerful means to promote personal development. Practitioners can be confident that well-designed, developmentally grounded service learning initiatives will engage students in personally meaningful learning that has the potential for lasting effects. Yet results may vary given the diversity of personal and contextual factors inherent to all complex human relations. That is to say, service learning pedagogies do not offer pinpoint learning outcomes that are easily captured. Part of the inherent power of the pedagogy stems from its rich complexity, built on what Perry (1970) described as the "risks of caring" (p. 200); little growth may happen in controlled, safe environments, yet such contexts may bring uncertainties. Not all service learning placements can be structured to enhance developmental outcomes through just the right mix of challenge and support. When we hit the mark, development may flourish; when we miss, service learning can be flat or even prompt unwanted outcomes: conclusions that the poor are lazy or that engagement is frustrating and ineffective. Thus, practitioners need to maintain a close watch on the learning processes and build in consistent assessment opportunities, especially because personal development aspects may be less salient than content outcomes, and, therefore, not as openly discussed.

In the studies reviewed in the previous section, much was learned about best practices; however, a detailed summary is beyond the scope of this chapter. Salient factors include quality placements (providing both challenge and support), reflection opportunities, and appropriate assessment with feedback. While it might be assumed that long-term engagement is necessary for sustaining personal development, short-term involvements may trigger responses that foster a trajectory of growth about which practitioners are unaware at the close of the formal learning opportunity (Bowman, Brandenberger, Mick, & Toms Smedley, 2010).

Overall, the literature reviewed suggests the need for a developmental sensitivity on the part of administrators, faculty, and community partners as they design community-based activities. To think developmentally in the context of service learning is to ask consistently: What do students bring to the encounters offered? What personal factors will be activated? And how may interaction lead to growth over time? Thinking in this way also leads to further assessment and research questions.

Future Research Directions

Early research on service learning had roots in program evaluation and efforts to document impacts in order to advance the pedagogy (Eyler, 2010). During the 1990s, methodologies evolved to include sophisticated designs and instruments, grounding an expansion of research, much of it focused on personal development outcomes (Bringle & Steinberg, 2010; Eyler et al., 2001). Drawing from a variety of literature, Bringle, Phillips, and Hudson (2004) present an array of well-documented research scales to assess student experience and outcomes. It is interesting to note, given the maturity and breadth of the field, that the majority of the instruments they include focus on personal development (including, for example, measures of personal values, moral development, self-esteem, identity, empathy, hope, life orientation, civic attitudes, and the like), suggesting an implicit focus within the field on personal development outcomes. The field needs further scale development, especially instruments finely tailored to key constructs (see, for example, the scale developed by Hatcher, 2008, assessing attributes of the civic-minded professional).

Most studies, including many reviewed in this chapter, are limited by sample size and a short-term focus. Many employ pre- and post-designs built around a course or program. Showing effects from a short-term intervention is challenging, so outcomes that are confirmed underscore the power of service learning. Yet studies in the field are too often conducted with a singular focus on the pedagogy or outcome of interest without examination of individual differences and contextual factors. Similarly, studies are too often atheoretical and lack grounding in developmental theory (Brandenberger, 1998).

Research on the personal development outcomes of service learning and engaged learning has made progress yet faces developmental challenges (pun intended) ahead. The next decade of research must be characterized by research rigor, including attention to theory development, refined use of constructs, direct (i.e., behavioral) measures, and longitudinal designs. Recommendations for research that would address the previously noted limitations and deepen our understanding follow.

Theory Building

Research in the coming years should be more fully grounded in theory and account for the complexity of personal development. Many scholars have recommended this (Bringle, 2003; Bringle & Hatcher, 2000; Giles & Eyler,

1994; Speck & Hoppe, 2004; Yarbrough & Wade, 2002), but theoretical integration throughout a research initiative presents challenges of time, expertise, and scale. As noted, the work of Dewey and the cognitive/constructivist developmental paradigm based on Piaget and others (Brandenberger, 1998) are good points of entry because each is built on an understanding of individual-environment interactions. Similarly, Warter and Grossman (2002) apply developmental contextualism, built on the work of Bronfenbrenner, to service learning. Service learning practitioners need to draw from such theories to build a macro theory of engaged learning and then test theory components in research. Concurrently, research instruments used in the field need to be grounded in theory, not just item analyses and scale reliability.

The Trajectory of Development

Research should attend to personal growth as a developmental process. Too many studies examine growth over a short period of time without attention to how one experience may build readiness for future learning. Flanagan (2004) notes that "relatively little attention has been paid to the developmental timing or sequence of different types of service experiences" (p. 722) that may reinforce or inhibit personal development. Dewey (1916) emphasized that a primary criterion for judging the effectiveness of education is the extent in which it "creates a desire for continued growth and supplies means for making the desire effective in fact" (p. 62). To understand the trajectories of personal development, researchers need to examine more fully the role that early experience and selection effects play. Similarly, longitudinal designs are still too rare. Using previous records and existing databases and then conducting follow-up surveys with previous participants in service learning is an effective means to extend research. For example, many colleges have access to early student data about their alumni via first-year and senior surveys (that included markers for service-related activities) from the Higher Education Research Initiative (see Bowman, Brandenberger, Lapsley, et al., 2010). By developing longitudinal studies that track students beyond college, service learning researchers can draw more fully on theories of emerging adulthood (e.g., Arnett, 2000) and adult development (e.g., Mezirow & Associates, 2000).

Holistic Perspectives

Pascarella and Terenzini (2005) summarize an extensive review of research in higher education by noting that "multiple forces shape student learning"

(p. 629). Service learning is not the only means to an identified end, though studies of the pedagogy may, unintentionally, frame it this way. College offers a myriad of opportunities for personal growth, including cooperative learning, undergraduate research, diversity education, and discovery learning. Future research should address how service learning may factor into a complex equation of student growth, perhaps as a mediating influence. Similarly, research on service learning needs to expand the use of instruments and paradigms from other lines of social science research (e.g., the study of character and moral development). The field would also benefit from research that examines how student, pedagogical, institutional, and community factors interact to facilitate students' personal development.

Who Is Served—Justice or Just Us?

Research should further attend to the reciprocal nature of service learning and examine how it may function for those less likely to participate (males, minority groups) and how it may affect the recipients of service. Framing service learning as a means to personal development is consistent with theories in positive psychology, but potential conflicts (and unfortunate dichotomies) abound. For whom do service learning programs exist: those served or those serving? Although many in the academy advocate for reciprocity and support for the community partners and citizens who foster student growth, service learning often remains the province of the privileged and may engage a "hidden curriculum" (Swaminathan, 2008). Those on both sides of the (implicit) serve/receive agreements may sense such tensions, yet research exploring such challenges is limited. Are there contexts in which personal gain for service learning participants is offset by a sense of ignominy experienced by the recipients? To address such questions, service learning practitioners and researchers need to be consistently aware of their personal worldviews and build initiatives in which diverse groups can address mutually important problems as equals. This is not easy work. The work of Freire (1970) has important implications here. Building on Freire, Rivage-Seul (1987) points out that most challenges to the status quo and a great deal of moral insight originate from those in less privileged positions. Research that illuminates such processes and addresses the social justice implications of service learning is critical (Butin, 2008). Similarly, service learning research needs to be understood within cultural frames; Butin (2005) suggests that service learning can be conceptualized as technical, cultural, political, or postmodern, with resulting implications for understanding research findings.

A related line of research would examine those who do not participate in service learning opportunities when presented. Why might students of lower socioeconomic status or males be reticent to participate? How can service learning experiences be designed so that those who are not inclined to participate can have meaningful growth experiences (Bringle, 2005)? Does service learning differentially attract students with particular learning styles? Further research on such questions may help tailor future curricular offerings and methods of recruitment.

Process Versus Product

Future research should emphasize and analyze process variables associated with service learning. More is known about service learning outcomes than how the associated changes take place (Eyler, 2010). Examining pedagogical processes presents methodological challenges; it is not sufficient to survey students at the start and end of a course or program. What first caught students' attention about a social concern, and how did the students' thinking begin to change? Delve, Mintz, and Stewart (1990) presented an early service learning process model, noting five phases (from exploration to realization). Future research toward this end should employ various creative means (e.g., participant observation, journaling) to assess students' thought processes throughout service learning and beyond.

Modeling and Moral Elevation

An underexplored research area concerns the influence of community leaders and other adults as role models for service learning participants and the effect of engaging in something larger than the self that has the power to inspire. Youth seek adults who stir their imagination and present them with models for life worthy of their talents and imminent commitments (Parks, 1986). Service learning can provide a context for positive modeling (from both adults and peers). To explore such processes, researchers may want to examine the concept of moral elevation. Haidt (2003) presents research suggesting that positive moral emotions are triggered when people observe acts of virtue, gratitude, "moral beauty" (p. 276), and life improvement. Experiencing such moral emotions, Haidt suggests, is associated not only with physical sensations (e.g., warmth in the chest) but also with strong desires to do likewise, to serve the common good. Such moral elevation is seen as the opposite of social disgust caused by witnessing negative deeds (and accompanied by a tendency to feel sick, cynical, or distant) and can lead to strong "positive contamination" (p. 285). Perhaps the powerful stories of transformation that often accompany students' participation in a positive service learning experience can be explained in part by processes of moral elevation (even hearing such stories second hand can be motivating for others, including parents and instructors). Research on such processes may dovetail nicely with examinations of eudaimonia and purpose as discussed earlier in this chapter.

Will, Purpose, and Skill Development

Much of the research with respect to personal development focuses on student attitudes and orientations. Less understood are effects on students' conative and motivational dispositions: the *will* necessary to address complex social concerns. Perry (1970) suggests that "students' ultimate purpose is . . . to find those forms [of thought] through which they may best understand and confront with integrity the nature of the human condition" (p. 201). This may be one of the most important service learning outcomes: fostering a sense of purpose toward the common good. Bowman, Brandenberger, Lapsley, et al. (2010) provide a framework for longitudinal exploration of purpose orientations in relation to service engagement.

In addition, research needs to focus on skill development. Awareness and outlook are incomplete; skills are critical yet difficult to build into short-term offerings and challenging to assess. Service learning researchers may draw from the work of Narvaez and Lapsley (2005), who have identified skills necessary for each of the components of Rest's model of moral functioning. Examples include identifying a cultural perspective, managing fear, monitoring one's reasoning, nurturing tolerance, and attending to human needs. What elements should be built into a service learning initiative designed to enhance such skills?

Conclusion

Since the late 1980s, service learning research on personal development has evolved and demonstrated significant outcomes. Many of the qualities and constructs assessed have a moral or prosocial focus, appropriate for the public goals inherent in service learning. The field is now poised to build toward more mature frames and methods. To advance the agenda outlined here, research will need to be theoretically grounded and integrated with cognate fields, using best practices in the social sciences. Studies often will require a multisite and longitudinal focus, with implications for funding. Building such research programs calls for vision and collaboration across constituencies. A powerful pedagogy with personal development implications needs to be tested and refined through significant research efforts.

Recommended Reading

Brandenberger, J. W. (2005). College, character, and social responsibility: Moral learning through experience. In D. Lapsley & F. C. Power (Eds.), *Character psychology and character education* (pp. 305–334). Notre Dame, IN: University of Notre Dame Press.

Butin, D. W. (Ed.). (2008). *Service-learning and social justice education: Strengthening justice-oriented community based models of teaching and learning.* New York, NY: Routledge.

Dewey, J. (1916). *Democracy and education: An introduction to the philosophy of education.* New York, NY: Macmillan.

Flanagan, C. (2004). Volunteerism, leadership, political socialization and civic engagement. In R. Lerner & L. Steinberg (Eds.), *Handbook of adolescent psychology* (2nd ed., pp. 721–746). New York, NY: John Wiley & Sons.

Freire, P. (1998). *Pedagogy of freedom: Ethics, democracy, and civic courage.* Lanham, MD: Rowman & Littlefield.

Warter, E. H., & Grossman, J. M. (2002). An application of developmental-contextualism to service-learning. In A. Furco & S. H. Billig (Eds.), *Service-learning: The essence of the pedagogy* (pp. 83–102). Greenwich, CT: Information Age.

References

Andolina, M., Meents-DeCaigny, E., & Nass, K. (2006). College students, faith and the public realm: The relationship between religious attitudes and civic and political engagement. *Journal of College & Character, 8*(1), 1–10. Retrieved from http://journals.naspa.org/jcc/

Armstrong, K. (2009). *The case for God.* New York, NY: Knopf.

Arnett, J. J. (2000). Emerging adulthood: A theory of development from the late teens through the twenties. *American Psychologist, 55,* 469–480.

Aronson, K. R. (2006). How prevention science can inform service-learning research. *International Journal of Teaching and Learning in Higher Education, 18*(1), 5–16. Retrieved from http://www.isetl.org/

Astin, A. W. (1993). *What matters in college: Four critical years revisited.* San Francisco, CA: Jossey-Bass.

Astin, A. W., & Sax, L. J. (1998). How undergraduates are affected by service participation. *Journal of College Student Development, 39,* 251–263.

Astin, A. W., Vogelgesang, L. J., Ikeda, E. K., & Yee, J. A. (2000). *How service learning affects students.* Los Angeles, CA: Higher Education Research Institute, UCLA.

Astin, A. W., Vogelgesang, L. J., Misa, K., Anderson, J., Denson, N., Jayakumar, U., . . . Yamamura, E. (2006). *Understanding the effects of service-learning: A study of students and faculty.* Los Angeles, CA: Higher Education Research Institute, UCLA. Retrieved from http://www.gseis.ucla.edu/heri/publications-brp.php

Bandura, A. (Ed.). (1995). *Self-efficacy in changing societies.* New York, NY: Cambridge University Press.

Barber, B. (1992). *An aristocracy of everyone: The politics of education and the future of America.* New York, NY: Ballantine Books.

Batchelder, T. H., & Root, S. (1994). Effects of an undergraduate program to integrate academic learning and service: Cognitive, prosocial cognitive, and identity outcomes. *Journal of Adolescence, 17,* 341–355.

Blasi, A. (1993). The development of identity: Some implications for moral functioning. In G. G. Noam & T. E. Wren (Eds.), *The moral self* (pp. 99–122). Cambridge, MA: MIT Press.

Boss, J. A. (1994). The effect of community service work on the moral development of college ethics students. *Journal of Moral Education, 23*(2), 183–198.

Bowen, H. R. (1997). *Investment in learning: The individual and social value of American higher education.* Baltimore, MD: Johns Hopkins University Press.

Bowman, N. A., & Brandenberger, J. W. (2012). Experiencing the unexpected: Toward a model of college diversity experiences and attitude change. *Review of Higher Education, 35*(2), 179–205.

Bowman, N. A., Brandenberger, J. W., Lapsley, D. K., Hill, P. L., & Quaranto, J. C. (2010). Serving in college, flourishing in adulthood: Does community engagement during the college years predict adult well-being? *Applied Psychology: Health and Well-Being, 2*(1), 14–34. doi:10.1111/j.1758–0854.2009.01020.x

Bowman, N. A., Brandenberger, J. W., Mick, C. S., & Toms Smedley, C. (2010). Sustained immersion experiences and student orientations toward equality, justice, and social responsibility: The role of short-term service-learning. *Michigan Journal of Community Service Learning, 17*(1), 20–31.

Brandenberger, J. W. (1998). Developmental psychology and service learning: A theoretical framework. In R. G. Bringle & D. K. Duffy (Eds.), *With service in mind: Concepts and models for service-learning in psychology* (pp. 68–84). Washington, DC: American Association for Higher Education, American Psychological Association.

Brandenberger, J. W. (2005). College, character, and social responsibility: Moral learning through experience. In D. K. Lapsley & F. C. Power (Eds.), *Character psychology and character education* (pp. 305–334). Notre Dame, IN: University of Notre Dame Press.

Brandenberger, J. W., & Bowman, N. A. (in press). From faith to compassion? Reciprocal influences of spirituality, religious commitment and prosocial development during college. In M. J. Mayhew & A. N. Rockenbach (Eds.), *Spirituality enacted in higher education.* New York, NY: Routledge.

Bringle, R. G. (2003). Enhancing theory-based research on service-learning. In S. H. Billig & J. Eyler (Eds.), *Deconstructing service-learning: Research exploring context, participation, and impacts* (pp. 3–21). Greenwich, CT: Information Age.

Bringle, R. G. (2005). Designing interventions to promote civic engagement. In A. Omoto (Ed.), *Processes of community change and social action* (pp. 167–187). Mahwah, NJ: Erlbaum.

Bringle, R. G., & Hatcher, J. A. (1999). Reflection in service-learning: Making meaning of experience. *Educational Horizons, 77*(4), 179–185.

Bringle, R. G., & Hatcher, J. A. (2000). Meaningful measurement of theory-based service-learning outcomes: Making the case with quantitative research [Special issue]. *Michigan Journal of Community Service Learning, Fall,* 68–75.

Bringle, R. G., Phillips, M. A., & Hudson, M. (2004). *The measure of service learning: Research scales to assess student experiences.* Washington, DC: American Psychological Association.

Bringle, R. G., & Steinberg, K. S. (2010). Educating for informed community involvement. *American Journal of Community Psychology, 46,* 428–441.

Buettner, C. K., Andrews, D. W., & Glassman, M. (2009). Development of a student engagement approach to alcohol prevention: The pragmatics project. *Journal of American College Health, 58*(1), 33–38.

Butin, D. W. (2005). Service learning as postmodern pedagogy. In D. W. Butin (Ed.), *Service-learning in higher education: Critical issues and directions* (pp. 89–104). New York, NY: Palgrave Macmillan.

Butin, D. W. (Ed.). (2008). *Service-learning and social justice education: Strengthening justice-oriented community based models of teaching and learning.* New York, NY: Routledge.

Campbell, D. E. (2000). Social capital and service learning. *PS: Political Science and Politics, 33,* 641–645.

Chickering, A. W., Dalton, J. C., & Stamm, L. (2006). *Encouraging authenticity and spirituality in higher education.* San Francisco, CA: Jossey-Bass.

Chickering, A. W., & Reisser, L. (1993). *Education and identity* (2nd ed.). San Francisco, CA: Jossey-Bass.

Colby, A., Beaumont, E., Ehrlich, T., & Corngold, J. (2007). *Educating for democracy: Preparing undergraduates for responsible political engagement.* San Francisco, CA: Jossey-Bass.

Colby, A., Ehrlich, T., Beaumont, E., & Stephens, J. (2003). *Educating citizens: Preparing America's undergraduates for lives of moral and civic responsibility.* San Francisco, CA: Jossey-Bass.

Damon, W., Menon, J., & Bronk, K. C. (2003). The development of purpose during adolescence. *Applied Developmental Science, 7*(3), 119–128.

Deci, E. L., & Ryan, R. M. (2008). Hedonia, eudaimonia, and well-being: An introduction. *Journal of Happiness Studies, 9*, 1–11.

Delve, C. I., Mintz, S. D., & Stewart, G. M. (1990). Promoting values development through community service: A design. *New Directions for Student Services, 1990*(50), 7–29. doi:10.1002/ss.37119905003

Des Marais, J. D., Yang, Y., & Farzanehkia, F. (2000). Service-learning leadership development for youths. *Phi Delta Kappan, 81*, 678–680. Retrieved from http://www.jstor.org/stable/20439760

Dewey, J. (1916). *Democracy and education: An introduction to the philosophy of education.* New York, NY: Free Press.

Dewey, J. (1934). *Art as experience.* New York, NY: Berkeley Publishing.

Dewey, J. (1938). *Experience and education.* New York, NY: Macmillan.

Dugan, J. P. (2006). Involvement and leadership: A descriptive analysis of socially responsible leadership. *Journal of College Student Development, 47*, 335–343.

Eisenberg, N., Carlo, G., Murphy, B., & van Court, P. (1995). Prosocial development in late adolescence: A longitudinal study. *Child Development, 66*, 1179–1197.

Eisenberg, N., Cumberland, A., Guthrie, I. K., Murphy, B. C., & Shepard, S. A. (2005). Age changes in prosocial responding and moral reasoning in adolescence and early adulthood. *Journal of Research on Adolescence, 15*, 235–260.

Erikson, E. (1950). *Childhood and society.* New York, NY: Norton.

Erikson, E. (1975). *Life history and the historical moment.* New York, NY: Norton.

Eyler, J. S. (2010). What international service learning research can learn from research on service learning. In R. G. Bringle, J. A. Hatcher, & S. G. Jones (Eds.), *International service learning: Conceptual frameworks and research* (pp. 225–242). Sterling, VA: Stylus.

Eyler, J. S., & Giles, D. E., Jr. (1999). *Where's the learning in service-learning?* San Francisco, CA: Jossey-Bass.

Eyler, J. S., Giles, D. E., Jr., Stenson, C. M., & Gray, C. J. (2001). *At a glance: What we know about the effects of service learning on college students, faculty, institutions and communities, 1993–2000* (3rd ed.). Washington, DC: Learn and Serve America's National Service Learning Clearinghouse.

Flanagan, C. (2004). Volunteerism, leadership, political socialization and civic engagement. In R. Lerner & L. Steinberg (Eds.), *Handbook of adolescent psychology* (2nd ed., pp. 721–746). New York, NY: John Wiley & Sons.

Freire, P. (1970). *Pedagogy of the oppressed.* New York, NY: Continuum.

Giles, D. E., Jr., & Eyler, J. S. (1994). The theoretical roots of service-learning in John Dewey: Toward a theory of service-learning. *Michigan Journal of Community Service Learning 1*(1), 77–85.

Haidt, J. (2003). Elevation and the positive psychology of morality. In C. L. M. Keyes & J. Haidt (Eds.), *Flourishing: Positive psychology and the life well-lived* (pp. 275–289). Washington, DC: American Psychological Association.

Hao, Y. (2008). Productive activities and psychological well-being among older adults. *Journal of Gerontology: Social Sciences, 63*(B), S64–S72.

Hatcher, J. A. (2008). *The public role of professionals: Developing and evaluating the civic-minded professional scale* (Doctoral dissertation). Retrieved from ProQuest Dissertations and Theses database. (UMI No. 3331248)

Higher Education Research Institute. (2004). *The spiritual life of college students: A national study of college students' search for meaning and purpose.* Retrieved from http://spirituality.ucla.edu/docs/reports/Spiritual_Life_College_Students_Full_Report.pdf

Hill, P. L., Burrow, A. L., Brandenberger, J. W., Lapsley, D. K., & Quaranto, J. C. (2010). Collegiate purpose orientations and well-being in adulthood. *Journal of Applied Developmental Psychology 31*, 173–179. doi:10.1016/j.appdev.2009.12.001

Jones, S. R., & Abes, E. S. (2004). Enduring influences of service-learning on college students' identity development. *Journal of College Student Development, 45*(2), 149–166.

Kahne, J., & Westheimer, J. (2006). The limits of political efficacy: Educating citizens for a democratic society. *PS: Political Science and Politics, 39*, 289–296.

Keyes, C. L. M., & Haidt, J. (Eds.). (2003). *Flourishing: Positive psychology and the life well-lived.* Washington, DC: American Psychological Association.

Kohlberg, L. (1971). From is to ought: How to commit the naturalistic fallacy and get away with it in the study of moral development. In T. Mischel (Ed.), *Cognitive development and epistemology* (pp. 151–235). New York, NY: Academic Press.

Lama XIV, D. (1999). *Ethics for the new millennium.* New York, NY: Penguin Putnam.

Lapsley, D. K., & Narvaez, D. (2006). Character education. In A. Renninger & I. Siegel (Eds.), *Handbook of child psychology* (Vol. 4, pp. 248–296). New York, NY: Wiley.

Lundy, B. L. (2007). Service learning in life-span developmental psychology: Higher exam scores and increased empathy. *Teaching of Psychology, 34*, 23–27.

Markus, G. B. (1995). A call for more research on community service learning. In J. Galura, J. Howard, D. Waterhouse, & R. Ross (Eds.), *Praxis III: Voices in dialogue* (pp. 151–159). Ann Arbor, MI: OCSL Press, University of Michigan.

McEwen, M. K. (1996). Enhancing student learning and development through service-learning. In B. Jacoby (Ed.), *Service-learning in higher education: Concepts and practices* (pp. 53–91). San Francisco, CA: Jossey-Bass.

Mezirow, J., & Associates. (Eds.). (2000). *Learning as transformation: Critical perspectives on a theory in progress.* San Francisco, CA: Jossey-Bass.

Moely, B. E., McFarland, M., Miron, D., Mercer, S., & Ilustre, V. (2002). Changes in college students' attitudes and intentions for civic involvement as a function of service-learning experiences. *Michigan Journal of Community Service Learning, 9*(1), 18–26.

Muller, U., Carpendale, J. I. M., & Smith, L. (Eds.). (2009). *The Cambridge companion to Piaget.* New York, NY: Cambridge University Press.

Musick, M. A., Herzog, A. R., & House, J. S. (1999). Volunteering and mortality among older adults: Findings from a national sample. *Journal of Gerontology: Social Sciences, 54B*(3), S173–S180.

Narvaez, D., & Lapsley, D. K. (2005). The psychological foundation of moral expertise. In D. K. Lapsley & F. C. Power (Eds.), *Character psychology and character education* (pp. 140–165). Notre Dame, IN: University of Notre Dame Press.

Nash, R. J., & Murray, M. C. (2010). *Helping college students find purpose: The campus guide to meaning-making.* San Francisco, CA: Jossey-Bass.

Parks, S. (1986). *The critical years: The young adult search for a faith to live by.* San Francisco, CA: Harper & Row.

Pascarella, E. T., & Terenzini, P. T. (2005). *How college affects students: A third decade of research* (Vol. 2). San Francisco, CA: Jossey-Bass.

Penner, L. A., Dovidio, J. F., Piliavin, J. A., & Schroeder, D. A. (2005). Prosocial behavior: Multilevel perspectives. *Annual Review of Psychology, 56*, 365–392.

Perry, W. G. (1970). *Forms of intellectual and ethical development in the college years.* New York, NY: Holt, Rinehart, and Winston.

Piaget, J. (1932). *The moral judgment of the child* (M. Gabain, Trans.). London, UK: K. Paul, Trench, Trubner & Co. Ltd./Edinburgh Press.

Piaget. J. (1970). *Genetic epistemology* (E. Duckworth, Trans.). New York, NY: Columbia University Press.

Piliavin, J. A. (2003). Doing well by doing good: Benefits for the benefactor. In C. L. M. Keyes & J. Haidt (Eds.), *Flourishing: Positive psychology and the life well-lived* (pp. 227–247). Washington, DC: American Psychological Association.

Pratt, S. B. (2001). *Moral development in college students engaged in community service learning: A justice-care perspective* (Doctoral dissertation). Available from ProQuest Dissertations and Theses database. (UMI No. 3026608)

Pryor, J. H., Hurtado, S., DeAngelo, L., Sharkness, J., Romero, L. C., Korn, W. S., & Tran, S. (2008). *The American freshman: National norms for fall 2008.* Los Angeles, CA: Higher Education Research Institute, UCLA.

Radecke, M. W. (2007). Service-learning and faith formation. *Journal of College and Character, 8*(5), 1–28. Retrieved from http://journals.naspa.org/jcc/

Reeb, R. (2006). Community service self-efficacy: Research review. *Academic Exchange Quarterly, 10*(1), 242–248.

Rest, J., Narvaez, D., Bebeau, M. J., & Thoma, S. J. (1999). *Postconventional moral thinking: A neo-Kohlbergian approach.* Mahwah, NJ: Erlbaum.

Rivage-Seul, M. K. (1987). Peace education: Moral imagination and the pedagogy of the oppressed. *Harvard Educational Review, 57*(2), 153–169.

Ryff, C. D. (1989). Happiness is everything, or is it? Explorations on the meaning of psychological well-being. *Journal of Personality and Social Psychology, 57*, 1069–1081.

Saroglou, V., Pinchon, I., Trompette, L., Verschueren, M., & Dernelle, R. (2005). Prosocial behavior and religion: New evidence based on projective measure and peer ratings. *Journal for the Scientific Study of Religion, 44*, 323–348.

Serow, R. (1989). Community service, religious commitment, and campus climate. *Youth and Society, 21*(1), 105–119.

Sikula, J., & Sikula, A., Jr. (2005). Spirituality and service learning. *New Directions for Teaching and Learning, 2005*(104), 75–81. doi:10.1002/tl.216

Spears, L. (1996). Reflections on Robert K. Greenleaf and servant-leadership. *Leadership & Organization Development, 17*(7), 33–36. Retrieved from http://www.galegroup.com/

Speck, B. W., & Hoppe, S. L. (Eds.). (2004). *Service-learning: History, theory, and issues.* Westport, CT: Praeger.

Stewart, T. (2009). Community collaboration for underserved schools: A first-year honors service-learning seminar approach. *Journal for Civic Commitment, 13*(1), 1–16.

Stukas, A. A., Jr., Clary, E. G., & Snyder, M. (1999). Service learning: Who benefits and why. *Social Policy Report, 13*(4), 1–19.

Swaminathan, R. (2008). Educating for the "real world": The hidden curriculum of community service-learning. In D. Butin (Ed.), *Service-learning and social justice education: Strengthening justice-oriented community based models of teaching and learning* (pp. 34–43). New York, NY: Routledge.

Tan, A., Ho, V., Ho, E., & Ow, S. (2008). High school students' perceived creativity self-efficacy and emotions in a service learning context. *The International Journal of Creativity & Problem Solving, 18*(2), 115–126.

Tomkovick, C., Lester, S. W., Flunker, L., & Wells, T. A. (2008). Linking collegiate service-learning to future volunteerism: Implications for nonprofit organizations. *Nonprofit Management and Leadership, 19*(1), 3–26. doi:10.1002/nml.202

Vandenberg, B. (1991). Is epistemology enough? An existential consideration of development. *American Psychologist, 46*, 1278–1286.

Walker, T. (2002). Service as a pathway to political participation: What research tells us. *Applied Developmental Science, 6*(4), 183–188.

Warter, E. H., & Grossman, J. M. (2002). An application of developmental-contextualism to service-learning. In A. Furco & S. H. Billig (Eds.), *Service-learning: The essence of the pedagogy* (pp. 83–102). Greenwich, CT: Information Age.

Waterman, A. S. (1993). Two conceptions of happiness: Contrasts of personal expressiveness (eudaimonia) and hedonic enjoyment. *Journal of Personality and Social Psychology, 64*, 678–691.

Yarbrough, D. B., & Wade, R. C. (2002). Using program theory to build and evaluate service-learning programs. In A. Furco & S. H. Billig (Eds.), *Service-learning: The essence of the pedagogy* (pp. 103–123). Greenwich, CT: Information Age.

Yates, M., & Youniss, J. (1996). Community service and political-moral identity in adolescents. *Journal of Research on Adolescence, 6*, 271–284.

Youniss, J., & Yates, M. (1997). *Community service and social responsibility in youth.* Chicago, IL: University of Chicago Press.

FRAMING AND ASSESSING STUDENTS' INTERCULTURAL COMPETENCE IN SERVICE LEARNING

Darla K. Deardorff and Kathleen E. Edwards

Every serious account of the major forces transforming our world today includes the word
globalization. . . . These developments have created a more urgent need than ever before for
Americans to develop intercultural understanding and an ability to live and work productively
and harmoniously with people having very different values, backgrounds, and habits.

—(Bok, 2009, p. ix)

Harvard President Emeritus Derek Bok's words reinforce those of U.S. President Barack Obama who, at the 2009 commencement address at Notre Dame, declared that "our very survival has never required greater cooperation and understanding among all people from all places than at this moment in history" (Obama, 2009). Institutions of higher education are increasingly addressing this urgent need by including such outcomes as intercultural competence (ICC), global citizenship, and intercultural learning in their mission statements, general education programs, and curricular reform efforts (Brewer & Cunningham, 2009; Gacel-Ávila, 2005). Not only is ICC an important outcome in programs that focus on global engagement (e.g., study abroad, foreign languages, international studies), but it is just as necessary in the lives of students who neither learn a foreign language nor travel abroad (Díaz-Martínez & Duncan, 2009; Haeckl & Manwell, 2009; Lewin, 2009). Throughout the academy, there is the recognition that without some degree of ICC, students are ill equipped to contribute to their communities or their professions, either domestically or internationally (Slimbach, 1996); in other words, there is a serious, and dangerous, risk of intercultural *incompetence* if ICC is not intentionally attended to as a curricular learning objective. Furthermore, ICC is a necessary component of global citizenship, which calls on all people to join together in addressing the pressing issues facing our world today, such as poverty, global health, and the environment (Gacel-Ávila, 2005; Lewin, 2009; Plater, 2011).

How, then, can post-secondary institutions help students develop and hone ICC? Regardless of the field or discipline, service learning is especially well suited to contribute significantly to the development of the knowledge, skills, and attitudes that comprise ICC because it provides experiential and reflective opportunities for learning with and about diverse persons that are not easily replicable in classroom settings alone. Service learning typically "involve[s] students in relationships across human differences, e.g., gender, race, age, economic status, national origin, faith, sexual [orientations], and/ or educational attainment" (Slimbach, 1996, p. 102). Such relationships ensure that some exposure to difference will occur; the question becomes: Will that exposure perpetuate unexamined stereotypes or open students to more appropriate and complex views about and interactions with other people and cultures? Answering this question requires recognizing and leveraging the links among research, assessment, and practice within service learning. For example, in order for its potential contribution to students' ICC to be realized, service learning must be designed to include effective and adequate preparation for intercultural interaction, relationship-building opportunities with people from diverse backgrounds, intentional reflection on experiences that is oriented toward intercultural learning, and multidimensional assessment of participants' ICC (Bringle, Hatcher, & Jones, 2011). Inquiry into such processes and their associated outcomes is needed to enhance understanding of when and why service learning experiences can achieve intended ICC learning goals.

This chapter explores research on ICC, within service learning and in other fields, in order to advance understanding of this key outcome within higher education generally and in service learning in particular. It provides a consensus-based definition of ICC and uses a framework built on that definition, as well as contact hypothesis theory, to emphasize relevant considerations to practitioners and researchers who want to assess elements of ICC within service learning courses and programs. The chapter also reviews key studies in order to uncover how and in what forms ICC has been framed and assessed within service learning. It explores strategies and methods for assessing ICC, implications for practice related to integrating assessment of ICC within service learning, and questions that can inform future research.

Theoretical and Conceptual Frameworks

To assess the development of students' ICC in the context of service learning effectively, it is first necessary to define ICC clearly. ICC is often used either interchangeably with or referenced alongside related terminology— *multicultural competence, global citizenship, transnational competence, intercultural communication,* and *cross-cultural skills,* to name a few—but there are slight distinctions among these terms (Deardorff, 2006). Once it is defined precisely, specific measurable outcomes can be developed for a service learning experience or project, and planning can occur to increase the likelihood that such outcomes are indeed achieved (Deardorff, 2006, 2009).

Several questions emerge in attempting to define ICC. First, from whose perspective is ICC being defined and, consequently, what are the goals and specific objectives of ICC development within the service learning context? For example, is ICC seen as a means to the end of a more effective service learning experience in terms of community impact or in terms of the students' civic learning or personal development, or both? Does it set the stage for deeper relationships with community members or a more powerful professional growth opportunity for students? Is the goal of ICC development to enhance global citizenship? Is the goal to deepen students' understanding of their discipline in the context of its international dimensions? Given the disciplinary and professional contexts of service learning, it is important to consider how various fields (e.g., engineering, social work, health care) understand and define ICC. To illustrate: Engineers may refer to *global competence* and emphasize the context of working with international engineering teams, social workers may prefer the term *cultural competence* and focus on the context of relationships with culturally diverse clients, and the presence or absence of ICC in a health care context can even have life-or-death consequences (Anand & Lahiri, 2009; Fong, 2009; Grandin & Hedderich, 2009).

More than 50 years of scholarly work on defining ICC in the United States has produced numerous definitions and models. Work on this concept initially focused on the identification of predictor variables (Ruben, 1976;

Ruben & Kealey, 1979), such as factors and elements that predict an individual's successful intercultural interactions, particularly on overseas assignments. Later scholarly work, especially in the United States, moved beyond examining predictor factors to explore processes related to the acquisition of ICC. For example, Kim (1992) positioned adaptability at the heart of ICC and defined ICC as "the individual's capacity to suspend or modify some of the old cultural ways, and learn and accommodate some of the new cultural ways, and creatively find ways to manage the dynamics of cultural difference/unfamiliarity, intergroup posture, and the accompanying stress" (p. 377). Bennett (1993) developed an oft-cited model of intercultural sensitivity that highlights six developmental stages of an individual's worldview related to cultural difference; the first three stages of this model (denial, defense, and minimization of difference) are considered to be ethnocentric stages, while the latter three (acceptance, adaptation, and integration of difference) are considered to be ethnorelative. Spitzberg and Changnon (2009) provide a comprehensive review of some of the primary definitions of and models for ICC.

An Emerging Framework for Intercultural Competence

Deardorff (2006, 2009) conducted the first research study that documented consensus among leading scholars of ICC within the United States. The consensus-based definition of ICC derived from that study is *effective and appropriate behavior and communication in intercultural situations.* This study categorized the specific, agreed-upon elements of ICC into attitudes, knowledge, skills, international outcomes, and external outcomes, all of which are further elaborated next.

Attitudes

Three key attitudes emerged as part of the consensus documented in the Deardorff (2006, 2009) study: respect, openness, and curiosity/discovery. Respect for others involves demonstrating that they are valued, including through showing interest in them and listening attentively to them. Openness and curiosity/discovery both imply a willingness to risk and to move beyond one's personal comfort zone in interacting with others. All of these key attitudes are foundational to the further development of the knowledge and skills needed for ICC. One way to move individuals toward these requisite attitudes is to challenge their assumptions about their own worldviews and the ways in which they perceive others (Adler, 1991; Barna, 1985; Deardorff, 2008; Ting-Toomey, 1999).

Knowledge

Scholars of ICC in Deardorff's (2006, 2009) study concurred on the following broad categories of knowledge: cultural self-awareness (awareness of the ways in which one's culture has influenced one's identity and worldview); culture-specific knowledge (knowledge relevant to a particular cultural context); deep cultural knowledge (understanding other worldviews); and sociolinguistic awareness (perceptions related to language usage). For the purposes of this discussion, culture is defined as the values, beliefs, and norms held by a group of people that shape how individuals communicate and behave— that is, how they interact with others. Note that here a group does not necessarily refer to a national or an ethnic group. Understanding the world from others' perspectives has significant implications for service learning: How do service learning experiences help participants consider others' perspectives? What needs to be incorporated into service learning courses to ensure that participants are indeed able to recognize, explain, respect, value (or thoughtfully critique) others' perspectives? And in terms of assessment, what would constitute evidence of the extent to which students are able to understand others' perspectives? Perspective taking is especially critical in developing ICC (Tomasello, Kruger, & Ratner, 1993).

Skills

The skills identified in Deardorff's (2006, 2009) study are related to processing knowledge: observing, listening, evaluating, analyzing, interpreting, and relating. These skills align with Bok's (2009) emphasis on the importance of thinking interculturally. Reflection in service learning is essential to the development and assessment of ICC skills because it is the intentional act of reflection that may generate and deepen learning associated with using and refining these skills (Whitney & Clayton, 2011).

Internal Outcomes

The Deardorff (2006, 2009) study documents scholars' view that the attitudes, knowledge, and skills just discussed ideally lead to internal outcomes that include flexibility, adaptability, empathy, and an ethnorelative perspective. Individuals may reach this outcome with varying degrees of success. For example, if individuals enter into service learning situations with some degree of openness or curiosity or respect, or have some acquired knowledge and skills, then they can be somewhat adaptable and flexible; if they have a higher degree of openness, curiosity, and respect, then they can be more adaptable and flexible.

External Outcomes

The summation of the attitudes, knowledge, skills, and internal outcomes is thought to be demonstrated through the visible behavior and communication of the individual, thus the consensus-based definition yielded by the Deardorff (2006, 2009) study: ICC is effective and appropriate behavior and communication in intercultural situations. This definition is predicated on particular requisite attitudes, knowledge, and skills as just presented, and it calls particular attention to the implications of the adjectives *effective* and *appropriate* as descriptors of behavior and communication. Whereas *effectiveness* can be determined by the individual engaging in the behavior or communication, *appropriateness* can be determined only by the other person(s) in the interaction (Spitzberg & Cupach, 1984), who judges whether the individual was communicating and behaving appropriately based on his or her own (i.e., the other's) cultural norms. Appropriateness is directly related to cultural sensitivity and adherence to the cultural norms of the other person(s) with whom the individual is interacting.

Intercultural Competence Model

The relationship among the five elements discussed here can be visualized through the model of ICC expressed in Figure 2.5.1, which provides a framework to guide efforts to develop students' ICC, starting with attitudes, which this study (Deardorff, 2006, 2009) suggests are crucial as a starting point for further ICC development. A student's degree of intercultural competence depends on the degree of acquired attitudes, knowledge/comprehension, and skills. As indicated by the arrow in the top left corner, the framework begins with attitudes; it moves from individual level (attitudes) to interaction level (outcomes). This model can also be used in developing more specific and assessable ICC outcomes, tailored to a specific learning or intercultural context. For example, if perspective taking is a key outcome in a service-learning experience, this can be stated more precisely in the outcomes, with specific criteria provided for evaluating the degree to which the participants engage in perspective taking in that situation. As illustrated by this model, developing ICC is a lifelong process (noted by "Process Orientation"): There is no final stage of development. Further, this process does not occur in a vacuum but, rather, through interactions with and in relation to persons who are from diverse backgrounds. And as further noted by "Process Orientation" in this framework, reflection and mindfulness (Ting-Toomey, 1999) are necessary for individuals to be aware of the process of developing ICC; through

FIGURE 2.5.1
Process Model of Intercultural Competence (Deardorff, 2006, 2009)

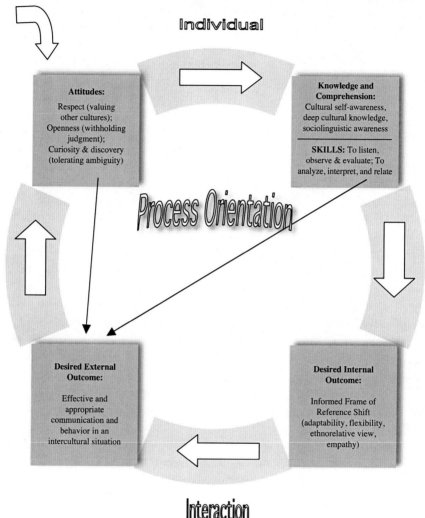

critical reflection, individuals become more self-aware as well as more aware of how they are intentionally developing specific aspects of ICC.

One limitation of this model is that it represents a U.S.-centric perspective because it was created through Deardorff's (2006, 2009) search for consensus among U.S. scholars. Given that a key element of ICC is viewing the world from others' perspectives, it behooves us to explore how those in other cultures define ICC. Arab, African, and Latin American scholars often discuss the importance of relationship building and the ways in which one's very identity is found in relation to others (Medina & Sinnigen, 2009; Nwosu, 2009; Zaharna, 2009). This viewpoint is distinct from the primarily individualistic nature of Western frameworks and definitions of ICC. Ting-Toomey (2009) discusses the dichotomy of individualistic versus collectivist cultures, suggesting that people in more collectivist, or group-oriented, cultures "think of themselves as individuals with interlocking connections with others" (p. 108). Ashwill and Duong (2009), writing from a Vietnamese perspective, note the importance of ICC in providing "the necessary skills to make . . . real, interpersonal connections—to forge deep, mutually beneficial and lasting cross-cultural personal bonds" (p. 156). They discuss American and Vietnamese ideas of ICC, pointing out the interconnectedness of global citizens who "think and feel themselves as part of something much grander and all-inclusive than one culture or nationality" (p. 155). Some non-Western conceptions of ICC emphasize the interconnectedness of political, historical, and social contexts. For example, Medina and Sinnigen (2009), in writing about Latin American perspectives on ICC, raise key questions regarding the role of equity and power in ICC as well as the impact of such historical contexts as colonialism on indigenous cultures. Situating ICC within these various cultural contexts is fundamental to understanding its complexity within service learning courses and also demonstrates various overlaps with characteristics of effective service learning, such as reflection, diversity, collaboration, reciprocity, and community voice (Eyler & Giles, 1999; Mintz & Hesser, 1996), once again illustrating the crucial element of being able to see the world from others' perspectives.

Within service learning contexts, the ICC framework of attitudes, skills, knowledge, internal outcomes, and external outcomes (see Figure 2.5.1) can be useful both in designing the experience and in assessing students' development of ICC, whether in domestic or international settings. ICC per se has most often been assessed in international service learning settings (see Camacho, 2004; Kiely, 2004; Merrill & Pusch, 2007; Urraca, Ledoux, & Harris, 2009; Whitney & Clayton, 2011), whereas in domestic service learning contexts such assessment is referred to differently: diversity assessment (Baldwin, Buchanan, & Rudisill, 2007), assessment of cultural responsiveness (Brown & Howard, 2005), or assessment of multicultural learning (Boyle-Baise, 2002; Paoletti, Segal, & Totino, 2007). Utilizing the structure(s) within ICC theories (e.g., Bennett, 1993; Deardorff, 2006) in both domestic and international service learning settings may help intentionally frame the articulation of learning objectives, project planning, community engagement, and critical reflection. ICC models can help service learning practitioners and researchers identify specific characteristics of ICC that can be assessed in service learning outcomes.

Contact Hypothesis Theory

One additional theoretical perspective that supports effective integration of conceptual models for ICC with service learning is contact hypothesis theory (Allport, 1954). This theory was developed by social psychologists to "examine and evaluate the various conditions under which face-to-face contact would promote greater personal and social understanding between members of different ethnic and racial groups" (Erickson & O'Connor, 2000, p. 63). According to Allport (1954), contact alone is not sufficient to produce such understanding; rather, in order to maximize the impact of contact among individuals from different cultural backgrounds, the following criteria need to be characteristic of an experience:

- Equal status: All groups have what Allport (1954) refers to as "equal status contact" (p. 281) in the relationship.
- Common goals: People work on a problem or task together and share the outcome as a common goal.
- Intergroup cooperation: The task must be structured so that individual members of all groups are interdependent to achieve this common goal.
- Mutual support of authorities, laws, or customs: All groups acknowledge and define social norms that support the contact and interactions among the groups and members, which may mean negotiating and achieving a new way of working together rather than adapting a set of social norms directly connected to one particular group.

This set of characteristics is very important in service learning experiences given that participants need to enter into such experiences with cultural humility and respect, valuing service learning partners and all that they bring to the relationship. Erickson and O'Connor (2000) build on Allport's (1954) criteria, specifically considering contact hypothesis theory's application in service learning. The conclusions of their conceptual analysis, using generalized service learning pedagogies considered best practices, emphasize the importance of incorporating all conditions of contact theory in order to lessen the likelihood of students engaging in ego-defensive strategies that inhibit their development of intercultural attitudes, knowledge, and skills. Therefore, if ICC development is an identified learning outcome, it may be helpful if the service learning course or program is thoughtfully constructed within a framework that supports common goals among faculty, students, and community partners; emphasizes equitable status contact of all engaged in the interactions associated with the community service; or supports students in critically reflecting on the absence or insufficiency of these conditions.

Evaluation of Past Research

A review of some of the literature on assessing ICC in service learning reveals interesting patterns that scholars need to be aware of in designing future research in this area. Overall, most studies have utilized qualitative inquiry methods, especially textual analysis of reflection papers and other assignments as well as field observations at service learning sites. Very few studies have sought indirect information from community partners (Boyle-Baise & Kilbane, 2002) or used previously developed quantitative assessment tools (e.g., the Modern Racism Scale or the Intercultural Development Inventory) (see Fitch, 2004, 2005). Most studies have concentrated on assessing immediate learning outcomes achieved at the end of semester-long courses, whereas longitudinal studies (Kiely, 2004) and studies assessing long-term effects (Merrill & Pusch, 2007) have not been as common. Most research has targeted students who are White, traditional-age, middle-class, and born in the United States, which significantly limits generalizing to other populations; however, it is difficult to overcome this challenge given that, even with multiple efforts to diversify student populations in higher education, most service learning participants are, in fact, White and middle-class (Davi, 2006).

One of the most commonly assessed student populations is pre-service teachers (Baldwin et al., 2007; Boyle-Baise & Kilbane, 2002; Brown & Howard, 2005). The development of ICC is greatly valued and emphasized in teacher candidate programs because the majority of pre-service teachers are "white, monolingual, middle-class, and female" (Baldwin et al., 2007, p. 316), whereas the U.S. K–12 student population is increasingly growing more multilingual and racially, ethnically, and socioeconomically diverse. In a qualitative study, Boyle-Baise and Kilbane (2002) identified specific intercultural learning outcomes for K–12 pre-service teachers, including "building cross-group relations, disrupting stereotypes, gaining awareness of community resources and problems, and learning to work positively with diverse youth" (p. 57). They evaluated student attainment of these outcomes, in terms of both appropriateness (i.e., behavior received as respectful, given the cultural context) and effectiveness (i.e., the goal or outcome accomplished), through focus groups, interviews with community partners, and analysis of student reflection products. Whereas students reported growth in some interpersonal areas, broader understanding of community resources and problems—a key indicator of ICC—was weak among students in the teacher education curriculum. The investigators concluded that the implementation of service learning needs to be reconfigured in order for the goals of ICC development to be fully realized within the pedagogy. In other words, assessing ICC in service learning involves more than just developing methods for that assessment. In some cases it also requires redesign of particular elements of projects, experiences, or courses; this could include building stronger relationships with community partners and altering curriculum to include material beyond course content.

Utilizing reflection questions and interviews, Sallee and Harris (2007) examined aspects of ICC among East Asian international students enrolled in a service learning education course in the United States. Their research identified as particularly important these elements of service learning practices: faculty familiarity with students' cultural backgrounds, student preparation for the differences that they may encounter between cultures, and clear establishment of guidelines with community partners and students before the service begins (pp. 57–58).

As Fitch (2005) acknowledged, more research is needed to document the development of ICC among students in service learning courses. However, current findings are promising. Service learning can promote intercultural learning (Berry, 1990), it can lead students to identify and challenge their own preconceived ideas about community members with whom they are engaging (Baldwin et al., 2007), and intentional intercultural contact through service learning can lead students to adapt their behavior in different cultures (Fitch, 2005). ICC research outside the field of service learning, particularly in study abroad, also yields similar findings, such as that individuals can move from a place of ethnocentrism to being more culturally sensitive (Bennett, 1993) and can develop more openness to cultural diversity (Clarke, Flaherty, Wright, & McMillen, 2009). These findings documenting the development of ICC through study abroad reinforce the importance of adequate preparation, reflection, and intervention strategies during the experience as well as sufficient debriefing after the experience (Bringle et al., 2011; Lou & Bosley, 2008; Paige, 1993; Vande Berg, 2007).

In sum, an examination of assessment and research focused on ICC within the service learning community identifies promising trends. At the same time, it reveals numerous limitations, including lack of (a) specificity in defining outcomes related to ICC, (b) diversity within the student populations being assessed, (c) clear reasons for conducting assessment, (d) use of assessment data to provide guidance to students, (e) substantive and intentional interventions for achieving ICC outcomes in service learning, (f) use of multiple measures to assess this complex construct, (g) intercultural assessment within domestic settings, and (h) longitudinal studies to understand the long-term impact of service learning experiences on the development of ICC. These identified gaps of assessing ICC within service learning are similar to the gaps identified in assessing ICC in general (Deardorff, 2009). For example, definitions of ICC may be limited to only a few aspects of intercultural learning without consideration of the full range of elements that comprise it or selection of particular elements on which to focus. Sometimes definitions may not be used at all, and, if they are, they are often derived without consulting the nearly five decades of scholarly work on this concept in the United States or considering multiple cultural perspectives on the construct.

Methods and Measurements

Research has shown that although it is possible to assess students' ICC, such assessment is complex because of the nature of ICC (Deardorff, 2009). Recall the broad definition of ICC discussed earlier in this chapter: effective and appropriate behavior and communication in intercultural situations. Given that the emphasis on appropriate and effective attitudes, knowledge, and skills in ICC requires accessing not only self-perspective but also others' perspectives of the individual's degree of competence, a "multi-method and multi-perspective . . . approach must be used to adequately assess intercultural competence" (Deardorff, 2009, p. 483).

Based on our review of the service learning literature, student self-report is a common assessment tool that is rarely paired with data from other methods or perspectives. Although this approach is potentially useful for assessing effectiveness from the student's point of view, it is not able to assess appropriateness given that appropriateness can be assessed only by others. To overcome the associated limitations (e.g., biased and insufficient data), research on ICC should utilize a multiperspective approach that solicits evidence from both students and people with whom they interact. Additionally, the evidence will be stronger if some of it is demonstrated (e.g., via observation of student performance or problem-solving interviews) rather than reported (e.g., via responses to survey or interview questions that evoke statements regarding the extent to which learning has occurred).

Design issues to consider when conducting quantitative ICC assessment and research include adequate sample size, sufficiently designed intervention studies, rigorous research design including the use of a control group, and use of longitudinal studies. Van de Vijver and Leung (2009) also highlight causality and validity as two research design issues to address when conducting such studies.

Education abroad is one sector within higher education that has greatly expanded both assessment of and research on ICC development in recent years. The number of research studies in education abroad exceeds 500 (Bolen, 2007), with many of those focused on ICC learning outcomes within the study abroad experience. More than 100 tools have been developed in various fields to measure specific attitudes, skills, and knowledge of ICC; these tools vary in their reliability and validity (Fantini, 2009; Paige, 2004; Stuart, 2008). Suggested strategies and tools from education abroad include the use of a multimethod approach, which involves collecting both direct and indirect evidence of the extent to which specific intercultural outcomes have been achieved. Depending on how they are designed, indirect measures may include self-assessment instruments, interviews, and focus groups; direct measures may include e-portfolios, observations (e.g., by instructors, host family members, community members), and performance reviews (Kiely, 2011; Kiely & Hartman, 2011).

A specific measurement approach within service learning is student reflection, which can be used alone or in combination with other approaches (i.e., reflection is usually part of the e-portfolio approach) to measure ICC, given that reflection is fundamental to ICC development and to learning more generally in service learning. Well-designed reflection can serve as the key component of the pedagogy for producing many of the learning outcomes identified for the service learning experience as well as for providing data for assessment (Whitney & Clayton, 2011). The emphasis here is on *well-designed* reflection in order to gather high-quality data as well as to provide a meaningful process through which participants have a greater opportunity to achieve the articulated ICC learning outcomes. As Whitney and Clayton (2011) state, "Conducting meaningful research on and through reflection . . . requires thoughtful, intentional design" (p. 149); therefore, it is important to establish strong reflection elements before considering how to utilize reflection for the purpose of assessment. Without strong design of the reflection process, the quality of data collected will be less helpful for assessment purposes.

Well-designed reflection goes beyond journal writing (although that may be an aspect of it); it is an "intentional, structured, and directed process that facilitates exploration for deeper, contextualized meaning linked to learning outcomes" (Rice & Pollack, 2000, p. 124). Through effective reflection, students can engage in an examination of their personal opinions, attitudes, perspectives, and positionalities; explore their relations to community members, their service site, and the activities in which they are engaged; and connect their day-to-day interactions with individuals to broader social and cultural issues (O'Grady, 2000; Rice & Pollack, 2000). Such reflection can provide a rich source of data for research on students' ICC development within service learning and can help inform a rigorous research design.

A challenge of some ICC assessment tools (e.g., commercial assessment instruments; see Fantini, 2009 and Stuart, 2008 for further discussion of such instruments) is that they may not measure the aspects of ICC articulated in any particular assessment plan; it is important that the assessment tools align with the specific outcomes of the particular assessment plan (Deardorff, 2009; see also chapter 2.2). For example, a specific outcome in a service learning assessment plan could be as follows: Students will be able to describe two major challenges encountered by the service learning partner from the partner's perspective. This outcome illustrates perspective taking. Evidence of the extent to which this outcome has been achieved could be documented through a student's writing assignment, a video documentary produced by the student, or a visual collage, which would then be graded by a well-developed rubric, including verification by the partner's feedback on the student's work. The student's work, along with the feedback from the partner and the rubric, could be placed in the student's e-portfolio.

Regardless of which particular tools and measures are used, the following recommendations can inform assessment practices:

- Articulate specific, measurable intercultural learning outcomes based on course goals and defined terms (i.e., which specific elements of ICC are being assessed?).

- Ensure that specific outcomes and tools are aligned; with more than 100 assessment tools that measure varying elements of ICC, knowing learning outcomes can be key in identifying appropriate tools (i.e., tools that measure those outcomes specifically).
- Utilize a multimeasure (including both direct and indirect measures), multiperspective approach in assessing ICC and make sure that this approach is integrated throughout the service learning course (i.e., not just as a pre- and post-assessment).
- Collect only evidence that will be utilized (e.g., for student feedback, for program improvement) and make sure that there is a plan in place for using the data collected.
- Ensure that intentional interventions are in place to help students achieve intercultural learning outcomes.
- Review the entire set of interventions and the assessment process for ways to improve them in the future.

Table 2.5.1 provides a set of questions that summarizes some of the discussion thus far and can help guide ICC research and assessment. Although some of the questions are applicable to assessment in general (i.e., questions 3–7, 15, and 16), others are specific to the assessment of ICC (i.e., questions 1 and 2, 8–14) and need to be taken under special consideration. Responses to these questions can help tailor assessment and research to specific programs or courses.

Implications for Practice

The ICC framework and contact hypothesis theory as well as our review of research and methods reveal the complexity of fostering the development of ICC. Within the research literature there are helpful recommendations for future researchers and practitioners creating service learning projects that include a focus on the development of ICC. The following eight recommendations and subsequent discussion of two particular arenas of practice implications (critical reflection and preparation) provide support for incorporating and assessing learning outcomes related to ICC within service learning.

1. Clearly articulate the reasons for engaging in assessment of ICC within service learning. Possible reasons include understanding how the development of ICC contributes to other areas of students' academic, civic,

TABLE 2.5.1
Assessment Guide for Intercultural Competence

Based on the research and findings from "The Identification and Assessment of Intercultural Competence as a Student Outcome of Internationalization at Institutions of Higher Education in the United States" (Deardorff, 2004), the following questions can be utilized in designing an approach to assessing ICC:

1. Has ICC been defined utilizing existing definitions in the literature?
2. From whose perspective is ICC being assessed? What are the cultural biases of the evaluator(s)?
3. Who is the locus of the evaluation?
4. What is the context of the ICC assessment?
5. What is the purpose of the ICC assessment?
6. How will the assessment results be used? Who will benefit from the assessment?
7. What is the time frame of the assessment (e.g., one point, ongoing)? In other words, is the assessment formative and not summative?
8. What is the level of abstraction, or, in other words, will the assessment be more general or will it assess more specific components of ICC?
9. Do the assessment methods match the working definition and stated objectives of ICC?
10. Have specific indicators been developed for the ICC assessment?
11. Is more than one method being used to assess ICC? If so, do the methods involve more than one evaluator's perspective?
12. Are the degrees of ICC being assessed? What is to be done with those not meeting the minimal level of ICC?
13. Does the assessment account for multiple competencies and multiple cultural identities?
14. Has the impact of situational, social, and historical contexts been analyzed in the assessment of ICC?
15. How do the assessment methods impact the measurement outcomes? Have the limits of the instruments/measures been accounted for?
16. Have student/participant goals been considered when assessing ICC?

and personal learning (e.g., understanding and counteracting racism) and reinforcing commitment to community partnerships in order to more successfully work toward reciprocity, mutuality, and knowledge co-generation.

2. Articulate specific ICC learning objectives (e.g., identify and interrogate false assumptions of persons of different cultures; engage with ideas, habits, and values from different perspectives; evaluate material conditions that contribute to diverse identities; identify resources and assets of different

cultures; locate social conditions within communities that influence individuals' lived experiences; develop skills to effectively and appropriately work and collaborate across cultures) within any service learning experience. Clear outcomes will guide the design of appropriate learning interventions as well as assessment procedures.

3. Explore how multiple perspectives can be incorporated into service learning experiences, courses, and programs. This could include shifting course meetings to community spaces when possible; facilitating group reflection so that students can hear each other's experiences; inviting community members to join in these reflection activities; and requesting feedback from community members and organizations about the attitudes, knowledge, and skills related to the desired ICC learning outcomes (the method for accessing this feedback should reflect the cultural norms of the community).

4. Design service learning with careful attention to variables that provide desired positive intercultural learning or active contradiction of stereotypes, including quality of contact, length of contact, and incorporation of preparation and reflection (Fitch, 2005), as well as criteria discussed in Allport's (1954) contact hypothesis theory (i.e., equal status; common goals; intergroup cooperation; and mutual support of authorities, laws, or customs). Intentional incorporation of these criteria is what distinguishes between exposure and engagement for students within service learning. Exposure is what most students will gain simply from the act of participating in service learning; however, engagement requires reflection, information about communities and about underlying causes of inequities, continual dialogue between students and community members, and ongoing feedback from instructors to students regarding their learning and their participation in projects (Erickson & O'Connor, 2000).

5. Intentionally develop community partnerships to support robust intercultural learning opportunities. Cruz and Giles (2000) acknowledge that voices of the community are rarely represented in service learning research. However, many community organizations are deeply aware of and committed to creating environments in which diversity is valued (Lin, Schmidt, Tryon, & Stoecker, 2009). Developing deeper relationships with community partners, including designating community partners as co-teachers in the classroom and collaborating with community partners in construction of field-based tasks (Boyle-Baise & Kilbane, 2002), can enhance assessment of students' intercultural development because of the capacity to

gain more perspectives. This may be helpful in intercultural preparation of students as well.

6. Develop an integrated, multimethod, multiperspective longitudinal assessment approach—not just pre- and post-assessment—and plan for measuring participants' ICC development. Such an approach provides for richer data and a more holistic picture that can be used to identify turning points and critical experiences that reveal students' progression of development for the ICC learning outcomes.

7. Use the assessment process to provide feedback to students as they move through the service learning course. Contact hypothesis theory maintains that for reduction of stereotypes and positive attitude changes to occur, the social norms of the privileged community (i.e., ethnocentric norms) must be challenged (Erickson & O'Connor, 2000). In the case of service learning, that community may be reflected in the classroom, and the ongoing feedback that instructors provide through integrated and longitudinal assessment approaches can deepen the critical reflection necessary to disrupt social norms that perpetuate stereotypes of different cultural identities and practices.

8. Undertake professional development to build capacity for cultivating and investigating ICC through service learning. Faculty articulation of specific ICC learning outcomes can be challenging if faculty themselves do not possess a strong foundation in intercultural theories and knowledge of ICC models, including ways to incorporate these outcomes into their curricula and ways to guide students through the process of developing ICC. Researchers' familiarity with intercultural theories provides an important foundation in establishing assessment strategies (Merrill & Pusch, 2007).

Critical Reflection

There are numerous reasons why critical reflection should be incorporated as a central component of service learning and intercultural learning as well as utilized in the assessment process itself. Perpetuating stereotypes, cultural misunderstandings, reinforcement of ethnocentrism, and inadequate consideration of the multiple and intersecting dynamics that construct individual positionalities within cultural contexts are all potential undesired outcomes of service learning. Critical reflection can help both to prevent these outcomes and to identify them in order to address and work through them (Ash & Clayton, 2009; Jones, Gilbride-Brown, & Gasiorski, 2005; Whitney & Clayton, 2011). Whitney and Clayton (2011) identify specific variables that can create challenges for reflection in international service learning contexts—distance, proximity, intensity, structure, culture, comfort zone, technology, language, and entry/exit—and highlight reflection opportunities within these challenging variables (pp. 163–165). Additionally, they offer guidance for establishing both a reflection strategy (e.g., Who will be involved in designing, participating in, and offering feedback on the reflection exercises? How do the reflection exercises support the learning outcomes? How will learning be assessed via the reflection exercises?) and reflection mechanisms that comprise that strategy (e.g., journaling, group processing, problem-solving narratives, integrated writing assignments, visual and embodied portrayals of experiences).

Preparation

Intentionally incorporating adequate intercultural preparation for students, faculty, and community members prior to the service learning experience is key to tapping its potential to generate ICC (Fitch, 2004). This preparation should address issues such as underlying cultural values, communication styles, and historical/social/political contexts with an emphasis on how these contexts are related to actual interactions and behaviors (Deardorff, 2009). Fitch (2004) and Deardorff (2009) recommend intentional preparation and interspersed reflection on specifically articulated intercultural topics in any intercultural community engagement. Intentional preparation may include readings, assignments, experiences, activities, dialogues, and lectures related to intercultural learning, guided by the stated intercultural learning objectives. In the preparation phase, it is important to address the more complex aspects of culture; in other words, instructors need to go beyond discussion of language, food, and music and help students understand the importance of exploring underlying cultural values, communication styles, worldviews, and cultural/historical/social/political/economic contexts, as well as the extent to which those underlying invisible elements influence the situations that students may encounter in service learning experiences. Specific to service learning, challenging privileged stereotypes before, during, and after community engagement is necessary for more thorough and deep reflection on both individual and systemic issues of power.

Future Research Agenda

The findings in previous research on ICC in service learning help inform the most important questions to ask in future research. Some of these questions are focused on assessing specific student learning outcomes related to the attitudes, knowledge, and skills elemental to ICC, whereas others relate broadly to the role of ICC in service learning (including partnership development and course design) and the learning of various persons engaged in the process (including faculty and community members as well as students).

In considering future research on ICC-related outcomes of service learning, researchers can think about and explore the following questions as catalysts:

- How can components of service learning courses and programs—including conytent, community-based experience, and critical reflection—best be designed to help students "interrogate issues of power, racism, oppression, or social injustice" (O'Grady, 2000, p. 14)? What are the conditions under which this interrogation is most supported (e.g., length of time, type of engagement, reflection strategy and mechanisms, integrated involvement of community partners)?
- How do the cultural, ideological, and disciplinary perspectives held by the individuals who design, implement, and assess the ICC learning outcomes of service learning influence the ways that they conceptualize ICC learning outcomes and approach service learning design, including partnership development?
- What are the service learning design, implementation, and assessment implications of using contact hypothesis theory's characteristic of "equal status contact" in contexts and cultures where equal status may be viewed differently (i.e., is constructed differently owing to cultural conditioning)? Constructs that should be considered include power, distance, and hierarchy as underlying cultural concepts, including intercultural situations in which "equal status" may not be desired.
- What are the long-term results of ICC development in service learning? Exploring this question requires engaging in longitudinal studies that examine students' lifestyle choices, degree of civic engagement, and so on (see Paige, Fry, Stallman, Josic, & Jon, 2009, as an example of how to set up such a longitudinal study). Lifestyle choices could include practices around voluntary service, philanthropic practices, diversity of friends and colleagues, and the choices to live simply and to buy fair trade when possible.
- To what extent does prior significant intercultural or international experience influence service learning participants' ICC development and intercultural interactions? For example, what is the influence of

service learning on students' ICC development if they were not raised
in the United States (i.e., if they are refugees or immigrants or are
international students studying in the United States)? If they study
abroad? If they work with immigrant groups domestically? If they
have multiple experiences rather than only one?

- What are the optimal conditions and criteria (e.g., variables include
  length of encounter, amount of quality contact, approach to development and maintenance of relationships) for a service learning experience that most fully develops students' ICC?
- How does adequate intercultural preparation (or lack thereof) influence students' relationships with others within the service learning context? Furthermore, what constitutes adequate intercultural
  preparation?
- What are the results of intercultural *incompetence* in the service learning context? For example, what are the short- and long-term consequences within a community if students behave in interculturally
  incompetent ways during their service learning experience?
- How would ICC outcomes be expressed if they were conceptualized
  using relational rather than individualistic orientations? What are the
  similarities and differences between these two orientations? How
  might the design and implementation of service learning differ
  between these two orientations?
- Under what conditions can service learning participants transcend
  key identity issues, moving beyond in/out group dichotomies to
  embrace and respect others' differences as well as commonalities?
- What are the opportunities for and barriers to intra-institutional (i.e.,
  interdepartmental, multiunit, cross-program) collaboration, articulation, and assessment of ICC? Is there value added to an integrated
  approach relative to isolated implementation?

Conclusion

All behavior is influenced by culture. Including an emphasis on the development of ICC in service learning courses, programs, assessment, and research
is, therefore, both readily done and imperative. Students cannot help but
have ICC-related encounters, but the quality of their learning is contingent
on a range of factors that are not yet fully understood. This chapter has
discussed some of the key literature, frameworks, and studies that can inform

scholars and practitioners in moving this work forward within the service learning context. Given that ICC has different meanings in various professional and academic fields, it is incumbent upon researchers to consider how to attract scholars from a wide variety of disciplines to collaborate on this research within service learning. Research on the intercultural aspects of service learning will further enhance understanding of student development processes more generally. Furthermore, service learning's best practices—collaboration, mutuality and reciprocity, critical reflection, attention to community interests—may provide a robust context within which ICC can be further developed and investigated. Such research on ICC can enhance understanding of how humans relate to one another. This last point may be the most important lesson of all, given the challenges that the human race must confront in the twenty-first century. Service learning, and hence intercultural learning, can provide one avenue for learning to live together in today's world.

Recommended Reading

Deardorff, D. K. (Ed.). (2009). *The SAGE handbook of intercultural competence.* Thousand Oaks, CA: SAGE.

Merrill, M., & Pusch, M. (2007). Apples, oranges, and kumys: Models for research on students doing intercultural service learning. In S. B. Gelmon & S. H. Billig (Eds.), *From passion to objectivity: International and cross-disciplinary perspectives on service learning research* (pp. 21–40). Greenwich, CT: Information Age.

O'Grady, C. (2000). *Integrating service learning and multicultural education in colleges and universities.* Mahwah, NJ: Erlbaum.

Slimbach, R. (1996). Connecting head, heart, and hands: Developing intercultural service competence. In R. Sigmon (Ed.), *Journey to service-learning: Experiences from independent liberal arts colleges and universities* (pp. 99–111). Washington, DC: Council of Independent Colleges.

Whitney, B. C., & Clayton, P. H. (2011). Research on and through reflection in international service learning. In R. G. Bringle, J. A. Hatcher, & S. G. Jones (Eds.), *International service learning: Conceptual frameworks and research* (pp. 145–187). Sterling, VA: Stylus.

References

Adler, N. J. (1991). *International dimensions of organizational behavior* (2nd ed.). Boston, MA: PWS-KENT.

Allport, G. (1954). *The nature of prejudice.* Cambridge, MA: Addison-Wesley.

Anand, R., & Lahiri, I. (2009). Developing skills for interculturally competent care. In D. K. Deardorff (Ed.), *The SAGE handbook of intercultural competence* (pp. 387–402). Thousand Oaks, CA: SAGE.

Ash, S. L., & Clayton, P. H. (2009). Generating, deepening, and documenting learning: The power of critical reflection in applied learning. *Journal of Applied Learning in Higher Education, 1*(1), 25–48.

Ashwill, M. A., & Duong, T. H. (2009). Developing globally competent citizens: The contrasting cases of the United States and Vietnam. In D. K. Deardorff (Ed.), *The SAGE handbook of intercultural competence* (pp. 141–157). Thousand Oaks, CA: SAGE.

Baldwin, S., Buchanan, A., & Rudisill, M. (2007). What teacher candidates learned about diversity, social justice, and themselves from service-learning experiences. *Journal of Teacher Education, 58*, 315–327.

Barna, L. (1985). Stumbling blocks in intercultural communication. In L. Samovar & R. Porter (Eds.), *Intercultural communication: A reader* (4th ed., pp. 345–352). Belmont, CA: Wadsworth.

Bennett, M. J. (1993). Toward ethnorelativism: A development model of intercultural sensitivity. In R. M. Paige (Ed.), *Education for the intercultural experience* (pp. 109–135). Yarmouth, ME: Intercultural Press.

Berry, H. A. (1990). Service-learning in international and intercultural settings. In J. Kendall (Ed.), *Combining service and learning: A resource book for community and public service* (Vol. I, pp. 311–313). Raleigh, NC: National Society for Internships and Experiential Education.

Bok, D. (2009). Foreword. In D. Deardorff (Ed.), *The SAGE handbook of intercultural competence* (pp. ix–xx). Thousand Oaks, CA: SAGE.

Bolen, M. C. (Ed.). (2007). *A guide to outcomes assessment in education abroad.* Carlisle, PA: Forum on Education Abroad.

Boyle-Baise, M. (Ed.). (2002). *Multicultural service learning: Educating teachers in diverse communities.* New York, NY: Teachers College Press.

Boyle-Baise, M., & Kilbane, J. (2002). What really happens? A look inside multicultural service learning. In M. Boyle-Baise (Ed.), *Multicultural service learning: Educating teachers in diverse communities* (pp. 55–73). New York, NY: Teachers College Press.

Brewer, E., & Cunningham, A. (Eds.). (2009). *Integrating study abroad into the curriculum: Theory and practice across the disciplines.* Sterling, VA: Stylus.

Bringle, R. G., Hatcher, J. A., & Jones, S. G. (Eds.). (2011). *International service learning: Conceptual frameworks and research.* Sterling, VA: Stylus.

Brown, E., & Howard, B. (2005). Becoming culturally responsive teachers through service-learning: A case study of five novice classroom teachers. *Multicultural Education, 12*(4), 2–8.

Camacho, M. (2004). Power and privilege: Community service learning in Tijuana. *Michigan Journal of Community Service Learning, 10*, 31–42.

Clarke, I., III, Flaherty, T. B., Wright, N. D., & McMillen, R. M. (2009). Student intercultural proficiency from study abroad programs. *Journal of Marketing Education, 31,* 173–181.

Cruz, N., & Giles, D. E., Jr. (2000). Where's the community in service-learning research? [Special issue]? *Michigan Journal of Community Service Learning, Fall,* 28–34.

Davi, A. (2006). In the service of writing and race. *Journal of Basic Writing, 25*(1), 73–95.

Deardorff, D. K. (2004). Internationalization: In search of intercultural competence. *International Educator, 8*(2), 13–15.

Deardorff, D. K. (2006). Identification and assessment of intercultural competence as a student outcome of internationalization. *Journal of Studies in International Education, 10,* 241–266.

Deardorff, D. K. (2008). Intercultural competence: A definition, model and implications for education abroad. In V. Savicki (Ed.), *Developing intercultural competence and transformation: Theory, research, and application in international education* (pp. 32–52). Sterling, VA: Stylus.

Deardorff, D. K. (Ed.). (2009). *The SAGE handbook of intercultural competence.* Thousand Oaks, CA: SAGE.

Díaz-Martínez, A. M., & Duncan, L. A. (2009). Beyond the classroom: An experiential model for developing multicultural competence. In R. Gurung & L. Prieto (Eds.), *Getting culture: Incorporating diversity across the curriculum* (pp. 341–350). Sterling, VA: Stylus.

Erickson, J., & O'Connor, S. (2000). Service-learning: Does it promote or reduce prejudice? In C. O'Grady (Ed.), *Integrating service learning and multicultural education in colleges and universities* (pp. 59–70). Mahwah, NJ: Erlbaum.

Eyler, J. S., & Giles, D. E., Jr. (1999). *Where's the learning in service-learning?* San Francisco, CA: Jossey-Bass.

Fantini, A. (2009). Assessing intercultural competence: Issues and tools. In D. K. Deardorff (Ed.), *The SAGE handbook of intercultural competence* (pp. 456–476). Thousand Oaks, CA: SAGE.

Fitch, P. (2004). Effects of intercultural service-learning experiences on intellectual development and intercultural awareness. In S. H. Billig & M. Welch (Eds.), *New perspectives in service-learning: Research to advance the field* (pp. 107–126). Greenwich, CT: Information Age.

Fitch, P. (2005). In their own voices: A mixed methods approach to studying outcomes of intercultural service-learning with college students. In S. Root, J. Callahan, & S. H. Billig (Eds.), *Improving service-learning practice: Research on models to enhance impacts* (pp. 187–211). Greenwich, CT: Information Age.

Fong, R. (2009). Culturally competent practice in social work. In D. K. Deardorff (Ed.), *The SAGE handbook of intercultural competence* (pp. 350–361). Thousand Oaks, CA: SAGE.

Gacel-Ávila, J. (2005). The internationalisation of higher education: A paradigm for global citizenry. *Journal of Studies in International Education, 9*(2), 121–136.

Grandin, J., & Hederich, N. (2009). Global competence for engineers. In D. K. Deardorff (Ed.), *The SAGE handbook of intercultural competence* (pp. 362–373). Thousand Oaks, CA: SAGE.

Haeckl, A. E., & Manwell, E. A. (2009). Cool cities: Kalamazoo and Carthage—the intersection of service-learning and intercultural learning. In E. Brewer & K. Cunningham (Eds.), *Integrating study abroad into the curriculum: Theory and practice across the disciplines* (pp. 121–136). Sterling, VA: Stylus.

Jones, S. R., Gilbride-Brown, J., & Gasiorski, A. (2005). Getting inside the "underside" of service-learning: Student resistance and possibilities. In D. Butin (Ed.), *Service-learning in higher education* (pp. 3–24). New York, NY: Palgrave Macmillan.

Kiely, R. (2004). A chameleon with a complex: Searching for transformation in international service-learning. *Michigan Journal of Community Service Learning, 10*(2), 5–20.

Kiely, R. (2011). What international service learning research can learn from research on international learning. In R. G. Bringle, J. A. Hatcher, & S. G. Jones (Eds.), *International service learning: Conceptual frameworks and research* (pp. 243–274). Sterling, VA: Stylus.

Kiely, R., & Hartman, E. (2011). Qualitative research methodology and international service learning: Concepts, characteristics, methods, approaches, and best practices. In R. G. Bringle, J. A. Hatcher, & S. G. Jones (Eds.), *International service learning: Conceptual frameworks and research* (pp. 291–318). Sterling, VA: Stylus.

Kim, Y. (1992). Intercultural communication competence: A systems-theoretic view. In W. Gudykunst & Y. Kim (Eds.), *Readings on communicating with strangers: An approach to intercultural communication* (pp. 371–381). New York, NY: McGraw-Hill.

Lewin, R. (2009). *The handbook of practice and research in study abroad: Higher education and the quest for global citizenship.* New York, NY: Routledge.

Lin, C., Schmidt, C., Tryon, E. A., & Stoecker, R. (2009). Service learning in context: The challenge of diversity. In R. Stoecker & E. A. Tryon, (Eds.), *The unheard voices: Community organizations and service learning* (pp. 116–135). Philadelphia, PA: Temple University Press.

Lou, K., & Bosley, G. (2008). Dynamics of cultural contexts: Meta-level intervention in the study abroad experience. In V. Savicki (Ed.), *Developing intercultural competence and transformation: Theory, research, and application in international education* (pp. 276–296). Sterling, VA: Stylus.

Medina, A., & Sinnigen, J. (2009). Interculturality versus intercultural competence in Latin America. In D. K. Deardorff (Ed.), *The SAGE handbook of intercultural competence* (pp. 249–263). Thousand Oaks, CA: SAGE.

Merrill, M., & Pusch, M. (2007). Apples, oranges, and kumys: Models for research on students doing intercultural service learning. In S. B. Gelmon & S. H. Billig (Eds.), *From passion to objectivity: International and cross-disciplinary perspectives on service learning research* (pp. 21–40). Greenwich, CT: Information Age.

Mintz, S., & Hesser, G. (1996). Principles of good service learning. In B. Jacoby (Eds.), *Service-learning in higher education: Concepts and practices* (pp. 26–52). San Francisco, CA: Jossey-Bass.

Nwosu, P. O. (2009). Understanding Africans' conceptualizations of intercultural competence. In D. K. Deardorff (Ed.), *The SAGE handbook of intercultural competence* (pp. 158–178). Thousand Oaks, CA: SAGE.

Obama, B. (2009). *Remarks by the President in commencement address at the University of Notre Dame.* Retrieved from http://www.whitehouse.gov/the_press_office/ Remarks-by-the-President-at-Notre-Dame-Commencement/

O'Grady, C. (2000). Integrating service learning and multicultural education: An overview. In C. O'Grady (Ed.), *Integrating service learning and multicultural education in colleges and universities* (pp. 1–19). Mahwah, NJ: Erlbaum.

Paige, R. M. (Ed.). (1993). *Education for the intercultural experience.* Yarmouth, ME: Intercultural Press.

Paige, R. M. (2004). Instrumentation in intercultural training. In D. Landis, J. M. Bennett, & M. J. Bennett (Eds.), *Handbook of intercultural training* (3rd ed., pp. 85–128). Thousand Oaks, CA: SAGE.

Paige, R. M., Fry, G. W., Stallman, E. M., Josic, J., & Jon, J. (2009). Study abroad for global engagement: The long-term impact of mobility experiences. *Intercultural Education, 20*(S1–S2), 29–44.

Paoletti, J. B., Segal, E., & Totino, C. (2007). Acts of diversity: Assessing the impact of service-learning. *New Directions for Teaching and Learning, 2007*(111), 47–54. doi:10.1002/tl.285

Plater, W. M. (2011). The context for international service learning: An invisible revolution is underway. In R. G. Bringle, J. A. Hatcher, & S. G. Jones (Eds.), *International service learning: Conceptual frameworks and research* (pp. 29–56). Sterling, VA: Stylus.

Rice, K., & Pollack, S. (2000). Developing a critical pedagogy of service learning: Preparing self-reflective, culturally aware, and responsive community participants. In C. O'Grady (Ed.), *Integrating service learning and multicultural education in colleges and universities* (pp. 115–134). Mahwah, NJ: Erlbaum.

Ruben, B. D. (1976). Assessing communication competency for intercultural competency for intercultural adaptation. *Group & Organizational Studies, 1,* 334–354.

Ruben, B. D., & Kealey, D. J. (1979). Behavioral assessment of communication competency and the prediction of cross-cultural adaptation. *International Journal of Intercultural Relations, 3*(1), 15–47.

Sallee, M. W., & Harris, S. C. (2007). An Eastern perspective on Western education: The experiences of international students engaged in service-learning. In

S. B. Gelmon & S. H. Billig (Eds.), *From passion to objectivity: International and cross-disciplinary perspectives on service learning research* (pp. 41–62). Greenwich, CT: Information Age.

Slimbach, R. (1996). Connecting head, heart, and hands: Developing intercultural service competence. In R. Sigmon (Ed.), *Journey to service-learning: Experiences from independent liberal arts colleges and universities* (pp. 99–111). Washington, DC: Council of Independent Colleges.

Spitzberg, B. H., & Changnon, G. (2009). Conceptualizing intercultural competence. In D. K. Deardorff (Ed.), *The SAGE handbook of intercultural competence* (pp. 2–52). Thousand Oaks, CA: SAGE.

Spitzberg, B. H., & Cupach, W. R. (1984). *Interpersonal communication competence.* Beverly Hills, CA: SAGE.

Stuart, D. (2008). Assessment instruments for the global workforce. In M. Moodian (Ed.), *Contemporary leadership and intercultural competence* (pp. 175–190). Thousand Oaks, CA: SAGE.

Ting-Toomey, S. (1999). *Communicating across cultures.* New York, NY: Guilford Press.

Ting-Toomey, S. (2009). Intercultural conflict competence as a facet of intercultural competence development: Multiple conceptual approaches. In D. K. Deardorff (Ed.), *The SAGE handbook of intercultural competence* (pp. 100–120). Thousand Oaks, CA: SAGE.

Tomasello, M., Kruger, A., & Ratner, H. (1993). Cultural learning. *Behavioral and Brain Sciences, 16,* 495–511.

Urraca, B., Ledoux, M., & Harris, J. (2009). Beyond the comfort zone: Lessons of intercultural service. *Clearing House, 82*(6), 281–289.

Vande Berg, M. (2007). Intervening in the learning of U.S. students abroad. *Journal of Studies in International Education, 11,* 392–399.

Van de Vijver, F. J. R., & Leung, K. (2009). Methodological issues in researching intercultural competence. In D. K. Deardorff (Ed.), *The SAGE handbook of intercultural competence* (pp. 404–418). Thousand Oaks, CA: SAGE.

Whitney, B. C., & Clayton, P. H. (2011). Research on and through reflection in international service learning. In R. G. Bringle, J. A. Hatcher, & S. G. Jones (Eds.), *International service learning: Conceptual frameworks and research* (pp. 145–187). Sterling, VA: Stylus.

Zaharna, R. S. (2009). An associative approach to intercultural communication competence in the Arab world. In D. K. Deardorff (Ed.), *The SAGE handbook of intercultural competence* (pp. 179–195). Thousand Oaks, CA: SAGE.

PART THREE

RESEARCH ON FACULTY AND SERVICE LEARNING

INVESTIGATING FACULTY DEVELOPMENT FOR SERVICE LEARNING

Nancy Van Note Chism, Megan M. Palmer, and Mary F. Price

Fundamentally, advocates of any particular innovative approach to instruction are strongly motivated by the potential of that pedagogy to promote more extensive or deeper student learning of content in comparison with more traditional pedagogical approaches. They may also be excited about additional, related outcomes; in the case of service learning, these may include student civic learning, benefits to the community, and campus-community relationships. However, if intentional faculty development strategies are not adopted, the implementation of any particular pedagogy may or may not lead to the desired outcomes or additional anticipated benefits. In the case of service learning, it has been argued that the success of a course is closely tied to its design (Ash & Clayton, 2009; Bringle & Hatcher, 1999; Clayton & O'Steen, 2010; Howard, 2000, 2001; Part Two of this volume), which, in turn, is dependent on the understanding and effectiveness of both faculty and those who provide them with professional development and support. Given the central role of the faculty member in implementing the pedagogy and its unfamiliar (Abes, Jackson, & Jones, 2002), counternormative nature (Clayton & Ash, 2004; Howard, 2000), when faculty development activities are nonexistent, haphazard, or based on faulty assumptions about the pedagogy, strong implementation of service learning courses can be assumed to be less likely to occur. Intentional faculty development, therefore, is an important focus of service learning practice and research. Professionals who seek to advance service learning practice and scholars who investigate service learning processes and outcomes need to understand how faculty become interested and engaged in service learning (see chapter 3.2) as well as the consequences of faculty development activities on student and community outcomes and what and how faculty learn about and through service learning (see chapter 3.3). These are key issues to understanding how effective implementation of the pedagogy can be facilitated through faculty development and to guiding the design of faculty development activities.

The Professional and Organizational Development Network in Higher Education (POD, 2007), the leading professional organization in the United States for faculty developers, offers the following definition of *faculty development*:

> Faculty Development refers to those programs which focus on the individual faculty member. The most common focus for programs of this type is the faculty member as a teacher. Faculty development specialists provide consultation on teaching, including class organization, evaluation of students, in-class presentation skills, questioning and all aspects of design and presentation. (para. 1)

Faculty development is frequently an aspect of programs to advance faculty as scholars and professionals. Furthermore, the faculty member as a person is an additional emphasis (POD, 2007).

In this chapter, the focus is on theories that undergird the work of faculty development, assessment of the impact of faculty development, and suggestions for how service learning professionals might assess faculty development activities through investigating outcomes of various constituencies. The chapter also includes implications for practice and recommendations for future research.

Theoretical Frameworks

Although faculty development as an activity has likely existed as long as institutions of higher education have, its status as an organized professional network across campuses is less than 50 years old (Sorcinelli, Austin, Eddy, & Beach, 2006). To augment or coordinate the faculty support activities situated in academic units, campuswide teaching centers and faculty mentoring programs were established during the 1970s and 1980s, often launched with funding from major foundations such as Lilly and Danforth

(Sorcinelli et al., 2006). Today, faculty development, referred to in various contexts as academic, educational, or professional development, is an international profession with a coordinating association, The International Consortium for Educational Development, and professional journals (e.g., *To Improve the Academy, The Journal of Faculty Development*, and *International Journal for Academic Development*).

Although there is a tendency to emphasize its practical dimensions, from time to time faculty developers discuss the theoretical bases of their work. Some authors, such as McKeachie (1991), approached this issue head-on, suggesting that, although developers may accomplish worthwhile outcomes even without an explicit theory, theories are helpful in many ways. McKeachie pointed out that many theories used by faculty developers are focused predominantly on teaching and learning, rather than on faculty growth and how to nurture it. He offered his own theory of faculty development, stating that development in teaching proceeds in stages from an early concern with self to a focus on task and, finally, to a focus on the learner. The implication that follows is that developers need to tailor their approaches to the stages of the faculty with whom they are working, recognizing their entry point and, in turn, their particular interests and needs. Baume (2002, 2004) promoted using theory explicitly and aligning faculty development practice with teaching practice, recommending the use of experiential learning models as the basis for faculty development.

Because the work of faculty development is complex, situated in varying contexts, and focused on a wide range of goals, the theories that can inform it are correspondingly diverse. For example, the following theoretical bases may all be useful for faculty developers, depending on the specific context:

- Theories of individual learning and development, including theories of adult learning, faculty learning, and learning over the career and life span. These can be used by developers to conceptualize how to work with faculty as learners.
- Theories of organizational learning and development, including models of organizations in general and of higher education organizations specifically, and theories of organizational culture and change. These can be used to anticipate and address the role of context in supporting faculty work.
- Theories of teaching and learning, including theories of cognition, motivation, and teaching and learning styles. These can be especially useful when working with faculty on topics related to instructional design.

Theories focused on the individual faculty members include those related to how faculty change and grow. These range from stage theories that describe how different phases of the faculty career influence focus and motivation (Baldwin, 1996; Bland & Bergquist, 1997; Seldin, 2006) to theories that describe progression in developing teaching expertise from less to more sophisticated conceptions (Kugel, 1993; Ramsden, 2003; Robertson, 2000). These theories are helpful in identifying key characteristics of faculty at various points in their development and generating implications for faculty developers.

By far, the most widely used and directly related theoretical basis for faculty development emanates from theories of individual learning, the major theory base described in this chapter. Especially helpful have been professional growth models rooted in the work of social psychologist Lewin (1947); discussions on the nature of learning by Dewey (1933); and the model of experiential learning offered by Kolb (1984), with its cycle consisting of abstract conceptualization, active experimentation, concrete experience, and reflective observation. Schön (1983) and Eraut (1994) have discussed the importance of reflection on experience in professional learning. Proponents of action research, such as Carr and Kemmis (1986) and Zuber-Skerritt (1992), have adopted the conceptual basis for all of these approaches in the field of education. Within educational development, faculty developers such as Chism (2004, 2005), Sharp (2004), and Weimer (2010) have all drawn upon this theoretical tradition.

Although each of these theories uses different language and emphasizes different dimensions, the following represents a synthesis that provides a framework for implementing and investigating faculty development:

1. *The entry point as felt need.* Whether based on Lewin's (1947) phase of *unfreezing* in which learners question prior assumptions, Dewey's (1933) notion of the *problem* that stimulates learners to begin to examine experience, or Schön's (1983) emphasis on *reflection on action* that describes moments when professionals reflect on their practice, these theories all emphasize the primacy of attention to the need to learn by a faculty member. This attention can be triggered by an external demand, such as an organizational agenda (e.g., general education) or mandate, or it can come from within the individual in response to personal experiences. Often these experiences arise from dissatisfaction with student performance (e.g., low test scores or performance) or the logistics of teaching (e.g., stress connected with time pressures, boredom with routines, limited resources).

2. *The formulation of a plan to change practice.* During this phase, different possibilities for a change in practice are entertained. Faculty may draw on past experience and ideas in the surrounding environment (e.g., colleagues, other courses), weighing different options and how effective each might be, how much energy would be required, and the barriers to adoption. As a result, faculty position themselves to select and design a course of action that will be the basis for the next phase.

3. *Active experimentation with the selected idea.* Faculty use the changed or new teaching practice in their teaching environment, constituting a natural experiment. They create a new set of learning experiences for addressing the need and observe how effectively they do this. When well implemented, this stage includes designing a way to determine the extent to which the intervention is successful in meeting desired outcomes.

4. *Observation of the impact of the new practice.* Faculty gather data that will form the basis for their decisions to keep the practice, modify it, or discard it as ineffective. In Kolb's cycle, this is the phase of reflective observation. Given that a pedagogy may fail to produce desired outcomes because of flawed design or implementation, this process evaluation includes considering how effectively the new teaching practice was implemented according to principles of good practice. The strategy for gathering evidence of outcomes will be based on the desired goals for the intervention, but it should also have the capacity to evaluate unanticipated positive and adverse outcomes, possibly by using mixed-methods (chapter 1.2).

5. *Reflection and implications for future teaching.* Having gathered information on process and outcomes, faculty determine implications for future practice, including modifying the intervention or discarding it as ineffective. In Kolb's (1984) model of experiential learning, this is the stage of abstract conceptualization in that the evidence is interpreted for its implications for future practice. The learning that results from the analysis of evidence leads to new engagement in practice (i.e., active experimentation anew), demonstrating that this model is cyclic, rather than linear, a feature also present in the work of theories of action research (Carr & Kemmis, 1986). The interpretation of evidence may not only have implications for revising the particular course but also have applicability to different course contexts and more broadly to other forms of teaching and learning. As such, the evidence provides a basis for the scholarship of teaching and learning, and dissemination of the results will provide a basis for others to improve their practice.

In applying this framework to the specific instance of learning to use instructional technology well, Chism (2004) commented on its utility for faculty developers: "The power of this learning is that it arises from a felt need. The experimentation ensures that the learning is authentic rather than imposed, and the observation and reflection ensure the innovation is monitored and adapted to fit the need" (p. 40).

How have faculty developers in the service learning context used these various theoretical foundations to assess the impact of their work and to refine their practice? The following section explores this question.

Critical Evaluation of Past Research on Faculty Development for Service Learning

Interestingly, the criteria used for faculty development impact studies are somewhat different from those used in service learning. A major difference lies in the level of impact that is the focus of most studies: Whereas faculty developers are most concerned with the direct effect on the faculty member, service learning developers focus more on student and community impact (Carracelas-Juncal, Bossaller, & Yaoyuneyong, 2009). Educational developers and training specialists more generally have suggested several levels at which the impact of their work might be assessed. The most cited of these is Kirkpatrick (1998), who, along with Guskey (2000), lists four levels: satisfaction, learning of the teacher, application by the teacher, and benefit to the organization and its mission. Chism and Szabo (1998) list similar levels: change in teaching beliefs/knowledge, change in teaching behaviors, and change in student learning. Smith (2004) suggests that impact can occur at the level of the individual participants, their careers, their students' experiences, and their department and the institution. Perhaps the most comprehensive list is provided by Kreber and Brook (2001), who assert that impact can be assessed at six levels: (a) participants' perceptions of and satisfaction with the intervention, (b) their beliefs about teaching and learning, (c) their teaching performance, (d) students' perceptions of the participants' teaching performance, (e) students' learning, and (f) changes in or contributions to the culture of the institution.

As Driscoll, Holland, Gelmon, and Kerrigan (1996) point out, community outcomes are an additional category of consideration in the service learning context, and this has implications for the range of potential outcomes of faculty development that are important to consider. In their enumeration of the criteria that might be used to assess faculty-related issues in service learning, they include items comparable with those in the faculty development literature, such as change in faculty beliefs and practices and student learning, but add criteria concerning change in faculty beliefs about their role in the community and in their actual engagement with the community. These authors also add engagement in further professional development as a faculty impact.

These different levels at which impact of faculty development can be assessed suggest important perspectives from which to survey existing literature. Chism and Szabo (1998) found that much of the literature on evaluation of faculty development in general focuses on participation rates in faculty development activities, such as workshops, or on faculty satisfaction with these activities. They found that some studies explored the extent to which new faculty learning or implementation of a new practice occurred, yet fewer addressed the extent to which increased student learning was directly connected to faculty development interventions. As participants in the Chism and Szabo (1998) study evaluating faculty development interventions attest, tracing the impact of faculty development strategies beyond the first-order effect on faculty is extremely difficult. Determining the impact of faculty development on an entire institution or community is even more challenging. McKinney's (2002) review offered similar findings:

> What do these studies show? For much of this evaluation research of instructional development, a variety of beneficial outcomes are reported. An increased sense of collaboration and community about teaching and high levels of participant satisfaction are outcomes reported in most of the studies. A third fairly common finding is that instructors' attitudes about teaching change. For example, instructors become more self-confident, more positive, and more concerned with students. In a few of these studies, changes in teaching behaviors are reported. . . . Rarely are student perceptions measured. . . . Most of the work, however, is descriptive and correlational in nature, and focuses on instructor use of services, instructor satisfaction with services, changes in instructors' attitudes, and instructor perceptions of [their own] behavior changes. (p. 230)

In addition, often these studies were conducted in the context of a single program at one institution by the same person or team who implemented the faculty development program being evaluated.

The service learning literature that addresses faculty development contains a few important studies about faculty motivation to engage in service learning (e.g., Abes et al., 2002; Bannerjee & Hausafus, 2007; McKay &

Rozee, 2004; chapter 3.2) and some studies of faculty development interventions. Of the published sources identified as addressing faculty impact in *At a Glance: What We Know About the Effects of Service Learning on College Students, Faculty, Institutions and Communities, 1993–2000* (Eyler, Giles, Stenson, & Gray, 2001), only four—Hammond (1994), Hesser (1995), Stanton (1994), and Ward (1996)—focused on faculty per se as an object of study. Of these, only Stanton's analysis took the results of a faculty development intervention, in this case a faculty seminar, as its point of analysis. The other three studies focused on self-reported data regarding factors influencing faculty participation and satisfaction with service learning.

Overall, of the studies that addressed faculty development interventions, some attempted to measure the impact of the specific intervention (e.g., Abes et al., 2002; Bloomgarden & O'Meara, 2007; Harwood et al., 2005; O'Meara & Niehaus, 2009; Pribbenow, 2005; Rice & Stacey, 1997). Others offered conceptual models or frameworks to guide faculty development programming (Butin, 2007; Mundy, 2004; Wade & Demb, 2009; Zlotkowski, 1998). Other authors described an intervention and argued for its efficacy without reporting the results of actually using that faculty development approach (e.g., Bringle & Hatcher, 1995; Kecskes & Spring, 2006; Varlotta, 2000). In some cases (Henderson, Fair, Sather, & Dewey, 2008), the focus of reporting related to a specific faculty development intervention situated faculty learning primarily as a vehicle for improving student learning outcomes; in such cases, faculty learning is not valued in equal measure as an important outcome unto itself. Our focus here is on studies of faculty interventions, which are grouped by type of activity. The three most common forms of development practice are singled out for discussion: communities of practice, consultation, and changes in teaching assignments.

Communities of Practice

Faculty developers have found that sustained interaction within a group of faculty members over the course of an academic semester or year is an approach that yields high returns for promoting change in conceptualizations about teaching and learning and teaching behaviors. Although the specific names of programs and their formats vary, they can be considered generically in terms of Wenger's (1998) communities of practice, groups of practitioners engaged in examination and often action projects on a common issue or problem.

Stanton (1994) used a community of practice model in a national weeklong institute on service learning. He first assessed initial level of motivation through examining learning plans submitted for the institute and later through retrospective interview questions. In assessing outcomes through a follow-up survey, he labeled 6 of the 12 participants as *high implementers* who not only taught service learning courses but also supported their colleagues in doing the same. Stanton also reported that three of the participants were *medium implementers* who taught service learning courses but did not serve as advocates or mentors, and the remaining three were *low implementers* who neither implemented service learning courses nor served as advocates. Thus, Stanton's measure of the impact of the faculty development institute was not only the subsequent implementation of service learning by participants but also their mentoring of others.

Rice and Stacey (1997) also used a community of practice model. Their Faculty Fellows program involved regular seminars over the course of an academic year that engaged faculty in developing an understanding of the pedagogy and designing service learning courses. Their measure of impact for multiple offerings of the seminar was continued use of service learning in courses by the Faculty Fellows, which was the case for 70% of the 14 participants.

Bringle, Games, Foos, Osgood, and Osborne (2000) reported on the Indiana Campus Compact Faculty Fellows program, in which cohorts of faculty were engaged in teaching a service learning course while attending regular retreats and conducting research on their courses. They found that Faculty Fellows in an academic year program reported improving their knowledge base of service learning and becoming more confident in seeking leadership roles in service learning. Participants reported benefiting from the social and professional support afforded them by means of the Fellows program. Finally, faculty reported that "participation in the program moved them toward becoming professionally more complete and connected" (p. 891).

Harwood et al. (2005) outlined a two-year Faculty Fellows program that exposed faculty to literature about teaching and learning and about the impact of service learning courses on students as well as to tips and strategies for designing service learning courses. In their report of the outcomes of the program, the leading finding from surveys, meeting notes, and final reports of each course project was that participants found the collegial aspect of the program of great benefit because it served as a means to garner support for the pedagogical approach and provided opportunities for networking and mentoring. The next most significant reported gain was that faculty involvement helped advance the participants' scholarship related to teaching and learning. Other reported benefits of this faculty development intervention

included personal growth, enhanced student learning outcomes, and a positive contribution to the community at large.

Carracelas-Juncal et al. (2009) examined narratives written by faculty in
a semester-long Faculty Fellows program in which participants were engaged
in revising or planning a new service learning course and attending seminars
in which service learning was explored. These investigators reported that
despite their different disciplines, participants each went through the same
three-stage process of change: (a) initial enthusiasm and conviction, (b)
encounter with reality, and (c) subsequent recommitment to service learning
as an effective pedagogy.

Consultation

In contrast to the faculty development literature that devotes much attention
to various consultation strategies and their impacts on faculty (Piccinin,
1999; Piccinin & Moore, 2002), there are few references to consultation
in the service learning literature. One might assume that within programs
involving other strategies, such as communities of practice, faculty developers do consult with faculty. Bringle, Hatcher, Jones, and Plater (2006) identified consultation as one form of intervention used at the institutional level
but did not discuss outcomes associated with it. Clayton and Ash (2004)
implied that those promoting service learning can assist faculty in understanding the significant challenges involved by helping them to reflect on
differences from traditional modes of teaching, but their discussion did not
document gains obtained from the actual use of this type of consultation.

Changes in Teaching Assignments (e.g., Teaching Venue, Type of Teaching)

An indirect method of faculty development often naturally occurs when
changes in teaching assignments take place. These provide the *felt need* for
change that triggers development under supportive conditions. For example,
in a focus group follow-up study, faculty who were teaching in learning
community courses that involved service learning reported that teaching in
the learning communities had been professionally revitalizing, provided an
opportunity to get updated technical skills, and was a means to engage in
their own lifelong learning (Hodge, Lewis, Kramer, & Hughes, 2001). Thus,
a change in teaching venue or assignment alone was reported to have had a
positive influence on faculty.

Observations on the Literature

As this review indicates, scant attention has been paid to the impact of various approaches to faculty development for service learning, much less to comparative investigation of those approaches. No discussion of theoretical rationales for the interventions used was encountered in the literature explored for this chapter. Extrapolating from the practices that were described, one can assume that theory on service learning and reflection are both important components, aligning approaches to faculty development for service learning with the theories of experiential learning described earlier (i.e., Kolb, 1984). The social environment for learning is also stressed in several of the studies described here, underscoring the belief in the importance of peer support during faculty experimentation and reflection. In addition, the studies attend to the organizational environment for learning in speaking to the obstacles that faculty face in their time commitments, reward systems, and lack of community connections.

Methodologically, studies of the outcomes of faculty development activities within the context of service learning suffer from the same limitations as those on faculty development more generally (Chism & Szabo, 1998; McKinney, 2002). The studies included in this review all focused on a relatively small number of faculty, they were conducted by the same people who offered the intervention, and they generally relied only on self-report surveys or interviews that assessed satisfaction or extent of subsequent implementation of the pedagogy. The research strategies were particularly weak, with a prevalence of posttest only designs (see chapter 1.2) and no investigations that compared approaches to faculty development.

A major difference between the general faculty development impact studies and research on outcomes done within the service learning context, however, is the limited inclusion of faculty in the latter. Just like most of assessment in higher education has been focused on student learning, most research on service learning has focused on student learning and other student outcomes (Eyler et al., 2001). Although it is natural to think that this is the correct balance because service learning is a teaching strategy at its core, several scholars (e.g., Bringle, Clayton, & Price, 2009; Clayton & Ash, 2005; Clayton, Bringle, Senor, Huq, & Morrison, 2010) suggest that service learning is potentially transformative not only for students but for faculty, staff, community members, community organizations, and institutions as well and call for investigating a broader set of stakeholder outcomes. It is difficult to identify from student impact studies the factors that help engage faculty in undertaking service learning, implementing it well, and remaining committed to its use, or not. The fact that the National Service Learning Clearinghouse still lacks a strong, visible presence for organizing and presenting research and assessment on faculty professional development in relation to service learning and community engagement more than 10 years after Driscoll's (2000) call for increased study in this area is significant—it indicates that as a field, service learning developers and researchers have yet to embrace fully her call.

In both higher education generally and service learning in particular, when faculty development is studied, the research seldom if ever links student outcomes to faculty interventions. Figure 3.1.1 depicts what has been asked about faculty development activities and what could be asked. The contrast between the two diagrams highlights the need to focus on agency in the process: How does the faculty member acquire and use the capacity to conceptualize and implement service learning? Addressing this broader set of research questions is integral to understanding faculty development as an intervention that can have a broad set of outcomes.

Measurement Approaches

What measures best capture the outcomes of faculty development interventions? Should developers gather evidence of faculty learning and growth in addition to participation in and satisfaction with faculty development activities (e.g., workshops, communities of practice, consultations)? Should the focus be on increased understanding and use of the pedagogy, scholarly publications and presentations, improved student learning outcomes, or evidence of higher quality relationships with community members? What about the influence of interventions that target curricular revision not only at the course level but also at the departmental level (Kecskes, Gelmon, & Spring, 2006)? What is the impact of faculty development activities on other constituencies in addition to students and faculty and on the resulting relationships between and among these constituencies (Bringle et al., 2009; Clayton et al., 2010)? What would be effective measures of any of these outcomes?

Baseline measures for participation in faculty development activities are simple counts, yet changes over time and different participation rates across gender, discipline, institutional context, and type of activity can provide descriptive information that guides tailoring programs to particular audiences and determining who is not participating, why, and what else might

FIGURE 3.1.1
Current Approach to Research on the Outcomes of Service Learning (top) and Proposed Approach That Includes Faculty Development (bottom)

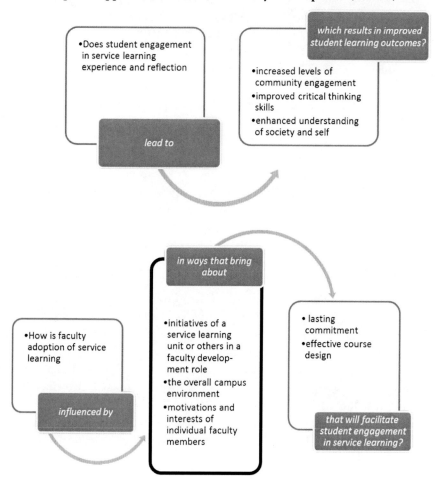

be done to reach various audiences on campus. Several faculty development centers have described their systems for keeping and using such statistics in analyzing participation rates by demographic variables (Plank, Kalish, Roh-dieck, & Harper, 2005). Documenting these patterns among service learning faculty and examining cross-institutional patterns would provide reference points for developing a better understanding of whom these programs are reaching and how participation varies by context (e.g., disciplinary, institutional, timing).

Expressed satisfaction with faculty development activities and continued participation in faculty development activities are relevant types of evidence that can provide information to improve future activities. Implementation of service learning, once or in an ongoing fashion, is also important evidence of outcomes. Electronic surveys completed by participants after undertaking faculty development activities can yield high rates of return, yet most programs that include time at the end of the program to complete an evaluation get the best response rates. Follow-up telephone interviews can also provide quantitative and qualitative information about outcomes.

For assessing change in faculty members' understanding of service learning, both quantitative and qualitative measures are appropriate. Instruments that assess beliefs and attitudes regarding the importance of service learning or civic engagement more generally may be administered before and after faculty development interventions or before and after teaching a course with service learning in order to gauge change. Faculty can be surveyed over time as they engage in designing and delivering service learning to measure continuing change. Such surveys can include questions to faculty about how they are conceptualizing service learning; their rationale for specific elements of course design; issues that they encountered in teaching the course; how they handled those issues; and what personal, student, and community outcomes they were able to document and how they assessed them. Finally, qualitative methods, such as interviews, observation, and document analysis, can produce insights into faculty members' knowledge base of the principles of service learning. In addition to the topics listed for surveys, interviews can probe for reflections on how the specific faculty development intervention influenced the reported changes. Observations of classroom performance or participation during faculty development sessions and examination of documents that faculty produce, such as reflective essays, journals, or planning outlines, can also provide good data on outcomes. Faculty who give conference presentations or publish about their service learning experiences produce additional artifacts to examine in assessing growth in understanding. At the institutional level, Pike, Bringle, and Hatcher (in press) suggest ways in which institutional data can be used to assess the impact of service learning faculty development programs. For all of these methods, it will be important to tie the outcomes to the faculty development program through matching specific activities to outcomes, ideally through the use of control groups and pre- and post-measurements but more practically through self-report combined with pre- and post-measurements.

The best methods for assessing the impact of faculty development interventions on the implementation of service learning would go beyond counts of participation or reports of satisfaction and actually focus on the quality of the course design and of that course's outcomes. Such an assessment would link the type of support that the faculty member received with the nature of the service learning course that was implemented. For this type of study, rubrics or checklists that are aligned with the course development activities, lists of service learning characteristics that were stressed in the faculty development activities, and lists of more general principles of course design or learning theory that were taught as part of the faculty development intervention can serve as instruments for ascertaining whether and to what extent the design of the course was influenced by the faculty development activity in question. Fine-grained examination of a small sample of cases, purposefully sampled to reflect varying conditions and contexts, may be most practical because these assessments may entail examination of course documents such as the syllabus, observation of practice, and interviews of faculty as well as students and community members. As with all qualitative research, depth can compensate for breadth as detailed descriptions of specific cases begin to accrue in the literature. Although experimental design that calls for random assignment of participants to intervention and control of extraneous variables is difficult to employ in faculty development settings owing to practical programmatic constraints, studies employing experimental or quasi-experimental designs could contribute much to the existing knowledge base (see chapter 1.2). These designs are particularly suitable when participation numbers are large enough to allow assignment of faculty to different intervention strategies so that approaches can be compared.

Investigating the impact of faculty development on student learning gains, by connecting the actions of the faculty developer with learning of the faculty member, and in turn that of the student, poses a very challenging set of conceptual as well as methodological questions for researchers. Service learning practitioner-scholars have focused on documenting student gains through a variety of measures (see Part Two), such as the use of self-report surveys, scales that elicit responses related to attitudes and behaviors, and reflective journals and other student products. Might some of these same approaches be used effectively not only to assess faculty learning but to enable investigation of its relationship with student learning? Establishing linkages between student outcomes and the faculty choices and actions that were informed by faculty development activities will be an important addition to the research on service learning (Jameson, Clayton, Jaeger, & Bringle, 2012; McGuire et al., 2009; chapter 3.3).

Although the focus to this point has been on the individual faculty member, it is also important to understand the changes in academic units (see chapter 5.2), institutions (see chapters 5.1 and 5.3), and communities (see Part Four) that are associated with faculty development for service learning. Measures can include counts of participation; examination of patterns of participation; in-depth analysis of the quality of courses across a curriculum; learning associated with service learning within each context; and exploration, likely through qualitative means, of the factors within each context that support or constrain the implementation of service learning. With any of these approaches, however, the link with the faculty development intervention needs to be made explicit; doing so entails tracing the influence of the faculty developer's actions on the ensuing results, a difficult research task that involves tracking multiple sets of data and challenges in making causal inferences about changes.

These methods and measures all focus on assessing the impact of faculty development. A key additional use for assessment, however, is needs analysis. Studies of faculty in the process of deciding to use service learning, designing or implementing courses, and undertaking scholarship of teaching and learning within the context of service learning can lead to rich insights for faculty developers about what motivators are the most powerful, what aspects of design and implementation are most challenging, and how faculty can best be supported in inquiring about practice within this context. Traditional approaches such as midcourse interviews, videotaped classroom teaching with feedback, and reflection among faculty participants can produce insights into how to facilitate faculty learning about service learning. Other sources of information may include student feedback; independent evaluation of student service learning products; and evaluation by community members, potentially including staff at community organizations and those whom they serve (e.g., of student performance, of faculty role in projects, of partnership dynamics).

In framing these measures, the conceptual framework presented earlier (e.g., need, design, implementation, feedback, revision) or other theories relevant to faculty development and change can be used to design measures that encompass indicators of various outcomes of the process of faculty development. Models of how individuals and organizations (e.g., academic departments) learn and change are important anchors that may inform choice of methods and the particular measures used in studying faculty development. In assessing a service learning faculty development intervention, different means of engaging faculty (e.g., small grant program, release time for course development, communities of practice versus one-on-one consultation) can be explored.

Implications for Practice

Faculty developers can work from the theoretical basis of experiential learning to determine how and when various interventions (e.g., workshops, communities of practice, consultations) might be used most effectively to stimulate and strengthen faculty learning. Specific faculty development activities for service learning have been organized and developed based on Kolb's (1984) conceptual approach to learning, a cycle that includes four interactive dimensions (i.e., abstract conceptualization, active experimentation, concrete experience, reflective observation). Bringle et al. (2006) present examples of interventions that are predominantly abstract (e.g., workshops), active experimentation (e.g., engaged department grants), concrete experiences (e.g., engaging faculty in community service or service learning immersions), and reflective observation (e.g., engaging faculty in professional presentations and scholarship). They point out that Kolb's experiential learning model can be applied at different organizational levels (e.g., individual faculty, cohorts of faculty, departments, schools/colleges, institutions) and can target different audiences (e.g., new faculty, newly tenured faculty, doctoral students, non–tenure track faculty) (Bringle et al., 2000, 2006; Bringle & Hatcher, 1995).

When a faculty member is examining possible changes in teaching practice, faculty development activities such as workshops or printed or Web-based resources that describe a variety of innovative approaches can increase the range of options that the faculty member can consider. One-on-one consultation can help the faculty member to explore possibilities, and cohort-based interventions or communities of practice can bring the added value of dialogue with colleagues. While an instructor is making changes in a course, faculty developers can provide technical support on how to design the course (e.g., structure service, develop service activities, design reflection, assess outcomes), implement the pedagogical changes, and handle challenging situations. They can help collect information on the impact of changes systematically by offering assistance with data gathering or suggesting tools for assessment, serve as sounding boards for reflection as the implications of the data are considered, and link instructors with peers who can provide insights during the reflective appraisal of the outcomes of the innovation.

Faculty developers can also use theories of experiential learning in their practice by examining approaches to fostering change, such as role modeling and idea seeding (Chism, 2005), in terms of the challenges and opportunities of their own context. As an example of the latter, although the common practice of offering brief workshops may not produce immediate or long-lasting change in participants' teaching, it may be effective for enlarging the pool of ideas from which instructors can choose when they are subsequently experiencing a need to make a change in practice.

Finally, faculty developers can use these theories to evaluate processes and impacts. They can look at processes used in a specific instance of faculty development and ask whether they began with felt needs and then supported the experiential learning of the faculty who were involved. They can use theories of teacher growth (Kugel, 1993; Ramsden, 1994; Robertson, 2000) to generate markers to use in assessing whether specific interventions helped increase the complexity of faculty members' thinking about teaching. And they can use theories of learning (Kolb, 1984; Marton & Säljö, 1976a, 1976b; Ramsden, 1994) to conceptualize studies of the growth that students experience as a result of faculty members' actions in order to improve their own approaches to faculty development.

Regardless of the extent to which faculty developers use theories of experiential learning in their work, there are many challenges associated with advancing research on faculty development in service learning. Not all colleges and universities have full-time faculty developers who promote and support service learning courses and related research; this may set significant limitations on the extent to which someone in the role of introducing faculty to service learning can design, develop, manage, and monitor systems to evaluate the effectiveness of distinct types of interventions (Clayton & O'Steen, 2010). An additional responsibility that some faculty developers in service learning carry, but that faculty developers more generally usually do not, is relationship building with community members. The activities involved in relationship building require extensive time commitments and may further limit the time a lone faculty developer can devote to investigating program outcomes. Another factor that may inhibit the growth of systematic data collection and research on faculty development in service learning is the variation in how campuses conceptualize and administer service learning, sometimes as a student activity, usually housed in Student

Affairs, and sometimes as faculty work, more often based in Academic Affairs or in academic units. The choices that institutions make regarding the administration and staffing of faculty development and of service learning are important organizational factors that may contribute to the exchange of resources and scholarship between the two.

In any case, institutional leaders should recognize that investments in research to study the results of faculty development activities focused on service learning can yield long-term payoff in the effectiveness and efficiency of activities to promote and support service learning as well as in the quality of student and community outcomes. Furthermore, individuals and units that provide faculty development and support in service learning need to attend to related theories and assessment methods and establish patterns of documenting and investigating outcomes, not only in terms of student learning and community change but also in terms of faculty learning and change.

Research Agenda

The theoretical framework of experiential learning as applied to faculty development described earlier (e.g., need, design, implementation, feedback, revision), along with the literature on levels of impact, can be used productively by practitioners and scholars to generate directions for future practice and additional research. For example, one might design a qualitative study to gain insight into what served as the catalyst for faculty to become involved in service learning and how that contributed to the cycle of their professional development. A study such as this would use the literature about individual change as a theoretical underpinning and could thus help service learning professionals know how best to design faculty development activities.

In studying faculty engagement and growth associated with service learning, an important element to consider is how the felt need that stimulates participation in faculty development activities is established and produces cycles of change for the faculty member. How can dissatisfaction with existing practice, stress, altruism, desire for change, or other levers be employed as opportunities for the introduction of service learning? What arguments or rationales make sense to faculty at different career stages and in different institutional and disciplinary contexts? How does interest in community issues or professional service by faculty stimulate interest in integrating community service into courses? Studies that investigate the influence of demographic factors, personal values, disciplinary perspectives, or theoretical perspectives on adopting service learning could also be instructive for recruiting participants for faculty development activities. For example, are faculty more likely to develop and sustain interest in service learning at one phase of their careers rather than another? Does the level of sophistication of a faculty member's conceptualization of learning influence interest in or implementation of service learning? How do assumptions about teaching practice in general influence faculty attitudes toward service learning? Case studies, needs analyses, and analyses of institutional data can be used to develop research on these questions. Motivation theories offer additional insights for conceptualizing these studies (see chapter 3.2). For example, studies might address the efficacy of extrinsic motivators (e.g., grants, awards, promotion, tenure) in encouraging faculty to invest in professional development for service learning and ask whether or not initial commitment is sustained after the reward ends.

How can faculty who have become interested in service learning be supported effectively in learning about service learning and experimenting with it? Under what conditions are communities of practice or other forms of facilitated conversations a valuable vehicle for helping faculty to enrich their vision of possibilities and to explore options for addressing challenges? What faculty development strategies are most effective at different stages, in different disciplines, and with different learning styles? What approaches are best suited for building readings into one-on-one consultations and into small-group discussions in order to maximize faculty members' application and analyze various service learning principles of good practice? These questions might be studied by taking an ethnographic approach to observing and understanding the cultures of faculty learning communities or by producing detailed descriptions and analyses of the ways in which consultants interact with faculty who are implementing service learning.

Working from the feedback point in the experiential learning cycle, the next questions would focus on how faculty can be supported in assessing the impact of their service learning activities. What is the relative effectiveness of offering support in terms of measurement instruments, help with research design, and resources for data collection and analysis? Are there institutional sources of data (e.g., surveys, student products) that can be used across service learning courses (Bringle & Hatcher, 2009)? Are there specific student learning objectives for which indicators can be developed (Ash & Clayton, 2009; see chapter 2.2)? The collaborative partnership between the faculty member and the service learning professional is also a key area to investigate. Descriptive studies that document faculty approaches to assessment and the impact of various supportive resources (e.g., consultation, funds, tools) on their work would be helpful in understanding how to support faculty growth at the feedback point in the development cycle.

The next area of the cycle focuses on reflection, that is, how to help faculty reflect on their goals, design choices, and behavior for the sake of their professional development and the improvement of their professional work. What approaches to reflection are best suited to supporting critical inquiry into practice in such a way that enhances motivation, establishes connections between past patterns and future possibilities, and generates questions for faculty members' scholarship? Many of the insights and tools that have been generated in service learning practice to help students reflect meaningfully on their experiences may be adapted for use in faculty development (Bringle & Hatcher, 2000; Clayton & Ash, 2005; Clayton & O'Steen, 2010; chapter 3.3).

Beyond the learning cycle of the individual faculty member is an interest in focusing on engaging entire academic departments in service learning (Kecskes et al., 2006; see chapter 5.2). In addition to using frameworks of experiential education, research about the role of faculty development in cultivating engaged departments would be strengthened by conceptualizing the interventions and the results of such activities in light of theories of organizational change (e.g., Beckhard, 2006; Mayhew, 2006). The efficacy of various ways of working with academic departments might also be addressed through studies that explore the relative effects of faculty development interventions (e.g., workshops, communities of practice, consultations) not only on individual faculty outcomes (e.g., attitudes, practice, knowledge) but also at the departmental level (e.g., curriculum, assessment, collaboration, climate). Insights into the extent to which various organizational factors (e.g., campus mission, resources, culture of teaching and learning, rewards systems, student population, faculty work conditions) influence and are influenced by the adoption of service learning can also be obtained from studies that use an organizational change analysis perspective (e.g., culture audits, force field analysis) (Beckhard, 2006; chapters 5.1 and 5.3).

Conclusion

The literature on faculty development in colleges and universities draws on an eclectic theory base that also has relevance for faculty development within the context of service learning. Of particular importance are theories related to how faculty learn and innovate. Theories relevant to the faculty career cycle, to motivation, and to conceptions of learning as well as theories of organizational change are relevant to understanding the complexities of faculty growth. To date, neither faculty developers in general nor those within the particular context of service learning have drawn on these theoretical frameworks to a sufficient degree. As these fields mature, however, theory-based studies are an important step.

Particularly within the arena of assessing the impact of faculty development, both general faculty development studies and those on service learning have used relatively informal methods, such as faculty satisfaction questionnaires, or have focused on issues other than authentic evidence of faculty growth and the processes that facilitate it. Most have been single program or single institution studies and have not drawn on benchmarking information or engaged in comparative analysis. There is a clear need for fuller and richer studies at all levels of impact.

The opportunity for thoughtful, theoretically based studies about faculty development strategies used to advance service learning will help build a literature base that can positively influence future practice. Such studies at both the individual and organizational level can draw on a wide array of methods and research designs. The resulting body of knowledge can complement studies of the impact of service learning on students, which are growing in number and sophistication.

The centrality of the faculty role in designing, implementing, and assessing service learning is obvious. Understanding how to facilitate faculty learning and engagement is complex, yet it is key to more widespread adoption of service learning that is likely to achieve the high ideals of fostering rich student learning, civic engagement, and community and institutional change. The literature on faculty development offers models and examples that can be adopted effectively in the service learning context; in turn, faculty developers working in the broader teaching and learning context can learn from those studying faculty development processes in the context of service learning. This partnership can enrich not only both fields but also the scholarship of practice that is still in its early years.

Recommended Reading

Bringle, R. G., Hatcher, J. A., Jones, S. G., & Plater, W. M. (2006). Sustaining civic engagement: Faculty development, roles, and rewards. *Metropolitan Universities, 17*(1), 62–74.

Chism, N. (2004). Using a framework to engage faculty in instructional technologies. *EDUCAUSE Quarterly, 27*(2), 39–45.

Kreber, C., & Brook, P. (2001). Impact evaluation of educational development programs. *International Journal for Academic Development, 6*(2), 96–108.

Sharp, R. (2004). How do professionals learn and develop? Implications for staff and educational developers. In D. Baume & P. Kahn (Eds.), *Enhancing staff and educational development* (pp. 134–153). London, UK: RoutledgeFalmer.

References

Abes, E. S., Jackson, G., & Jones, S. R. (2002). Factors that motivate and deter faculty use of service-learning. *Michigan Journal of Community Service Learning, 9*(1), 5–17.

Ash, S. L., & Clayton, P. H. (2009). *Teaching and learning through critical reflection: A tutorial for service-learning students (instructor version)*. Raleigh, NC: Authors.

Baldwin, R. G. (1996). Faculty career stages and implications for professional development. In D. E. Finnegan, D. Webster, & Z. F. Gamson (Eds.), *Faculty and faculty issues in colleges and universities* (pp. 551–561). Needham Heights, MA: Simon & Schuster.

Bannerjee, M., & Hausafus, C. (2007). Faculty use of service-learning: Perceptions, motivations, and impediments for the human services. *Michigan Journal of Community Service Learning, 14*(1), 32–45.

Baume, D. (2002). Scholarship, academic development and the future. *International Journal for Academic Development, 7*(2), 109–112.

Baume, D. (2004, June). *Professional development, professional recognition and professional standards for higher education teachers and developers.* Paper presented at the conference of the International Consortium for Educational Development, Ottawa, Canada.

Beckhard, R. (2006). What is organizational development? In J. V. Gallos (Ed.), *Organizational development: A Jossey-Bass reader* (pp. 3–38). San Francisco, CA: Jossey-Bass.

Bland, C., & Bergquist, W. (1997). The vitality of senior faculty members: Snow on the roof—fire in the furnace. *ASHE Higher Education Report, 25*(7). San Francisco, CA: Jossey-Bass.

Bloomgarden, A. H., & O'Meara, K. A. (2007). Faculty role integration and community engagement: Harmony or cacophony? *Michigan Journal of Community Service Learning, 13*(2), 5–18.

Bringle, R. G., Clayton, P. H., & Price, M. F. (2009). Partnerships in service learning and civic engagement. *Partnerships: A Journal of Service Learning & Civic Engagement, 1*(1), 1–20.

Bringle, R. G., Games, R., Foos, C. L., Osgood, R., & Osborne, R. (2000). Faculty Fellows Program: Enhancing integrated professional development through community service. *American Behavioral Scientist, 43*, 882–894.

Bringle, R. G., & Hatcher, J. A. (1995). A service-learning curriculum for faculty. *Michigan Journal of Community Service Learning, 2*(1), 112–122.

Bringle, R. G., & Hatcher, J. A. (1999). Reflection in service-learning: Making meaning of experience. *Educational Horizons, 7*(4), 179–185.

Bringle, R. G., & Hatcher, J. A. (2000). Institutionalization of service learning in higher education. *Journal of Higher Education, 71*, 273–290.

Bringle, R. G., & Hatcher, J. A. (2009). Innovative practices in service learning and curricular engagement. *New Directions for Higher Education, 2009*(147), 37–46. doi:10.1002/he.356

Bringle, R. G., Hatcher, J. A., Jones, S. G., & Plater, W. M. (2006). Sustaining civic engagement: Faculty development, roles, and rewards. *Metropolitan Universities, 17*(1), 62–74.

Butin, D. W. (2007). Focusing our aim: Strengthening faculty commitment to community engagement. *Change: The Magazine of Higher Learning, 39*(6), 34–37.

Carr, W., & Kemmis, S. (1986). *Becoming critical: Knowing through action research.* Geelong, Australia: Deakin University Press.

Carracelas-Juncal, C., Bossaller, J., & Yaoyuneyong, G. (2009). Integrating service-learning pedagogy: A faculty reflective process. *InSight: A Journal of Scholarly Teaching, 4*, 28–44.

Chism, N. (2004). Using a framework to engage faculty in instructional technologies. *EDUCAUSE Quarterly, 27*(2), 39–45.

Chism, N. (2005). Evaluating approaches to faculty development in the use of learning technologies. *Journal of Faculty Development, 20*(1), 31–36.

Chism, N., & Szabo, B. (1998). How faculty development programs evaluate their services. *Journal of Staff, Program, and Organization Development, 15*(2), 55–62.

Clayton, P. H., & Ash, S. L. (2004). Shifts in perspective: Capitalizing on the counter-normative nature of service-learning. *Michigan Journal of Community Service Learning, 11*(1), 59–70.

Clayton, P. H., & Ash, S. L. (2005). Reflection as a key component in faculty development. *On the Horizon, 13*(3), 161–169.

Clayton, P. H., Bringle, R. G., Senor, B., Huq, J., & Morrison, M. (2010). Differentiating and assessing relationships in service-learning and civic engagement: Exploitative, transactional, and transformational. *Michigan Journal of Community Service Learning, 16*(2), 5–21.

Clayton, P. H., & O'Steen, W. L. (2010). Working with faculty: Designing customized developmental strategies. In B. Jacoby & P. Mutascio (Eds.), *Looking in—reaching out: A reflective guide for community service-learning professionals* (pp. 95–135). Boston, MA: Campus Compact.

Dewey, J. (1933). *How we think: A restatement of the relation of reflective thinking to the educative process.* Lexington, MA: Heath.

Driscoll, A. (2000). Studying faculty and service learning: Directions for inquiry and development [Special issue]. *Michigan Journal of Community Service Learning, Fall*, 35–41.

Driscoll, A., Holland, B. A., Gelmon, S. B., & Kerrigan, S. (1996). An assessment model for service-learning: Comprehensive case studies of impact on faculty, students, community, and institution. *Michigan Journal of Community Service Learning, 3*(1), 66–71.

Eraut, M. (1994). *Developing professional knowledge and competence.* London, UK: Routledge.

Eyler, J. S., Giles, D. E., Jr., Stenson, C. M., & Gray, C. J. (2001). *At a glance: What we know about the effects of service learning on college students, faculty, institutions and communities, 1993–2000* (3rd ed.). Washington, DC: Learn and Serve America's National Service Learning Clearinghouse.

Guskey, T. R. (2000). *Evaluating professional development.* Thousand Oaks, CA: SAGE.

Hammond, C. (1994). Integrating service and academic study: Faculty motivation and satisfaction in Michigan higher education. *Michigan Journal of Community Service Learning, 1*(1), 21–28.

Harwood, A. M., Ochs, L., Currier, D., Duke, S., Hammond, J., Moulds, L., Werder, C. (2005). Communities for growth: Cultivating and sustaining service-learning teaching and scholarship in a faculty fellows program. *Michigan Journal of Community Service Learning, 12*(1), 41–51.

Henderson, S., Fair, M., Sather, P., & Dewey, B. (2008). Service learning research as a feedback loop for faculty development. In M. A. Bowdon, S. H. Billig, & B. A. Holland (Eds.), *Scholarship for sustaining service learning and civic engagement* (pp. 113–138). Charlotte, NC: Information Age.

Hesser, G. (1995). Faculty assessment of student learning: Outcomes attributed to service-learning and evidence of changes in faculty attitudes about experiential education. *Michigan Journal of Community Service Learning, 2*(1), 33–42.

Hodge, G., Lewis, T., Kramer, K., & Hughes, R. (2001). Collaboration for excellence: Engaged scholarship at Collin County Community College. *Community College Journal of Research and Practice, 25*, 675–690.

Howard, J. (2000). Academic service learning: Myths, challenges and recommendations. *Essays on Teaching Excellence, 12*(3), 12–19.

Howard, J. (2001). *Service learning course design workbook.* Ann Arbor, MI: OCSL Press.

Jameson, J. K., Clayton, P. H., Jaeger, A. J., & Bringle, R. G. (2012). Investigating faculty learning in the context of community engaged scholarship. *Michigan Journal of Community Service Learning, 18*(2), 40–55.

Kecskes, K. J., Gelmon, S. B., & Spring, A. (2006). Creating engaged departments: A program for organizational and faculty development. In S. Chadwick-Blossey & D. R. Robertson (Eds.), *To improve the academy: Resources for faculty, instructional, and organizational development* (Vol. 24, pp. 147–165). Bolton, MA: Anker.

Kecskes, K. J., & Spring, A. (2006). Continuums of engagement at Portland State University: An institution-wide initiative to support departmental collaboration

for the common good. In K. Kecskes (Ed.), *Engaging departments: Moving faculty culture from private to public, individual to collective focus for the common good.* Bolton, MA: Anker.

Kirkpatrick, D. (1998). *Evaluating training programs: The four levels* (2nd ed.). New York, NY: Berrett-Koehler.

Kolb, D. (1984). *Experiential learning: Experience as the source of learning and development.* Upper Saddle River, NJ: Prentice-Hall.

Kreber, C., & Brook, P. (2001). Impact evaluation of educational development programmes. *International Journal for Academic Development, 6*(2), 96–108.

Kugel, P. (1993). How professors develop as teachers. *Studies in Higher Education, 18,* 315–328.

Lewin, K. (1947). Group decision and social change. In T. N. Newcomb & E. L. Hartley (Eds.), *Readings in social psychology* (pp. 197–211). New York, NY: Holt, Rinehart, & Winston.

Marton, F., & Säljö, R. (1976a). On qualitative differences in learning I: Outcome and process. *British Journal of Educational Psychology, 46*(1), 4–11.

Marton, F., & Säljö, R. (1976b). On qualitative differences in learning II: Outcome as a function of the learner's conception of the task. *British Journal of Educational Psychology, 46*(2), 115–127.

Mayhew, E. (2006). Organizational change processes. In B. B. Jones & M. Brazzel (Eds.), *The NTL handbook of organizational development and change: Principles, practices, and perspectives* (pp. 104–120). San Francisco, CA: Wiley.

McGuire, L., Strong, D., Lay, K., Ardemagni, E., Wittberg, P., & Clayton, P. H. (2009). A case study of faculty learning around reflection: A collaborative faculty development project. In B. E. Moeley, S. H. Billig, & B. A. Holland (Eds.), *Creating our identities in service-learning and community engagement* (pp. 53–72). Charlotte, NC: Information Age.

McKay, V. C., & Rozee, P. D. (2004). Characteristics of faculty who adopt community service learning pedagogy. *Michigan Journal of Community Service Learning, 10*(2), 21–33.

McKeachie, W. J. (1991). What theories underlie the practice of faculty development? In K. Zahorski (Ed.), *To improve the academy* (Vol. 10, pp. 3–8). Stillwater, OK: New Forums Press.

McKinney, K. (2002). Instructional development: Relationships to teaching and learning in higher education. In D. Lieberman & C. Wehlburg (Eds.), *To improve the academy: Resources for faculty, instructional, and organizational development* (Vol. 20, pp. 225–237). Bolton, MA: Anker.

Mundy, M. F. (2004). Faculty engagement in service learning: Individual and organizational factors at distinct institutional types. In M. Welch & S. H. Billig (Eds.), *New perspectives in service-learning: Research to advance the field* (pp. 169–193). Greenwich, CT: Information Age.

O'Meara, K. A., & Niehaus, E. (2009). Service learning is . . . : How faculty explain their practice. *Michigan Journal of Service Learning, 16*(1), 17–32.

Piccinin, S. (1999). How individual consultation affects teaching. *New Directions for Teaching and Learning, 1999*(79), 71–84. doi:10.1002/tl.7908

Piccinin, S., & Moore, J. P. (2002). The impact of individual consultation on the teaching of younger versus older faculty. *International Journal for Academic Development, 7*(2), 123–135.

Pike, G. R., Bringle, R. G., & Hatcher, J. A. (in press). Assessing civic engagement at Indiana University–Purdue University–Indianapolis [Special issue]. *New Directions for Institutional Research.*

Plank, K. M., Kalish, A., Rohdieck, S. V., & Harper, K. A. (2005). A vision beyond measurement: Creating an integrated data system for teaching centers. In S. Chadwick-Blossey & D. Robertson (Eds.), *To improve the academy: Resources for faculty, instructional, and organizational development* (Vol. 23, pp. 173–190). Bolton, MA: Anker.

Pribbenow, D. A. (2005). The impact of service-learning pedagogy on faculty teaching and learning. *Michigan Journal of Community Service Learning, 11*(2), 25–38.

Professional and Organizational Development Network in Higher Education. (2007). *What is faculty development?* Retrieved from http://www.podnetwork.org/faculty_development/definitions.htm

Ramsden, P. (1994). Using research on student learning to enhance educational quality. In G. Gibbs (Ed.), *Improving student learning: Theory and practice.* Oxford, UK: Oxford Centre for Staff Development. Retrieved from www.londonmet.ac.uk/deliberations/ocsld-publications/isltp-ramsden.cfm

Ramsden, P. (2003). *Learning to teach in higher education* (2nd ed.). London, UK: Routledge.

Rice, D., & Stacey, K. (1997). Small group dynamics as a catalyst for change: A faculty development model for academic service-learning. *Michigan Journal of Community Service Learning, 4*(1), 64–71.

Robertson, D. R. (2000). Professors in space and time: Four utilities of a new metaphor and developmental model for professors-as-teachers. *Journal on Excellence in College Teaching, 11*(1), 117–132.

Schön, D. A. (1983). *The reflective practitioner: How professionals think in action.* New York, NY: Basic Books.

Seldin, P. (2006). Tailoring faculty development programs to faculty career stages. In S. Chadwick-Blossey & D. Robertson (Eds.), *To improve the academy* (Vol. 24, pp. 137–146). Bolton, MA: Anker.

Sharp, R. (2004). How do professionals learn and develop? Implications for staff and educational developers. In D. Baume & P. Kahn (Eds.), *Enhancing staff and educational development* (pp. 134–153). London, UK: RoutledgeFalmer.

Smith, H. J. (2004). The impact of staff development programmes and activities. In D. Baume & P. Kahn (Eds.), *Enhancing staff and educational development* (pp. 96–117). London, UK: RoutledgeFalmer.

Sorcinelli, M. D., Austin, A. E., Eddy, P. L., & Beach, A. L. (2006). *Creating the future of faculty development: Learning from the past, understanding the present.* Bolton, MA: Anker.

Stanton, T. K. (1994). The experience of faculty participants in an instructional development seminar on service-learning. *Michigan Journal of Community Service Learning, 1*(1), 7–20.

Varlotta, L. (2000). Service as text: Making the metaphor meaningful. *Michigan Journal of Community Service Learning, 7*(1), 76–84.

Wade, A., & Demb, A. (2009). A conceptual model to explore faculty community engagement. *Michigan Journal of Community Service Learning, 15*(2), 5–16.

Ward, K. (1996). Service-learning and student volunteerism: Reflections on institutional commitment. *Michigan Journal of Community Service Learning, 3*(1), 55–65.

Weimer, M. (2010). *Inspired college teaching: A career-long resource for professional growth.* San Francisco, CA: Jossey-Bass.

Wenger, E. (1998). *Communities of practice: Learning, meaning and identity.* Cambridge, UK: Cambridge University Press.

Zlotkowski, E. (1998). A service learning approach to faculty development. *New Directions for Teaching and Learning, 1998*(73), 81–89. doi:10.1002/tl.7310

Zuber-Skerritt, O. (1992). *Action research in higher education: Examples and reflections.* London, UK: Kogan Page.

3.2

RESEARCH ON FACULTY MOTIVATIONS FOR SERVICE LEARNING AND COMMUNITY ENGAGEMENT

KerryAnn O'Meara

F aculty become interested and involved in service learning and community engagement for many reasons, and this range of motivations has been an important area of study over the last 20 years. The concept of motivation arises from the field of psychology and human development and refers broadly to the reasons that individuals take actions toward particular goals. Such reasons might be intrinsic, related to personal goals and individuals' knowledge of what they do well; or extrinsic, related to what their external environment encourages them to do or establishes as a consequence of the action (Austin & Gamson, 1983; Blackburn & Lawrence, 1995). The study of motivation has been enriched by perspectives from multiple disciplines—including organizational behavior, sociology, political science, anthropology, education, cultural studies, and human resources—that have revealed the myriad, layered, and complex nature of human motivation. Specifically, these perspectives contribute to an understanding of motivation as not only an individual-level but also a collective-level phenomenon, emerging from communities, social movements, generational dynamics, political ideologies, workplaces, policies, and socialization processes.

Over the last two decades, scholars who study service learning in particular and higher education faculty more generally have documented a wide variety of motivations for faculty involvement in community engagement.

At the individual level these motivations include but are not limited to teaching goals, gender, race and ethnicity, experiences growing up working-class, epistemology or orientation to knowledge, a desire for learning, and a desire to enact commitments to specific community organizations or issues (Abes, Jackson, & Jones, 2002; Banerjee & Hausafus, 2007; Colbeck & Janke, 2006; Jaeger & Thornton, 2006; McKay & Rozee, 2004; O'Meara, 2008; O'Meara & Niehaus, 2009; Parkins, 2008). Investigations of the institutional settings and cultures that act as scaffolding or support for motivation have shown that discipline, institution type, perception of institutional support, and type of appointment all act as motivating forces (Vogelgesang, Denson, & Jayakumar, 2010).

Studying the factors that contribute to and inhibit faculty motivation for service learning and community engagement is important for several reasons. First, although there is a national imperative to advance the public dimensions of institutional missions by linking teaching and research with public issues (Boyer, 1990; Bringle & Hatcher, 2000), service learning and most community engagement activities are still widely considered discretionary activities within academic reward systems (O'Meara, 2002, 2004, 2008). Research on motivation can inform how scarce resources are best dedicated to recruit, support, and reward faculty involvement in community engagement. Second, the academic profession is in a major transition in terms of faculty demographics, work roles, types of appointments, and reward systems (O'Meara, Terosky, & Neumann, 2008). Research that considers how motivation may differ not only by institution type and discipline but also as a function of these shifts can contribute to college and university planning for faculty engagement. Such planning might focus on resources for faculty development, incentives for recruitment, and support for those involved. Finally, studying faculty motivation is important for service learning and community engagement because some of the most important questions are yet unanswered. Much of the early research identified the characteristics of faculty involved in service learning and then assumed that many of these characteristics were related to motivation. Applying Astin's (1993) input-environment-output (IEO) model broadly to faculty demonstrates that individual (e.g., gender), institutional (e.g., support for engagement), and environmental (e.g., social movement or political ideology) characteristics serve as starting points for involvement. Understanding how these starting points and faculty members' experiences in their work influence and are influenced by the potential outcomes of their work—outcomes such as learning, strengthened commitment, or increased social capital—is key to designing professional development that supports them in achieving these outcomes.

This analysis helps us understand and advance faculty participation in service learning as a form of professional growth, as well as faculty work that needs to be better regarded in academic reward systems, in part by considering new theories and methods to use in future research. The chapter begins with a presentation of perspectives related to motivation generally and then provides an overview of dimensions of professional growth (learning, agency, professional relationships, and commitments) that might enrich future research. Astin's (1993) IEO model is used to frame the process of faculty motivation for community engagement. Subsequent sections synthesize and critique research to date and consider implications for faculty developers and institutions. The chapter also provides an agenda for future research on faculty motivation for service learning and community engagement. In this analysis, service learning is considered one key expression of community engagement.

Theoretical and Conceptual Frameworks

The study of the academic profession is by its very nature interdisciplinary, and scholars who study faculty borrow from a wide range of conceptual frameworks (Creamer, 1998; Daly & Dee, 2006; O'Meara et al., 2008; Pallas, 2001; Perna, 2001). As Blackburn and Lawrence (1995) observe, "There is no conclusive framework for understanding this occupational group" (p. 282). The study of community engagement likewise requires epistemological flexibility and willingness to consider multiple methods and frameworks. This is especially true in the study of faculty motivation for service learning because faculty work (a) often crosses boundaries—across teaching and research roles (if community-based research or the scholarship of teaching and learning is involved), across race and class, and across language, country, and culture in the case of international service learning; (b) involves multiple skill sets (teaching, community development, institutional savvy, assessment); and (c) engages faculty and students in nontraditional kinds of work that are often interdisciplinary.

There is a rich and long history of using theories of motivation from the fields of psychology, organizational psychology, and human development to consider the intrinsic and extrinsic factors that come together to motivate individuals toward particular behaviors. Bess (2003) identified schools of motivation theories that are particularly applicable to faculty: need theories such as those by Maslow (1970) and Herzberg (1959), motive theories (McClelland, 1971), job enrichment theories (Hackman & Oldham, 1980), and equity theories (Adams, 1965; O'Meara, 2011). Most of these theories assume that individual faculty members have innate needs (such as a desire to achieve), acquire other needs, and are motivated by institutions—such as through reward systems—that help them meet needs and achieve personal and professional goals (O'Meara, 2011). One of the best examples of the interdisciplinary application of motivational theory of faculty was conducted by Blackburn and Lawrence (1995), who posit that a dynamic interaction between self-knowledge, or knowledge of what one does well and is skilled at doing, and social knowledge, or knowledge of the priorities of one's employer and workplace, influences motivation and behavior. Colbeck and Wharton-Michael (2006) apply motivational systems theory (Ford, 1992)— which assumes motivation is the result of individual goals, beliefs about capabilities, and beliefs about the supportiveness of one's contexts—to the study of public scholarship. Colbeck and Wharton-Michael (2006) conclude that although many engaged scholars are drawn to community engagement by individual goals and preferences, their institutions play a key role in enhancing faculty sense of self-efficacy and in sending messages that they prioritize and value the work. Although they are useful in research on faculty involvement in community engagement because they focus attention on the unique features of the individual and the intrinsic and extrinsic reasons that they make decisions, such theories can also be limiting in that they may overemphasize the role of individual motivation within the complex ecosystem of faculty work lives.

Social science theory on professional growth—especially as focused on the four synergistic dimensions of learning, agency, professional relationships, and commitments—has only recently begun to be tapped in research on faculty motivation for service learning and community engagement, but it has much to offer (O'Meara et al., 2008). This framework offers a broad perspective on faculty professional growth, bringing together theories of organizational culture and behavior, economic theories of human and social capital, the sociological concept of agency, and human development and motivational theories related to professional growth and career. Each of these clusters of theory can be used to study faculty motivation at an individual, a department/college, an institutional, or a national/international level. Research suggests that academic environments that cultivate professional growth in these four areas (learning, agency, professional relationships, and commitments) will lead to increases in organizational commitment and retention, motivation, satisfaction, and performance (Blackburn & Lawrence, 1995; Gappa, Austin, & Trice, 2007; Hagedorn, 2000), in part because workers, including faculty, thrive when they take control of their own growth, work toward purpose-driven mastery, and engage in positive professional relationships (Dweck, 2006; Laird, 2006; Pink, 2009).

Learning

In recent years scholars who study the academic profession have drawn on theories of learning from the fields of education and human development to extend understanding of how and what faculty learn (Creamer & Lattuca, 2005; Neumann, 2009a, 2009b; chapter 3.3). Among the central tenets of such work is how learning is supported and generated by one's identity and work context. Studies of faculty widely document that opportunities for learning in their respective fields and the prospect of making significant contributions and receiving recognition for those achievements are among the factors that draw faculty into academic careers (Hagedorn, 2000; Hermanowicz, 2009; Neumann, 2009a, 2009b). At the same time, faculty struggle for resources to support their learning, and they often feel pulled away from opportunities to learn by other responsibilities (e.g., administrative work, balance of work and family) (Neumann, 2009a, 2009b). Faculty change what they are learning, and how they are learning it, throughout their careers. The more that is known about the kinds of learning faculty are acquiring and the structures and cultures that are most likely to support that kind of learning, the more faculty development interventions, reward systems, and accountability measures can be designed to support them.

Agency

Sen (1985) defines *human agency* as "the ability to act on behalf of goals that matter to [oneself]" (p. 203). Theories of agency posit that individuals' sense of agency is (a) highly connected to their social context in any given situation, (b) a key ingredient of their well-being, and (c) temporal—that is, it changes over time and is influenced by their assessment of past, current, and future social capital (Alkire, 2005; Marshall, 2000; O'Meara & Campbell, 2008). Boyte (2008) observes that a sense of civic agency, or confidence in one's ability to make a difference as a citizen, is critical not only to student civic engagement but to faculty civic engagement as well. Many factors are likely to enhance faculty members' sense of self-efficacy in their work environment, in the community, and in advancing scholarship. For example, faculty may feel greater self-efficacy in facilitating conversations about race and poverty with students after having been part of a faculty learning community studying how to approach these issues. Alternatively, faculty may feel more comfortable doing the same if they have greater knowledge from their community partner about how these issues are playing out in the specific community in which their students are working. Understanding what factors are most likely to enhance faculty members' sense of agency and how these factors may differ by career stage, discipline, and individual identity yields important insights into motivation.

Professional Relationships

Several qualitative research studies on faculty motivation for service learning and community engagement have shown the significant growth and fulfillment that faculty derive from having close personal ties and networks, or allies, involved with them (Bloomgarden, 2008; Bloomgarden & O'Meara, 2007; O'Meara, 2002; O'Meara & Niehaus, 2009; Ward, 2010). Research on careers (Lin, 2001a, 2001b) and collegial networks (Milem, Sherlin, & Irwin, 2001) demonstrates that faculty advance at least in part through tapping the human and social capital embodied in professional relationships and networks (Becker, 1993; Laird, 2006). Therefore, theory and research on networks and professional relationships (Kadar, 2005; Laird, 2006) can contribute to a better understanding of whether and how community-engaged faculty are in fact motivated for the work by relationships with students, other faculty, and community partners.

Commitments

Perry (1968) defines *commitment* as "affirmation of personal values or choice" and "a conscious act or realization of identity and responsibility" (p. 135). Drawing on theories of human development and the work of developmental psychologists and sociologists, one might further define commitments as "long-term, conscious, personal, and professional investments that scholars make in certain people, programs, places, and social concerns through concrete activity that furthers the goals of higher education" (O'Meara et al., 2008, pp. 30–31). Specifically, faculty who make commitments to service learning and community engagement do so as a matter of conscious choice, which is followed up by specific behaviors that make specific contributions to a cause, an individual, or a community (O'Meara et al., 2008). There is an important connection here with epistemology, or how we understand knowledge. Research has shown that faculty who have a humanistic orientation (Vogelgesang et al., 2010), feminist perspective (Ward, 2010), or constructivist/solidarity approach (Colbeck & Wharton-Michael, 2006) tend to be overrepresented among faculty involved in community engagement, which may thus be the extension of these epistemological commitments. Such theories that explore commitments (e.g., Daloz, Keen, Keen, & Parks, 1996), how they develop over time, and their connections to epistemology can enrich not only the research on service learning and engagement but also conversations among faculty developers about how to support faculty long term in this work. For example, commitments to community engagement that originate in socialization about the role of the discipline in the world require different kinds of supports and networks to grow than commitments to teaching well or to student development.

Synthesis: Input-Environment-Output

In line with the synergistic implications of these four dimensions of professional growth, research on faculty has found that it is the *dynamic interaction* among an individual's characteristics (e.g., demographics and identity characteristics, socialization, work effort, preferences such as teaching goals, and sense of agency), institutional factors (e.g., culture; climate; rewards for community engagement in departments, colleges/schools, and the institution overall), and environmental factors (e.g., their standing in and interactions with colleagues external to the institution in disciplines and networks) that influences retention, satisfaction, growth, and performance (Blackburn & Lawrence, 1995; Creamer, 1998; Gappa et al., 2007). As in the case of general studies of faculty, the literature on faculty motivations for service learning and community engagement could benefit from conceptual models that explore the interactions among factors. This chapter offers such a conceptualization of faculty motivations for community engagement, drawing on Astin's (1993) IEO model. Created to underscore the influence of entering student characteristics and previous experiences and beliefs on later outcomes and to call attention to the ways in which the college environment (e.g., size, public or private status, diversity of the institution) mediates student learning outcomes, Astin's model focuses on inputs, processes, and outcomes that are common to many theories of change. The model has been used in conjunction with systems theory to consider the impact of classrooms on civic outcomes (O'Meara, Jaeger, & Giles, 2009) and to frame academic reward systems (O'Meara, 2011); it is a useful tool for conceptualizing all of the potential influences on faculty motivation at different points in a process such as involvement with service learning. Figure 3.2.1 outlines many of the starting points, or potential inputs, for faculty motivation for service learning and community engagement, aspects of the experience or process of being involved in it that may influence motivation, and some of the outcomes that may influence motivation. These outcomes cycle back and become inputs as they become new motivational forces. This conceptualization is not an exhaustive representation; rather, it is meant to be illustrative of the major conceptual elements in the study of faculty motivation.

What We Know About Faculty Motivation for Community Engagement

Drawn from both empirical studies and literature reviews, Table 3.2.1 outlines the major influences on faculty motivation for service learning and community engagement as identified in the extant research, categorized into individual, institutional, and environmental factors with examples of studies that have shown each factor to be important.

Over the last five years several major studies of faculty and reviews of literature were conducted on the state of the academic profession (Gappa et al., 2007; O'Meara et al., 2008; Schuster & Finkelstein, 2006). These studies revealed major shifts in (a) faculty demographics (or who faculty are), (b) appointment types, (c) the nature of faculty work, and (d) reward systems, all of which influence faculty motivation for community engagement. In terms of demographics, increasingly, baby boomers are retiring and being replaced with Generation X (born between 1965 and 1982) and Y (born between 1980 and 1994) faculty. Generation X faculty, women faculty, and faculty of color appear to have a greater interest in teaching methods that use active learning and that engage students in higher-order cognitive skill building (Umbach, 2006, 2007). Although these subpopulations of faculty may not yet be in the most prestigious faculty positions, the growing diversity of the professoriate seems likely to result in increased participation in service learning and community engagement as these groups are also more likely to hold teaching goals and epistemologies that act as motivators for this work (Vogelgesang et al., 2010).

Non–tenure track appointments are becoming more predominant. Tenure-ineligible, full-time appointments account for 30% of the academic workforce, and part-time appointments account for more than 40% of the academic workforce and 65% of recent appointments (Gappa et al., 2007;

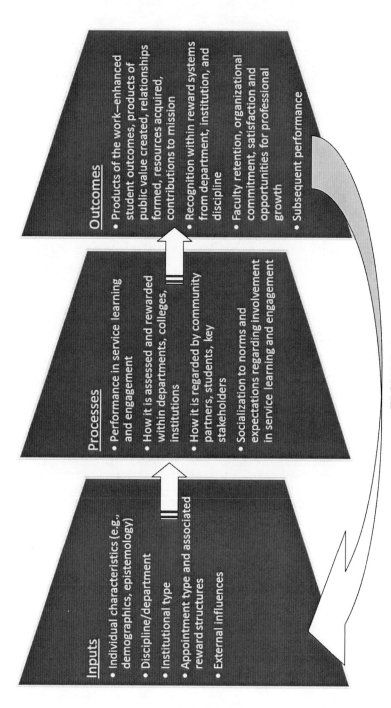

Inputs

- Individual characteristics (e.g., demographics, epistemology)
- Discipline/department
- Institutional type
- Appointment type and associated reward structures
- External influences

Processes

- Performance in service learning and engagement
- How it is assessed and rewarded within departments, colleges, institutions
- How it is regarded by community partners, students, key stakeholders
- Socialization to norms and expectations regarding involvement in service learning and engagement

Outcomes

- Products of the work—enhanced student outcomes, products of public value created, relationships formed, resources acquired, contributions to mission
- Recognition within reward systems from department, institution, and discipline
- Faculty retention, organizational commitment, satisfaction and opportunities for professional growth
- Subsequent performance

FIGURE 3.2.1

Conceptual Model for Faculty Motivation for Service Learning and Community Engagement

TABLE 3.2.1
Extant Research on Faculty Motivations for Service
Learning and Community Engagement

Individual Factors	Themes and Citations
Demographics: gender, race and ethnicity, early career and first-generation college and working-class background	Participation in and commitment to service learning and community engagement has been self-reported as higher among women, faculty of color, and early and career faculty (Aguirre, 2000; Antonio et al., 2000; Astin et al., 2006; Baez, 2000; Colbeck & Wharton-Michael, 2006; González & Padilla, 2008; O'Meara, 2008; Parkins, 2008; Ward, 2010; WRCCC, 2009).
Personal commitment to service learning and epistemology	Participation in service learning and community engagement has been found to be higher among faculty who report having a personal commitment to service learning and engagement (Jaeger & Thornton, 2006), social change and humanistic orientations (Antonio et al., 2000; Astin et al., 2006), and constructivist approaches to knowledge (Colbeck & Wharton-Michael, 2006).
Teaching goals	Participation in service learning has been found to be higher among faculty who think it adds to student learning (Abes et al., 2002; Bringle & Hatcher, 2000; Bringle, Hatcher, & Games, 1997; Hammond, 1994; McKay & Rozee, 2004; Parkins, 2008), develops disciplinary knowledge and skills, is an effective form of experiential learning, and shapes moral and civic dispositions (O'Meara & Niehaus, 2009).
Career stages	Participation in service learning and community engagement has been found to be influenced by career stage and different professional learning and development needs at early, mid, and late career such as training on reflection versus assistance with publishing on student outcomes (Baldwin, 1990; Baldwin & Chang, 2005; Colbeck & Wharton-Michael, 2006; O'Meara, 2004).
Identity and professional experience	Participation in service learning and community engagement has been found to be associated with a sense of civic agency, commitment, and prior experience with community engagement (Baez, 2000; Colbeck & Janke, 2006; Daloz et al., 1996; Hatcher, 2008; O'Meara & Niehaus, 2009; Ward, 2010).

Institutional Factors	*Themes and Citations*
Institutional type, context, and reward system	Participation in service learning and community engagement has been found to be negatively associated with institutional reward systems that do not prioritize service learning and engagement (Astin et al., 2006; Bloomgarden & O'Meara, 2007; Colbeck & Wharton-Michael, 2006; Fairweather, 2005; Holland, 1999; Jaeger & Thornton, 2006; O'Meara, 2002, 2004; O'Meara & Niehaus, 2009; Peters et al., 2008; Ward, 2003). In addition, more faculty from private, Catholic, and other religious institutions report being involved in service learning and engagement than those at public institutions (Antonio et al., 2000; Vogelgesang et al., 2010).
Appointment type/rank	Participation in service learning and community engagement has been found to be influenced by appointment type and rank within an institutional context (Abes et al., 2002; Antonio et al., 2000; Bellas & Toutkoushian, 1999; Parkins, 2008).
Environmental Factors	
Discipline	Participation in service learning and community engagement has been found to be associated with disciplinary socialization and approaches to knowledge, and the desire to achieve disciplinary goals in teaching. Specifically, faculty in the social sciences and professional programs such as health and social work are more likely to self-report participation in service learning and engagement than those in the hard sciences and humanities (Abes et al., 2002; Antonio et al., 2000; Colbeck & Wharton-Michael, 2006; O'Meara & Niehaus, 2009; Vogelgesang et al., 2010; Zlotkowski, 2000).
Nature of the community partnership and partnership identity	Participation in service learning and community engagement has been found to be motivated by faculty desire to participate in and learn from community partnerships (Colbeck & Janke, 2006; Janke, 2009).

Schuster & Finkelstein, 2006). Although appointment type acts as a key working condition that motivates faculty behavior and productivity (Bland, Center, Finstad, Risbey, & Staples, 2006), it is not yet clear whether the major shifts from tenure track to non–tenure track and from full-time to part-time positions will increase participation in service learning and community engagement overall.

There have also been major shifts in the nature of faculty work, requiring faculty to do more with technology and to work within settings that are increasingly diverse as well as in ways that are interdisciplinary and entrepreneurial (Gappa et al., 2007; O'Meara et al., 2008; Schuster & Finkelstein, 2006). Other key trends in work include faculty increasing the number of hours worked per week, being part of two-career households, and struggling to find the best balance between work and family (O'Meara et al., 2008). Finally, as state and federal funding decline, faculty have lost critical resources to support their teaching, research, professional development, and community engagement. These shifts in how faculty go about their work and in the nature of the work they undertake pose both opportunities and constraints related to community engagement. For example, many campuses are developing new interdisciplinary research centers and projects, revising general education curriculum, and providing opportunities for study abroad and uses of technology that have never existed before—all of which can have synergy with service learning and community engagement.

Although overall satisfaction levels among faculty are high in comparison to other professions, they are nonetheless declining (Gappa et al., 2007; O'Meara et al., 2008). This decrease in satisfaction has been linked to increased demands on faculty time and accountability measures, pressure to excel in all areas of faculty work with fewer institutional resources, and appointments with less job security (Gappa et al., 2007). Few studies of faculty motivation have been able to infer how these different work and appointment conditions may be influencing faculty community engagement.

The research base summarized in Table 3.2.1 is not without its contradictions. For example, much research suggests that in comparison with their male counterparts, women faculty are more likely to self-report involvement in service learning and community engagement, to believe campuses should work with the community, and to endorse a service learning requirement (Antonio et al., 2000; Astin et al., 2006; Hurtado, Ponjuan, & Smith, 2003; Vogelgesang et al., 2010). Yet several studies show that when other factors—such as career stage and rank, discipline, and institutional type—are controlled for, gender is no longer a significant predictor of faculty involvement

(Bellas & Toutkoushian, 1999; Parkins, 2008). The same is true for faculty of color being more involved in community engagement (Antonio et al., 2000; Baez, 2000; Parkins, 2008; Vogelgesang et al., 2010). Furthermore, because faculty of color are disproportionately represented in academic ranks, disciplines, and institution types more likely to participate in this work; because they have also been found more likely to hold teaching goals conducive to service learning (Umbach, 2006), it is not always clear whether it is race and ethnicity or other aspects of identity that are dominant in predicting involvement. Likewise, some studies have shown that involvement in and commitment to service learning is higher among faculty who are non–tenure track and pre-tenure (Antonio et al., 2000; O'Meara, 2002), whereas others suggest that pre-tenure faculty are less apt to be involved, likely because of their focus on getting tenure through traditional forms of scholarship (Abes et al., 2002). Part of the contradiction in findings is no doubt the result of the facts that the field of study is still new and that different definitions of service learning and community engagement have been used with different methods employed to arrive at findings.

The topic of professional growth, including the specific dimensions of learning, agency, professional relationships, and commitments developed through service learning and engagement, has also been understudied. However, issues of long-term support and professional development (as opposed to short-term workshops or recruitment) have begun to emerge more frequently in studies of faculty motivation. In chapter 3.3 Clayton, Hess, Jaeger, Jameson, and McGuire explore faculty learning, including the role it plays in sustaining motivation; they suggest that understanding how and in what settings faculty learn is key to strengthening faculty commitment to service learning and community engagement. Several studies have documented the motivation that exemplary engaged faculty have gained from participation in national and international relationships developed through community engagement (O'Meara, 2008; Peters et al., 2008). Although some qualitative studies have revealed the importance of learning and relationships gained from service learning and engagement (e.g., Janke, 2009), very little research has explored how they translate back into particular outcomes such as student learning, development of partnerships, collaborative scholarship, or long-term institutional change and support.

In sum, changes in the contexts that surround faculty and in the nature of their work offer not only opportunities for and constraints on service learning and community engagement but also different incentives and contexts in which faculty might be motivated in this work via recruitment, support, and reward. Often, research on faculty motivation does not take this milieu into account, therefore providing only a partial picture of the motivational process. Given the importance of solid research designs in achieving more complete understanding, the following section considers approaches that have been used to study faculty motivation and suggests new approaches as well.

Critique of Past Research Methods and New Approaches

Three common methods are used to study faculty motivation for service learning and community engagement—quantitative surveys, qualitative interviews, and narrative analysis—and each has strengths and limitations. Much of what is known about faculty motivation for and involvement in this work comes from survey research at individual, regional, and national levels (e.g., Abes et al., 2002; Antonio et al., 2000; Hammond, 1994; Hatcher, 2008; Vogelgesang et al., 2010; Western Region Campus Compact Consortium [WRCCC], 2009). For example, Hammond (1994) surveyed 250 service learning faculty members across 23 institutions in order to gather data about their demographic characteristics, their interests, and their courses. Respondents reported that they were primarily drawn to service learning by curricular concerns. That is, as also found in subsequent work (e.g., Abes et al., 2002; O'Meara & Niehaus, 2009), faculty were motivated to integrate service learning into their courses by a desire to teach content more effectively and thereby enhance student learning outcomes.

To compare the characteristics of faculty involved in service learning with those not involved (see also Abes et al., 2002; Banerjee & Hausafus, 2007; Patel, 2004; WRCCC, 2009), Parkins (2008) surveyed 3,000 full-time tenured and tenure track faculty at five research institutions using the Faculty Survey of Individual and Motivational Factors. Ethnicity (being from an underrepresented minority), rank (having tenure and being higher in rank), and teaching goals (having a specific set of teaching goals related to student learning, civic education, and connecting teaching and scholarly agenda) were found to be significant factors in the use of service learning pedagogy, after controlling for other key variables such as institution type and discipline.

A major contributor to understanding the factors that predict faculty involvement in community engagement has been analysis of data from the Higher Education Research Institute's Faculty Survey (e.g., Antonio et al.,

2000; Astin et al., 2006; Vogelgesang et al., 2010). In terms of individual characteristics (e.g., humanistic orientation) and gender appear to be critical predictors of faculty involvement, as do certain disciplinary (e.g., education versus mathematics) and institutional (e.g., Catholic versus research-oriented) environments. Regardless of the specific discipline or institution type, however, this data set confirms that perception of institutional support matters in faculty involvement in service learning and community engagement (Vogelgesang et al., 2010).

Strengths of these studies include the use of multivariate statistics and regression to control for individual, institutional, and disciplinary characteristics when asking questions about the relationship between any one factor, such as humanistic orientation, and community engagement. Vogelgesang et al. (2010) suggest that the broad definitions of service learning and community engagement that are generally used in faculty surveys constitute another strength in that they allow a wide range of respondents to locate their work within this arena contextually. An associated shortcoming of such imprecise definitions, however, may be that it is less possible to trace whether a particular kind of community engagement (e.g., community-based research, service learning) is more or less related to a particular characteristic, behavior, or motivation. As the field moves forward, this tension point between inclusiveness and the clarity, consistency, and continuity in measurement that could result from using more specific and perhaps common definitions (such as that provided by Campus Compact or the Carnegie Foundation in the elective classification for Community Engagement) will need further attention.

There has also been important qualitative work on faculty motivation for service learning and community engagement (e.g., Bloomgarden, 2008; Bloomgarden & O'Meara, 2007; Janke, 2009; Peters et al., 2008). In some of the more in-depth examples (Bloomgarden, 2008; Janke, 2009), researchers interviewed not only faculty but also their colleagues, students, and community partners to develop either individual qualitative portraits or case studies of faculty within specific institutional contexts. Three examples are presented here for illustration; although not a central focus, each of these examples also touches on faculty experiences of professional growth in community engagement activities, which serves as motivation for continued involvement.

Bloomgarden (2008) analyzed 15 exemplary engaged scholars in selective liberal arts institutions. A community partner and a departmental colleague were also interviewed regarding each faculty member's engagement and how they saw it work within the context of the institutional and community settings, and archival documents (e.g., syllabi, grant applications, project descriptions, personal statements) were also collected. Bloomgarden found these faculty to be motivated by aspects of their own autobiographies related to race, gender, socioeconomic status, and professional and personal experiences as well as by disciplinary goals and desires to integrate their scholarly and personal commitments.

Peters et al. (2008) interviewed and gathered background materials on the careers and community engagement of 44 faculty members (31 men and 13 women) across a range of demographics, disciplines, and career stages at a state college of agriculture, life sciences, and environmental sciences regarding the origins of and motivations for their community engagement. The authors found that the institution's land-grant mission played a large role in the faculty members' motivations and that the faculty shared a desire to make their work relevant beyond their disciplines and to bring new knowledge from practice settings back into their classrooms and their research.

Ward (2010) conducted a qualitative study of 11 women who received the Lynton Award for the Scholarship of Engagement to examine motivations for community engagement and the nature of faculty interactions with academic reward systems. In-depth semi-structured interviews, personal promotion and tenure narratives, and other written documents served as the data sources. In addition to learning of significant bias against community-engaged scholarship in reward systems and sexism in work settings, Ward found that the women's community-engaged scholarship was deeply rooted in not only gender but also other identities (e.g., as immigrants, women of color, faculty from working-class backgrounds) as well as in their epistemology and ontology. Ward's work is an excellent example of teasing apart motivation tied to one factor (gender) from motivations tied to other aspects of identity and institutional context. This is key because the approach taken in much of the literature—describing characteristics of faculty involved in service learning and community engagement and then assuming that because more engaged faculty than non-engaged faculty have these characteristics they must be motivating factors—confuses correlation with causation and often fails to examine any one characteristic in terms of its complex relationship to others.

Qualitative designs such as these three examples have the benefit of in-depth analysis of the intersections between various motivations. Both a strength and a limitation of such an approach is that it reveals how these motivations played out in very specific institutional, disciplinary, and career stage contexts—providing depth but lacking generalizability. The samples were intentionally small to provide rich detail, and the sampling method usually selected heavily engaged faculty, thus rendering this approach less well suited than larger studies to generalizing to the overall population of faculty in terms of the characteristics that may best predict faculty involvement in community engagement.

A third method of studying faculty motivation for service learning and community engagement involves narrative or content analysis of personal essays and materials—such as journals, project descriptions, and analyses of outcomes—produced, for example, by exemplary engaged faculty or faculty participants in professional development activities (e.g., Faculty Fellows programs). This approach was used to study faculty who had won or been nominated for the Thomas Ehrlich Civically Engaged Faculty Award (O'Meara, 2008; O'Meara & Niehaus, 2009). O'Meara and Niehaus (2009) found dominant teaching and learning motivations for faculty involvement in service learning (e.g., a desire for students to learn disciplinary knowledge and skills and to learn through experience, to shape student civic and moral dispositions, to expose students to diversity). An advantage of this approach is that the participants had often thought deeply about their motivations and interests in community engagement in crafting the materials that served as data sources; thus, the data can be much richer than responses to on-the-spot interview questions. On the other hand, there is a halo effect wherein faculty are likely to frame their motivations and interests in overly altruistic ways to play to what they believe potential readers (e.g., award committees) want to hear.

Implications for Practice

Review of the research and literature on faculty motivations for service learning and community engagement reveals several important implications for faculty developers and administrators who support or seek to expand and deepen faculty involvement (see chapter 3.1). The previously noted finding from Vogelgesang et al.'s (2010) study—that even after controlling for such factors as demographic characteristics, discipline, and institution type, faculty perception of institutional support for community engagement is the primary predictor of involvement—suggests that institutions have a major role to play in creating environments that motivate faculty toward this work.

There are at least three critical areas in which institutions could make a significant difference. First, research suggests that faculty are likely to be drawn to service learning and motivated to become more deeply engaged if they expect and find out (a) that they are learning something important for their professional and personal lives and (b) that their teaching goals are being met. Therefore, professional development programs that emphasize deep reflection as part of the learning process (Clayton & Ash, 2005; chapter 3.3) and faculty developers and administrators who help faculty assess the degree to which their individual teaching goals are being met are more likely to see those faculty stay involved. Likewise, opportunities to connect service learning and community engagement with scholarship, and to publish and disseminate on the work and its impact, will likely result in greater faculty motivation for the pedagogy.

Second, the individual, institutional, and environmental contexts that surround faculty are key to their motivation for this work and should be considered in designing programs. For example, the Lilly Teaching Fellows Program for early career faculty in research universities (Austin, 2002) and the Preparing Future Faculty program for doctoral students (Gaff, 2005) were successful because of the focus on specific teaching and career content (such as teaching with technology or integrating diversity into the curriculum) and the identification of a common career stage (pre-career or early career). Thus, faculty developers may want to create and implement programs that focus on engaging, motivating, and supporting faculty cohorts at specific career stages (Jameson, Clayton, & Jaeger, 2011), within engaged departments (Kecskes, 2006), and perhaps even by identification with particular epistemological or political stances (e.g., convening faculty who share feminist, critical race, social justice, or civic action reasons for this work).

Third, theory on agency and emerging studies of learning through professional relationships and networks make clear that the webs of support that faculty can develop through community engagement are meaningful and important in and of themselves. If faculty developers can connect faculty both to an on-campus community that maintains regular communication (e.g., through blogs or brown-bag lunches) to share resources, ideas, failures, and successes and to peers off campus doing this work in their own disciplines motivation will be significantly enhanced.

Recommendations for Future Research

This discussion of relevant theoretical perspectives and of extant research results and methods related to the study of faculty motivation for service learning and community engagement leads to the questions: Where does the field stand, and what are some important future directions for research on faculty motivation? Overall, quantitative studies have done much to reveal personal and professional characteristics of faculty committed to and engaged in this work, and qualitative studies have revealed why and how they are involved. Yet there are persistent limitations across most research designs (quantitative and qualitative) that could be improved upon in future research. One straightforward improvement that any researcher in this field can attend to—and that would add significantly to the quality and utility of data sets—is consistently taking care to ask participants for and document critical background characteristics, such as gender, discipline, career stage, generation, appointment type, and institutional context. This approach would allow researchers to more easily identify common themes across research studies such as motivations linked to generation, mission, and gender identity.

The remainder of this section lays out five key directions for new research on faculty motivation for service learning and community engagement. The first is that the quality and usefulness of research on motivation will be improved when there is thicker application of social science theory to the examination of faculty involvement. In some instances, attention has been given to a particular social science framework in analyzing findings. O'Meara and Niehaus (2009) used the strategy of critical discourse analysis to frame faculty motivations for this work. Discourse analysis sheds a critical spotlight on how what is said and written about service learning and community engagement represents a particular social context, identity, beliefs, and values and actively produces and legitimates a given reality. Furthermore it reveals individual perceptions of subject or power relationships and priorities in the work. The concept of identity, including racial identity (Baez, 2000), civic identity (Hatcher, 2008), partnership identity (Janke, 2009), and gender identity (Ward, 2010), has been used to frame faculty involvement and motivation for engagement. Yet overall there have been more exploratory and descriptive studies than in-depth uses of theory to shape research (e.g., to frame research questions, develop survey items, form interview questions, or conduct content analysis of written documents).

As part of better mobilizing theory to enrich research on faculty motivation, scholars might tap the four dimensions of professional growth presented earlier. A better understanding of what structural and cultural conditions increase faculty members' sense of agency and how it in turn motivates their behaviors related to community engagement is needed. Does having a tenured appointment, professional development experience with colleagues, or support from one's department chair make the biggest difference, or even a significant difference, in this regard? If so, how and why? Do these conditions perhaps increase the level of social capital faculty feel confident in drawing upon? Likewise, scholars have critiqued the individualized silos of the academic culture (O'Meara et al., 2008) and noted that they prefer to live a life that is more connected to colleagues (Palmer, 2007). What kinds of relationships are more generative for facilitating learning and strengthening faculty commitments to service learning and community engagement? What kinds of community engagement have the potential to initiate the most significant learning experiences?

A second direction for future research relates to Figure 3.2.1 and the interactions among faculty inputs or starting points, faculty members' subsequent experiences in service learning and community engagement, and the outcomes of those experiences. The conceptual framework expressed in Figure 3.2.1 can serve as the basis for a variety of important research questions: Which outcomes and products of service learning and community engagement are most likely to strengthen ongoing motivation? Are there certain groups of faculty for whom reward system recognition matters less and other outcomes matter more? Future research might also examine the cumulative effect of becoming more involved in this work and how ever-deepening involvement changes motivations over time. For example, a study of faculty exemplars (O'Meara, 2008) documented a cumulative effect of success on ongoing participation: As the faculty became known for their work on their campuses as well as regionally and nationally, their motivation for and commitment to it increased and changed (becoming more focused on specific communities and partnerships and furthering the number of engaged faculty on their campuses). Under what conditions does this dynamic hold for other faculty? Also of interest is the question of the conditions under which faculty begin but then discontinue involvement in service learning and community engagement.

Issues related to the appointment structures that support motivation for service learning and community engagement comprise an important third future direction for research. Given what is known about differences in rates of adoption of active learning strategies among part-time, non–tenure track, and tenure track faculty and about the role of appointment types more generally in faculty work and rewards (O'Meara, 2011), as the academic labor force moves to a predominantly non–tenure track system it will be more important than ever to shift research focus toward contract systems and other incentives within non–tenure track appointments in terms of how they support or thwart this work. Are there major differences between tenure track and non–tenure track faculty in the quality of their implementation of service learning and community engagement? Are there differences in the quality of the support they receive from their institutions? Are there different motivations and outcomes that can be correlated with appointment type? Relatedly, if community engagement increasingly becomes segregated in the faculty roles of those off the tenure track, will this thwart institutionalization on campus? With more than half of higher education students in community colleges, understanding motivations for faculty, both part-time and full-time, at these institutions is particularly important to completing the portrait of faculty motives. Given the rapid increase in the non–tenure track and unbundled faculty roles, the influence of appointment structures on faculty motivations for service learning and community engagement remains a very important area for future research.

A fourth important direction for studies of motivation relates to the intersections among individual, institutional, and environmental forces and the need to understand how they work synergistically to motivate faculty involvement in particular kinds of community engagement. One example involves institutions that have received the Carnegie classification for community engagement status. Arguably these institutions are trying to provide institutional support for this work. Does this mean that they are attracting more faculty who want to undertake service learning and community engagement? Or were those faculty already there, pushing the institution to go after the classification? Likewise, how does the current resource-limited environment of higher education influence both institutional and individual faculty efforts? Just as we should not assume that an institution with a high *U.S. News & World Report* ranking provides a high-quality learning experience for students simply on the basis of that ranking, we need comparative research that considers the intersections of faculty motivation at the individual level; the institutional mission, contexts, and supports; and the social, political, and economic forces influencing higher education.

A second example of an approach to investigating such intersections would be to use the lens of generation (e.g., Bova & Kroth, 2001) and consider how Generation X and Y faculty, versus older faculty, may be predisposed toward service learning and community engagement by virtue of a more participatory or constructivist epistemology. Studies of engaged graduate students and early career faculty could reveal much about similarities and differences across generations of faculty and how the nature of motivation for this work may be shifting. The Next Generation Engagement Project (Saltmarsh, Zlotkowski, & Horowitz, 2010) has begun such inquiry, asking questions about differences in epistemology and approaches to teaching and research among Generation X and Y collaborators. Additional questions of interest relate to the dynamic interactions among gender, race, epistemology, interdisciplinarity, political orientation, and community engagement.

A final recommendation for future research involves moving beyond the historical overreliance on self-report surveys. Although responses to such surveys have been found to be related to actual behaviors, their value is constrained by the inherent limitations of respondents' recollections of the past and predictions of the future. The field needs to develop greater expertise in such methods as participant observation and ethnography. Very few studies have followed faculty into classrooms where service learning is framed and discussed or into the field where faculty interact with students and community partners. Classroom observation and ethnographic approaches could reveal previously undocumented motivations embedded in relationships and learning processes, some of which faculty may not even be fully aware of by virtue of being so immersed in the work (O'Meara et al., 2009; O'Meara, Sandmann, Saltmarsh, & Giles, 2011). Such approaches would help address many of the limitations associated with the halo effect in describing this work and personal motivations for it. Such research would also serve an immediate practical purpose of providing richer descriptions of the processes of faculty involvement in service learning and community engagement, including but also transcending the variables that influence faculty members' motivations for the work.

Conclusion

As Syracuse University president Nancy Cantor (2010) has observed, higher education institutions are among the last remaining anchor institutions in communities struggling in the new global economy. If executed effectively, faculty integration of service learning into teaching enhances student learning while serving critical community needs. This can lead to other forms of community engagement and their integration into faculty research and professional service roles. However, faculty are motivated toward specific kinds of work activities by a diversity of factors, including their own socialization and training in disciplines, perception of the support of their institution, and individual characteristics such as epistemology—all of which must be better understood if the pedagogy is to realize its full potential through systematic and high-quality institutionalization.

Although the knowledge base is growing, there are many opportunities to deepen the capacity of the field for scholarly inquiry. Research to date has not been rich in the use of theory, and the focus has tended to be on faculty starting points for service learning and community engagement rather than also on what keeps faculty involved after they step through the door, and what is associated with discontinuing engagement activities. Social science theory related to professional growth offers a valuable perspective for investigating the factors that keep faculty involved and that deepen their commitments. Future research needs to go beyond exploring how single factors, such as gender, attract faculty to this work and also examine the ways in which such aspects of their identity actually shape the work. Furthermore, the working conditions of academics are changing quickly. Future research must factor in such contextual variables as appointment type, institutional resources, and competing demands for faculty time on faculty members' motivation to become involved, and then to stay involved, in service learning and community engagement. Otherwise, we risk losing a prime opportunity to understand better and, in turn, support the participation of current and especially future generations of practitioner-scholars in work that is increasingly recognized as central to our mission both as academics and as citizens.

Recommended Reading

Blackburn, R. T., & Lawrence, J. H. (1995). *Faculty at work: Motivation, expectation, satisfaction.* Baltimore, MD: The Johns Hopkins University Press.
Colbeck, C., & Wharton-Michael, P. (2006). Individual and organizational influences on faculty members' engagement in public scholarship. *New Directions for Teaching and Learning, 2006*(105), 17–26. doi:10.1002/tl.221
O'Meara, K., & Niehaus, E. (2009). Service-learning is . . . : How faculty explain their practice. *Michigan Journal of Community Service Learning, 16*(1), 1–16.
O'Meara, K., Terosky, A. L., & Neumann, A. (2008). Faculty careers and work lives: A professional growth perspective. *ASHE Higher Education Report, 34*(3). San Francisco, CA: Jossey-Bass.
Vogelgesang, L. J., Denson, N., & Jayakumar, U. M. (2010). What determines faculty-engaged scholarship? *The Review of Higher Education, 33*, 437–472.

References

Abes, E. S., Jackson, G., & Jones, S. R. (2002). Factors that motivate and deter faculty use of service-learning. *Michigan Journal of Community Service Learning, 9*(1), 5–17.

Adams, J. S. (1965). Inequity in social exchange. In L. Berkowitz (Ed.), *Advances in experimental social psychology* (pp. 267–299). New York, NY: Academic Press.

Aguirre, A., Jr. (2000). Women and minority faculty in the academic workplace: Recruitment, retention, and academic culture. *ASHE-ERIC Higher Education Report, 27*(6). San Francisco, CA: Jossey-Bass.

Alkire, S. (2005). Subjective quantitative studies of human agency. *Social Indicators Research, 74*(1), 217–260.

Antonio, A. L., Astin, H. S., & Cress, C. M. (2000). Community service in higher education: A look at the nation's faculty. *The Review of Higher Education, 23,* 373–397.

Astin, A. W. (1993). *What matters in college.* San Francisco, CA: Jossey-Bass.

Astin, A. W., Vogelgesang, L. J., Misam, J., Anderson, J., Denson, N., Jayakumar, U., Yamamura, E. Y. (2006). *Understanding the effects of service-learning: A study of students and faculty.* Los Angeles, CA: Higher Education Research Institute.

Austin, A. E. (2002, November). *Aspiring and early career faculty: What do we know? What do we need to know?* Paper presented at the Annual Meeting of the Association for the Study of Higher Education, Sacramento, CA.

Austin, A. E., & Gamson, Z. F. (1983). Academic workplace: New demands, heightened tensions. *ASHE-ERIC Higher Education Research Report No. 10.* Washington, DC: Association for the Study of Higher Education.

Baez, B. (2000). Race-related service and faculty of color: Conceptualizing critical agency in academe. *Higher Education, 39,* 363–391.

Baldwin, R. G. (1990). Faculty career stages and implications for professional development. In J. H. Schuster, D. W. Wheeler, & Associates (Eds.), *Enhancing faculty careers: Strategies for development and renewal* (pp. 20–40). San Francisco, CA: Jossey-Bass.

Baldwin, R. G., & Chang, D. (2005). Reinforcing our keystone faculty. *Liberal Education, 92*(4), 28–35.

Banerjee, M., & Hausafus, C. O. (2007). Faculty use of service-learning: Perceptions, motivations, and impediments for the human sciences. *Michigan Journal of Community Service Learning, 14*(1), 32–45.

Becker, G. S. (1993). *Human capital.* Chicago, IL: University of Chicago Press.

Bellas, M. L., & Toutkoushian, R. K. (1999). Faculty time allocations and research productivity: Gender, race and family effects. *The Review of Higher Education, 22,* 367–390.

Bess, J. L. (2003, November). *Changing times, changing motivations: The impact of new organizational conditions on worker effort and will.* Paper presented at the annual meeting of the Association for the Study of Higher Education, Portland, OR.

Blackburn, R. T., & Lawrence, J. H. (1995). *Faculty at work: Motivation, expectation, satisfaction.* Baltimore, MD: The Johns Hopkins University Press.

Bland, C., Center, B., Finstad, D., Risbey, K., & Staples, J. (2006). The impact of appointment type on the productivity and commitment of full-time faculty in research and doctoral institutions. *The Journal of Higher Education, 77*(1), 89–123.

Bloomgarden, A. (2008). *Prestige culture and community-based faculty work* (Doctoral dissertation). Available from ProQuest Dissertations and Theses database. (UMI No. 3336986)

Bloomgarden, A., & O'Meara, K. (2007). Harmony or cacophony? Faculty role integration and community engagement. *Michigan Journal of Community Service Learning, 13*(2), 5–18.

Bova, B., & Kroth, M. (2001). Workplace learning and Generation X. *Journal of Workplace Learning, 13*(2), 57–65.

Boyer, E. L. (1990). *Scholarship reconsidered: The priorities of the professoriate.* Princeton, NJ: Carnegie Foundation for the Advancement of Teaching.

Boyte, H. C. (2008). Against the current: Developing the civic agency of students. *Change: The Magazine of Higher Learning, 40*(3), 8–15.

Bringle, R. G., & Hatcher, J. A. (2000). Institutionalization of service learning in higher education. *The Journal of Higher Education, 71*, 273–290.

Bringle, R. G., Hatcher, J. A., & Games, R. (1997). Engaging and supporting faculty in service learning. *Journal of Public Service and Outreach, 2*(1), 43–51.

Cantor, N. (2010, March). *Academic excellence and civic engagement: Constructing a third space for higher education.* Paper presented at the Association of American Colleges and Universities Conference on Faculty Roles in High-Impact Practices, Philadelphia, PA.

Clayton, P. H., & Ash, S. L. (2005). Reflection as a key component in faculty development. *On the Horizon, 13*(3), 161–169.

Colbeck, C., & Janke, E. (2006, November). *If not for the rewards . . . why? Theory-based research about what motivates faculty to engage in public scholarship.* Paper presented at the annual conference of the Association for the Study of Higher Education, Anaheim, CA.

Colbeck, C., & Wharton-Michael, P. (2006). Individual and organizational influences on faculty members' engagement in public scholarship. *New Directions for Teaching and Learning, 2006*(105), 17–26. doi:10.1002/tl.221

Creamer, E. G. (1998). Assessing faculty publication productivity: Issues of equity. *ASHE-ERIC Higher Education Report, 26*(2). Washington, DC: The George Washington University Graduate School of Education and Human Development.

Creamer, E. G., & Lattuca, L. R. (Eds.). (2005). Advancing faculty learning through interdisciplinary collaboration [Special issue]. *New Directions for Teaching and Learning, 2005*(102).

Daloz, L. A., Keen, C. H., Keen, J. P., & Parks, S. D. (1996). *Common fire: Lives of commitment in a complex world.* Boston, MA: Beacon Press.

Daly, C., & Dee, J. (2006). Greener pastures: Faculty turnover intent in urban public universities. *The Journal of Higher Education, 77*, 776–803.

Dweck, C. (2006). *Mindset: The new psychology of success.* New York, NY: Random House.

Fairweather, J. S. (2005). Beyond the rhetoric: Trends in the relative value of teaching and research in faculty salaries. *The Journal of Higher Education, 76,* 401–422.

Ford, M. E. (1992). *Motivating humans: Goals, emotions, and personal agency beliefs.* Newbury Park, CA: SAGE.

Gaff, J. (2005). Preparing future faculty and multiple forms of scholarship. In K. A. O'Meara & R. E. Rice (Eds.), *Faculty priorities reconsidered: Encouraging multiple forms of scholarship* (pp. 66–71). San Francisco, CA: Jossey-Bass.

Gappa, J. M., Austin, A. E., & Trice, A. G. (2007). *Rethinking faculty work: Higher education's strategic imperative.* San Francisco, CA: Jossey-Bass.

González, K., & Padilla, R. (2008). *Doing the public good: Latina/o scholars engage in civic participation.* Sterling, VA: Stylus.

Hackman, J. R., & Oldham, G. R. (1980). Work design in organizational context. In B. M. Staw & L. L. Cummings (Eds.), *Research in organizational behavior* (Vol. 2, pp. 389–402). Greenwich, CT: JAI.

Hagedorn, L. S. (2000). Conceptualizing faculty job satisfaction: Components, theories and outcomes. *New Directions for Institutional Research, 2000*(105), 5–20. doi:10.1002/ir.10501

Hammond, C. (1994). Integrating service and academic study: Faculty motivation and satisfaction in Michigan higher education. *Michigan Journal of Community Service Learning, 1*(1), 21–28.

Hatcher, J. A. (2008). *The public role of professionals: Developing and evaluating the Civic-Minded Professional Scale* (Doctoral dissertation). Available from ProQuest Dissertations and Theses database. (UMI No. 3331248)

Hermanowicz, J. C. (2009). *Lives in science: How institutions affect academic careers.* Chicago, IL: University of Chicago Press.

Herzberg, F. (1959). *The motivation to work.* New York, NY: John Wiley & Sons.

Holland, B. A. (1999). Factors and strategies that influence faculty involvement in public service. *The Journal of Public Service and Outreach, 4*(1), 37–43.

Hurtado, S., Ponjuan, L., & Smith, G. (2003, May). *Women and faculty of color on campus: Campus diversity and civic engagement initiatives.* Paper presented at the Association for Institutional Research conference in Tampa, FL. Retrieved from http://www.umich.edu/~divdemo/Final%20Women%20and%20Faculty%20of%20Color_2.pdf

Jaeger, A., & Thornton, C. (2006, November). *Neither honor nor compensation: Faculty and public service.* Paper presented at the Association for the Study of Higher Education annual meeting, Philadelphia, PA.

Jameson, J. K., Clayton, P. H., & Jaeger, A. J. (2011). Community-engaged scholarship through mutually transformative partnerships. In L. Harter, J. Hamel-Lambert, & J. Millesen (Eds.), *Participatory partnerships for social action and research* (pp. 259–277). Dubuque, IA: Kendall Hunt.

Janke, E. (2009). Defining characteristics of partnership identity in faculty-community partnerships. In B. E. Moely, S. H. Billig, & B. A. Holland (Eds.), *Creating our identities in service-learning and community engagement* (pp. 75–102). Charlotte, NC: Information Age.

Kadar, R. S. (2005). *Peer-mentoring relationships: Toward a non-hierarchical mentoring approach for faculty women* (Doctoral dissertation). Available from ProQuest Dissertations and Theses database. (UMI No. 3175699)

Kecskes, K. (Ed.). (2006). *Engaging departments: Moving faculty culture from private to public, individual to collective focus for the common good.* Bolton, MA: Anker.

Laird, P. W. (2006). *Pull: Networking and success since Benjamin Franklin.* Cambridge, MA: Harvard University Press.

Lin, N. (2001a). Building a network theory of social capital. In N. Lin, K. Cook, & R. S. Burt (Eds.), *Social capital: Theory and research* (pp. 3–29). New York, NY: Aldine De Gruyter.

Lin, N. (2001b). *Social capital: A theory of social structure and action.* New York, NY: Cambridge University Press.

Marshall, V. (2000, August). *Agency, structure, and the life course in the era of reflexive modernization.* Paper presented at the American Sociological Association annual meeting, Washington, DC.

Maslow, A. (1970). *Motivation and personality* (Vol. 2). New York, NY: Harper & Row.

McClelland, D. C. (1971). *Assessing human motivation.* Morristown, NJ: General Learning Press.

McKay, V. C., & Rozee, P. D. (2004). Characteristics of faculty who adopt community service learning pedagogy. *Michigan Journal of Community Service Learning, 10*(2), 21–33.

Milem, J. F., Sherlin, J., & Irwin, L. (2001). The importance of collegial networks to college and university faculty. In E. G. Creamer (Ed.), *Working equal: Academic couples as collaborators* (pp. 146–166). New York, NY: RoutledgeFalmer.

Neumann, A. (2009a). *Professing to learn: Creating tenured lives and careers in the American research university.* Baltimore, MD: The Johns Hopkins University Press.

Neumann, A. (2009b). Protecting the passion of scholars in times of change. *Change: The Magazine of Higher Learning, 41*(2), 10–15.

O'Meara, K. (2002). Uncovering the values in faculty evaluation of service as scholarship. *The Review of Higher Education, 26*(1), 57–80.

O'Meara, K. (2004). Reframing incentives and rewards for community service-learning and academic outreach. *Journal of Higher Education Outreach and Engagement, 8*(2), 201–220.

O'Meara, K. (2008). Motivation for public scholarship and engagement: Listening to exemplars. *Journal of Higher Education Outreach and Engagement, 12*(1), 7–29.

O'Meara, K. (2011). Inside the panopticon: Studying academic reward systems. In J. C. Smart & M. B. Paulsen (Eds.), *Higher education: Handbook of theory and research* (Vol. 26, pp. 161–220). New York, NY: Springer.

O'Meara, K., & Campbell, C. (2008, November). *Can I, should I, will I? Faculty sense of agency in decisions about work and family.* Paper presented at the annual conference of the Association for the Study of Higher Education, Jacksonville, FL.

O'Meara, K., Jaeger, A., & Giles, D. E., Jr. (2009, November). *Civic learning and the classroom: How and in what contexts classroom experience enhances civic action.* Paper presented at the annual Association for the Study of Higher Education conference, Vancouver, CA.

O'Meara, K., & Niehaus, B. (2009). Service-learning is . . . : How faculty explain their practice. *Michigan Journal of Community Service Learning, 16*(1), 17–32.

O'Meara, K., Sandmann, L. R., Saltmarsh, J., & Giles, D. E., Jr. (2011). Studying the professional lives and work of faculty involved in community engagement. *Innovative Higher Education, 36*(2), 83–96.

O'Meara, K., Terosky, A. L., & Neumann, A. (2008). Faculty careers and work lives: A professional growth perspective. *ASHE Higher Education Report, 34*(3). San Francisco, CA: Jossey-Bass.

Pallas, A. (2001). Preparing education doctoral students for epistemological diversity. *Educational Researcher, 30*(5), 6–11.

Palmer, P. J. (2007). A new professional: The aims of education revisited. *Change: The Magazine of Higher Learning, 39*(6), 6–13.

Parkins, L. C. (2008). *Predicting faculty participation in service-learning pedagogy at research universities* (Doctoral dissertation). Available from ProQuest Dissertations and Theses database. (UMI No. 3306616)

Patel, H. S. (2004). Assessment of the personal and professional attributes of educators who utilize service-learning. *Dissertation Abstracts International: Section A. The Humanities and Social Sciences, 65*(07), 2479.

Perna, L. W. (2001). Sex and race differences in faculty tenure and promotion. *Research in Higher Education, 42*, 541–567.

Perry, W. G. (1968). *Forms of intellectual and ethical development in the college years: A scheme.* Orlando, FL: Holt, Reinhart, and Winston.

Peters, S. J., Alter, T. R., & Schwartzbach, N. (2008). Unsettling a settled discourse: Faculty views of the meaning and significance of the land-grant mission. *Journal of Higher Education Outreach and Engagement, 12*(2), 33–66.

Pink, D. H. (2009). *Drive: A whole new mind.* New York, NY: Riverhead Books.

Saltmarsh, J., Zlotkowski, E., & Horowitz, K. (2010, April). *Students as colleagues in the next generation of civic engagement.* Paper presented at the New England Regional Campus Compact Conference, Burlington, VT.

Schuster, J. H., & Finkelstein, M. J. (2006). *The American faculty: The restructuring of academic work and careers.* Baltimore, MD: The Johns Hopkins University Press.

Sen, A. K. (1985). Well-being, agency and freedom: The Dewey Lectures 1984. *Journal of Philosophy, 82*(4), 169–221.

Umbach, P. D. (2006). The contribution of faculty of color to undergraduate education. *Research in Higher Education, 47,* 317–345.

Umbach, P. D. (2007). How effective are they? Exploring the impact of contingent faculty on undergraduate education. *The Review of Higher Education, 30*(2), 91–123.

Vogelgesang, L. J., Denson, N., & Jayakumar, U. M. (2010). What determines faculty-engaged scholarship? *The Review of Higher Education, 33,* 437–472.

Ward, E. (2010). *Women's ways of engagement: An exploration of gender, the scholarship of engagement, and institutional rewards policy and practice* (Doctoral dissertation). ProQuest Dissertations and Theses database. (UMI No. 3420073)

Ward, K. (2003). Faculty service roles and the scholarship of engagement. *ASHE-ERIC Higher Education Report, 29*(5). San Francisco, CA: Jossey-Bass.

Western Region Campus Compact Consortium (WRCCC). (2009). *Faculty engagement in service learning and community based research.* Bellingham, WA: Washington Campus Compact.

Zlotkowski, E. (2000). Service-learning in the disciplines [Special issue]. *Michigan Journal of Community Service Learning, Fall,* 61–67.

3·3

THEORETICAL PERSPECTIVES AND RESEARCH ON FACULTY LEARNING IN SERVICE LEARNING

Patti H. Clayton, George R. Hess, Audrey J. Jaeger,
Jessica Katz Jameson, and Lisa E. McGuire

ervice learning faculty[1] can, do, and should learn. Sigmon's (1979)
seminal essay outlining the defining principles of service learning
made explicit the foundational dynamic whereby the students, community members, and faculty members involved in service learning are all
learners. Subsequent explorations of the counternormative nature of service
learning (Howard, 1998) examine the ways in which service learning
pedagogy requires and fosters learning—often transformational, paradigm-
shifting learning—on the part of everyone involved, including faculty (Clayton & Ash, 2004). As service learning faculty ourselves, we have reflected on
our experiences with the pedagogy and have become more aware of some of
the dynamics of faculty learning, at least as they have emerged in our own
work. Our recent examinations of community-campus engagement have
emphasized the power of "inductive, reflective, and co-creat[ive]" (Hess et
al., 2011, p. 374) approaches to partnership building and the value of designing associated scholarship as a "shared developmental journey" (Jameson,
Clayton, & Jaeger, 2011, p. 269) that explicitly positions faculty, students,
and community members as learners.

The authors gratefully acknowledge Barbara Harrison and Kathleen Edwards for their contributions to
our thinking.

The central tenet of Sigmon's (1979) early thinking about the relationship among participants in service learning has come to be expressed with the term *reciprocity*. Minimally, reciprocity requires that everyone involved in the process benefit. Beyond mutual benefit, reciprocity in its "thick" (Jameson et al., 2011, p. 264) form means that students, community members, and faculty share voice and authority in determining questions, defining approaches, and contributing to knowledge construction and dissemination; through their interactions with one another they all experience learning that leads to new ways of thinking, perceiving, and acting (Donahue, Bowyer, & Rosenberg, 2003; Saltmarsh, Hartley, & Clayton, 2009). In other words, reciprocity in service learning ultimately means that all participants are co-educators, co-learners, and co-generators of knowledge (Hess et al., 2011; Jameson et al., 2011; Kirby, 2010; Mondloch, 2009).

Most fundamentally, faculty positioning themselves explicitly as learners in service learning requires that they have identities as learners: Faculty members must see themselves as learners and value their own learning. Deeply ingrained norms in the academy, however, reinforce the distinct identities of faculty as educators and generators of knowledge, students as learners, and community members as recipients of academic expertise. Institutional language (e.g., in faculty handbooks, in promotion and tenure guidelines) commonly describes the teaching role of faculty in terms of the transmission of knowledge from faculty to students and to communities, whereas inquiry (and, therefore, learning) is associated primarily with faculty members' role as creators of knowledge. However, faculty—indeed, all participants—may take on a broader and more interconnected set of identities in service learning than those traditionally attributed. Here, we are most interested in faculty identity as learner and its associated dynamics in the context of teaching, specifically with service learning.

As is the case with student learning, maximizing faculty learning in the context of service learning depends to a large extent on intentionality with respect to both outcomes and process, and the investigation of that learning similarly involves inquiring into the content of faculty members' learning and the processes through which they learn. The range of largely unfamiliar activities associated with service learning—teaching and learning through critical reflection on experience, assessing learning as demonstrated through reflection products, integrating knowledge from multiple and nontraditional sources, partnering with individuals and organizations whose expertise may not have been acknowledged previously, integrating academic with civic learning—both requires and fosters faculty learning (Clayton & Ash, 2004).

The *content* of that learning is complex. Faculty learn new techniques, skills, practices, and ways of interacting with students and community members, but they also, perhaps more importantly, learn new ways of being and knowing. The *processes* through which that learning occurs are similarly multifaceted. Faculty learning in the context of service learning can be a transformative process that involves refocusing the lenses through which faculty make meaning of their work, its connections to the world around them, their students, their institutions, and themselves.

In many ways, faculty learning may be conceptualized similarly to student learning in service learning (Part Two). Its outcomes may include metacognitive development (e.g., critical thinking, transference; see chapter 2.1), academic learning (e.g., the content and perspectives of faculty members' disciplines; see chapter 2.2), civic learning (e.g., dynamics of community building, change agency, and power both inside and outside the classroom; see chapter 2.3), personal growth (e.g., faculty members' sense of identity, their skills, their personal and professional development goals and processes; see chapter 2.4), and intercultural competence (e.g., faculty members' interpretation of the effectiveness and appropriateness of their behaviors in intercultural settings; see chapter 2.5). In addition, as with students, faculty may learn through the process of critical reflection on their own and others' experiences. Faculty learning may have other relationships with student learning as well, including a multidirectional, causal one in which the learning of each frames, feeds into, and strengthens the learning of the other. And there may be important ways in which the learning of faculty is different from or in tension with that of students, linked to differences in the cultural norms and organizational contexts that define and support learning in these two populations and perhaps as well a function of preferred learning styles, of advanced disciplinary training, or of age- and experience-related cognitive and affective development.

Once we have explored faculty identity as learner and considered both what and how faculty learn—in effect, once practitioner-scholars in service learning have caught up in our thinking about faculty learning to where we arguably are in our thinking about student learning—we can begin to examine the dynamics of faculty as co-learners. By co-learning we mean not only that faculty learn *too* (i.e., in addition to students) but that they learn *with* their students and community partners in service learning; their learning is a dimension and an emergent outcome of being in partnerships with other learners, and it is interdependent with the learning of others.

Lattuca (2005) notes that "research on the role of learning in faculty members' lives is critical because the success of faculty members' learning experiences has real consequences for students, scholarly communities, and the larger society that is informed by their work" (p. 14). Neumann (2005) adds that investigating faculty learning can contribute to understanding how faculty practice, including teaching, can change through time. This is especially important in service learning because implementation of the initially unfamiliar pedagogy, at least in our experience, evolves and improves while keeping us continually on a learning edge. As with students, the learning that faculty undertake can be—and perhaps often is—transformational, not only for themselves but for the organizations and systems of which they are a part. Ultimately, as faculty members' ways of being, knowing, and engaging change and evolve, so too does the nature of their work and its effects on the world around them.

In this chapter we consider how the academy has and might understand and investigate the nature of learning among faculty in their role as educators. We focus on theory and research about learning that can contribute to understanding faculty as learners and co-learners in the context of service learning and community engagement, highlighting key conceptual frameworks, methods, and questions that hold potential to advance the field's ability to assess and investigate learning well beyond the usual focus on students.

Theoretical and Conceptual Frameworks

This section examines several frameworks that are useful for thinking about faculty learning: faculty identity as learner in service learning, typologies for organizing what and how they learn, and the dynamics of co-learning.

Faculty Identity as Learner in Service Learning

Fundamental to the investigation of faculty learning is the conviction that faculty are, in fact, learners—including in their role as designers of learning experiences. As noted, this starting point is not as clear or simple as it may at first appear because it implicates complex questions of identity and identity formation as well as norms and roles that are deeply ingrained in the academy and in Western society more generally. Neumann examines the role of learning in the daily lives of faculty, including in scholarly identity development, subject matter expertise, and teaching (Neumann, 2000, 2005; Neumann & Peterson, 1997). O'Meara, Terosky, and Neumann (2008) suggest that faculty have various opportunities to learn in their work and position that learning as one of four defining aspects of faculty professional growth (the other three being agency, relationships, and commitments); learning serves as a foundational component and a focus of how faculty develop throughout their careers in this model of professional growth.

Equally central to the investigation of faculty learning in service learning per se is the conviction that the pedagogy often requires and fosters faculty members' learning—that it can confront faculty with learning opportunities and challenges and that its defining dynamics are congruent with the characteristics of effective adult learning contexts. O'Meara and Terosky (2010) suggest that "faculty members' learning happens only when they have a hand in making that learning happen" and that "such learning and agency occur and are reinforced in the context of the relationships faculty have" (p. 45). In the case of both students and faculty, maximizing learning through participation in service learning requires understanding the pedagogy as a vehicle for learning and using it intentionally as a means to cultivate learning.

This understanding of the learning potential of service learning is grounded in a particular conceptualization of the pedagogy, one that is aligned with principles of best practice and embodied in emerging consensus (Bringle & Clayton, 2012; chapter 1.1). Rather than defining service learning as courses in which students volunteer to meet community needs as an add-on to the core learning strategies and course content, service learning is conceptualized here as having the potential for significant faculty (and student and community member) learning in part because of its intentional— and intentionally capitalized on—counternormative nature, its use of critical reflection on experience to generate and document learner-articulated learning outcomes, and its insistence on critical thinking within and across multiple categories of learning (e.g., civic and academic learning). Furthermore, this learning potential exists because the requisite power sharing and co-creation of processes and goals by all participants evokes identity and role shifts; because the attention paid to historical and contemporary context and to future possibilities explicitly invites taking multiple, sometimes conflicting, perspectives; and because understanding the interconnections that it encourages investigation of demands interdisciplinary, systems thinking.

Conceptualizing the Content and Process of Faculty Learning

Neumann (2005) notes, "Talk and thought about learning is vague and insubstantial without taking into account what is being learned" (p. 64).

What, then, do faculty learn and need to learn as teachers, specifically in the context of service learning? A casual review of service learning workshop and conference session titles surfaces such topics as defining service learning, partnering with community members, designing reflection, and assessing student learning (Bringle & Hatcher, 1995). Clayton and O'Steen (2010) suggest that as service learning staff design professional development activities for faculty, the learning goals might include integrating the pedagogy into courses, ensuring that it is academically grounded, fostering civic as well as academic learning, using reflection to improve the quality of both learning and service, bringing the full range of stakeholder voices into the process, and building student capacity for undertaking service learning successfully. Investigating faculty learning, however, requires not only topical lists of subjects to be learned but also systematic ways of organizing and conceptualizing the content of that learning.

The overlapping categories of academic learning, civic learning, and personal growth that comprise the learning goals of service learning (Ash & Clayton, 2009b; Felten & Clayton, 2011; chapter 1.1) provide one useful framework for organizing the content of faculty learning (Clayton, Bacon, Hess, Moore, & Snow, 2010). Faculty may, for example, learn more about the content of their discipline (academic), the public purposes of their field of study and practice and the work of organizations in their communities (civic), and their own personal characteristics as individuals, as educators, as scholars, and as citizens (personal growth). In an alternate framing, service learning faculty may learn definitions, models, and techniques related, for example, to reflection; become better at writing assessable learning objectives and giving students feedback; and come to value community members' contributions to student learning—thus, as with students, their learning may be categorized into knowledge, skills, and attitudes (alternately, dispositions or values). They may learn policies on their own campuses and in community organizations and build their capacity to critique and advocate for changes in those policies; again as with students, their learning may be factual and it may be at a higher level of reasoning and integrated with commitment to action.

Furthermore, faculty may learn nonhierarchical ways of relating with others in the classroom and in the community and develop their abilities to recognize and influence power dynamics in these and other settings; they may become more cognizant of the influence of multiple epistemologies and cultures on knowledge construction; and they may revisit and revise their own sense of identity, their assumptions about teaching and learning, and their expectations of students and themselves. In other words, their learning—like that of their students—may involve the shifts in perspective and practice that service learning both requires and fosters (Clayton & Ash, 2004); it may transform the lenses through which they view the world and their ways of being and knowing within it. Mezirow and associates (2000) and Cranton (2006) speak of transformational learning as occurring through processes of examining, questioning, validating, and revising perspectives; individuals change their frames of reference by reflecting critically on their assumptions and beliefs and consciously making and implementing plans that bring about new ways of defining their worlds. Cranton (2006) posits "authentic relationships" as a context for such learning and describes them as occurring within educational systems when teachers and students "choose to act so as to foster the growth and development of each other's being" (p. 7); consistent with the discussion here of service learning, Cranton suggests that these relationships can result in learning on the part of everyone involved. Angelo (1999) and Baxter Magolda (2012) both suggest that the transformational learning many educators desire for students depends on the transformational learning—the shift to new frames of mind—of the educators themselves.

The three frameworks related to learning, behavior, and change summarized next may provide useful insight regarding how to organize inquiry into faculty learning, highlight connections between the content and the process of faculty members' learning, and suggest ways that identity is implicated in that learning. Each of these frameworks offers three interconnected domains or levels, distinguishing between—as we frame it concisely here—learning focused on (a) *what*, (b) *how*, and (c) *why* and *who*.

Single-, Double-, and Triple-Loop Learning

Originally in the context of organizational learning, Argyris and Schön (1974) distinguish among single-, double-, and triple-loop learning. In *single-loop learning* the learner modifies actions when the outcome from them was not as expected (i.e., learns new skills or develops new abilities). *Double-loop learning* involves examining the underlying assumptions, values, policies, and other influences that led to action and to the expectation of particular consequences—revealing previously unseen patterns so that the learner becomes aware of and able to modify second-order influences and thus begins to be free from uncritical adherence to norms and habits. *Triple-loop learning*—learning that examines and enhances the learning process itself—includes understanding how the learner's own behavior or actions influenced the situation and critically evaluating alternative responses; at this level, the learner examines and often modifies his sense of purpose or identity, which can lead to changes in the principles on which action is based. Single-loop learning focuses on technique and improving practice by asking *what* questions but does not include challenging the status quo. Double-loop learning involves asking *how* questions and lends itself to understanding the complexity of situations and improving underlying processes. Triple-loop learning is a function of asking *why* and *who* questions and is transformational, fundamentally shifting the learner into new ways of being and knowing and new identities.

Content, Process, and Premise Reflection

Reflection is an important foundation for work on adult learning. Mezirow (1991) distinguishes three levels of reflection: content (which involves *what* questions), process (which involves *how* questions), and premise (which involves *why* questions). Kreber and Cranton (2000) suggest that Mezirow's three levels can operate within each of three domains of knowledge about teaching: instructional (i.e., possessing a technical understanding of what strategies are used in teaching), pedagogical (i.e., understanding how students learn), and curricular (i.e., understanding "why we teach the way we teach," p. 481). Thus, faculty learning about teaching can include, for example, faculty members' asking content (*what*) questions in each domain— "What should I do in course design?" (instructional), "What do I know about how students learn?" (pedagogical), and "What do I know about the goals and rationale for my courses/program?" (curricular)—and their asking premise (*why*) questions in each domain—"Why does it matter what methods, materials, or course design I use?" (instructional), "Why does it matter if I consider how students learn?" (pedagogical), and "Why do our goals and rationale matter?" (curricular) (p. 485).

Technical, Contextual, and Dialectical Reflection

Taggart and Wilson's (2005) synthesis of multiple scholars' conceptualizations of reflection distinguishes among technical, contextual, and dialectical levels of reflection and can similarly serve to connect the content and the process of faculty learning. Describing *technical* reflection—focused on *what* questions—they write, "Outcomes for practitioners reflecting at a technical level may involve appropriate selection and implementation of lessons to achieve objectives. The objectives are not problematic, nor does the practitioner deliberate on the context of the situation" (p. 2). The second, *contextual*, level of reflection—focused on *how* questions—involves "clarification of and elaboration on underlying assumptions and predispositions of classroom practices as well as consequences of strategies used, . . . establish[ing] congruency between theory and practice, . . . [and] understanding personal and environmental interactions" (p. 4). *Dialectical* reflection, or critical reflexivity—focused on *why* and *who* questions—involves the teacher in contemplation of the ethical and political dimensions of instruction, systemic analysis of the relationships between theories, and concern for the broader contexts and consequences of teaching and learning; it is oriented as well toward self-understanding, self-efficacy, and self-actualization.

The Dynamics of Co-Learning

The literature on adult education and critical pedagogy provides a conceptual framework for examining faculty learning that is particularly relevant to co-learning in service learning. Freire (1970) conceptualizes learning as an egalitarian partnership and highlights the reciprocal process between teachers and students: "The teacher-of-the-students and the students-of-the-teacher cease to exist and a new term emerges: teacher-student with student-teachers. The teacher is no longer merely the-one-who-teaches, but one who is . . . taught in dialogue with the students" (p. 80). Such dialogical learning— distinct from one-way communication or asynchronous, back-and-forth monologues—involves continual engagement with others' ideas in a process of questioning, interrogating evidence, and iteratively revising understanding. Freire's adult education theory has political, philosophical, and epistemological implications that grow from the praxis that occurs during these reciprocal relationships between learners: "Knowledge emerges only through invention and re-invention, through the restless, impatient, continuing, hopeful inquiry human beings pursue in the world, with the world, and with each other" (p. 72). As such, it may imply not only collaborative learning processes but also transformational learning processes and outcomes that reframe learners' interpretive lenses, identities, and ways of being and knowing. Service learning invites dialogical learning processes that bring faculty, students, and community members together in co-constructing knowledge and practice.

Lattuca and Creamer's (2005) discussion of interdisciplinary collaboration among faculty may provide useful insights regarding co-learning in service learning. They define *collaboration* as "a social [i.e., relational] inquiry practice that promotes learning" (p. 5). Moving beyond an instrumental view of collaboration that emphasizes the efficiency and effectiveness of working together rather than individually to produce outcomes and that, thus, "overlook[s] the learning that occurs as faculty produce what is delivered," (p. 3), the authors examine interdisciplinary collaboration through the lens of its learning dimensions. "These types of collaborative activities," they write, "typically require faculty to apprehend, understand, and use concepts, theories, and methods from disciplines or fields other than their own" (p. 4). Collaboration among faculty from multiple disciplines—analogous, for the purposes of this discussion, to collaboration among faculty, students, and community members in service learning—requires faculty (and all partners) to "create new ways of working together, as well as develop new ways to perceive and understand the phenomenon of interest to them" (p. 4). Lattuca and Creamer (2005) reference Petrie (1986) to suggest that faculty collaborating with one another across communities of practice are required by the nature of the activity to "learn something about the cognitive maps of their collaborators, at least their ways of looking at and interpreting phenomena and concepts" (Petrie, as cited in Lattuca & Creamer, 2005, p. 8). As a result, they conclude, ways of thinking intersect, new understandings are created, and reflectiveness about learning increases. When we use the language of this chapter, interdisciplinary faculty collaboration is both a context for co-learning among faculty and a model of the dynamics of co-learning as it may characterize faculty learning through partnerships in service learning.

Review of Research Studies and Methods

Driscoll (2000) identified the paucity of research around the critical role of faculty in service learning pedagogy and articulated a research agenda grounded in the conviction that "the future growth and sustainability of service-learning depends to a large extent on the faculty" (p. 39). She referred to the impact of faculty on the pedagogy and the impact of the pedagogy on faculty, which imply but do not specifically identify faculty learning as an arena of inquiry. Gelmon, Holland, Driscoll, Spring, and Kerrigan (2001) offer a compilation of tools for assessing service learning, including a section on faculty, framed to include, for example, motivation for and barriers to using service learning, the influence of service learning on scholarship, and satisfaction by faculty with their service learning experiences. Suggested approaches include surveys and interviews, classroom observation, and analyses of artifacts related to the service learning experience (e.g., syllabi, faculty journals, curriculum vitae). Many of the noted indicators of faculty impact —for example, influence on teaching and on scholarship—can be viewed as implying that faculty learning has occurred, but there are few if any probes that address it explicitly.

Perhaps the most obvious approach to learning about the content and process of faculty learning in the arena of teaching with service learning is simply to ask faculty. Domagal-Goldman's (2010) dissertation included semi-structured interviews with 15 faculty participants in Pennsylvania State University's Public Scholarship Associates program. The investigator examined the impact of participation in the program on teaching civic engagement with questions such as "Have your ideas about education and teaching changed at all as a result of your participation in this group? How?" (p. 261). The investigator found that the more deeply engaged faculty were in the program, the more strongly they reported aligning their beliefs about civic engagement with their teaching. Some participants reported changes not only to how they taught but also their sense of identity. Domagal-Goldman organized evidence of faculty learning through participation in the Public Scholarship Associates program into three categories: adopting new language, replicating others' civic engagement practices, and developing identities as public scholars. Another recent project (Carter & Brockerhoff-Macdonald, 2011) gathered data related to faculty learning from interviews and focus groups with recipients of teaching awards on a campus in Canada. The investigators examined how participants learned about teaching at the beginning of their careers and later in their careers. Analysis of the self-reported data suggests that these faculty learned about teaching at the beginning of their teaching careers primarily through interactions with their colleagues and from student feedback; later in their careers, they learned about teaching through professional resources such as conferences and journals, student feedback, and experimentation with new strategies in the classroom. From the perspective of the conceptual frameworks reviewed earlier, these two studies were concerned more with the process of faculty learning than the content, and the first was more explicitly focused than the second on the relationship between identity formation (the *who* level) and learning. Although the Canadian investigators organized their results using Kreber and Cranton's (2000) typology of domains of teaching-related knowledge (instructional, pedagogical, and curricular), they did not design the study to elicit information regarding whether participants' learning occurred at the *what*, *how*, or *why/who* levels.

Four recent studies that are explicitly focused on faculty learning in service learning and community engagement are examined next in terms of the methods used and the conceptual frameworks that we have summarized.

Faculty Development of Competencies for Community-Engaged Scholarship

Blanchard et al. (2009) report on the development and assessment of faculty competencies for community-engaged scholarship (CES) as it has been advanced under the auspices of Community-Campus Partnerships for Health (CCPH). General CES competencies that all academics should develop, as determined by the Community-Engaged Scholarship for Health Collaborative, include knowledge (e.g., definitions of CES), skills (e.g., the ability to evaluate CES products), and values (e.g., respect for the significance of CES). Specific competencies for faculty undertaking CES were originally categorized into novice, intermediate, and advanced categories, including understanding concepts of community engagement and CES and familiarity with basic literature and history of CES (novice), ability to work effectively in and with diverse communities (intermediate), and ability to mentor students and junior faculty in establishing and building a CES-based portfolio (advanced).

The set of competencies offers a basis for assessing the learning outcomes of faculty development programs. As one example, the University of North Carolina at Chapel Hill's Faculty Engaged Scholars Program (Blanchard, Strauss, & Webb, 2012) incorporated participant self-assessment at the end of each year on 14 competencies using a 6-point scale from *minimal* (a) to *complete mastery* (f). Participants also rated their accomplishments within eight areas (e.g., "I have enriched and deepened my community partnerships"; p. 106) throughout the program using a 3-point scale from *not at all* (1) to *fully* (3) and responded to open-ended questions about their experience in the program. Blanchard et al. (2012) provide a descriptive summary of participants' self-assessment ratings and indicate several patterns that emerged in the first three years of the program. Among the 24 participants, none rated themselves as having achieved complete mastery of any competency. Participants felt most proficient (*advanced*) in "ability to work effectively in and with diverse communities" ($n = 14$), "ability to negotiate across community-academic groups" ($n = 11$), and "understanding of the various contributors to community issues" ($n = 10$) (p. 113). Participants rated themselves lowest (*no* or *minimal mastery*) on four competencies: "understanding of the policy implications of CES and ability to work with communities in translating the process and findings of CES into policy" ($n = 13$);

"knowledge of review, promotion, and tenure process and its relationship with community engaged scholarship, ability to serve on review, promotion, and tenure committee" (n = 13); "ability to write grants expressing community-engaged scholarship principles and approaches" (n = 12); and "knowledge and successful application of definitions, benchmarks . . . and measures of quality" (n = 12) (Blanchard et al., 2012, p. 113).

This approach to assessing faculty learning encompasses some of the content but none of the process by which participants learned. Its primary contribution is the use of specific competencies to define and document learning outcomes of interest. Implemented only at the conclusion of the program in this study, this approach did not offer participants or investigators a way to watch—metacognitively—the learning process. Although the categorization of competencies into novice, intermediate, and advanced was later eliminated (Blanchard et al., 2012) and was never framed by the investigators in these terms, we find it intriguing to consider the potential relationship between this categorization and the earlier discussed frameworks that posit levels of learning. For example, familiarity with the literature and history of CES is a matter of the *what* (single-loop, content, technical), while working effectively across diversity may well involve attending to the *how* of underlying processes and relationships (double-loop, process, contextual) if not also the *why* level of learning associated with transforming sense of purpose and identity (triple-loop, premise, dialectical).

This study also relied exclusively on self-report. While self-report measures are useful as indications of perceived learning, work on assessing student learning in service learning has criticized overreliance on self-report and called for direct evidence of learning (Bowman & Brandenberger, 2010; Eyler, 2000; Steinke & Buresh, 2002; Steinke & Fitch, 2008). The two studies described next attempted to incorporate direct evidence into their investigation of faculty learning, using mixed-methods approaches.

Faculty Learning Around Reflection and Critical Thinking

A study in the context of a service learning faculty development initiative at Indiana University–Purdue University Indianapolis included investigation of both student and faculty learning and preliminary exploration of the relationship between them (McGuire et al., 2009). Five faculty members from four disciplines formed a learning community grounded in use of the DEAL Model for Critical Reflection (Ash & Clayton, 2009a, 2009b; see chapter 2.2). They learned the model and its associated rubrics for critical thinking and higher-order reasoning through a series of workshops and refined their understanding of critical reflection through reflective implementation of DEAL in their courses and through related scholarship projects.

While individually and collectively analyzing student reflection products for evidence of critical thinking, the investigators simultaneously examined their own work products—syllabi, assignment prompts, and feedback to students—for evidence of the content of their own learning and convened a doctoral student-led focus group for further exploration of their learning processes. A lightly structured content analysis of their communication with students before and during their involvement with the faculty learning community revealed enhanced specificity and tighter connections between feedback and learning objectives. The instructors' learning was demonstrated, for example, in reflection prompts becoming more precisely worded and structured to facilitate student learning of course content and in feedback becoming more precisely and transparently linked to critical thinking. Faculty learning about standards of critical thinking (Paul, 1993; Paul & Elder, 2006) and about the use of Bloom's Taxonomy (1956) to structure student learning objectives and design associated student learning activities led faculty to make documentable changes in their teaching practices (specifically in how they communicated with students). These changes were aimed at helping students to develop critical thinking skills; the students generated products that, in turn, were refined through the instructors' enhanced abilities to provide critical feedback. The investigators were able to compare the depth of learning evidenced in student products from before and during the faculty development initiative only anecdotally but provided some direct evidence of faculty members' own learning (e.g., comparison of their own feedback on student products across time) as well as themes from their collaborative reflection on their own learning process and outcomes.

This study's key contribution is that it explicitly conceptualized a causal relationship between faculty learning and student learning and began to develop mechanisms for investigating that relationship that go beyond self-report: Faculty learned about critical thinking through professional development activities, evidence of that learning was provided by comparing their feedback on student products before and after that professional development, and evidence of students' critical thinking abilities was provided through the application of a rubric to their reflection products. A focus group directed faculty participants' attention to their understanding of themselves as learners and as educators and invited the participants to identify process improvements. This allowed the investigators to access some of the double-loop, process, contextual learning—*how*-level issues—that the professional development activities were designed to generate. The investigators also considered some of the dynamics of co-learning in the context of faculty learning communities. Significant limitations of this study included the lack of rigorous content analysis of faculty products (e.g., their feedback, their reflection prompts) and the small size of the faculty sample. Both the professional development and the assessment processes would have benefited from more focused and better articulated goals for faculty learning using the three levels outlined in the previous discussion of theoretical frameworks, including development of associated rubrics to apply to faculty products.

Faculty Learning Through the EDGES Learning Community

Jameson, Clayton, Jaeger, and Bringle (2012; Jaeger, Jameson, & Clayton, 2012) investigated faculty learning in the context of a learning community called Education and Discovery Grounded in Engaged Scholarship (EDGES), which included four cohorts: doctoral students, early career faculty, recently tenured faculty, and late career faculty. The learning goals for EDGES participants included understanding the foundational concepts of CES; analyzing the dynamics of partnerships in CES; and developing abilities to collaborate with students and with community members as co-educators, co-learners, and co-generators of knowledge.

EDGES Scholars completed a 25-item CES competencies scale developed from the CCPH work discussed previously in this chapter. The self-report instrument was used at the beginning of the program and twice at its conclusion (a posttest and a retrospective pretest, which assessed their competency levels before the program began). This pre-post-then strategy, developed by G. S. Howard and Dailey (1979), accounts for response-shift-bias: the tendency to overestimate competence before experiencing an intervention through which one realizes what one does not know. The assessment strategy also involved written reflection activities at the beginning, middle, and end of the program; reflection prompts asked participants to define, apply, and evaluate key concepts (providing demonstrations of enhanced understanding rather than report of same) as well as to report their perceptions of changes in their understanding. Through qualitative analysis of these reflection products, investigators found examples of faculty learning that were categorized into three major themes. Participants used new vocabulary for the engaged scholarship process and described how this new language helped them talk about learning goals with their students, negotiate community partnerships, and discuss the value of their work with colleagues. Participants provided insight into how they learned by describing surprises and new discoveries through the EDGES program, such as challenges to the assumption that research is supposed to be neutral or the belief that community engagement is a one-way dissemination of expertise from the university to the community. Finally, reflection products revealed that participation in EDGES influenced participants' identity as scholars as the participants realized there was a community of scholars doing community-engaged research and recognized, in some cases for the first time, that they wanted to make a contribution to the community rather than limit their research contribution to their discipline and professional associations.

EDGES was designed to cultivate higher level learning (e.g., synthesis across realms of faculty work, evaluation of partnerships and scholarship products), challenge and reframe institutional and faculty norms (e.g., technocratic models for student-faculty and community-campus relationships), transform identities (e.g., from instructors and researchers to co-educators, co-learners, and co-generators of knowledge), and build capacity for systems change (e.g., of institutional culture and discourse). In summary, it was designed for faculty to learn about and through all three levels discussed previously: *what*, *how*, and *why/who*. The CES competencies scale contained items from each of the conceptual levels examined earlier, ranging from, for example, "familiarity with the basic literature and history of community engaged scholarship" (technical, *what* level) to "ability to collaborate with students [and community members] as co-educators, co-learners, and co-generators of knowledge" (dialectical, *why/who* level). Several items, for example "ability to work effectively with diverse communities," arguably involve learning across all three levels, but the instrument did not provide a way to parse the learning referred to in such items into its associated levels. The study's use of reflection to provide direct evidence of learning focused largely on the content of faculty learning; the subset of the reflection prompts designed to elicit self-reported data provided access to faculty members' thinking about the processes through which the faculty learned.

As with the first study that we discussed, a strength of the CES competencies instrument is that it allows investigators to identify the specific content areas in which participants report the most and least learning. Significant limitations are that it does not provide any information about the processes whereby the learning occurred, and as with any self-report measure, it also only provides participants' perceptions of their learning, not direct evidence of learning. Although the written reflection products provided additional insights to interpret the quantitative data, decreased participation over time and the lack of a rubric that clearly defined and operationalized learning outcomes limited the claims that could be made about faculty learning. An implication of this study is that rubrics should be applied to reflection products in the assessment of faculty learning just as in the assessment of student learning.

Faculty Autoethnography

Tilley-Lubbs's (2009) autoethnographic examination of her "transformative journey" (p. 59) with service learning is an example of how faculty reflection can both generate and document learning. The author's course, Crossing the Border, involved Spanish and education students in a semester-long project supporting Spanish-speaking immigrant families as they learned English and transitioned to life in the United States. Tilley-Lubbs marshaled perspectives from feminist post-structuralism and critical theory as lenses through which to analyze a workday early in the semester during which students brought donated clothing and furniture to the families' homes. Data sources included students' journals and the author's own field notes and personal journal from the Fall 2002 implementation of the course; the author positioned herself as both the investigator and the investigated and used as data others' responses to her, which led her to reinterpret her own actions and the meaning that she originally ascribed to them and thereby to learn through a process of self-reflexivity.

Tilley-Lubbs (2009) traced the evolution of her understanding of her role, her views of reciprocity, her relationships with community members and students, her course design, and her sense of the integrity of the project. In doing so she documented several examples of the content and the process of her learning; she examined her own learning, much of it transformational, occurring at the level of *why/who* (triple-loop, premise, dialectical). Tilley-Lubbs used her own contemporaneous description of the workday to explain her core learning: the ways that her approach to service learning unintentionally cultivated hierarchy between her students and community members. The content of her learning is documented by her application of service learning theory to some of the potentially problematic aspects of service in her own experience. The process of her learning is documented by her detailed discussion of the ways in which "that class shook [her] beliefs about the rightness of the workday as students critically evaluated the practice" (p. 63). Tilley-Lubbs recalls from that experience:

> For the first time class members critically questioned my practices [and] at that point, I subconsciously began to confront my motives, but I chose to

> remain cloaked in denial and irritation, unable to acknowledge the situation I had created. Fortunately, I had created a class that encouraged questioning, even if I had not intended to be the object of the questions. (p. 63)

Evidence of Tilley-Lubbs's learning—arguably at all three levels—was further provided by her identification of specific changes to her practice that resulted from that learning (e.g., replacing the workday with a meet-and-greet potluck event, arranging for her students and the families to decide together how best to identify and address community concerns) and by the speculative connections that she made between these changes and changes in the behaviors of her community partners (e.g., being less accommodative of student preferences in scheduling, determining topics they want to talk about with students from semester to semester).

This autoethnography contributed to and revealed the transformational nature of the author's learning as she recognized the influence of and engaged critically with the norms of "the world that shaped [her]" (Tilley-Lubbs, 2009, p. 61) and began to change her previous perspective. As she notes:

> The patriarchal society in which I grew up promotes charitable acts as beneficent and virtuous. I am a member of a church that considers service to humankind to be of the highest calling. . . . Inadvertently . . . I converted my sense of caring into perceiving need among the families, subconsciously developing a deficit notion about the families. . . . I was appalled to recognize that my entire perspective about the world and the workdays contributed to the oppressive behavior I abhor. (pp. 62–64)

The author's description of her new awareness of herself and her students as co-learners provided additional evidence of the transformational nature of her learning:

> Up to that point, my vision included facilitating a class to foster change within students, causing them to become agents of change in society. I never once considered they could serve as agents of change for me through what I perceived at the time to be probing, hurtful criticisms. . . . The irony of this narrative is that the continuum of my transformational journey was precipitated by student questioning, a journey that changed me from enacting a deficit notion of the community, which I in turn implicitly had been communicating to the students. (pp. 63–64)

The study by Tilley-Lubbs, like the study by McGuire et al. (2009), demonstrates intentional inquiry by faculty into their own learning. More so than the methods of the other three studies surveyed here, Tilley-Lubbs's method provides access to learning at the third level (triple-loop, premise, dialectical). This autoethnographic analysis could be supplemented with the perspectives of students and community partners, explicitly applying the conceptual framing of co-learning, because the events that provide the context for the study clearly lent themselves to the possibility of co-learning.

Implications for Practice

The conceptual frameworks discussed earlier—which provide perspectives on faculty identity as learner; learning at the levels of *what, how,* and *why/ who*; and co-learning—and the review of studies investigating faculty learning have implications for the design of interventions aimed at faculty learning. Neumann (2000) suggests that faculty development opportunities "rarely position individual professors as potential sources of their own professional development, assuming, instead, that development is best done to them" (p. 1). This is a useful reminder that the faculty learning interventions explored next may be informal or formal; self-directed or designed and guided by others; and, of course, co-created within a community of co-learners.

Kreber and Cranton (2000) list a variety of illustrative actions that faculty may undertake as they learn about teaching at each of Mezirow's (1991) three levels (content, process, premise) in each of the three domains of learning (instructional, pedagogical, curricular). Learning in the first domain, for example, may result from discussing ideas with students or colleagues, keeping a log of methods used, and reading articles on teaching strategies (the *what* level) and soliciting peer review of course-related materials (the *how* level). Learning in the pedagogical domain may result from administering inventories to students (the *what* level), conducting research on student learning (the *how* level), and reading about and writing critiques related to the relevance of various learning-related theory (the *why* level). These activities both support faculty in learning and serve as indicators of their engagement in the scholarship of teaching. The range of activities they discuss is similar to that proposed by Clayton and O'Steen (2010) in their overview of potential approaches to faculty development that can be used by service learning professionals, which range from providing access to resources for faculty to read to facilitating multidisciplinary learning communities of faculty engaged in long-term research on student learning. Mapping types of activities designed to generate learning with the levels of learning desired is complicated by the reality that any one activity, depending on its content but more importantly on how the learner engages with it, might cultivate learning at any of the three levels we have been discussing. While reading examples of service learning definitions or projects may lead some faculty members to learn at the single-loop/content/technical level—asking *what* the pedagogy consists of—it may lead others to learn at the triple-loop/premise/dialectical level—asking *why* they teach and *who* they are as educators.

Faculty learning in collaboration with others, whether other faculty, students, or community members, may be advanced through careful attention to the design of collaborative learning environments; and that design may be maximized when it is informed by principles of best practice regarding both collaboration and learning. As one intriguing example, Baxter Magolda (2012) offers her Learning Partnership Model as an aid to supporting the transformational learning that educators need to undertake as requisite to and part of facilitating such learning among their students. The components of the model include respecting one another's thoughts and feelings, helping one another view experiences as opportunities for growth, collaborating to analyze problems, discouraging simplistic solutions and instead attending to complexity, encouraging the development of personal authority, and encouraging one another to share expertise while working together. Examining groups that have acted on such an orientation to mutual learning, she highlights such approaches as developing common standards and shared visions (for both the work and the collaboration that generates the work) and establishing a strong sense of community that can provide support for risk taking.

As with student learning, critical reflection that links experience with theory is a key dimension of faculty learning. Faculty learning about service learning may be cultivated through a wide variety of approaches to critical reflection. One example that may be particularly powerful involves immersion as students in a service learning activity (integrating content, service, and critical reflection), especially if that opportunity includes metalevel reflection on the activity as a microcosm of the design and implementation choice points involved (Clayton & O'Steen, 2010). Jameson et al. (2012) discuss the value such an approach would have added to the implementation of EDGES in terms of its potential to frame critical reflection as a vehicle for learning and, thereby, establish the rationale for participants' ongoing meaning making throughout the program. Insofar as critical reflection is to be used to generate, assess, and investigate faculty learning, the extent to which faculty value it as a learning tool and have the ability to undertake it effectively will determine its utility (as with students). Building the capacity to learn through reflection is an ongoing process, but if it is not undertaken carefully, there can be significant negative consequences for the generation and assessment of learning with faculty (again, just as with students). Structuring reflection prompts so as to provide a scaffold for faculty (as for student) learning may be useful in this process. The reflection strategy used in the EDGES program discussed earlier, for example, included prompts designed to evoke thinking across all levels of Bloom's Taxonomy (1956)—from such lower level prompts as "How do you define partnerships?" to such higher level prompts as "How are your work with students and your community-engaged scholarship aligned and how are they in tension?" The designers of the EDGES program point out that more frequent reflection, undertaken in a more explicitly cumulative fashion, in addition to more support for the participants in learning how to learn through reflection, would have significantly strengthened both the learning outcomes achieved and the value of faculty reflection products as sources of evidence of faculty learning (Jameson et al., 2012).

Finally, there is the issue of cultivating faculty identity, not only as learner but also as co-learner. Jameson et al. (2011) discuss conditions under which the transformative potential of CES can be tapped as all partners come to see themselves and be seen by the others as co-educators, co-learners, and co-generators of knowledge, suggesting that "because such 'co-' roles are highly counter-normative . . . they require and foster paradigm shift" (p. 260). Among the conditions they posit as helpful in the process of making the associated shifts in perspective, practice, and identity are renegotiation of typical power relationships and attention to language. If faculty are to see themselves as and be seen as learners, both alongside and in partnerships with students and community members, the elements of hierarchy that have often characterized their relationships with both populations (Saltmarsh et al., 2009) must be replaced with more egalitarian power dynamics in which all partners assume—and assume responsibility for—shared power and in which no one's contributions are marginalized. Further, what the authors refer to as "shedding some of our traditional, all-too-often deficit-based language and intentionally choosing more egalitarian, participatory, and democratic language" (Jameson et al., 2011, p. 272)—for example, shifting from "for" to "with" and from "they" to "we"—is equally key to nurturing relationships and environments that are conducive to co-learning among the partners in service learning. These conditions that foster co-learning, intriguingly, themselves require faculty (and student and community member) learning, arguably at all three of the levels that we have discussed. For example, faculty must learn *what* power shift consists of and attend to *what* language they and others use; they must consider *how* power dynamics and language hinder and support collaborative processes; and they must engage with *why* they and others do and do not assume and share power readily and do and do not default to democratic language, in terms of the underlying systems and paradigms at work and their influence on the formation of co- (and not co-) identities (*who*).

Most fundamentally, reflecting critically on the experience of teaching with service learning is likely the best opportunity for faculty to learn about it and about themselves as learners (and co-learners) and educators (and co-educators). Clayton and Ash (2004) describe a process of supporting faculty in reflection on the paradigmatic shifts in perspective and practice that teaching with service learning evokes, among the faculty themselves as well as among their students. The contrast between technocratic and democratic paradigms (Jameson et al., 2011; Saltmarsh et al., 2009) can be applied to faculty members' experiences teaching with service learning, for example, as a workshop activity. Doing so not only can highlight the learning that faculty may desire as they seek to challenge the dominant norms of the academy in their teaching but also can frame the learning that they are accomplishing (e.g., *what* is meant by reciprocity; *how* they might relate with students and community members in less hierarchical ways; *why* their students resist and embrace democratic engagement; and *who* they want to be as co-educators, co-learners, and co-generators of knowledge). The scholarship of teaching and learning, including presentations and publications, and the dossier preparation process are two leading examples of structures that can explicitly support such faculty reflection and, simultaneously, yield products that provide evidence of learning. Similarly, research that involves faculty in the inquiry process—whether focused on faculty learning per se, as in the studies reviewed here, or on other service learning processes and outcomes (Clayton, Bringle, Senor, Huq, & Morrison, 2010)—can itself be a catalyst to their learning.

Future Research Agenda

Faculty learning is an underdeveloped yet ripe arena for research in service learning. In this section we propose research questions suggested by the earlier discussion of relevant theory and extant research, suggest potential investigations of relationships between student and faculty learning, and consider possibilities for gathering and analyzing both direct and indirect evidence of faculty learning.

Sample Research Questions

Examples of meaningful questions for investigation include the following:

- What are the indicators of faculty identity as learner? As co-learner? What specific constructs are most useful in gauging the extent to which an individual faculty member has developed either or both of these identities? Is there a set of such indicators and constructs that apply to student and community member—as well as to faculty—identities as learner and co-learner?
- Under what conditions do faculty hold an identity as learner? What factors in their prior experience (e.g., graduate school) might predict the development of this identity, shed light on key sources of identity formation among faculty, and help determine individual- and systems-level inhibitors of identity as learner? What institutional structures and norms support and hinder the development of such identities among faculty?
- What are the moderating variables that most influence the content and the process of faculty learning in service learning? Prior experience with service learning or with other nontraditional pedagogies? Career stage? Institution type? Degree of integration among roles desired by faculty? Characteristics of their student partners? Of their community partners? Discipline? Sense of place (e.g., rootedness in a particular community)? What determines the relative influence of these variables in any given instance?
- What is the relationship between learning outcomes and learning processes for faculty? For example, is there added value in learning about service learning through immersion in the service learning process as students rather than as only instructional designers, in learning about reflection through reflective approaches, in developing capacities as co-learners through co-learning activities? Under what conditions? In what ways, if any, is reflectively teaching with service learning (as distinct from other pedagogical approaches) unique, either in learning process or in learning outcomes, for faculty?
- What are the similarities and differences between the processes by which faculty learn in their discipline and those by which they learn about service learning and community engagement? Between the

processes of inquiry that they use as researchers and the processes that they use to learn as educators?

- What faculty development interventions most effectively cultivate faculty learning at each of the three levels discussed here—*what, how,* and *why/who*? For faculty with what characteristics (e.g., Is there a relationship with level of experience in service learning?)? Under what conditions (e.g., Is there a relationship with the faculty developer's own identity as a learner or co-learner?)? What difference does it make if the faculty learner enters the faculty development process aware of these levels? Having set goals for learning in accordance with these levels? Participating in an assessment process explicitly mapped to these levels?

- What are the obstacles—individual, interpersonal, institutional, systemic, paradigmatic (Edwards & Clayton, 2012)—to faculty learning in the context of service learning? Beyond their sense of identity (or not) as learners and co-learners, what motivates faculty to attend to their own learning, in light of these obstacles? What specific variables in the conceptualization and design of service learning per se present obstacles to faculty learning? Encourage faculty learning?

- What is involved in faculty developing the perspectives, practices, and identities associated not only with learning in their roles as service learning educators but also with co-learning? Are there particular *why/who* level learning outcomes that they need to achieve in order to become "co-"? Are there stages through which this process of faculty (and students and community partners) becoming co-learners occurs? If so, how are they similar to and different from those through which student partners and community partners move? What are the indicators of movement through these stages? What supports and what hinders faculty in the process of becoming co-learners? Which specific dimensions of the perspectives, practices, and identities associated with co-learning change as the context changes and which transcend context?

- How do and might faculty use what they know about student learning to conceptualize, generate, and investigate their own learning?

Investigating Relationships Between Student and Faculty Learning

O'Meara et al. (2008) emphasize the value of understanding the connections between faculty learning and student learning and state that "researchers have a long way to go in conceptualizing the nature of the possible connections that may (and may not) exist between the teacher's learning and her [or his] teaching and the learning of the individuals in her or his classroom" (p. 168). Given the development of constructs with which to gauge the extent to which an individual (faculty member, student, community member) has an identity as learner and, further, as co-learner, research that links faculty identity and learning outcomes with student identity and learning outcomes can proceed. For example, do students taught by faculty with a deep identity as co-learners themselves tend to demonstrate such an identity, and to the extent that they do, is this because they are attracted to such faculty or because their relationships with such faculty help to cultivate this student identity (or both)? What specific relationship dynamics between such faculty and students mediate the development of student identity as co-learner? What is the relationship between faculty identity as co-learner and student learning outcomes in service learning (see Part Two)? Does that relationship vary across categories of student learning outcomes (e.g., cognition, academic learning, civic learning, personal development, intercultural competence)? What student characteristics (e.g., age) and what qualities of interaction (e.g., frequency, closeness) between students and the faculty member in question most strongly influence this relationship? Practitioner-scholars in service learning can use the foundation provided by years of work on assessing student learning and more recent work on assessing faculty learning to develop quantitative, qualitative, and mixed-methods approaches to investigating the relationship between faculty learning outcomes (e.g., understanding critical thinking, demonstrating critical thinking, being able to provide feedback to students in accordance with standards of critical thinking) and student learning outcomes (e.g., understanding critical thinking, demonstrating critical thinking, being able to assess their own and others' thinking in terms of standards of critical thinking).

Future research might also focus on the similarities and differences between the content of student and faculty (and community member) learning in the context of service learning and in so doing contribute to the understanding of what the most salient learning goals for each partner category are as well as what learning is being achieved by each under what conditions. Such understanding would support the design of professional development opportunities for members of each partner category separately and for combinations of them participating together. For example, the general categorization of learning goals into academic enhancement, civic learning, and personal growth—potentially inclusive of or to be supplemented with metacognition, intercultural competence, and professional development, for example—has been used (Clayton, Bacon et al., 2010) and might be developed further as a conceptual framing for faculty and community partner learning as well as student learning. Models of civic learning as developed at Indiana University–Purdue University Indianapolis (Bringle & Steinberg, 2010; Bringle, Studer, Wilson, Clayton, & Steinberg, 2011; Hatcher 2008; Steinberg, Hatcher, & Bringle, 2011) that have overlapping but distinct elements in their application to students (e.g., civic-minded graduate) and to community engagement practitioner-scholars (e.g., civic minded professional) might be further refined for specific application to service learning faculty and used to guide professional development as well as assessment of learning outcomes. Researchers might find that there are commonalities across partner categories—key examples of civic knowledge, skills, or attitudes, for example—that, if intentionally set as learning goals, are important precursors to reciprocal partnerships.

Another area of inquiry regards similarities and differences between students and faculty (and community members) in terms of the processes through which they learn. It is frequently said that faculty tend to be abstract learners whereas students often learn best through concrete experience—a difference that could hinder co-learning dynamics. Whether it was ever that simple or not, changing faculty demographics—including especially the experiences with and expectations of community-campus engagement that new faculty increasingly bring to their roles (New England Resource Center for Higher Education, 2012; O'Meara et al., 2008)—may have implications for the relationships between student and faculty learning styles and preferences. Work by Marchese (1997), Chickering and Gamson (1991), and Kuh (2008) comprises a body of promising practices related to the design of learning environments and pedagogies for students, such as learner independence, timely feedback, active involvement, collaboration, challenge, and guided practice. Future research might determine how these principles are best operationalized with faculty given a commitment to co-learning among all participants in service learning. Work applying Kolb's (1984) learning cycle to the design of faculty development (Bringle & Hatcher, 1995; Bringle, Hatcher, Jones, & Plater, 2006) and exploring promising practices in faculty development for service learning (Bringle, Games, Ludlum, Osgood, & Osborne, 2000; Clayton & Ash, 2005; Clayton & O'Steen, 2010) strongly suggests that faculty learning can be maximized through structured reflection on experience. Future research might examine the utility and consequences of faculty using the same reflection strategies and mechanisms that they design for their students as tools to generate and deepen their own learning: Does such a practice lead faculty to learn about reflection and examine and revise their reflection assignments to achieve deeper student learning? Does it lead them to understand their students' challenges with learning through reflection?

Obtaining Evidence of Faculty Learning

Syllabi, statements of course learning goals and objectives, assignments, project descriptions, reflection prompts, and feedback to students are all examples of course-related faculty products that can serve as data sources, providing direct and authentic evidence of their learning. As discussed in the critique of the McGuire et al. (2009) and Jameson et al. (2012) studies, practitioner-scholars need to develop rubrics that specify levels of learning and that are aligned with objectives for faculty learning. For example, rubrics to measure the extent to which faculty feedback on student products is aligned with standards of critical thinking (e.g., Paul, 1993; Paul & Elder, 2006) or the extent to which assignment prompts are expressed in assessable (i.e., Bloom-based; Bloom, 1956) language could be developed and applied to faculty products before and after a workshop series or other professional development activity to assess faculty learning and, in turn, investigate questions regarding the conditions under which faculty best learn. Observations of faculty language and behaviors, including from students and community members, can also provide additional evidence of learning outcomes in the context of service learning courses.

Bloom-based rubrics for designing reflection prompts for faculty and assessing their understanding of any of a wide range of concepts associated with service learning and community engagement could easily be developed, drawing on the work of Ash and Clayton (2009a). Table 3.3.1 offers an illustrative, preliminary example for the sample learning goal: Faculty will understand the typology of scholarship offered by Boyer (1996). Similar rubrics might also be designed using the *what, how, why/who* structure provided by the distinctions among single-, double-, triple-loop; content, process, premise; and technical, contextual, dialectical. Combined with Bloom-based rubrics, these could be used to investigate the relationship between higher order reasoning, on the one hand, and the three levels, on the other. Such rubrics could be applied to such faculty products as grant proposals, publications, and dossiers as well as to reflection products.

Work on assessing student learning suggests a particularly intriguing approach to generating direct evidence of faculty learning to which such

TABLE 3.3.1
Sample Bloom-Based Rubric for the Goal of Faculty Understanding the Typology of Scholarship Offered by Boyer (1996)

Level 1	Identifies Boyer's categories of scholarship
Level 2	Explains Boyer's categories of scholarship in his or her own words
Level 3	Gives an example of each of these types of scholarship from his or her own work or that of his or her colleagues
Level 4	Compares and contrasts these examples of different types of scholarship with one another and with an exemplar CES project (What do they have in common and how are they distinct?)
Level 5	Revises his or her own working definition of CES as needed to take into account the perspectives offered by Boyer's typology and to capture the nuances of the exemplar project
Level 6	Critiques his or her original working definition of CES and the definition of CES used in the faculty development program in light of his or her Boyerized definition (What should be changed in any or all of these definitions and why?) and evaluates the utility of Boyer's typology as an aid to establishing a clear and meaningful conceptualization of CES

rubrics could be applied: the use of problem scenarios. Steinke and Fitch (2003) developed problem-based scenarios to document student learning, and Steinberg, Hatcher, and Bringle (2011) and Bullock and Clayton (2010) integrated self-report scales with problem-solving narratives. The work of these investigators suggests that a common multidisciplinary problem scenario might be posed to faculty or that faculty might be asked to identify a relevant problem individually, but in either case they would then engage with the problem using predetermined prompts designed to evoke and provide evidence of the categories of learning of interest (e.g., knowledge, skills, and attitudes or academic, civic, personal) and levels of thinking desired. As one example, participants in a faculty development program could be given a problem scenario related to teaching a service learning course as a pre- and post-instrument. A rubric embodying the *what, how,* and *why/who* levels of learning could be applied to the problem resolutions to assess learning, to examine some of the questions posed in this chapter, and to enhance development of theory related to faculty learning.

Conclusion

As is the case with student learning, investigating faculty learning in service learning—in all its multidimensionality, which has only been hinted at here—holds the potential to inform theory and practice well beyond the realm of service learning. Our own journeys with service learning practice and scholarship have been extraordinary learning opportunities that have regularly invited us to expand and deepen not only our understanding of the *what*s and *how*s of the pedagogy but also our willingness and our capacity to inquire into the *why*s and *who*s of our work more generally. One of the many counternormative implications of service learning as we have experienced it is that it calls into question whose learning is at stake and provides an answer that is broader, deeper, and more integrated than the academy's characteristic focus on student learning—without, however, suggesting any diminishment of the significance of student learning. Its answer highlights the ways that student learning is bound up in the learning of faculty and community members.

Reflecting on their experiences as student and faculty learners and co-learners in service learning, Whitney, McClure, Respet, and Clayton (2007) posit that "ultimately, students best undertake [service learning as] a developmental journey when those who support and mentor them are also striving for growth through the same process" (p. 195). Faculty who understand themselves as learners and co-learners, actively engage in learning opportunities, and inquire into their own learning may be in a particularly strong position to support and challenge their students' learning. Such faculty may be likely to relate with students and community members (as well as with one another) as partners in service learning—as people from whom and with whom they can learn—and thereby nurture not only their own learning but also a more empowered stance on the part of those partners and in turn a more democratic way of being in community-campus engagement and in the public realm more generally.

Note

1. The term *faculty* herein refers to all members of the academy who serve as educators.

Recommended Reading

Clayton, P. H., & Ash, S. L. (2004). Shifts in perspective: Capitalizing on the counter-normative nature of service-learning. *Michigan Journal of Community Service Learning, 11*(1), 59–70.

Creamer, E. G., & Lattuca, L. R. (Eds.). (2005). Advancing faculty learning through interdisciplinary collaboration [Special issue]. *New Directions for Teaching and Learning, 2005*(102).

Jameson, J. K., Clayton, P. H., Jaeger, A. J., & Bringle, R. G. (2012). Investigating faculty learning in the context of community-engaged scholarship. *Michigan Journal of Community Service Learning, 18*(2), 40–55.

Mezirow, J. (1991). *Transformative dimensions of adult learning.* San Francisco, CA: Jossey-Bass.

O'Meara, K., & Terosky, A. L. (2010). Engendering faculty professional growth. *Change: The Magazine of Higher Learning, 42*(6), 44–51.

References

Angelo, T. (1999, July). *Doing academic development as though we valued learning most: Transformative guidelines from research and practice.* Paper presented at the HERDSA Annual International Conference, Melbourne, Australia.

Argyris, C., & Schön, D. (1974). *Theory in practice: Increasing professional effectiveness.* San Francisco, CA: Jossey-Bass.

Ash, S. L., & Clayton, P. H. (2009a). Generating, deepening, and documenting learning: The power of critical reflection in applied learning. *Journal of Applied Learning in Higher Education, 1*(1), 25–48.

Ash, S. L., & Clayton, P. H. (2009b). *Learning through critical reflection: A tutorial for service-learning students (instructor version).* Raleigh, NC: Authors.

Baxter Magolda, M. B. (2012). Building learning partnerships. *Change: The Magazine of Higher Learning, 44*(1), 32–38.

Blanchard, L. W., Hanssmann, C., Strauss, R. P., Belliard, J. C., Krichbaum, K., Waters, E., & Seifer, S. D. (2009). Models for faculty development: What does it take to be a community-engaged scholar? *Metropolitan Universities, 20*(2), 47–65.

Blanchard, L. W., Strauss, R. P., & Webb, L. (2012). Engaged scholarship at the University of North Carolina at Chapel Hill: Campus integration and faculty development. *Journal of Higher Education Outreach and Engagement, 16*(1), 97–128.

Bloom, B. S. (Ed.). (1956). *Taxonomy of educational objectives book 1: Cognitive domain.* White Plains, NY: Longman.

Bowman, N. A., & Brandenberger, J. W. (2010). Quantitative assessment of service-learning outcomes: Is self-reported change an adequate proxy for longitudinal change? In J. Keshen, B. A. Holland, & B. E. Moely (Eds.), *Research for what? Making engaged scholarship matter* (pp. 25–43). Charlotte, NC: Information Age.

Boyer, E. (1996). The scholarship of engagement. *Journal of Public Outreach, 1*(1), 11–20.

Bringle, R. G., & Clayton, P. H. (2012). Civic education through service learning: What, how, and why? In L. McIlrath, A. Lyons, & R. Munck (Eds.), *Higher education and civic engagement: Comparative perspectives* (pp. 101–124). New York, NY: Palgrave Macmillan.

Bringle, R. G., Games, R., Ludlum, C., Osgood, R., & Osborne, R. (2000). Faculty Fellows Program: Enhancing integrated professional development through community service. *American Behavioral Scientist, 43,* 882–894.

Bringle, R. G., & Hatcher, J. A. (1995). A service-learning curriculum for faculty. *Michigan Journal of Community Service Learning, 2*(1), 112–122.

Bringle, R. G., Hatcher, J. A., Jones, S. G., & Plater, W. M. (2006). Sustaining civic engagement: Faculty development, roles, and rewards. *Metropolitan Universities, 17*(1), 62–74.

Bringle, R. G., & Steinberg, K. S. (2010). Educating for informed community involvement. *American Journal of Community Psychology, 46,* 428–441.

Bringle, R. G., Studer, M. H., Wilson, J., Clayton, P. H., & Steinberg, K. S. (2011). Designing programs with a purpose: To promote civic engagement for life. *Journal of Academic Ethics, 9*(2), 149–164.

Bullock, B., & Clayton, P. H. (2010, March). *International MS education and dual degrees in forestry: The Atlantis Program.* Paper presented at the University Education in Natural Resources Conference, Blacksburg, VA.

Carter, L. M., & Brockerhoff-Macdonald, B. (2011). The continuing education of faculty at a mid-sized Ontario university. *The Canadian Journal for the Scholarship of Teaching and Learning, 2*(1), Article 4. Retrieved from http://ir.lib.uwo.ca/cjsotl_rcacea/vol2/iss1/4

Chickering, A. W., & Gamson, Z. F. (1991). *Applying the seven principles for good practice in undergraduate education.* San Francisco, CA: Jossey-Bass.

Clayton, P. H., & Ash, S. L. (2004). Shifts in perspective: Capitalizing on the counter-normative nature of service-learning. *Michigan Journal of Community Service Learning, 11*(1), 59–70.

Clayton, P. H., & Ash, S. L. (2005). Reflection as a key component in faculty development. *On the Horizon, 13*(3), 161–169.

Clayton, P. H., Bacon, D., Hess, G., Moore, A., & Snow, C. (2010, February). *Who's doing the learning: Faculty and community partners as learners in service-learning.* Paper presented at the Pathways to Achieving Civic Engagement Conference, Elon, NC.

Clayton, P. H., Bringle, R. G., Senor, B., Huq, J., & Morrison, M. (2010). Differentiating and assessing relationships in service-learning and civic engagement: Exploitive, transactional, and transformational. *Michigan Journal of Community Service Learning, 16*(2), 5–21.

Clayton, P. H., & O'Steen, W. L. (2010). Working with faculty: Designing customized developmental strategies. In B. Jacoby & P. Mutascio (Eds.), *Looking in—reaching out: A reflective guide for community service-learning professionals* (pp. 95–135). Boston, MA: Campus Compact.

Cranton, P. (2006). Fostering authentic relationships in the transformative classroom. *New Directions for Adult and Continuing Education, 2006*(109), 5–13. doi:10.1002/ace.203

Domagal-Goldman, J. M. (2010). *Teaching for civic capacity and engagement: How faculty members align teaching and purpose* (Doctoral dissertation). Available from ProQuest Dissertations and Theses database. (UMI No. 3436063)

Donahue, D. M., Bowyer, J., & Rosenberg, D. (2003). Learning with and learning from: Reciprocity in service learning in teacher education. *Equity & Excellence in Education, 36*(1), 15–27.

Driscoll, A. (2000). Studying faculty and service-learning: Directions for inquiry and development [Special issue]. *Michigan Journal of Community Service Learning, Fall*, 35–41.

Edwards, K. E., & Clayton, P. H. (2012, February). *Talking our talk: The power of words in community engagement.* Workshop presented at Berea College, Berea, KY.

Eyler, J. S. (2000). What do we most need to know about the impact of service learning on student learning? [Special issue]. *Michigan Journal of Community Service Learning, Fall*, 11–17.

Felten, P., & Clayton, P. H. (2011). Service-learning. *New Directions for Teaching and Learning, 2011*(128), 75–84. doi:10.1002/tl.470

Freire, P. (1970). *Pedagogy of the oppressed.* New York, NY: Continuum.

Gelmon, S. B., Holland, B. A., Driscoll, A., Spring, A., & Kerrigan, S. (2001). *Assessing service-learning and civic engagement: Principles and techniques.* Providence, RI: Campus Compact.

Hatcher, J. A. (2008). *The public role of professionals: Developing and evaluating the civic-minded professional scale* (Doctoral dissertation). Available from ProQuest Dissertations and Theses database. (UMI No. 3331248)

Hess, G., Blank, G., Clayton, P. H., Connors, J., Ramsey, J., Reis, K., Wallace, J. (2011). Perspectives on partnership evolution: From passionate people to committed organizations. In L. Harter, J. Hamel-Lambert, & J. Millesen (Eds.), *Participatory partnerships for social action and research* (pp. 349–376). Dubuque, IA: Kendall Hunt.

Howard, G. S., & Dailey, P. R. (1979). Response-shift bias: A source of contamination of self-report measures. *Journal of Applied Psychology, 64*(2), 144–150.

Howard, J. (1998). Academic service learning: A counternormative pedagogy. *New Directions for Teaching and Learning, 1998*(73), 21–29. doi:10.1002/tl.7303

Jaeger, A. J., Jameson, J. K., & Clayton, P. H. (2012). Institutionalization of community engaged scholarship at a land grant, research extensive university: Examining the paradox of identity. *Journal of Higher Education Outreach and Engagement, 16*(1), 149–167.

Jameson, J. K., Clayton, P. H., & Jaeger, A. J. (2011). Community engaged scholarship as mutually transformative partnerships. In L. Harter, J. Hamel-Lambert, &

J. Millesen (Eds.), *Participatory partnerships for social action and research* (pp. 259–277). Dubuque, IA: Kendall Hunt.

Jameson, J. K., Clayton, P. H., Jaeger, A. J., & Bringle, R. G. (2012). Investigating faculty learning in the context of community-engaged scholarship. *Michigan Journal of Community Service Learning, 18*(2), 40–55.

Kirby, E. L. (2010). The philosophy of "co-": Acting "with" to maximize potential in participatory partnerships. In L. Harter, J. Hamel-Lambert, & J. Millesen (Eds.), *Participatory partnerships for social action and research* (pp. 377–384). Dubuque, IA: Kendall Hunt.

Kolb, D. (1984). *Experiential learning: Experience as the source of learning and development.* Upper Saddle River, NJ: Prentice Hall.

Kreber, C., & Cranton, P. A. (2000). Exploring the scholarship of teaching. *The Journal of Higher Education, 71,* 476–495.

Kuh, G. D. (2008). *High-impact educational practices: What they are, who has access to them, and why they matter.* Washington, DC: Association of American Colleges and Universities.

Lattuca, L. R. (2005). Faculty work as learning: Insights from theories of cognition. *New Directions for Teaching and Learning, 2005*(102), 13–21. doi:10.1002/tl.193

Lattuca, L. R., & Creamer, E. G. (2005). Learning as professional practice. *New Directions for Teaching and Learning, 2005*(102), 3–11. doi:10.1002/tl.192

Marchese, T. J. (1997). The new conversations about learning: Insights from neuroscience and anthropology, cognitive science and work-place studies. In American Association for Higher Education (Ed.), *Assessing impact: Evidence and action* (pp. 79–95). Washington, DC: American Association for Higher Education.

McGuire, L., Strong, D., Lay, K., Ardemagni, E., Wittberg, P., & Clayton, P. H. (2009). A case study of faculty learning around reflection: A collaborative faculty development project. In B. E. Moeley, S. H. Billig, & B. A. Holland (Eds.), *Creating our identities in service-learning and community engagement* (pp. 53–72). Charlotte, NC: Information Age.

Mezirow, J. (1991). *Transformative dimensions of adult learning.* San Francisco, CA: Jossey-Bass.

Mezirow, J., & Associates. (Eds.). (2000). *Learning as transformation: Critical perspectives on a theory in progress.* San Francisco, CA: Jossey-Bass.

Mondloch, A. S. (2009). One director's voice. In R. Stoecker & E. A. Tryon (Eds.), *The unheard voices: Community organizations and service learning* (pp. 136–146). Philadelphia, PA: Temple University Press.

Neumann, A. (2000, April). *Toward a profession of learning: Exploring how university professors learn through their subjects through teaching.* Paper presented at the meeting of the American Educational Research Association, New Orleans, LA.

Neumann, A. (2005). Observations: Taking seriously the topic of learning in studies of faculty work and careers. *New Directions for Teaching and Learning, 2005*(102), 63–83. doi:10.1002/tl.197

Neumann, A., & Peterson, P. L. (1997). *Learning from our lives: Women, research, and autobiography*. New York, NY: Teachers College Press.

New England Resource Center for Higher Education. (2012). *Next Generation Engagement Project*. Retrieved from http://www.nerche.org/index.php?option =com_content&view=article&id=355&Itemid=96

O'Meara, K., & Terosky, A. L. (2010). Engendering faculty professional growth. *Change: The Magazine of Higher Learning, 42*(6), 44–51.

O'Meara, K., Terosky, A. L., & Neumann, A. (2008). Faculty careers and work lives: A professional growth perspective. *ASHE Higher Education Report, 34*(3). San Francisco, CA: Jossey-Bass.

Paul, R. (1993). *Critical thinking: What every student needs to survive in a rapidly changing world*. Dillon Beach, CA: Foundation for Critical Thinking.

Paul, R., & Elder, L. (2006). *Critical thinking: Tools for taking charge of your learning and your life* (2nd ed.). Saddle River, NJ: Prentice Hall.

Petrie, H. G. (1986). Do you see what I see? The epistemology of interdisciplinary inquiry. In D. E. Chubin, A. L. Porter, F. A. Rossini, & T. Connelly (Eds.), *Interdisciplinary analysis and research: Theory and practice of problem-focused research and development* (pp. 115–130). Mt. Airy, MD: Lomond.

Saltmarsh, J., Hartley, M., & Clayton, P. H. (2009). *Democratic engagement white paper*. Boston, MA: New England Resource Center for Higher Education.

Sigmon, R. L. (1979). Service-learning: Three principles. *Synergist, 9–11*.

Steinberg, K. S., Hatcher, J. A., & Bringle, R. G. (2011). A north star: Civic-minded graduate. *Michigan Journal of Community Service Learning, 18*(1), 19–33.

Steinke, P., & Buresh, S. (2002). Cognitive outcomes of service-learning: Reviewing the past and glimpsing the future. *Michigan Journal of Community Service Learning, 8*(2), 5–14.

Steinke, P., & Fitch, P. (2003). Using written protocols to measure service learning outcomes. In S. H. Billig & J. S. Eyler (Eds.), *Deconstructing service learning: Research exploring context, participation, and impacts* (pp. 171–194). Greenwich, CT: Information Age.

Steinke, P., & Fitch, P. (2008). Assessing service-learning. In S. Shalini (Ed.), *Service learning: Perspectives and applications*. Punjagutta, India: Icfai University Press.

Taggart, G., & Wilson, A. (2005). *Promoting reflective thinking in teachers: 50 action strategies*. Thousand Oaks, CA: Corwin Press.

Tilley-Lubbs, G. A. (2009). Good intentions pave the way to hierarchy: A retrospective autoethnographic approach. *Michigan Journal of Community Service Learning, 16*(1), 59–68.

Whitney, B. C., McClure, J. D., Respet, A., & Clayton, P. H. (2007). Service learning as a shared developmental journey: Tapping the potential of the pedagogy. In L. McIlrath & I. MacLabhrainn (Eds.), *Higher education and civic engagement: International perspectives* (pp. 185–196). Burlington, VT: Ashgate.

ABOUT THE CONTRIBUTORS

Sarah L. Ash is professor and coordinator of the undergraduate nutrition program in the Department of Food, Bioprocessing and Nutrition Sciences at North Carolina State University (NCSU), where she advises more than 100 students and teaches close to 1,000 students each year in courses ranging from introductory and advanced human nutrition to U.S. food history. Her scholarly work examines the role of critical reflection in enhancing learning outcomes; along with colleagues she developed the DEAL Model for Critical Reflection, an internationally recognized reflection and assessment model designed to produce high-quality written products via a rigorous framework. She has also provided leadership in many teaching-related initiatives, from general education reform to faculty development. Sarah received the UNC System Board of Governors Award for Excellence in Teaching, the NCSU Alumni Distinguished Undergraduate Professor Award, and the USDA Food and Agriculture Excellence in Teaching Award for the Southern Region. Her work with Cooperative Extension faculty on nutrition education programming for limited resource older adults was recognized with the Lawrence Green Paper of the Year Award from the journal *Health, Education, and Behavior.* She earned her PhD in nutrition from Tufts University.

Richard M. Battistoni is professor of political science and public and community service studies at Providence College. For more than 20 years, Rick has been a leader in the field of community service learning, especially as it relates to questions of civic learning and engagement. From 1994 to 2000, he served as the founding director of the Feinstein Institute for Public Service at Providence College, the first degree-granting program in the nation combining community service with the curriculum; he will be returning to the position of director of the Feinstein Institute in the fall of 2012. A scholar in the field of political theory with a principal interest in the role of education in a democratic society, Dr. Battistoni has written numerous articles as well as authored and co-edited a number of books, including *Civic Engagement Across the Curriculum: A Resource Book for Faculty in All Disciplines* (Campus Compact, 2002); *Experiencing Citizenship: Concepts and Models for Service-Learning in Political Science* (edited with William E. Hudson; Stylus, 1997);

and *Public Schooling and the Education of Democratic Citizens* (University Press of Mississippi, 1985). Another volume, *Education for Democracy: Citizenship, Community and Service* (Kendall Hunt, 1999), which he edited with Benjamin R. Barber, is a principal textbook used in service learning classes taught around the country. From 2001 to 2004, Rick was the director of Project 540, a national high school civic engagement initiative funded by a grant from The Pew Charitable Trusts. He is a member of the board of directors of the Bernard and Audre Rapoport Foundation and has served on a number of community and not-for-profit organization boards, including City Year Rhode Island and Habitat for Humanity. From 2007 to 2011 he served as an elected member of the Lincoln School Committee. Rick received his PhD in political science from Rutgers University.

Jay W. Brandenberger is the director of research and assessment at the Center for Social Concerns and a concurrent associate professor of psychology at the University of Notre Dame. He has been a member of the faculty at Notre Dame since 1992 and has facilitated a variety of academic initiatives and engaged scholarship there. His research interests include social cognition, moral and ethical theory/development, and assessment of outcomes in higher education. He serves on the review boards of various journals and has collaborated on national research initiatives examining means to enhance social responsibility, leadership, and moral development. His work has appeared in *Journal of Applied Psychology, The Review of Higher Education, Michigan Journal of Community Service Learning, Journal of College Student Development, Applied Psychology: Health and Well-Being, Advances in Service-Learning Research,* and other publications. He received his PhD in developmental and educational psychology from the University of Pittsburgh.

Robert G. Bringle is Kulynych-Cline Professor of Psychology at Appalachian State University and formerly chancellor's professor of psychology and philanthropic studies and executive director of the Center for Service and Learning at Indiana University–Purdue University Indianapolis. He has been involved in the development, implementation, and evaluation of educational programs directed at talented undergraduate psychology majors, high school psychology teachers, first-year students, and the introductory psychology course. His work as executive director has resulted in numerous national recognitions for his campus and himself. He has published *With Service in Mind: Concepts and Models for Service-Learning in Psychology* (edited with Donna Duffy; Stylus, 1998); *Colleges and Universities as Citizens* (edited with

Richard Games and Edward Malloy; Allyn & Bacon, 1999); *The Measure of Service Learning: Research Scales to Assess Student Experiences* (co-authored with Mindy Phillips and Michael Hudson; American Psychological Association, 2004); and *International Service Learning: Conceptual Frameworks and Research* (edited with Julie Hatcher and Steven Jones; Stylus, 2011). For his accomplishments and scholarship on service learning, Dr. Bringle was awarded the Ehrlich Faculty Award for Service Learning and was recognized at the International Service-Learning Research Conference. He was the Volunteer of the Year in 2001 for Boys and Girls Clubs of Indianapolis. The University of the Free State, South Africa, awarded him an honorary doctorate for his scholarly work on civic engagement and service learning. Dr. Bringle received his PhD in social psychology from the University of Massachusetts–Amherst.

Nancy Van Note Chism is professor emerita of higher education and student affairs at Indiana University–Purdue University Indianapolis (IUPUI). As former associate vice chancellor for academic affairs, she directed the Office for Professional Development, which consisted of the Centers for Research, Service, and Teaching and Learning at IUPUI. In 2011, she taught an international service learning course for doctoral students in Bangkok, Thailand. Dr. Chism's interests center on the faculty profession, faculty development, college teaching and learning, and international educational development. She has taught seminars and published widely in these areas, including recent books on peer review of teaching, the faculty profession, and learning spaces. She was president of the Professional and Organizational Development (POD) Network in Higher Education and received the Bob Pierleoni Spirit of POD Award as well as the Robert Menges Research Award and the Innovator Award from that organization. She is the recipient of the Burton Gorman Teaching Excellence Award of the Indiana University School of Education and is a member of the Faculty Colloquium on Excellence in Teaching at Indiana University. A former Fulbright scholar, she has consulted on professional development or college teaching and learning at more than 50 campuses in the United States and internationally. Dr. Chism earned her PhD in educational policy and leadership at Ohio State University.

Patti H. Clayton is an independent consultant and practitioner-scholar (PHC Ventures). She has more than 12 years of experience as a practitioner-scholar in community-engaged teaching and learning and in experiential education more generally. She serves as a senior scholar with the Center for Service and Learning at Indiana University–Purdue University Indianapolis, a visiting fellow with the New England Resource Center for Higher Education, and a visiting scholar at the University of North Carolina at Greensboro. Patti co-developed with students and faculty a leading critical reflection and assessment model (the DEAL Model for Critical Reflection), models for student leadership in service learning, and a variety of faculty development and curriculum development processes. She and her colleagues produced student and instructor versions of a tutorial called *Learning Through Critical Reflection,* and she co-authored the *Democratic Engagement White Paper* (with John Saltmarsh and Matthew Hartley; New England Resource Center for Higher Education, 2009). Patti's current scholarship interests include the relationships among student, faculty, and community member learning; transformational institutionalization; and the dynamics of "with-ness" in democratic partnerships that position all partners as co-educators, co-learners, and co-generators of knowledge. Patti is a board member of the International Association for Research on Service-Learning and Community Engagement and serves as a co-editor of the *Proceedings* of the association's annual conference. She is also an associate editor of *Michigan Journal of Community Service Learning* and serves on the editorial board of *Journal of Applied Learning in Higher Education.* She received her PhD from the Curriculum in Ecology at the University of North Carolina at Chapel Hill.

Darla K. Deardorff is executive director of the Association of International Education Administrators, a national professional organization based at Duke University, where she is also a research scholar in education. In addition, she is visiting professor at Leeds-Metropolitan University in the United Kingdom and is on the faculty of the prestigious Summer Institute of Intercultural Communication in Portland, Oregon. She receives numerous invitations from around the world to speak and consult on her research on intercultural competence and assessment as well as on global leadership and internationalization issues. Dr. Deardorff has published widely on topics in international education and intercultural learning and assessment. She is editor of *The SAGE Handbook of Intercultural Competence* (SAGE, 2009), editor of *The SAGE Handbook of International Higher Education* (with Hans de Wit, John Heyl, and Tony Adams; SAGE, 2012) and of *Building Cultural Competence* (with Kate Berardo; Stylus, 2012), and author of *Beneath the Tip of the Iceberg: Improving English and Understanding US American Cultural*

Patterns (University of Michigan Press, 2011). Dr. Deardorff holds a doctorate in higher education from North Carolina State University, where she focused on international education.

Kathleen E. Edwards is currently a PhD student in educational leadership and cultural foundations at the University of North Carolina at Greensboro (UNCG). She has worked in higher education for more than 12 years. Prior to returning to school, she was the assistant director in the Kernodle Center for Service Learning at Elon University, where she collaborated with and supported more than 60 student leaders involved in direct, indirect, and advocacy-based co-curricular service. Kathleen's work is motivated and deeply inspired by her involvement with communities—which has included serving as a volunteer coordinator at a homeless shelter, community organizing with tenants in low-income/subsidized housing, working with survivors of sexual assault, and training youth activists. Her scholarly interests are focused on examining the cultural foundations of popular education and the democratic potential of community engagement as well as exploring and bringing non-Western and critical perspectives to bear on traditional conceptions and practices of service learning and community engagement. For Kathleen, community-based research and other forms of community engagement are opportunities to learn with others and to work toward social justice transformation. Committed to reimagining the roles and work of emerging scholars, Kathleen is involved with the International Association for Research on Service-Learning and Community Engagement (IARSLCE) Graduate Student Network Steering Committee and the Public Scholarship Graduate Network at UNCG, and she serves as a senior editorial fellow producing the *Proceedings* of the IARSLCE conference. She earned her MEd in college student personnel from the University of Dayton.

Peggy Fitch is vice president for student development and professor of psychology at Central College, where she has taught developmental psychology courses, a first-year-experience course on human nature, and experimental psychology and has supervised students' research. Her research interests include service learning, intellectual development, assessment, and the development of intercultural competence. Since arriving at Central in 1992, she has served as a consultant to various committees and offices charged with evaluation and outcomes assessment. She collaborates with Pamela Steinke, PhD on many projects. Dr. Fitch earned her MA in counseling and student personnel administration from the University of Maryland at College Park and her PhD in developmental and child psychology from the University of Kansas.

Susan F. Folger is a graduate student working toward her PhD in clinical psychology at Miami University. She has a variety of research interests, which include both positive (e.g., posttraumatic growth) and negative (e.g., posttraumatic stress disorder) effects of traumatic experiences and the risk and resilience factors that may moderate or mediate these outcomes. She is also interested in prevention programs that can be implemented at the community level for various groups of people with mental health issues and in the utilization of students engaged in service learning to implement interventions or prevention strategies for clinical populations. Susan is co-author of "Self-efficacy in Service-Learning Community Action Research: Theory, Research, and Practice" (with R. Reeb, S. Langsner, C. Ryan, and J. Crouse; *American Journal of Community Psychology, 46*[3–4], 2010) and also of "Behavioral Summarized Evaluation: An Assessment Tool to Enhance Multidisciplinary and Parent-Professional Collaborations in Assessing Symptoms of Autism" (with R. Reeb and B. Oneal; *Children's Health Care, 38*[4], 2009). She received her MA in clinical psychology from the University of Dayton.

Andrew Furco is associate vice president for public engagement at the University of Minnesota, where he also serves as an associate professor in the College of Education and Human Development and as director of the University's International Center for Research on Community Engagement. Previously, he served 14 years as director of the Service-Learning Research and Development Center at the University of California Berkeley, where he completed more than two dozen studies on the impacts and institutionalization of service learning. Andy's publications include *Service-Learning: The Essence of the Pedagogy* (Information Age Publishing, 2001) and *Service-Learning Through a Multidisciplinary Lens* (Information Age Publishing, 2002), both edited with Shelley Billig, and more than 50 journal articles, book chapters, and technical reports that explore the practice and study of various forms of community engagement in K–12 and higher education systems in the United States and abroad. He currently serves as a member of the International Center for Service-Learning in Teacher Education Board of Directors, the National Review Board for the Scholarship of Engagement, and the Universidad de Monterrey's International Advisory Board of Student Affairs. He also serves on the editorial boards for *Michigan Journal of Community Service Learning* (United States), *Journal of University Teaching* *and Learning Practice* (Australia), and *Journal of Education as Change* (South Africa). He was the inaugural recipient of the John Glenn Service-Learning Scholar Award and also received the International Association for Research on Service-Learning and Community Engagement's 2003 Award for Outstanding Contributions to Service-Learning Research and the National Society for Experiential Education's 2006 Researcher of the Year Award. Andy received his doctoral degree in educational administration from the University of California, Berkeley.

Beth Gazley is associate professor of public and environmental affairs at Indiana University–Bloomington and also an adjunct faculty member in political science and philanthropic studies. She teaches public affairs courses and conducts research related to nonprofit and governmental management capacity, including the quality of government/nonprofit collaboration, the role of nonprofits in local government emergency planning, association management, public policies related to volunteerism, and effective service learning and volunteer management models. She has authored more than 30 publications, including articles in *Nonprofit and Voluntary Sector Quarterly, Public Administration and Development, Public Administration Review, Journal of Public Administration Research and Theory, Voluntas,* and *Nonprofit Management and Leadership.* Dr. Gazley was the 2012 recipient of the Thomas Ehrlich Award for Service-Learning, a statewide award given by the Indiana University Board of Trustees for distinguished teaching and research on service learning. She has also been engaged in a multiyear research partnership with the American Society of Association Executives on philanthropic activity within membership organizations. Before entering academia, Dr. Gazley served in the nonprofit sector as a fund-raiser, volunteer, board member, and management consultant. She received her MPA and her PhD in public administration and policy from the University of Georgia.

Julie A. Hatcher is executive director of the Center for Service and Learning and associate professor of philanthropic studies in the School of Liberal Arts at Indiana University–Purdue University Indianapolis (IUPUI). She has served as the director of undergraduate programs in philanthropic studies at IUPUI. Her research focuses on the role of higher education in civil society, civic learning outcomes in higher education, and the philanthropic motivations of professionals. She has collaborated on national projects such as the development of the Carnegie Foundation's Community Engagement classification and the development of the Association of American Colleges and

Universities' VALUE Rubric for civic engagement. In addition, she is an active member of the International Association for Research on Service-Learning and Community Engagement. Julie earned her PhD in philanthropic studies with a minor in higher education administration at Indiana University.

George R. Hess joined North Carolina State University's Department of Forestry and Environmental Resources in June 1996. He studies conservation planning for wildlife in suburbanizing areas and broader issues of open space conservation. George's research has evolved from a strictly science-based focus to a combination of science and policy inquiry, because he believes both tools are needed to get the job done. As a teacher, he focuses on finding and developing approaches such as inquiry-guided learning, service learning, and collaborative research that get students engaged in topical problems with the organizations and people working to solve them. He works to combine his teaching, research, and service activities at the undergraduate and graduate levels by creating exciting learning opportunities for his students and himself alike. George completed an MS in computer science at the Stevens Institute of Technology and received his PhD in biomathematics and ecology from North Carolina State University.

Barbara A. Holland is an internationally recognized higher education researcher and consultant, holding academic affiliations with Indiana University–Purdue University Indianapolis, Portland State University, and the University of Sydney. She has held executive roles at the University of Sydney, the University of Western Sydney, Northern Kentucky University, Portland State University, and the U.S. Department of Housing and Urban Development. She was director of the Learn and Serve America National Service-Learning Clearinghouse for seven years. Her presentations and publications reflect her expertise in organizational change in higher education, community engagement, service learning, and partnerships. In 2006, Barbara received the Research Achievement Award from the International Association for Research on Service-Learning and Community Engagement, and she currently serves as chair of the association's board. In 2008, she was one of the first two scholars recognized as an Honorary Fellow of the Australian Universities Community Engagement Alliance. She is a lead faculty member of the U.S.-based National Engagement Academy for University Leaders, a member of the National Review Board for the Scholarship of Engagement, a board member of the International Center for Service-Learning in Teacher

Education, and editor of *Metropolitan Universities*. Her current research and practice interests focus on leadership of change, linkage of engagement to other institutional strategies and priorities, enhancement of local and international partnerships, and tracking and measuring of community engagement's internal and external impact and outcomes. Barbara received her PhD in higher education policy from the University of Maryland, College Park.

Tara D. Hudson is a doctoral student in the Department of Leadership, Policy, and Adult and Higher Education at North Carolina State University as well as an academic advisor in the College of Education. Tara's research interests include critical race and feminist theories, multiple dimensions of identity, and assessment within student affairs. Her dissertation research is focused on the experiences of college students in interracial and interethnic close friendships. Prior to returning to graduate school, Tara worked at the Center for Gender in Organizations at Simmons College's School of Management in Boston. She received her MEd in higher education administration from North Carolina State University.

Barbara Jacoby is Faculty Associate for Leadership and Community Service Learning at the Adele H. Stamp Student Union–Center for Campus Life at the University of Maryland, College Park. In this role, she facilitates initiatives involving academic partnerships, service learning, and civic engagement. She is also a fellow of the university's Academy for Excellence in Teaching and Learning. She was previously a Center for Teaching Excellence–Lilly Fellow and director of the Office of Community Service-Learning at the university. Dr. Jacoby has served as Campus Compact's Engaged Scholar for Professional Development and was previously director of the National Clearinghouse for Commuter Programs. She is an affiliate associate professor of college student personnel in the Department of Counseling and Personnel Services, where she teaches doctoral and undergraduate courses. Dr. Jacoby's publications include six books: *The Student as Commuter: Developing a Comprehensive Institutional Response* (ASHE-ERIC Higher Education Reports, 1989); *Service-Learning in Higher Education: Concepts and Practices* (Jossey-Bass, 1996); *Involving Commuter Students in Learning* (Jossey-Bass, 2000); *Building Partnerships for Service-Learning* (Jossey-Bass, 2003); *Civic Engagement in Higher Education* (Jossey-Bass, 2009); and *Looking In, Reaching Out: A Reflective Guide for Community Service-Learning Professionals* (with Pamela Mutascio; Campus Compact, 2010). She has held many leadership positions in NASPA–Student Affairs Administrators in Higher Education and in

ACPA–College Student Educators International. Dr. Jacoby received her PhD in French language and literature from the University of Maryland, College Park.

Audrey J. Jaeger is an associate professor of higher education policy and co–executive director of the National Initiative for Leadership and Institutional Effectiveness at North Carolina State University (NCSU). For the past two years, she has served as NCSU's Office of Faculty Development Scholar on Community Engagement. Her research focuses on building capacity for engaged scholarship with future faculty, current faculty, and higher education administrators. She edited *Institutionalizing Community Engagement in Higher Education: The First Wave of Carnegie Classified Institutions* (Jossey-Bass, 2009) with Lorilee Sandmann and Courtney Thornton. She serves with several national organizations that focus on community engagement and is often called upon to address the preparation of graduate students in their pursuit of community-engaged research. Dr. Jaeger received her PhD in higher education administration from New York University.

Jessica Katz Jameson is associate professor and associate head of the Department of Communication at North Carolina State University (NCSU). Her research and teaching are primarily focused on organizational communication and conflict management, with increasing attention to conducting and institutionalizing community-engaged scholarship. Jessica is an Engaged Faculty Fellow at NCSU and a 2010 recipient of the Outstanding Faculty Service Extension Award and the Opal Mann Green Engagement and Scholarship Award. She is affiliated faculty and former Academic Council Chair with NCSU's Institute for Nonprofit Research, Education, and Engagement. She has co-authored several articles and book chapters on service learning and faculty engagement. Her work appears in *Journal of Higher Education Outreach and Engagement; Michigan Journal of Community Service Learning;* and edited volumes such as Harter, Hamel-Lambert, and Millesen's *Participatory Partnerships for Social Action and Research* (Kendall Hunt, 2011). Jessica received her PhD in communication from Temple University.

Emily M. Janke is the Special Assistant for Community Engagement in the Office of Research and Economic Development at the University of North Carolina at Greensboro (UNCG). In this position, she provides university-wide leadership to establish a collective vision as well as systems for excellence in community engagement. Previously, Emily served as the assistant director for service-learning in the UNCG Office of Leadership and Service-Learning, where she provided curricular, administrative, and partnership support to faculty and students to enhance their teaching, learning, research, and service through academic service learning and community-engaged scholarship. A visiting fellow with the New England Resource Center for Higher Education (NERCHE), Emily is a member of the Next Generation Engagement Project, a collaboration between NERCHE, the American Association of State Colleges and Universities, and Imagining America. She is a recipient of the Dissertation Award given by the International Association for Research on Service-Learning and Community Engagement for her dissertation titled *Shared Partnership Identity Between Faculty and Community Partners*. Emily's scholarship explores collaborative processes; the nexus among organizational, partnership, and social identities; institutionalization of community engagement; and the experiences of practitioner-scholars as engaged scholars. She received her PhD in higher education from The Pennsylvania State University.

Kevin Kecskes is associate vice provost for engagement and director for community-university partnerships at Portland State University (PSU). Prior to joining PSU's Center for Academic Excellence in 2002, he was regional program director of the Western Region Campus Compact Consortium. He teaches on civic leadership in the Hatfield School of Government Public Administration and Policy division and offers an international senior capstone course as well as other university studies courses. He is on the editorial board of *Journal of Public Scholarship in Higher Education*. Kecskes has advised numerous college and university campuses in the United States and globally; his current international work focuses primarily on the Middle East. His recent publications focus on engaging academic departments, the nexus between cultural theory and community-campus partnerships, faculty and institutional development for community engagement, student civic leadership development, building community-university engagement in Vietnam, and ethics and community-based learning. He edited *Engaging Departments: Moving Faculty Culture From Private to Public, Individual to Collective Focus for the Common Good* (Jossey-Bass, 2006). Kecskes received his PhD in public administration and policy from Portland State University.

Laura Littlepage is a member of the faculty at the School of Public and Environmental Affairs and Philanthropic Studies at Indiana University–

Purdue University Indianapolis (IUPUI) and a senior researcher at the Indiana University Public Policy Institute. She was named a Faculty Fellow in Service Learning in 2009 by the IUPUI Center for Service and Learning. Her classes in program evaluation and human resources include service learning components. One class that she has taught every year since 2007, called Do the Homeless Count, integrates service, teaching, and research through partnering with the Coalition for Homelessness Intervention and Prevention to count the homeless in Indianapolis as part of the Department of Housing and Urban Development's data collection activities. She is currently the principal investigator for several evaluations of nonprofit organizations. Littlepage is the principal author of numerous publications and several journal articles, including articles in *Nonprofit and Voluntary Sector Quarterly, Public Administration Review, Nonprofit Management and Leadership, Review of Public Personnel Administration,* and *Review of Public Personnel Management.* She has made national and international presentations. She holds an MPA from New York University.

Lisa E. McGuire is an associate professor and director of the Bachelor of Social Work Program at Indiana University–Purdue University Indianapolis (IUPUI) in the Indiana University School of Social Work. She serves as the principal investigator in a partnership between the university and the Indiana Department of Child Services to strengthen the workforce for public child welfare practice. She has utilized service learning pedagogy in courses since the late 1990s and has researched reflection in service learning as well as in traditional courses. Lisa was named a Boyer Scholar at IUPUI and received the Thomas Ehrlich Award for Service Learning from Indiana University in 2009. She has also served as senior scholar for the IUPUI Center for Service and Learning, focusing on qualitative methods in service learning research. In 2011, she edited (with Virginia Majewski) a special issue of *Advances in Social Work* on service learning and competency-based learning in social work. She received her MSW from Indiana University and her PhD in social welfare from Case Western Reserve University.

KerryAnn O'Meara is an associate professor of higher education in the College of Education and affiliate faculty in women's studies at the University of Maryland, College Park. She has been involved in the community engagement movement for more than 20 years, and she studies engaged scholars, academic reward systems, and how individuals and institutions create spaces to assume agency. She serves as higher education concentration coordinator at the University of Maryland and associate editor for *Michigan Journal of Community Service Learning* and *Journal of the Professoriate*. Prior to joining the faculty at the University of Maryland in the fall of 2007, she served on the higher education faculty at the University of Massachusetts–Amherst. Before taking that position she spent two years at the Harvard Project on Faculty Appointments (now COACHE) and five years as a professional in student affairs and academic affairs, directing service learning programs and undergraduate research and working in residence life. In 1998 she received the Emerging Leader Award from the National Society for Experiential Education; in 2003 the Teacher of the Year Award, School of Education, University of Massachusetts–Amherst; and in 2008 the Early Career Research Award from the International Association for Research on Service-Learning and Community Engagement, where she serves on the board. KerryAnn teaches courses on the academic profession, service learning and community engagement, women in higher education, ranking systems, history of American higher education, and organization and administration. She consults with institutions, national associations, and networks on issues of faculty development, reform in academic reward systems, and community engagement. She earned her PhD in education policy from the University of Maryland.

Megan M. Palmer is an assistant dean for faculty affairs and professional development and director of the Academy of Teaching Scholars at the Indiana University (IU) School of Medicine. She also serves as the director of faculty development in the health professions at Indiana University–Purdue University Indianapolis (IUPUI). Dr. Palmer holds faculty appointments in general internal medicine and educational leadership and policy studies at IU. Prior to her work with the IU School of Medicine, Dr. Palmer served as the director of the IUPUI Center for Teaching and Learning. She has published on faculty vitality, faculty development, student engagement in higher education, and college choice. Dr. Palmer teaches graduate-level courses in the higher education program, including Teaching and Learning in Postsecondary Education, Campus Environmental Theory and Assessment, Introduction to Educational Inquiry, and Introduction to College and University Administration. In her administrative role, Dr. Palmer supports faculty in teaching, promotion and tenure, orientation, work-life balance, and other aspects of faculty life in the schools of Medicine, Dentistry, Nursing and Health, and Rehabilitation Science. She received her master's in higher education from Colorado State University and her PhD in higher education administration from Indiana University.

William M. Plater served for 19 years as the chief academic officer of Indiana University–Purdue University Indianapolis (IUPUI) until July 2006, a period spanning more than half its existence as a campus of Indiana University. Earlier, he served as dean of the School of Liberal Arts at IUPUI and before that as associate director of the School of Humanities at the University of Illinois at Urbana–Champaign. At IUPUI, Plater played a major role in developing the civic mission of the campus, addressing the conditions of faculty work, expanding international programs, creating new fields of interdisciplinary inquiry, promoting the use of technology for learning, and establishing a habit of innovation in undergraduate learning. More recently, as chancellor's professor and director of International Community Development, he worked with the Center on Philanthropy, the Public Policy Institute, and International Affairs to extend IUPUI's civic engagement work into international dimensions. He has worked with national associations on projects and programs related to internationalization and civic engagement, including serving on the advisory panel for the Carnegie Foundation's Community Engagement classification. After retiring from IUPUI in 2010, he served as senior consultant for higher education for Epsilen (a learning technologies company owned by the *New York Times*) until 2012, when he became the senior advisor for international affairs for the Western Association of Schools and Colleges and senior advisor for educational strategies for Course Networking (a global learning technology system). Plater received his PhD in English from the University of Illinois at Urbana–Champaign.

Mary F. Price currently serves as the service learning specialist at the Indiana University–Purdue University Indianapolis Center for Service and Learning (CSL). Since coming to CSL in 2009, she has worked directly with individual faculty, staff, and departments to develop, implement, and assess service learning courses and to transform curricula. She also directs the Service Learning Assistant Scholarship Program, which partners service learning faculty with student leaders. Mary brings to her work at CSL more than 10 years of experience in faculty, student, and organizational development in undergraduate research, international study abroad, community-based learning, collaborative learning strategies, general education, and e-portfolios. Since coming to CSL she has led faculty development programs associated with improving the quality of civic learning in course and program designs, building practitioner capacity to integrate collaboration as a dimension of faculty and student work, assessing community partnerships, using e-portfolios to support longitudinal civic development, and designing international service learning programs. Mary also contributes to CSL's Research Collaborative, in which she and her colleagues are refining a set of tools to support reflection, assessment, and research on partnership relationships. In addition to her role at CSL, Mary is a doctoral candidate in anthropology at Binghamton University, State University of New York. Her disciplinary research interests include power, the micropolitics of social reproduction, practice theory and craft production, space and place, and the archaeology of technology. She expects to complete her doctorate in 2012.

Roger N. Reeb is a professor of psychology at the University of Dayton, where he serves as both the director of the clinical psychology graduate program and the director of graduate programs in Psychology. After completing the predoctoral internship at Brown University Clinical Psychology Internship Consortium, Dr. Reeb joined the faculty at the University of Dayton in 1993. Dr. Reeb received two awards from the American Psychological Association: Dissertation Award and Springer Award for Excellence in Research in Rehabilitation Psychology (Division 22). At the University of Dayton, he received the 2012 Faculty Award in Teaching, and previously he received two service learning awards (Outstanding Faculty Service-Learning Award and Service-Learning Faculty Research Award) and was nominated by the university's president for the National Ehrlich Faculty Award for Service-Learning. Dr. Reeb has several lines of research in clinical psychology (e.g., psychopathology), engaged scholarship (e.g., homelessness), and service learning (e.g., Community Service Self-Efficacy Scale). He published *Community Action Research: Benefits to Community Members and Service Providers* (Routledge, 2006) and edited a special issue on service learning research for *American Journal of Community Psychology*. He has also published approximately 25 refereed articles and several book chapters as well as offered more than 60 professional presentations at regional, national, and international conferences. In Montgomery County, Ohio, Dr. Reeb serves as a board member for the Homeless Solutions Board and for the National Alliance on Mental Illness. He received his PhD in clinical psychology from Virginia Commonwealth University.

Lorilee R. Sandmann is professor and program chair in the adult education program, Department of Lifelong Education, Administration, and Policy in the College of Education at The University of Georgia (UGA). Dr. Sandmann was previously the associate vice president for public service and outreach and executive director of the Georgia Center for Continuing Education, both at UGA. For more than 10 years, she was co-director of the National Review Board for the Scholarship of Engagement. She has been involved in designing and conducting several capacity-building programs related to the scholarship of engagement, including Virginia Tech's Engagement Academy for University Leaders, the University of New Hampshire's Engaged Scholars Academy, and the Houle Scholars Program. She has published widely in journals such as *The Review of Higher Education, Journal of Higher Education, Innovative Higher Education, Journal of Higher Education Outreach and Engagement, Michigan Journal of Community Service Learning,* and *Change: The Magazine of Higher Learning.* In 2009 she edited *Institutionalizing Community Engagement in Higher Education: The First Wave of Carnegie Classified Institutions* (with Courtney Thornton and Audrey Jaeger; Jossey-Bass). Dr. Sandmann has been inducted into the International Adult and Continuing Education Hall of Fame, was president of the American Association for Adult and Continuing Education, chaired what is now the Council of Engagement and Outreach for the Association of Public and Land-Grant Universities, was awarded UGA's Scholarship of Engagement Award, and is on the national advisory panel for the Carnegie Foundations' Community Engagement classification. She holds a PhD in adult education and business management from the University of Wisconsin–Madison.

Kathryn S. Steinberg was most recently employed as an academic assessment specialist at the Center for Service and Learning (CSL) at Indiana University–Purdue University Indianapolis (IUPUI). In this position she coordinated and served as a faculty member in the annual IUPUI Research Academy on service learning research. Her work at CSL involved conducting program evaluation and research on the student civic learning outcomes of service learning. She has given numerous presentations and published several articles on the conceptual framework and assessment of the civic-minded graduate. In addition, Kathy teaches on an adjunct basis in the Psychology Department at IUPUI. Before she began working at CSL, Kathy served for nine years as the assistant director of research at the Center on Philanthropy at IUPUI. In that capacity she was involved in research on methodology and measurement of giving and volunteering in the United States. Kathy holds a PhD in educational psychology and an MS in clinical psychology, both from Purdue University.

Pamela Steinke is currently the dean of academic affairs and institutional effectiveness at MacCormac College. Immediately prior to this position, she was director of research, planning and assessment at Meredith College. She has also worked as an assessment professional at North Carolina State University and at Lincoln Land Community College. Prior to her administrative positions she was a tenured psychology faculty member at Central College. Throughout her career she has been active in the regional accreditation process and has continued to present and publish on her scholarly interests, which include cognitive outcomes of service learning and outcomes assessment. She often collaborates with Peggy Fitch, PhD. Dr. Steinke received her MA and PhD in psychology from the University of California, Davis.

AAC&U. *See* Association of American
Colleges and Universities
AASCU. *See* American Association of State
Colleges and Universities
Abes, E. S., 139
academic departments. *See also* academic
units; community engagement in
higher education; service learning in
academic departments
change in higher education institutions
and, 473–74
collaboration of, 472
global citizenship preparation of, 472
as heart of higher education, 471
institutional theory, community and,
479–80
academic engagement leadership. *See* executive academic engagement leadership
academic institutions
as loosely coupled, 444
nature of, 443–45
organizational change theory and, 443–45
academic learning
in faculty learning, 106, 250
overview, 86
as service learning category, 86, 250
academic learning domains, 99–101
critical thinking in, 90–92, 96
disciplinary thinking in, 89, 90, 91
foundational knowledge in, 90, 91, 92–93
higher level learning in, 90, 91, 92–93
operationalizing, 102–4
overview, 90–93
academic learning in service learning, 250.
See also assessment of academic learning
in service learning; service learning
research on academic learning
learning outcomes in, 87
overview, 86–87
academic learning outcomes. *See also*
learning outcomes

conceptual framework for typology of,
90–93, 99–102
conceptual frameworks for, 87–93, 99–102
previous research review, 93–96
academic profession, 216
generation factors in, 222
research on, 217, 222
academic units. *See also* academic
departments
in community engagement institutionalization, 473
community engagement research rationale
for including, 473–75
cultural theory and partnerships between
community and, 477–78
organizational change theory and transformation in, 476–77
in service learning institutionalization,
473–74
service learning research rationale for
including, 473–75
acquisition, 579
active citizenship, 124
administrative leadership, 506
administrative service learning leadership
of CAOs, 506, 508–10
of CEOs, 506, 508–10
of department chairs/heads and deans,
506, 507–8
levels and contexts in, 505, 506–12
overview, 505, 506
of program/center directors, 506–7
administrators, service learning partnerships and campus, 540–42
ADP. *See* American Democracy Project
adult learning
reflection in, 252
theory, 253
adult-youth partnerships, 605
Afflerbach, P., 62

identity, 586, 604
learning theory, 189, 190
individual relationships
organizational partnerships as, 575
organizational relationships and, 575,
577–78
inference, as cognitive skill, 59
input-environment-output (IEO) model,
216, 217
faculty motivations for community
engagement and, 221
in faculty research, 221–22
inquiry
community-based, 67
narrative, 33, 365
naturalistic, 31, 363
principles in scientific process, 28, 34–35,
360, 366–67
institutions. *See also* academic institutions;
higher education institutions
accountability and community
engagement leadership research, 529–30
accountability and service learning leadership research, 529–30
anchor, 236
change in, 472
factors in faculty motivations for
community engagement, 216, 218, 221,
222, 225–33, 235
service learning in academic departments
and public purposes of, 475
institutional and managerial capacity. *See
also* community organization capacity
overview, 419
institutionalization. *See* community
engagement institutionalization; service
learning institutionalization
institutional leadership in service learning.
See also service learning research on
institutional leadership
overview, 505–6
institutional leadership theory and concepts
distributed leadership, 514
Kezar on, 512–14
overview, 512–15
institutional review boards (IRBs), 48–49,
380–81

institutional theory
community, academic departments and,
479–80
engaged departments and, 479–80, 481,
489–91
instruction
design, research and practice, 15, 347
developmental, 72–73, 78
instructors
service learning research benefits for, 4,
336
service learning research by, 3, 335
instruments. *See* measurement instruments
for service learning research
integrity
in interpersonal relationships, 545–46
in service learning partnerships, 542–43
intellectual development
in cognition theory and concepts, 59–61
critical thinking, cognitive processes and,
58, 59, 60
metacognition and, 63
overview, 59–61
service learning, cognitive processes and,
58, 62, 64–65
service learning and, 65–66
service learning pedagogy, cognitive processes and, 57
theory and personal epistemology, 59, 61
interaction. *See also* interpersonal
interactions
contemporary conceptualizations of, 391,
393–96
diathesis-stress model, 393–94
principle of reciprocal determinism,
393–94
intercultural competence (ICC). *See also
specific ICC topics*
assessment guide for, 171, 172
cultural definitions of, 164
definitions of, 159–60, 162, 164
global citizenship and, 158, 159
globalization and, 157
overview, 157–60
interinstitutional partnership typologies
cooperative relationships, 577
exchange relationships, 577
service relationships, 576, 577

nature of academic institutions and,
443–45
overview, 443
service learning research on institutionalization and, 441–56
organizational empowerment, 405, 406
organizational identity
overview, 584
in partnership entities research, 584–85
organizational learning, 582–83
Organizational Learning in Higher Education
(Kezar), 447
organizational partnerships. *See also* partnership entities; service learning
organizational partnerships
as individual relationships, 575
interorganizational, 574
as interorganizational relationships, 575
organizational-level partnership benefits,
577–78
as partnership entities, 575
United Way example, 573–75
organizational relationships. *See also* interorganizational relationships
individual relationships and, 575, 577–78
research on, 578–79
organizational research. *See also specific organizational research topics*
organizational theory and, 575
organizational theory
organizational research and, 575
service learning organizational partnerships and, 575–76
Orton, J. D., 445
Osborne, R., 195
Osgood, R., 195
O'Steen, W. L., 263

Palermo, A. G., 592
Parker-Gwin, R., 68
Parkins, L. C., 228
participatory citizenship, 114
participatory research, 33–34, 365–66
partnerships. *See also* organizational partnerships; service learning partnerships
as analysis unit in service learning partnerships, 576
definitions of, 600–601

identity, 585–86, 592
interinstitutional partnership typologies,
576–77
in relationships, 576
youth-adult, 605
among youths, 605
Partnership Assessment Tool (PAT), 554,
558–59
partnership entities
EITCP as, 574
interorganizational relationships
compared to, 578–80
organizational partnerships as, 575
service learning organizational partnerships as, 576
in service learning research on organizational partnerships, 575, 576, 578–80,
584–90, 592
partnership entities research, 575, 576,
578–80, 587–90. *See also* service learning
research on organizational partnerships
individual identity in, 586
organizational identity and, 584–85
overview, 584–86
partnership identity in, 585–86, 592
Partnerships Perspective, 576
partnerships research, 592–93. *See also* partnership entities research; service
learning partnerships research
Pascarella, E. T., 141, 142, 146
PAT. *See* Partnership Assessment Tool
Patton, M. Q., 10–11, 342–43
Paul, R., 61, 62, 66, 90, 91, 95, 98, 99
pedagogy. *See also* service learning pedagogy
critical, 253
pedagogical design
research and, 15, 16, 347, 348
service learning research and, 16, 348
peer education, 605
peer leadership, 605
Penner, L. A., 137
Perrow, C., 479
Perry, W. G., 66, 72, 144, 149, 220
personal epistemology and model of,
59–61
personal agency, 139
personal development. *See also* personal
growth

change compared to, 135
constructs of, 134
Dewey on, 135
moral development and, 134
overview of, 134, 135
personal growth and, 135
Piaget on, 135–36
prosocial development and, 134
personal development in service learning. *See also* service learning research on
personal development
overview, 133–34
personal development outcomes
in higher education, 134
overview, 134
service learning pedagogy goal of, 133
personal epistemology
definitions, 59
intellectual development theory and, 59, 61
Perry's model and, 59–61
personal growth. *See also* personal development; service learning research on
personal growth
as developmental process, 146
in faculty learning, 250
personal development and, 135
potentials in service learning pedagogy, 134
as service learning category, 86, 250
in service learning practice, 86, 134
perspective transformation, 140
PESM. *See* Psycho-Ecological Systems Model
Peters, S., 33, 230, 365, 475
Petrie, H. G., 254
Pew Charitable Trust, 116
phenomenology, 33, 365
Phillips, M. A., 145
Piaget, J., 135–36, 146
Pickeral, T., 578
Pike, G. R., 200
Piliavin, J. A., 137
Pinchon, I., 141
Pintrich, P. R., 59, 61
Plano Clark, V. L., 15, 347
Plater, William M., 196, 515, 516, 517

POD. *See* Professional and Organizational
Development Network in Higher
Education
political engagement, 118, 122
Political Engagement Project, 121, 122, 126
Portland State University (PSU), 119, 455–56, 474, 483
positive psychology, 138
Poulson, S. J., 16, 348
Powell, W. W., 479
practice. *See also* faculty development
practice; service learning practice
communities of, 194–96
design and, 10, 13, 342, 345
instructional design, research and, 15, 347
measurement and, 10, 13, 342, 345
overview, 15–17, 347–49
research and, 10, 11, 15–17, 342, 343, 347–49
theory and, 10, 13, 16–17, 342, 345, 348–49
practice implications for assessment
of academic learning in service learning, 99–102
of ICC in service learning, 171–75
practice implications for service learning
research. *See also* service learning
practice
on academic learning, 99–102
on civic learning, 121–23
on cognition, 71–74
on community organization capacity, 429–33
on community outcomes, 406–9
on engaged departments, 484–86
on faculty development, 203–5
on faculty learning, 263–66
on faculty motivations for community
engagement, 231–32
on ICC, 171–75
on organizational partnerships, 586–88
on partnerships and relationships, 556–59
on personal development, 144
on student partnerships, 608–10
on VMC, 429–33
practitioners
service learning research by practitioner-scholars, 3, 335
service learning researchers as, 17, 349

service learning research on student
   partnerships
benefits and influence of, 611
community-campus partnerships as
   models for, 606–8, 609
effective design lessons for, 610
forms of, 608–9
overview, 540–42, 599–602
programs, 599
social change and, 603
SOFAR model and, 599, 608, 611, 614
student development through, 603–5
student leadership in, 604
TRES and, 608, 611
student research. *See specific student related
   research topics*
*Students as Colleagues: Expanding the Circle of
   Service Learning Leadership* (Zlotkowski), 600
students in community engagement, 473. *See
   also* engaged departments; students in
   service learning
students in service learning. *See also*
   community organization capacity;
   student learning in service learning;
   students in community engagement;
   volunteer management capacity
engaged departments and, 473
student volunteerism. *See* community organization capacity; volunteer
   management capacity
studies. *See also* service learning research
international, 49, 381
multicampus, 49, 380
nonprofit, 85–86, 92, 93
Stukas, A. A., 143
supra macrosystem, 396
surveys
   in assessment of community engagement
      leadership, 521, 522, 523
   faculty, 228–29
   HERI's Life After College, 125
   one-shot or onetime, 37, 369
   self-report, 236
Syracuse University, 516, 522–23
systemic and transformative relationships,
   577
Szabo, B., 192, 193

Taggart, G., 252
teachers, and reciprocal process with
   students, 253
teaching. *See also* scholarship of teaching and
   learning
assignment changes, 196
examining approaches to learning and,
   105–6
practice and faculty development practice,
   189, 191
service learning research future and, 48,
   379–80
service learning research on ICC for
   candidates of, 166–67
technical reflection, 252
tenure, in faculty motivations for
   community engagement, 222, 226, 227,
   234–35
Terenzini, P. T., 141, 142, 146
Terosky, A. L., 249
theory. *See also specific theory topics*
adult learning, 253
agency, 219
assessment and, 12, 344
attributes and, 14, 346
constructs and, 13, 345
contact hypothesis, 165–66, 174
design and, 10, 13, 15, 342, 345, 347
of Dewey, 87–88, 135, 602
epistemology and intellectual development, 59
equity, 545–46
experiential learning, 13, 190, 191, 203, 204,
   205
grounded, 33, 365
identity, 547–49
individual learning, 189, 190
measurement and, 10, 13, 342, 345
moral development, 136–37
motivation, 217, 218
overview, 28, 360
of Piaget, 135–36
practice and, 10, 13, 16–17, 342, 345,
   348–49
professional relationships, 220
prosocial development, 137
research and, 10–13, 16, 28–29, 43, 342–45,
   348, 360–61, 375